The Cinema of Sergei Parajanov

Parajanov performs his own imprisonment for the camera. Tbilisi, October 15, 1984. Courtesy of Yuri Mechitov.

The Cinema of
Sergei Parajanov

James Steffen

The University of Wisconsin Press

Publication of this volume has been made possible, in part,
through support from the Andrew W. Mellon Foundation.

The University of Wisconsin Press
1930 Monroe Street, 3rd Floor
Madison, Wisconsin 53711-2059
uwpress.wisc.edu

3 Henrietta Street
London WC2E 8LU, England
eurospanbookstore.com

Printed in the United States of America

Library of Congress Cataloging-in-Publication Data
Steffen, James.
The cinema of Sergei Parajanov / James Steffen.
p. cm. — (Wisconsin film studies)
Includes bibliographical references and index.
ISBN 978-0-299-29654-4 (pbk. : alk. paper) — ISBN 978-0-299-29653-7 (e-book)
1. Paradzhanov, Sergei, 1924-1990—Criticism and interpretation. 2. Motion pictures—Soviet
Union. I. Title. II. Series: Wisconsin film studies.
PN1998.3.P356S74 2013
791.430947—dc23
2013010422

For my family.

Contents

Illustrations

Because of the importance of visual texture in Parajanov's films, production stills have been used when available and where they correspond closely to the specific scenes being analyzed. Otherwise, frame captures are used. Figures 0.1, 4.1, 4.3, 4.4, 4.5, 4.7, 4.8, 5.1, 5.2, 6.1, 6.2, 7.6, 8.2 are courtesy of the Sergei Parajanov Museum (Yerevan). Figures 1.3–1.8 and 3.1–3.4 are courtesy of the Oleksandr Dovzhenko National Centre (Kyiv). Figures 7.1, 7.3, 7.5, and 8.5 are courtesy of Yuri Mechitov. Figures 1.1, 1.2, 2.1–2.7, 4.2, 4.6, 7.2, 7.4, 8.1, 8.3, and 8.4 are frame captures from the author's collection.

Acknowledgments

Zaven Sargsyan and the staff at the Sergei Parajanov Museum in Yerevan not only opened up the rich trove of materials at the museum and answered countless questions, but helped with the logistics of my stays in Yerevan and Kyiv; for this I am endlessly grateful. The late Tetiana Derevianko at the Dovzhenko Film Studio Museum in Kyiv also shared many rare materials and provided a welcoming environment; she will be greatly missed. Liudmila Budiak, Dmitri Karavaev, and the staff at NII Kinoiskusstva (Moscow) allowed me to use their extensive library, screened 35mm prints, and helped obtain permission to access the Goskino files in RGALI. The Moscow scholars Valeri Fomin and Miron Chernenko also offered helpful insights and shared materials with me. The staff at the Russian State Archive of Art and Literature (RGALI) and the Russian State Archive of Contemporary History (RGANI) kindly facilitated access to their archival documents. Ivan Kozlenko at the Oleksandr Dovzhenko National Centre helped me obtain stills from several of Parajanov's Ukrainian films and DVDs of other key Ukrainian films. Serhiy Trymbach at the Dovzhenko National Centre and Eldar Shengelaia and the staff at the Georgia Film Studio (Tbilisi) screened 35mm prints of films and generously offered their insights. In Tbilisi, thanks also to Temur Palavandishvili at the Georgia Film Studio and Manana Chkonia for sharing insights and research materials with me. Adrian Curry at Zeitgeist Films enabled me to see the film *Swan Lake: The Zone*. The Widener Library and the Davis Center for Russian and Eurasian Studies at Harvard University helped access the Georgian newspaper *Literaturuli sakartvelo* and other Soviet-era periodicals. The outstanding interlibrary loan department at Emory's Woodruff Library has helped me obtain many other materials over the years. Irena Popiashvili hosted me during visits to Tbilisi and New York and introduced me to individuals such as Mark Polyakov and Yuri Mechitov; I am much indebted to her and her family. Elena Drozdova and Arch Getty at Praxis assisted with the logistics of my stay in Moscow. Galina Alexandrovna was an unforgettable host in Moscow. Taline Voskeritchian, besides being a delightful colleague and friend over the years, hosted me during the research trip to Harvard.

The Graduate School of Arts and Sciences at Emory University funded my initial research trips to Armenia and Georgia in 1996 and 1998; the Emory Internationalization Fund supported the main research trip from September 2000–February 2001 in Russia, Ukraine, and Armenia. My dissertation committee (David A. Cook, Angelika Bammer, Matthew Payne, and Karla Oeler) offered unflagging support and challenged me to think about the topic in new ways. The Woodruff Library at Emory granted temporary leave to complete work on the manuscript in the summer of 2011. The Russian, East European, and Eurasian Studies Program at Emory provided subvention funds to offset the cost of illustrations.

A number of individuals granted me interviews. Not all of them ended up in this book, but they will be used in a future biography of Parajanov. I would especially like to thank Svetlana Shcherbatiuk for her patience and generous spirit. Cora Tsereteli, Vigen Galstyan, Nairi Galstanian, Yuri Mechitov, Berj Kalayjian, and others offered invaluable feedback on the manuscript at various stages. In particular, the three anonymous readers offered genuinely helpful comments and recommendations. The editor Gwen Walker deserves a note of special thanks for her exemplary professionalism and her support, as does the rest of the excellent staff at the University of Wisconsin Press.

Chapter 3 is a revised version of the essay "*Kyiv Frescoes*: Sergei Parajanov's Unfinished Film Project," published in *KinoKultura* Special Issue 9: Ukrainian Cinema (December 2009): http://www.kinokultura.com/specials/9/steffen .shtml. The issue's editor, Vitaly Chernetsky, offered many insights into the script's culturally specific references, which have been incorporated into the notes of that essay and this book. Chapter 4 is a revised version of the essay "From *Sayat-Nova* to *The Color of Pomegranates*: Notes on the Production and Censorship of Parajanov's Film," published in the Parajanov special issue of the *Armenian Review* 47/48, nos. 3–4/1–2 (2001/2002): 105–47. Thanks to both journals for permission to reprint this material.

Finally, Cora Tsereteli deserves a special note of appreciation as the foundational Parajanov scholar, without whose timely and tireless efforts my work and that of other scholars would be impossible.

Note on Transliteration

The subject of this book poses special challenges for transliteration because it encompasses multiple languages and alphabets — primarily Russian, Ukrainian, Georgian, and Armenian. There is no easy solution to the problems that result, nor is it even feasible to achieve complete internal consistency. With this caveat in mind, the primary goal is to make the main body of the text accessible to a general readership.

In most cases, film titles are given in Russian and the names of film industry figures are transliterated according to Russian-based spellings. This is because the book looks at Sergei Parajanov's life and filmmaking primarily within a Soviet context and was conceived as a contribution to scholarship on Soviet cinema. It acknowledges the practical reality that Russian was the lingua franca of the former Soviet Union as a whole, and that much of the existing literature about Soviet cinema is in the Russian language. Thus, for example, I generally use the Russian-based "Nikolai" instead of the Ukrainian-based "Mykola" and likewise "Alexander" instead of "Oleksandr" when referring to individuals from Ukraine.

Parajanov's given name could be rendered variously as "Sergei," "Serhii," or "Sergo" depending on whether one is working with Russian-, Ukrainian-, or Georgian-language sources. I have opted for the Russian-based Sergei, because that was his official name within the Soviet state. For his surname I have chosen "Parajanov" rather than the older, French-based "Paradjanov" or the Russian-based "Paradzhanov." The single "j" represents the emerging standard spelling in English, is the preferred spelling of the Sergei Parajanov Museum in Yerevan, and corresponds to the hard "j" consonant used with his name in both Armenian and Georgian.

Exceptions inevitably remain. I have spelled some Russian names to match their English counterparts (e.g., Alexander instead of Aleksandr and Maria instead of Mariia). For readability, I have chosen not to include soft signs or hard signs, a distinctive feature of Russian and Ukrainian grammar, in proper names. In some cases I have retained spellings that are already commonly used in the West, such as Illienko (versus Il'enko). Slavic surnames that end with -ii or -yi are rendered simply with a -y, such as Tarkovsky. Given names are usually rendered with an -i at the end, such as Grigori. Names that begin with the letters "iu," "ia," or the voiced "e" are rendered with "y": thus Yuri instead of Iurii and Yevgeni instead of Evgenii. The endings of Armenian names are commonly transliterated as either "-ian" or "-yan." In most cases I use "-ian" unless the standard spelling for an individual's name in English dictates otherwise. For Armenian names that begin with "h," a sound that does not exist in Russian, I have preserved the initial "h" to ensure correct pronunciation; thus I have opted for "Hairian" instead of "Airian." I have also avoided Russifying the names of established literary figures such as Mykhailo Kotsiubynsky and Mykola Bazhan when they are already known by Ukrainian-based spellings in the West.

In the scholarly apparatus and in film titles I adhere to simplified Library of Congress transliteration rules in order to make it easier for researchers to locate the works cited.

Chronology

In addition to my own research, sources for this chronology include: Karen Kalantar, *Ocherki o Paradzhanove* (Yerevan: Izd-vo Gitutiun NAN RA, 1998); "Khronika zhizni i tvorchestva Sergeia Paradzhanova (Sargisa Paradzhaniantsa)," in Sergei Paradzhanov and Zaven Sarkisian, *Kaleidoskop Paradzhanova* (Yerevan: Muzei Sergeia Paradzhanova, 2008), 9–17; and "Khronika zhizni i tvorchestva," in *Sergei Paradzhanov: Kollazh na fone avtoportreta*, ed. Kora Tsereteli, 2nd ed. (Nizhnii Novgorod: Dekom, 2008), 17–21.

1890: Birth of Sergei Parajanov's father Iosif (Hovsep).

1894: Birth of mother Siran Bezhanova.

1917: Iosif and Siran married.

1922: Birth of sister Anna.

1923: Birth of sister Ruzanna.

January 9, 1924: Birth of Sergei Iosifovich Parajanov.

1932–1942: Studied in Tbilisi Russian Middle School No. 42.

1941–1943: Worked in the toy factory "Soviet Toy" in Tbilisi during the war.

1942: Enrolled in the Tbilisi Institute of Railway Transport. Left the Institute that winter.

1943–1945: Studied in the Voice Department at the Tbilisi Conservatory and performed in a concert troupe serving military hospitals. Also studied violin and dance.

1945: Applied and was admitted to the VGIK (All-Union State Institute of Cinematography), in the directing workshop of Igor Savchenko.

1947: Worked as an assistant on *The Third Strike* (dir. Igor Savchenko).

Summer 1948: Arrested in Tbilisi on charges of homosexuality in the Nikolai Mikava scandal, spent several months in jail.

1950: Worked as an assistant on *Taras Shevchenko* (dir. Igor Savchenko). The film was finished by Savchenko's students after he passed away. Alexander Dovzhenko took over the workshop at the VGIK.

January 1951: Married first wife, Nigyar Seraeva, in Moscow. She was killed on February 13, 1951. Parajanov subsequently shot diploma film, *A Moldovan Fairy Tale*, on location in Moldova.

June 28, 1952: Graduated from the VGIK. Sent to work at the Kyiv Film Studio as a director.

1952: Worked as an assistant on *Maximka* (dir. Vladimir Braun).

May 1955: First feature film *Andriesh* (co-directed by Yakov Bazelian) released.

November 1955: Married Svetlana Shcherbatiuk.

November 10, 1958: Birth of son Suren.

1958–1960: Shot the documentary shorts *Natalia Uzhvy*, *Dumka*, and *Golden Hands*.

July 1959: *The Top Guy* released.

September 1961: *Ukrainian Rhapsody* released.

1962: Death of father, Iosif.

March 1962: Divorce from Svetlana Shcherbatiuk.

September 1962: *The Flower on the Stone* released.

Winter 1964–1965: Wrote the initial literary scenario for *Kyiv Frescoes*. Project launched by the Dovzhenko Film Studio in spring 1965.

September 4, 1965: Political protest accompanied the Kyiv premiere screening of *Shadows of Forgotten Ancestors*.

October 1965: Shot the screen tests for *Kyiv Frescoes*.

Spring 1966: *Kyiv Frescoes* shut down by the authorities.

April 1966: Vahagn Mkrtchian, director of Armenfilm Studio, invited Parajanov to shoot *Sayat-Nova* (later retitled *The Color of Pomegranates*) in Armenia.

1967: Preparatory work on *The Color of Pomegranates*. Work begun on the autobiographical script *Confession*. Shot the documentary film *Hakob Hovnatanyan*.

1968: Wrote the script *Ara the Fair*.

1969: Wrote the script *The Slumbering Palace*. Completed the script *Confession*.

October 1969: *The Color of Pomegranates* released in Yerevan.

August 1970: *The Color of Pomegranates* released in Moscow in the version reedited by Sergei Yutkevich.

1971: Wrote the script *The Demon*.

Spring 1971–Spring 1972: Worked on the production *Intermezzo* (Dovzhenko Film Studio) until its cancellation.

December 1, 1971: Speech in Minsk.

1972: Wrote the script *The Golden Edge*.

December 1972–March 1973: Worked on the production *Inga* (alternate title *When a Person Smiled*), then was removed as director.

1973: Wrote the script for *A Miracle in Odense* in collaboration with Viktor Shklovsky. The film was launched into preproduction by Armenfilm in December 1973.

November 1973: Left Tbilisi for Kyiv because his son was gravely ill with typhus.

December 17, 1973: Arrest in Kyiv.

April 23–25, 1974: Trial and conviction.

July 1974–April 1975: Imprisonment in "severe regime" camp Gubnik (Vinnytsia Oblast, Ukraine).

February 1975: Death of mother, Siran.

April 1975–August 1976: Imprisonment in Strizhavka camp (Vinnytsia oblast).

August 1976–December 1977: Imprisonment in Perevalsk camp (Voroshilovgrad oblast).

December 30, 1977: Released from prison, returned to Tbilisi.

1978: Wrote letter to the authorities in Armenia requesting to film adaptations of *Ara the Fair* and *David of Sasun*.

August 4, 1978: Lilya Brik passed away. Parajanov attended her funeral in Moscow.

January 1980: Interview with the French reporter H. Anassian, published in the January 27 issue of *Le Monde*.

October 31, 1981: Attended the Artistic Council discussion of the play *Vladimir Vysotsky* at the Taganka Theatre in Moscow.

February 11, 1982: Arrest at apartment in Tbilisi, pretrial confinement at Ortachala prison.

September 22–October 5, 1982: Trial on bribery charges in Tbilisi. Freed with a suspended sentence on October 5.

November 1982: Invitation to direct *The Legend of the Surami Fortress*.

October 1983–February 1984: Shot *The Legend of the Surami Fortress*.

January 15, 1985: Opening of the first exhibition of Parajanov's artworks, in the lobby of the Union of Cinematographers of Georgia.

Spring 1985: Shot *Arabesques on the Theme of Pirosmani*.

July 1985: *The Legend of the Surami Fortress* shown out of competition at the Moscow Film Festival.

January 1986: *The Legend of the Surami Fortress* released in Tbilisi.

Summer 1986: Wrote the script *The Passion of Shushanik*. The project was cancelled in 1987 due to political controversy.

Summer 1987: Wrote the script *The Treasures at Mount Ararat*.

August 1987: Shooting of *The Demon* delayed; the film ultimately was never shot.

Fall 1987–February 1988: Shot *Ashik-Kerib*.

January 15, 1988: Opening day of the exhibition of Parajanov's artworks at the Museum of Folk Art in Yerevan.

February 1988: First trip outside the Soviet Union, to the Rotterdam Film Festival. Received the prize "Twenty Directors of the Future" and screened *Arabesques on the Theme of Pirosmani*.

April 1988: Plans approved for the creation of a home-museum for Parajanov in Yerevan. That same year Parajanov also received a state prize from the Armenian SSR for *The Color of Pomegranates* and *Hakob Hovnatanyan*.

June 1988: Attended the Munich Film Festival for the festival premiere screening of *Ashik-Kerib* and the first retrospective of his films.

September 1988: Attended the Venice Film Festival and later the New York Film Festival.

November 1988: Attended the retrospective of his films in Paris.

December 7, 1988: Earthquake in Armenia. Construction of the museum was delayed.

January 1989: Wrote brief prose treatment for an adaptation of *The Song of Igor's Campaign*.

February 1989: Attended the screening of *Ashik-Kerib* at the Fantasporto Film Festival (Porto).

April 1989: Attended the screening of *Ashik-Kerib* at the Istanbul International Film Festival. Received Special Jury Prize "for his contribution to contemporary art."

April 1989: Began shooting film *Confession* at family home in Tbilisi. The production was shut down due to illness, later diagnosed as lung cancer.

July 1989: Operation on lungs in Moscow; returned to Tbilisi.

December 1989–July 1990: Exhibit of new works at the Museum of Folk Art in Yerevan.

February 27, 1990: Named People's Artist of the Ukrainian SSR.

March 15, 1990: Traveled to Yerevan for medical care due to declining health.

May 20, 1990: Sent by plane to Paris for urgent medical treatment.

June 19, 1990: Named the People's Artist of the Armenian SSR.

July 1990: Returned to Yerevan.

Night of July 20–21, 1990: Passed away at the Yerevan hospital.

July 25, 1990: Funeral and burial in the Pantheon in Yerevan.

December 1990: Received four posthumous "Nika" awards for *Ashik-Kerib* in Moscow.

1991: Posthumously awarded the Taras Shevchenko Prize (Ukraine) for *Shadows of Forgotten Ancestors*.

July 27, 1991: Sergei Parajanov Museum opens in Yerevan.

1993: Memorial plaque by Nikolai Rapai placed at the entrance to the apartment building where he lived in Kyiv.

1996: *Ashik-Kerib* received its first commercial release in Armenia.

June 1997: Memorial statue unveiled at the Dovzhenko Film Studio. The presidents of Armenia and Ukraine attended.

November 6, 2004: Memorial statue by sculptor Vazha Mekaberidze unveiled in Tbilisi.

The Cinema of Sergei Parajanov

Introduction

Few film directors ever manage to create a single image that is truly unlike anything you have seen before. In that respect, Sergei Parajanov's films seem almost reckless in their generosity. We watch a tree falling on the man who has felled it—from the point of view of the tree. An androgynous robed figure pours a vat of wine over the chest of a dying poet. Wives in a fairy-tale sultan's harem fire toy automatic rifles into the air. Meticulously composed tableaux resembling medieval miniature paintings hide obscene visual puns that would make Luis Buñuel envious. We are treated to pageants of richly decorated folk art and an imaginary Orient where llamas and ostriches are as likely to appear as a camel, but we also hear the laments of peoples who have suffered for centuries under one empire after another.

Today one can spot the influence of Parajanov among directors from the former Soviet Union and Eastern Europe, in Iranian cinema, and even in music videos. After seeing *The Color of Pomegranates* (*Tsvet granata*, Armenfilm 1969), Jean-Luc Godard stated in an interview: "I think you have to live at least fifteen miles away and feel the need to walk there on foot to see it. If you feel that need and give it that faith, the film can give you everything you could wish. It is a film, by the way, which has given me a lot of faith in myself, since it confirmed some ideas I had about film technique."[1] Godard's comments speak not only to the admitted effort required to approach that film, but also to its underlying spiritual dimension and the often difficult circumstances that both the director and his films faced during much of his lifetime under the Soviet system. As the first English-language book about Parajanov's films, this study seeks to make the fifteen-mile journey a little less arduous by providing a basic framework to understand the films themselves, their creator, and the context in which he made them.

Born in 1924 to an Armenian family in Tbilisi, Georgia, Parajanov was profoundly shaped by the city's cosmopolitan atmosphere and more generally by the rich intersection of cultures in Transcaucasia, a region inhabited since the dawn of civilization. Watching his films, one is struck by the material presence of ancient peoples, of entire histories contained in the very objects depicted on-screen, but also by a style of acting that seems to come from a long-vanished era. His sources of visual inspiration include primitive and folk art, Armenian and Persian miniature painting, and early filmmakers such as Georges Méliès. In an interview with the French journalist and filmmaker Patrick Cazals, Parajanov stated, "I may have received this love for authentic texture in films thanks to Pasolini or Fellini, but through that truth which has it that when you film an old subject, the film acquires an archaic character and demands another style. You can't put on an old costume and walk around in a contemporary manner, unless you wish to produce an effect that way. My love for old things is not a hobby, it's my aesthetic conviction."[2] But Parajanov did something far more interesting than simply to tell old stories and show old things in an old way. Under the guise of this consciously archaic style, he cultivated a sophisticated form of poetic cinema that extended the experiments in editing, sound, and color initiated by earlier Soviet filmmakers such as Sergei Eisenstein, Vsevolod Pudovkin, and Alexander Dovzhenko. At the same time, he was very much conversant in contemporary European cinema and movements in modern art such as Surrealism. Ultimately, his great accomplishment was to bring the cultures of non-Russian republics such as Ukraine, Armenia, and Georgia onto the global cinematic stage through a lively synthesis of regional folk culture and literary traditions with avant-garde filmmaking techniques and sly personal touches.

His bigger-than-life personality and his tumultuous biography loom as large as the films themselves. A talented musician and a conservatory student, in 1945 he switched to filmmaking and enrolled at the VGIK (Vsesoiuznyi Gosudarstvennyi Institut Kinematografii or All-Union State Institute of Cinematography) in Moscow. In 1948 he was arrested in Tbilisi on charges of homosexuality, the first of three times he would face prison. In 1951 he married a young Tatar woman named Nigyar Seraeva who was apparently killed by family members in retaliation. Despite these terrible setbacks Parajanov completed his studies and established a career as a film director in Ukraine, where in 1955 he married Svetlana Shcherbatiuk, the daughter of a diplomat. The couple had a son named Suren, but divorced in 1962. After a series of routine genre films he directed his breakthrough feature, *Shadows of Forgotten Ancestors* (*Teni zabytykh predkov*, Dovzhenko Film Studio 1964). Noted for its abundant folkloric elements and virtuosic camerawork, the film earned several awards at international festivals and remains one of the key works of Ukrainian cinema alongside the films of Dovzhenko.

Parajanov's volatile, outspoken, and pranksterish public persona became both inseparable from his art and a perpetual source of alarm for the Soviet authorities. Despite the success of *Shadows of Forgotten Ancestors*, he ran into trouble over his next project, *Kyiv Frescoes* (*Kievskie freski*, Dovzhenko Film Studio 1965–1966), a semiautobiographical work that depicted vignettes of contemporary Kyiv twenty years after the city's liberation from the Germans. The film was ultimately cancelled, but the surviving screen tests and script give us some idea what it might have become. Over the next few years in Armenia he directed his masterpiece, the visually stunning *The Color of Pomegranates*: an elliptical, poetic biography of the eighteenth-century poet-troubadour Sayat-Nova. This film similarly faced a bitter censorship battle and received only a limited release within the Soviet Union.

In the early 1970s Parajanov attempted to get a number of projects off the ground but encountered one official roadblock after another. In December 1973, just as he was about to begin production on *A Miracle in Odense* (*Chudo v Odense*), a film about Hans Christian Andersen, he was arrested again on various charges related to homosexuality and given a five-year sentence. As this book argues, the charges were politically motivated and had mainly to do with his outspokenness and his influence among Ukrainian artists and intellectuals, which the authorities viewed as a threat during the ongoing political crackdown in Ukraine. At the same time, based on the available evidence Parajanov was probably bisexual with a preference for men, especially later in life. He made no great secret of his sexuality, and indeed one can find homoerotic elements in many of his mature films and artworks. Most likely the authorities viewed this as a weak point that could be exploited to take him out of circulation.

After an international campaign to secure his release, he was set free in December 1977 and returned to his home in Tbilisi, but he remained without work for the next few years. In February 1982 the authorities arrested him yet again, this time on the pretext of bribery. The advent of glasnost in the mid-1980s enabled his return to filmmaking with *The Legend of the Surami Fortress* (*Legenda Suramskoi kreposti*, Georgia Film Studio 1984) and *Ashik-Kerib* (Georgia Film Studio 1988), both of which were widely shown at international festivals.[3]

Toward the end of Parajanov's life, his artworks—mainly prison sketches, collages, and assemblages—drew critical attention in their own right. Figure 0.1

Figure o.1. Sergei Parajanov, *I Am Sixty*. Photo collage. Courtesy of the Sergei Parajanov Museum.

is a collage that Parajanov created from photos taken of him at different stages in life, at once autobiographical and highly characteristic of the kinds of art-works he liked to create. In the summer of 1989 he attempted to film a long-cherished autobiographical project entitled *Confession* (*Ispoved'*, Armenfilm 1989) but his health rapidly deteriorated and he was diagnosed with lung cancer. He passed away in Yerevan, Armenia, in July 1990. The following year, the Sergei Parajanov Museum opened in Yerevan; it continues to attract visitors from around the world.

Although Parajanov has become a cult figure in world cinema and his four major films have remained available on video more or less constantly in the

West since the late 1980s, until now no book-length study on his work has appeared in English. To be sure, a small collection of translated screenplays, a couple of art albums, and a special issue of the *Armenian Review* (edited by this author) have offered tantalizing glimpses.[4] The present study addresses this long-standing gap by providing a comprehensive overview of Parajanov's films and his many unrealized film scripts. It further provides the necessary historical and cultural context for understanding his work and, more broadly, it examines his contributions to global film aesthetics. To a much lesser extent the book also touches upon Parajanov's sizable body of collages and drawings, the bulk of which are on display at the Sergei Parajanov Museum. While these artworks are of significant interest in themselves, they did not impact his political fate within the former Soviet Union in the same way as his films, nor did they play quite the same role in establishing his international reputation.

In the last two decades since Parajanov's death, a number of books about him have been published in Russian and Ukrainian. Notable examples include the Georgian scholar Cora Tsereteli's collections of Parajanov's writings and reminiscences by acquaintances, a memoir by his close friend Vasili Katanian, a collection of Ukrainian documents, analyses of his works by the film critic Karen Kalantar and the filmmaker Levon Grigorian, and a recently published biography also by Grigorian.[5] This present study naturally draws upon that significant body of publications. One area where it breaks new ground is its use of previously unpublished archival documents from Soviet institutions such as Goskino USSR and the Central Committee of the Communist Party to examine Parajanov's relationship with the authorities. In that regard, it offers an unusually detailed, behind-the-scenes portrait of the politics of film production and censorship during the era of stagnation under Leonid Brezhnev, especially from the mid-1960s to the early 1970s, when a number of important films were cancelled, banned, or shelved. While Parajanov was in no way a typical Soviet film director, the vicissitudes of his career provide an effective "cardiogram of the time," to invoke a phrase occasionally used by the director himself.[6]

Ultimately, this book uses the figure of Parajanov as an especially productive case study to shed light on the complex relationship between nationality politics and aesthetics within the former Soviet Union. This interrelationship is crucial for understanding Parajanov and, more generally, the so-called poetic school of Soviet cinema to which he is commonly said to belong. Questions this book will attempt to answer include: Why did Parajanov run afoul of the authorities and, occasionally, other groups within Soviet society such as nationalist movements? Conversely, what factors enabled him to produce the kinds of films that he did within the Soviet film industry when he *was* allowed to work? How were his unique aesthetics understood and evaluated relative to prevailing aesthetic and ideological norms? And, given the significant role that nationality occupied both in his preferred subject matter and his aesthetics, what impact did it have on his career in general?

It has often been assumed that Parajanov's 1973 arrest was due either to the nonconformist nature of his directorial style or to coded nationalist messages within his films. Many critics in the West, particularly during the Cold War era, have emphasized the status of Parajanov's films as "dissident" texts that challenge Soviet ideological norms. *The Color of Pomegranates*, which was not seen widely in the West until after Parajanov's arrest, was especially susceptible in this regard not only because of the timing of its release, but also because of its heavy degree of encodedness as a text. In his review of a May 1978 screening of the film at the Cannes film festival, Ron Holloway speculated that the film "more than likely is only completely understandable to the Armenian nation and people." Briefly summarizing Armenia's historical sufferings, he added, "These nationalist threads and cultural heritage buried in beliefs and traditions course through *Sayat-Nova* like a rushing river from beginning to end."[7] In his 1982 review of the film, Frank Williams referred in passing to *Shadows of Forgotten Ancestors* as a "celebration of purely national values" and offered an explicitly nationalistic interpretation of *The Color of Pomegranates*: "According to an Armenian colleague, seeing the film creates a feeling of intense pride in the Armenians' ability to survive as a nation and retain their Christian culture despite catastrophe and oppression. There are specific images that are highly charged — blood-red juice spilling out onto a cloth and forming a stain in the shape of the boundaries of the ancient Kingdom of Armenia; dyers lifting hanks of wool out of vats in the colors of the national flag, and so on."[8] In Williams's account, Parajanov "represent[s] the church as the centre of resistance to alien imposition."[9] Williams further implied that the 1973 arrest was due to nationalistic and openly religious content in the film. Another film critic, Jeanne Vronskaya, attempted to tie the director's arrest to a purportedly banned film entitled *Kiev's Frescoes* (1971) [*sic*]. According to Vronskaya, the film described "the destruction by the Soviet authorities of the of the famous frescoes in the Kievan cathedrals, the oldest in Russia dating back to the golden age of Kievan art in the tenth and twelfth centuries."[10] As is now known, the unfinished project *Kyiv Frescoes* in fact dated to 1965–1966 and had to do with an altogether different topic.

Writing after Parajanov's death, the Ukrainian filmmaker and journalist Leonid Alekseychuk took care not to characterize Parajanov as a nationalist filmmaker per se, but rather as a "refined aesthete, disdainful of any politics in art."[11] Nonetheless, Alekseychuk implied an underlying connection between the "national" content of Parajanov's major films and their respective republics' struggle for independence: "While the authorities were imposing on the multinational country the artificial concept of a 'homogenous Soviet people, an historically new entity of nations,' Parajanov passionately defended those nations' diversity and uniqueness."[12] Alekseychuk further cited Parajanov's "unwelcome passion for national cultures — for their primordial stages"[13] and the director's obsession with the "genuine," which Alekseychuk juxtaposed to the counterfeit values of Soviet ideology. This account likewise needs to be qualified. While *Shadows of Forgotten Ancestors*, with its vivid representation of Ukrainian folk culture, did indeed become associated with Ukrainian nationalism in the mid-1960s, the same cannot really be said of *The Color of Pomegranates* in terms of Armenian nationalism. And though *The Legend of the Surami Fortress* would appear on the surface to have the most overtly nationalistic narrative elements of Parajanov's major films — a youth willingly immures himself in the wall of a fortress to help it stand against invaders — it was not exactly embraced by Georgian nationalist intellectuals upon its release in the mid-1980s.

I argue instead that Parajanov's troubles were due to a complex set of factors. His unique brand of poetic cinema indeed challenged the aesthetic norms of Soviet cinema, earned accusations of "formalism," and contributed to his eventual exclusion from work, but in other ways his films also reflected prevailing ideology. In particular, a closer look at the production and reception of his films reveals that he was not a nationalist dissident in the commonly understood sense but in some respects held fairly orthodox views, at least publicly, about the role of nationality in the Soviet Union. Other factors that contributed to his arrest and lengthy exclusion from work were his compulsion for attention-seeking, which included public statements criticizing and poking fun at the authorities; his status as a sexual outsider, which was not an immediate cause of the 1973 arrest but which provided a convenient pretext; and his personal entanglement in Ukrainian politics, which must be viewed separately from his films per se. The "national" content of his films was received in different ways depending on the specific political context of the individual republics in which the films were produced. The controversies surrounding Parajanov's reception as a cultural figure in the USSR embody underlying tensions and power struggles within the multinational Soviet state.

The book as a whole is organized in chronological order so as to provide a clear sense of the overall trajectory of Parajanov's life. Chapter 1 describes Parajanov's early years and his first films as a director in Ukraine. Chapter 2 analyzes *Shadows of Forgotten Ancestors* as an example of poetic cinema and traces the film's complicated reception against the background of nationality politics in Ukraine. Chapter 3 focuses on the unfinished project *Kyiv Frescoes*, which marked a turning point in Parajanov's artistic development and his relationship with the authorities. Chapter 4 focuses on *The Color of Pomegranates*, Parajanov's most rigorous example of poetic cinema, and the lengthy censorship battle it encountered. Chapter 5 describes the many unfinished projects Parajanov undertook during the 1970s. Chapter 6 examines the circumstances behind his 1973 arrest and imprisonment in Ukraine and his 1982 arrest in Tbilisi. Chapter 7 traces the reception of *The Legend of the Surami Fortress* during the rise of nationalism in Georgia. Chapter 8 focuses on *Ashik-Kerib*, its unusual conception of the Orient, how the film was affected by rising tensions between Armenia and Azerbaijan just before the breakup of the Soviet Union, and the final years of Parajanov's life.

The Soviet Film Industry

The first context in which Parajanov must be understood is the institutional structure of the Soviet film industry, especially its censorship mechanisms. As the film historian George Faraday has noted, the Soviet film industry was characterized by three main features: a state monopoly on all aspects of production, distribution, and exhibition; a highly bureaucratized system of control; and enforced aesthetic-ideological orthodoxy.[14] When considering the role of censorship in the career of Parajanov or other Soviet filmmakers, one must remember that censors did not function solely as some kind of external review board after a film was finished. Rather, censorship was thoroughly integrated within the film production process as a whole and extended into distribution and exhibition as well. All three traits — state monopoly, bureaucratization, and aesthetic-ideological control — were inextricably related. But as will become clear in the course of the book, the system was not monolithic, and controls were neither absolute nor even consistently applied.

The Soviet film industry functioned as a complex, highly stratified state bureaucracy. Goskino, or the State Committee of the USSR on Cinematography (Gosudarstvennyi komitet SSSR po kinematografii), oversaw all aspects of production, distribution, and exhibition within the Soviet Union as a whole.[15] From 1953 to 1963, the early period of Parajanov's career, the state filmmaking apparatus resided under the Ministry of Culture. Renamed Goskino in 1963, it was attached to the Council of Ministers for financial purposes but it still answered to the cultural section of the Central Committee of the Communist Party of the USSR on ideological issues.[16]

From the time when Parajanov made *Shadows of Forgotten Ancestors* (1964) up to the year before his arrest, the chair of Goskino was Alexei Romanov (1963–1972). Romanov had served previously as the deputy chair of the Propaganda Department for the Central Committee. The Russian émigré and former Mosfilm employee Val Golovskoy has described Romanov as concerned above all with "Party spirit" (*partiinost'*) and "extremely puritanical and ultra-sensitive about 'bedroom scenes.'" In 1972 the authorities replaced Romanov with Filipp Yermash, who was charged with developing a stronger slate of commercial films.[17] Yermash was in turn replaced by Alexander Kamshalov in 1986 as part of the overall shakeup in leadership and loosening of controls under perestroika and glasnost.

Departments within Goskino included the Main Administration for the Production of Feature Films, the Main Administration for Cinefication (*kinofikatsiia*) and Distribution,[18] and the Administration for External Relations. For our purposes, of particular interest was the Main Script-Editorial Board (Glavnaia stsenarno-redaktsionnaia kollegiia). All feature film studios within the Soviet Union had to submit their films to the Script-Editorial Board for approval at various stages, from the initial proposal to include a project in the studio's annual "thematic plan" (*tematicheskii plan*, or *templan*) to the finished screenplay and, ultimately, the finished film itself. One should note that the role of the script editor (*redaktor*) went beyond the conventional definition of censorship; in addition to monitoring a work's ideological content, editors offered advice on creative aspects. Editorial board members typically included experienced industry figures such as scriptwriters and film critics in addition to editors with permanent appointments.[19] Outside of Russia, the individual republics maintained their own state film committees that oversaw production, distribution, and exhibition at the republic level and acted as an intermediary between the individual studios and the central Goskino office in Moscow.

Each film studio had its own Script-Editorial Board and an Artistic Council (*khudsovet*), both of which closely examined films at all stages of production. Besides production crew members and other studio staff, the Artistic Council's membership typically included local Party officials, creative intelligentsia, factory workers, and members of the military. The actual meetings typically included invited attendees in addition to regular council members. Golovskoy describes Artistic Councils as "virtually powerless" bodies that approved films as a matter of routine, despite being "promoted as an outstanding example of democracy in action."[20] Additionally, the larger studios such Mosfilm, the Gorky Studio, Lenfilm, and the Dovzhenko Film Studio divided film production tasks into creative units (*tvorcheskie ob"edineniia*), which were self-contained production units that theoretically "allowed for the decentralizing of artistic-creative leadership and bringing it closer to the shooting crew."[21]

As should be clear at this point, to Faraday's schema one must add a fourth feature: the subdivision of the Soviet film industry into smaller units along national (that is, ethnic) lines. The absolute centrality of this fact remains relatively under-appreciated in much of Western scholarship on Soviet cinema. The closest parallel is perhaps to India, with the important difference that the Soviet state maintained a monopoly on all film production and consequently devoted massive state resources to the development of its multinational industry. In other words, as part of its broader nationality policies, the Soviet state established studios, trained creative personnel, and generally promoted the development of distinct national cinemas in each of the fifteen major republics. As a consequence, during the Soviet era nationalities with a relatively small population base (such as the Kyrgyz) were able to develop a distinct national cinema to an extent that would have been unimaginable on their own in the global marketplace. While the non-Russian film studios faced numerous structural disadvantages compared to their much larger and better-equipped Russian counterparts, during the Soviet era they nonetheless were able to access a broad distribution network, including international festival exposure. Indeed, the collapse of the Soviet Union has left many of these national cinemas in a state of long-term crisis, though this book is concerned mainly with the Soviet era when a more or less stable system remained in place.

Paradoxically, these same Soviet institutional structures that ultimately turned against Parajanov had enabled his development in the first place. Despite their unconventional style, films like *Shadows of Forgotten Ancestors* and *The Color of Pomegranates* reflected the fondness of the Soviet cultural apparatus for promoting the cultural heritage of the many peoples contained within the Soviet Union, and they required the allocation of considerable resources by the state. *The Color of Pomegranates* in particular did not run into trouble because it was about the great Armenian national poet Sayat-Nova. Rather, as archival documents reveal, officials both in the central Goskino office and in Armenia objected to it because they felt that its challenging style and poetic flights of fancy had failed to educate the public about Sayat-Nova in the way they wanted. The question was the extent to which a state-controlled industry should subsidize a highly idiosyncratic, "subjective" vision like Parajanov's.

Nationality and Soviet Cinema

In order to appreciate the full implications of the multinational Soviet film industry and how Parajanov's films were received within it, one must situate the industry both within the Soviet state's broader nationality policies and within the local cultural politics of the individual republics. Drawing upon the theories of historians such as Ernest Gellner, Anthony Smith, Eric Hobsbawm, and Benedict Anderson, some scholars have begun to rethink the extent to which nationality was "constructed" rather than "primordial" in the Soviet Union. Ronald Grigor Suny, analyzing the factors behind the Soviet Union's collapse, argues that the Soviet state "became the incubator of new nations" through its nation-building policies.[22] While the historical and cultural raw materials for national movements already existed within many ethnic groups in the Soviet Union, in Suny's view state policies — together with external trends such as demographic shifts — actually helped engender the paradoxical situation of a "peculiar historic formation of coherent, conscious nations in a unique political system that deliberately set out to thwart nationalism."[23] In his widely cited essay "The USSR as a Communal Apartment," Yuri Slezkine goes even farther in emphasizing what he calls the "chronic ethnophilia of the Soviet regime," which he argues "promoted ethnic particularism."[24] As Slezkine puts it, "'The world's first state of workers and peasants' was the world's first state to institutionalize ethnoterritorial federalism, classify all citizens according to their biological nationalities and formally prescribe preferential treatment of certain ethnically defined populations."[25] In the same vein, Terry Martin has written an in-depth study of early Soviet nationality policies tellingly entitled *The Affirmative Action Empire*.[26] Martin's book in particular stands out for its careful balance between the Soviet state's positive "affirmative action" policies and its more violent and repressive aspects, which included the forced relocation of entire ethnic groups.

In many respects Parajanov's situation reflected the complexities of nationality within the former Soviet Union, especially with regard to local politics and center-periphery relations. Coming from Tbilisi's sizable Armenian enclave, he spoke both Georgian and Armenian but was educated in a Russian-language school. (During the early Stalin era the Soviet State actively promoted education in local languages, but many people still considered fluency in Russian desirable for advancement.) The workshop in directing which he attended at the VGIK was headed by the Ukrainian filmmaker Igor Savchenko and included a mix of ethnic Russians, Jews, Armenians, a Georgian, a Hungarian, and an

Uzbek. Parajanov's filmmaking career began not in his home country of Georgia or in Moscow, but in Ukraine where he was first assigned along with several of his classmates. In 1963, around the time that *Shadows of Forgotten Ancestors* was in production, Petro Shelest rose to first secretary of the Communist Party of Ukraine. Shelest promoted an autonomous Ukrainian national culture. He also oversaw the first wave of crackdowns against Ukrainian dissidents shortly before *Shadows of Forgotten Ancestors* premiered in Kyiv. As a result, the screening became the focus of a protest against the recent arrests and Parajanov became involved in Ukrainian politics though he himself was not a nationalist in the usual sense. Twenty years later, the rise of Georgian separatist nationalism clouded the reception of *The Legend of the Surami Fortress*; his outsider status as an ethnic Armenian became a political liability and he was forced to abandon plans to film an adaptation of the medieval Georgian literary classic *The Passion of Shushanik*. In the late 1980s, the escalating conflict between ethnic Armenians and Azerbaijanis over Karabagh resulted in his last feature film, *Ashik-Kerib*, getting held up from distribution in Armenia for several years.

Parajanov's films further reflect the close relationship between nationality and Soviet cultural production as a whole. In *The Affirmative Action Empire*, Martin argues that the Soviet state "systematically promote[d] the distinctive national identity and national self-consciousness of its non-Russian populations," including through "the aggressive promotion of symbolic markers of national identity: national folklore, museums, dress, food, costumes, opera, poets, progressive historical events, and classic literary works."[27] The Soviet state also devoted much energy to official celebrations and festivals such as the All-Union Film Festival; some specific examples included "Ten Days (*dekad*) of Ukrainian literature and art in the RSFSR" and "Ten Days of Kazakh culture in the People's Republic of Hungary."[28] As such official celebrations suggest, the state was also careful to promote "internationalism" and the "friendship of the peoples" (*druzhba narodov*) through the principle of cultural exchange. In many respects, the Soviet film industry displayed the pervasive impact of state nationality policies as a whole. Some non-Russian republics already had a limited amount of film production before the revolution (e.g., Ukraine and Georgia), but others such as Moldova, Armenia, and the Central Asian republics lacked studio facilities and regular feature film production until the Soviet state established them.

In addition to genre films intended mainly for local consumption, the republic studios produced many prestige projects devoted to their national heritage, such as historical epics and literary adaptations. In fact the Soviet state expended considerable resources on literary adaptations, particularly of nineteenth-century Russian works, the most notorious example being Sergei

Bondarchuk's gargantuan version of Leo Tolstoy's *War and Peace* (*Voina i mir*, Mosfilm 1965–1967). Admittedly, adaptations produced in the non-Russian republics did not receive quite such generous budgets and logistical support. Nonetheless, they played an important role in disseminating knowledge about indigenous traditions, thus asserting cultural difference both within the Soviet sphere and globally. Given Parajanov's interests, it is not surprising that all four of his major features are literary adaptations or, in the case of *The Color of Pomegranates*, a film about a literary figure. The same was true for most of his unrealized scripts and projects, with the notable exceptions of *Kyiv Frescoes* and *Confession*, which were set in the present and had strong autobiographical elements. Literary adaptations provided him with a solid, preexisting structure upon which he could improvise and at the same time indulge his fascination with the past. Because they were heavily supported by the state, adaptations also potentially offered a reliable creative outlet. Indeed, Parajanov frequently attempted, though not always with success, to justify his films within this larger rubric of state-sponsored art celebrating traditional regional cultures.

Official discourse further evoked the formula of Soviet culture being "national in form, socialist in content" (*natsional'naia po forme, sotsialisticheskaia po soderzhaniiu*), as Joseph Stalin memorably phrased it, but what this actually meant in practice varied greatly depending on the immediate political circumstances. At times the emphasis shifted decisively toward the "national"; starting in the mid-1930s, editorials in the Soviet press extolled the "Great Russian people" and elevated them to the rank of "first among equals."[29] Around the same time, as Peter Kenez points out, the Soviet film industry began to produce openly nationalistic historical films such as Vladimir Petrov's *Peter the First* (*Pyotr Pervyi*, Lenfilm 1937–1938), Sergei Eisenstein's *Alexander Nevsky* (Mosfilm 1938), and Vsevolod Pudovkin's *Minin and Pozharsky* (*Minin i Pozharskii*, Gorky Film Studio 1939). During the war, Ukraine, Armenia, and Georgia also produced films on historical patriots to mobilize the population: Igor Savchenko's *Bohdan Khmelnytsky* (Kyiv Film Studio 1939), Hamo Bek-Nazarov's *David Bek* (Yerevan Film Studio 1944), and Mikhail Chiaureli's *Giorgi Saakadze* (Tbilisi Film Studio 1942–1943).[30] During the era of stagnation, even as the Soviet state clamped down hard on "bourgeois nationalist" separatist movements in republics such as Ukraine and Armenia, it tolerated the implicit nationalism behind the Village Prose literary movement in Russia and arguably xenophobic representations of the Other in historical films such as Leonid Osyka's *Zakhar Berkut* (Dovzhenko Film Studio 1972).

As these last examples suggest, representations of nationality occupied a complex and shifting, at times contradictory space within Soviet culture. The same is true of aesthetics, which the Soviets saw as intimately related to ideology. A characteristic expression of this discourse from the Brezhnev era is an essay by Alexander Karaganov, secretary of the Administration of the Union of Cinematographers of the USSR, entitled "Similarities and Differences" ("Skhodstva i razlichiia") and originally published in the October 10, 1982, issue of *Pravda*.

Karaganov opened the essay by defining the Soviet Union as "a voluntary union of equals—a multinational community of peoples, in which respect for the traditions and distinctive features of national cultures, mutual assistance, and reciprocity in relations among them [are] raised to the level of state policy."[31] He then extolled the "special role of Russia in the life of the multinational family of peoples of the USSR," which ranged from the revolutionary role of the Russian proletariat to the widespread cultural influence of the great Russian writers and composers of the nineteenth century. Nonetheless, Karaganov disavowed any connection between such influences and the "forcible Russification" of the Tsarist era.[32] Some of the practices that he cited as contributing to the development of a multinational cinema included "exchanging creative cadres" (that is, having filmmakers work in other republics besides their own); assigning more experienced (usually Russian) directors to serve as consultants to young directors in republics with developing industries; and setting up forms of institutionalized social interaction such as "creative conferences" and "joint trips by practitioners of the film arts from the various republics to large construction sites, factories, and agricultural areas."[33]

Karaganov further maintained that the most successful young filmmakers of the non-Russian republics managed to strike a balance between the need for modernization and the need to respect national traditions as a source of creative inspiration. To illustrate this, he alluded to the pasture-versus-helicopter metaphor from Tolomush Okeev's *The Sky of Our Childhood* (*Nebo nashego detstva*, Kyrgyzfilm 1966). (In the film, children living in a remote Kyrgyz yurt must leave home via helicopter to attend school.) Karaganov emphasized that "national traditions are not a code of laws but a process," and that young filmmakers such as Okeev made "the universal medium of the screen" into "their own living possession, to be then enriched by national tinctures and resonances."[34] Thus, he argued, "In the process, the best products of the national cinemas provide profound and finely nuanced examples of the living dialectic that marks the evolution of human personalities and relationships, an important component of which is the maturation under socialism of the 'primordial' national wellsprings of people's life."[35] Besides the Okeev film, other works Karaganov named as successful examples of this principle include the Turkmen director Khodzhakuli

Narliev's *Daughter-in-Law* (*Nevestka*, Turkmenfilm 1972) and the Georgian director Rezo Chkheidze's *The Father of a Solder* (*Otets soldata*, Georgia Film Studio
1964).

However, Karaganov suggested that not everything "national" was necessarily desirable and singled out an unnamed group of directors "in the republics" for becoming "overly enamored with the decorativeness of their national
styles, especially in their depiction of the past." According to him, "This sometimes leads to bombast, concentration on the externals of style, and obfuscation
of the essence of the action on the screen."[36] Here Karaganov clearly meant the
so-called "poetic school" of Soviet cinema, particularly the films of Parajanov
and the Ukrainian poetic school of the 1960s and 1970s discussed later. Karaganov also criticized filmmakers who "mute the national principle with stylistic
exercises that attempt to bring films up to 'general European standards'" — that
is, who imitated European art films. He capped this larger point as follows:
"What should be sought is not always to be found halfway between a delectation
[of] the past and national exotica on the one hand and a faceless portrayal of
national and social features on the other. What should be sought is a dynamism
in art, which reflects the dynamism of life and the socialist convergence [*sblizhenie*] and mutual enrichment of nationally distinct cultures."[37]

In other words, official discourse exhorted Soviet filmmakers — especially
those from non-Russian republics — to produce works accessible to a mass audience and to maintain a precise ideological and aesthetic balance along a tightrope of nationality, avoiding bland facelessness on the one hand, and excesses of
nationality and style on the other. The poetic school is of great interest precisely
because a number of its exponents, Parajanov among them, failed to walk this
tightrope successfully in the eyes of the Soviet state.

The Poetic School in Soviet Cinema

The term "poetic school" is most commonly associated with Ukrainian filmmakers of the 1960s and 1970s, especially Yuri Illienko and Leonid Osyka.
Other Ukrainian filmmakers sometimes included are Vladimir Denisenko,
Nikolai Mashchenko, and Boris Ivchenko.[38] However, it is important to note
that the term was not merely invented by critics after the fact. The filmmakers in question, especially Parajanov, regularly used terms such as "poetic"
and "poetry" to describe their own work. Although not Ukrainian himself,
Parajanov figures centrally in the Ukrainian poetic school because of *Shadows of Forgotten Ancestors*, which largely initiated that movement and served as a
model, alongside Dovzhenko's works from earlier decades. It remains the most

accomplished Ukrainian film of the postwar era, and today one can even find a statue of Parajanov facing that of Dovzhenko in the front courtyard of the Dovzhenko Film Studio.

Some scholars add to this list other non-Russian filmmakers such as Arta-vazd Peleshian (Armenia), Tengiz Abuladze and Otar Iosseliani (both Georgia), and Bolotbek Shamshiev (Kyrgyzstan). Anna Lawton further classifies Andrei Tarkovsky as "a northern offshoot of the poetic school,"[39] though one hesitates to diminish Tarkovsky's formative impact on his contemporaries by labeling him as an "offshoot." Still, this broader definition proposed by Lawton makes sense since the aforementioned directors all share a common interest in national cultures (especially folk culture or national myths) and stylistic experimenta-tion, at least in some of their films. Indeed, this tendency to link expressions of national particularity with a poetic style is the Soviet poetic school's defining trait.

At the same time, this school was informal at best, and the filmmakers from the republics outside of Ukraine did not even necessarily identify themselves as belonging to the same group. Nonetheless, their shared stylistic traits and thematic concerns enable us to consider the poetic school as a discrete phe-nomenon. What one *can* say is that during the period in question, a small group of directors from various (mostly non-Russian) republics attempted to develop new modes of cinematic expression within the context of Soviet feature film production and to expand the boundaries of narrative film form, commonly emphasizing a lyrical approach.

Jeanne Vronskaya, one of the earliest critics in the West to describe the school in a systematic manner, called it "the cinema of images." She argued that the school typically relied on "a slight story, and concentration on folklore, ethnography, exotic motifs and, in general, the visual elements of the film." She added, "These films resemble a beautiful painting, an old print or drawing, rather than the usual 'filmed play' [. . .] where a dramatic story is acted out on the screen."[40] While Vronskaya was right to point out the heightened signifi-cance of visual design in the poetic school, these filmmakers sought instead to achieve something more synthetic and more aesthetically sophisticated than a simple "painterly" visual style. Rather, poetic cinema as a genre also explores the parameters of sound and editing, producing meaning in new ways com-pared to ordinary dramatic narrative films.

One can trace the concept of poetic cinema in Soviet film theory at least as far back as 1927 with the literary critic Viktor Shklovsky's essay "Poetry and Prose in Cinematography." (Shklovsky, incidentally, took a great interest in Parajanov's work and even collaborated with him in the early 1970s.) In the essay, Shklovsky identifies "two basic film genres" — poetry and prose. He writes, "They are distinguished one from the other not by rhythm, or rather, not by rhythm alone, but by the fact that in a poetic film the technical-formal features predominate over the semantic features. The composition is resolved by formal techniques rather than by semantic methods. Plotless film is poetic film."[41]

Elsewhere in the essay, Shklovsky elaborates the concept as follows: "Possibly what basically distinguishes poetry from prose is its greater range of geometric devices; a whole series of arbitrary semantic resolutions can be replaced by purely formal, geometric resolution. The devices are geometrised, as it were."[42] As examples Shklovsky points to the use of parallelism and recurring images in Dziga Vertov's *One Sixth of the World* (*Shestaia chast' mira*, Goskino 1926) and poetic devices in Pudovkin's *Mother* (*Mat'*, Mezhrabpom-Rus 1926) such as the double exposure of "'moving' Kremlin walls," what he calls a device of "formal rather than semantic derivation."[43] These "geometric devices," as Shklovsky calls them, function as cinematic parallels to verbal poetry. The deployment of repetitions, parallelisms, and visual rhymes creates an underlying structure of meaning within the film text. Similarly, the double exposure to which Shklovsky alludes functions as a relatively straightforward visual metaphor. In the same way that poetry as a literary genre heightens awareness of the sensual and formal qualities of language through devices such as alliteration, assonance, rhyme, and repetition, cinematic poetry foregrounds film language as an expressive medium, freely mobilizing the elements of cinema: mise-en-scène, camerawork, editing, and the soundtrack.

Another concept by Shklovsky that sheds light on the aesthetic principles underlying Parajanov's films is that of *ostranenie*, translated variously as "defamiliarization," "estrangement," or "enstrangement." In his groundbreaking essay "Art as Device," Shklovsky writes: "And so, in order to return sensation to our limbs, in order to make us feel objects, to make a stone feel stony, man has been given the tool of art. [. . .] By 'enstranging' objects and complicating form, the device of art makes perception long and 'laborious.' The perceptual process in art has a purpose all its own and ought to be extended to the fullest. *Art is a means of experiencing the process of creativity*."[44] While Shklovsky saw this perceptual process as the purpose of *all* art, the extent to which Parajanov consistently foregrounds the strategy of *ostranenie* in his mature work is remarkable. This is in fact one of his main aesthetic strategies, regardless of whether he had Shklovsky's essay specifically in mind. The various Soviet film administrators who remarked how *The Color of Pomegranates* was difficult to "perceive" were absolutely right, but one must remember the ultimate aim and value of this process: to refresh and sharpen our perceptions of the world. Another important connection with Shklovsky's theory and Parajanov's poetic cinema is the desire to provoke the viewer into a more active stance toward the work of art and thus to experience and participate in the process of creativity. The deliberate self-reflexive elements in many of his films are one example of this.

The Color of Pomegranates, which is fittingly enough about an Armenian poet, stands out as Parajanov's most thoroughgoing attempt at cinematic poetry and arguably the most rigorous example of this genre in postwar Soviet cinema. Parajanov's achievement is all the more remarkable in that he was largely an intuitive artist and never elaborated his artistic agenda in a deliberate and theoretical manner as did Sergei Eisenstein, Dziga Vertov, or even Andrei Tarkovsky. While one can indeed meaningfully apply the term "poetic" to the aforementioned movement as a whole, most of the films in question are not radically poetic texts to the same extent as *The Color of Pomegranates*. A few other films of the school — namely, Parajanov's *Shadows of Forgotten Ancestors*, Illienko's *A Well for the Thirsty* (*Rodnik dlia zhazhdushchikh*, Dovzhenko Film Studio 1965), and Abuladze's *The Entreaty* (*Mol'ba*, Georgia Film Studio 1967) — function consistently as cinematic poetry, but in fact most represent something of a hybrid genre. One good example of this is Bolotbek Shamshiev's *The White Steamship* (*Belyi parokhod*, Kyrgyzfilm 1975); much of it functions in a fairly straightforward manner, albeit with lyrical touches that represent the boy protagonist's imagination. However, the episode in which the grandfather relates the Kyrgyz tribal origin myth of the Horned Deer Mother displays a marked shift in style and means of signification. For example, during the conversation between the Lame Old Pockmarked Woman and the Horned Deer Mother, Shamshiev uses normal color stock for the shots of the Deer Mother and toned monochromatic stock for those of the Lame Old Pockmarked Woman in order to signify the moral gulf between the two characters. Leonid Osyka's *A Stone Cross* (*Kamennyi krest*, Dovzhenko Film Studio 1968) similarly combines a straightforward narrative with painterly compositions, unconventional editing techniques, and symbolic visual motifs that are echoed over the course of the film.

To be sure, the films of the poetic school were not the only "national" films made during this period; the great bulk of such films adhered more or less closely to dominant ideological and aesthetic norms. One of the films mentioned by Karaganov offers a prime example: Chkheidze's *The Father of a Soldier*, a moving World War II drama about a Georgian peasant who travels to the front in order to locate his son, who has been wounded in battle. In addition to its monumental visual style (as befits a film commemorating the twentieth anniversary of the war), Chkheidze's film is noteworthy for the way it retains the conventional Socialist Realist narrative pattern of the hero's education and integration into the larger community: what Katerina Clark describes in her study on the Soviet novel as the "master plot" charting "the hero's ritual progress toward 'consciousness.'"[45] In this particular case, through the crucible of war the peasant Giorgi Makharashvili learns to see himself not just as a Georgian with narrow ties to his village, but as a citizen of the larger Soviet Union who still retains a distinct Georgian identity.

Nonetheless, for a number of Soviet filmmakers and critics, the poetic mode of cinema could express national particularity in a way that ordinary films could not. There are a few likely reasons why poetic cinema tended to become associated with "national" subject matter. First, ideological controls were generally looser in the non-Russian republics (the periphery) than in Russia itself (the center), with the notable exception of Ukraine. This included the level of tolerance for artistic experimentation; for example, a museum devoted to contemporary art opened in Armenia during the 1970s, when it would have been unthinkable in Russia. Similarly, Georgian cinema during the 1960s and 1970s tended to be more stylistically adventurous and less bound by ideological constraints than Russian cinema. Also, the sensitivity of the nationalities problem meant that some non-Russian intellectuals and artists — most notably, Chingiz Aitmatov — were able to engage in more direct criticism of Soviet society than their Russian counterparts.[46]

Second, the non-Russian studios were eager to attract audiences both within the Soviet Union and internationally. The success of films like *Shadows of Forgotten Ancestors* suggested to studios that poetic cinema might be a way to compete with better-funded and more widely distributed Russian films. In this respect, it is helpful to understand the basic mechanisms behind socialist economies. Katherine Verdery has characterized socialism as a "bureaucratic apparatus" that operates according to the principle of "rational redistribution" — that is, a "drive to maximize redistributive [or 'allocative'] power." Under this "supply-constrained" economic system, Verdery writes, "what counts most in the competition among social actors within allocative bureaucracies is *inputs to one's segment*, rather than outputs of production."[47] Applying this to the specific case of Parajanov, the Armenfilm Studio's support for *The Color of Pomegranates* — despite the film's manifest difficulty and Parajanov's intransigent behavior — was a rational decision insofar as the potential prestige and income of an international success could improve the studio's standing with Moscow. If the film had proved successful, Moscow might have allocated more funds for the studio and allowed them to produce more feature films per year.

Additionally, according to Verdery, ideology functioned as a form of capital

in the socialist state. Thus, in an explicitly multinational state such as the Soviet Union, the expression of ethnic or "national" difference and of the unique
cultural value of one's group—albeit correctly articulated within a socialist
framework—could serve as an effective claim for the allocation of resources to
one's particular "national" segment. However, experimental projects such as
The Color of Pomegranates carried a certain risk since ideological concerns, including ideologies of aesthetics, could override those of efficiency or profit in the
Soviet system. During the retrenchment of the Brezhnev era a number of films
were banned, "shelved," or deliberately under-distributed, even if it meant that
the state never recouped its financial investment.

A third likely reason for the association between "national" subject matter and the mode of poetic cinema was that setting films in the national past
simply gave Soviet directors more room to explore the aesthetic parameters of
cinema. This was not just due to the creative possibilities of folk costumes, myth,
ritual, and folk music. It also had a practical motivation: however concerned the
authorities may have been about representing the past, they were even more
concerned about representing the present or recent events such as the Great
Patriotic War (World War II). When Parajanov did undertake a film set in the
present and concerned with the legacy of the war—*Kyiv Frescoes*—it was widely
criticized and ultimately cancelled.

In sum, the poetic school occupied an ambivalent position within Soviet
cinema. On the one hand, both the value that the state placed on "national"
subject matter and the relative devaluation of market considerations in a socialist system meant that these filmmakers could launch ambitious studio productions that were also personal and experimental to an extent hardly possible in
the Hollywood studio system. Within the Soviet system they could even potentially muster significant resources from the state to realize them. Parajanov, for
instance, was able to borrow priceless artifacts from Etchmiadzin, the seat of
the Armenian Apostolic Church, in order to enhance the aura of historical and
aesthetic authenticity in *The Color of Pomegranates*. On the other hand, these same
filmmakers remained vulnerable, since conservative authorities might interpret
their "difficult" films as contrary to the principles of Socialist Realism, and
since excessive emphasis on national values and imagery risked accusations of
"bourgeois nationalism." Furthermore, unlike art cinema or avant-garde counterparts in the West, Soviet filmmakers had to contend with a bureaucratized
system of production, distribution, and exhibition that was wholly controlled
by the state and lacked alternative venues such as the underground samizdat
press for literature. This set of underlying structural contradictions shaped the
vicissitudes of Parajanov's career to a significant extent.

Of the filmmakers of the poetic school, Parajanov most fully embodies both its emphasis on national difference and its "poetic" mode of expression. However, he himself was hardly a nationalist in the usual sense. Rather, his aesthetics reflected a fascination with the particularities of national cultures, a cosmopolitan outlook, and a penchant for playing with cultural boundaries or sometimes even with the notion of authenticity itself, as this book shall argue. Because of Parajanov's complicated relationship with the idea of the national, his films did in fact tend to attract the attention of nationalists, but not always in a positive light. In other words, Parajanov's political fate was not just a story of the "poet and the tsar," or in this case the filmmaker and the repressive state apparatus. Both he and the Soviet state were in dialogue and sometimes in conflict with the emerging public sphere in the various republics.

All these things make Parajanov a fascinating entry point for examining the shifting ground between nationality and aesthetics in Soviet cultural politics. At the same time, thanks to his unique vision and the creative force with which he realized it, his artistic achievement stands above the bulk of the poetic school and ultimately makes him, alongside Andrei Tarkovsky, the most significant director in postwar Soviet cinema and a major figure of world cinema as well.

1

An Artist's Origins

Youth and Early Ukrainian Films

The story of Parajanov necessarily begins with Tbilisi, also known historically as Tiflis. The city's rich history and lore laid the foundations for his eclectic artistic sensibility and his outlook on life. Nestled in a picturesque valley of the Mtkvari (or Kura) River, Tbilisi is divided by a steep gorge. Although the region has a long history of human settlement, the city proper was established in the late fifth century by the Georgian king Vakhtang I (Vakhtang Gorgasali), who according to legend was attracted to the hot sulfur springs in the area. (In Georgian, *tbili* means "warm.") Already by the early fourth century, long before Vakhtang I's reign, both Georgia and its neighbor Armenia had adopted Christianity as the state religion, making them the first countries to do so. Tbilisi later became an important stop along medieval trade routes due to its location along the crossroads of Europe and Asia. Indeed, because of their geography, Georgia and the other countries of Transcaucasia fell under the influence — and at various times the direct subjugation — of the Persian, Byzantine, Ottoman, and Russian Empires. As a consequence, the peoples of Transcaucasia developed a complex mixture of Eastern and Western cultures that contributed to a sense of rich cultural diversity in the region and to periodic eruptions of ethnic and religious conflict. Both diversity and conflict ultimately shaped Parajanov's own artistic identity and the trajectory of his filmmaking career.

Baedeker's 1914 travel guide to Russia beautifully encapsulates the city's unique cosmopolitan flavor in the years leading up to the 1917 Revolution:

The streets are generally steep and often so narrow that two carriages cannot pass each other. The houses, mostly adorned with balconies, are perched one above the other on the mountain-slope, like the steps of a staircase. From sunrise to sunset, with the exception of the hot midday hours, the streets are crowded with a motley throng of men and animals, walkers, riders and carts. The most conspicuous elements of the population include the Georgian dealers in vegetables, fruit and fish, with their large wooden trays on their heads; the Persians, in their long caftans and their high black fur caps, often with red-dyed hair and finger-nails; the Tartar seïds and mullahs, in flowing raiment, with green and white turbans (tchalma); the smooth-shaven Tartars, in ragged clothing; the representatives of various mountain tribes, in their picturesque tcherkéskas and shaggy fur caps; and the porters, bearing heavy burdens on their backs. The Mohammedan women never appear in the street without their veils. Among other features are the lively little donkeys bearing heavy loads or ridden by one or more men, and the horses carrying waterskins, with their gaily-clad attendants.[1]

For our purposes, it is also important to remember that Tbilisi, with its prosperous Armenian merchant class and Armenian-language newspapers, book publishers, and theaters, was the real center of Armenian culture in the region. During the first half of the nineteenth century, Armenians in fact constituted a solid majority of the city's population. Due to rapid growth of the Georgian and Russian populations, the proportion of Armenians fell to 38 percent by 1897, though they still retained a plurality within the city for some time afterward.[2] Besides Parajanov, other famous Tbilisi Armenians include the playwright Gabriel Sundukian, the composer Aram Khachaturian, and the Hollywood director Rouben Mamoulian.

By 1924, the year of Parajanov's birth, Tbilisi had witnessed convulsive political and social changes: the fall of Tsarist Russia, a brief period of independence under the Social-Democratic Party, and the invasion of the Red Army and establishment of Bolshevik rule in 1921. The Soviet state then merged Georgia with Armenia and Azerbaijan into the Transcaucasian Federated Soviet Socialist Republic, which remained in place until 1936.

Despite all this, aspects of Old Tbilisi culture lingered through Parajanov's childhood. Like other residents of the city, he was well acquainted with the iconic folk art of painters such as Pirosmani and the social types of popular lore. One social type was the *ashugh* or *ashugi*, a poet-troubadour who performed on traditional instruments such as the *tar* (a kind of lute), the *chonguri* (a lute specific to Georgia), and the *kamancha* (an upright fiddle with a globe-shaped body). The *kinto* was a wily street vendor, usually dressed in baggy trousers with a silver belt, who balanced a tray of fruits or vegetables on his head. He was known for his distinctive songs and dances, his cunning, and his love of drinking and carousing. The *qarachokheli* was a craftsman, usually a guild member, who wore a black tunic and was often depicted wining and dining at a table with his friends. The city's cosmopolitan ethnic makeup and material culture likewise remained visible to a certain extent. In that regard, the scholar Giorgi Gvakharia argues that Parajanov's "ecumenical" aesthetic reflects both Tbilisi's diverse "traditions coexisting but almost never fusing" and its "thirst for openness and freedom, for the variegated colors and textures of the spectacular and carnivalesque."[3]

It has often been assumed that the Parajanov family name was Russified from Parajanian. Parajanov himself believed that to be the case, based on various verbal and written comments that he made over the years; he even signed the 1987 script *Treasures at Mount Ararat* (*Sokrovishcha u gory Ararat*) in Russian as "Sarkis Paradzhanian." A surviving birth certificate of his paternal aunt Astkhik indicates that the family name was instead Parajaniants, a historically attested family name in the region.[4] According to Karen Kalantar, the Parajaniants family came from Akhaltsikhe, a town west of Tbilisi, which at that time had a sizable Armenian majority. In the late 1870s or early 1880s, Parajanov's grandfather Sargis (Sergei) Parajaniants moved to Tbilisi. In order to join a merchant's guild he Russified his name to Sergei Parajanov, which was common practice under the Russian Empire. He and his wife Elizaveta had five children: Mkrtich (Mikich), Hovsep (Iosif), Haykaz (Aikaz), Astkhik, and Varvara. In 1920, when Haykaz and his family relocated to Armenia, his brother Iosif (Parajanov's father) moved into their house at 7 Kote Meskhi Street, located in the well-to-do Mtatsminda district.[5]

Iosif Parajanov (1890–1962) attended military cadet school before the Revolution, and later ran a commission shop that sold antiques and valuables. He and his wife Siran Davidovna Bezhanova (1894–1975) had two daughters, Anna (1922–1985), and Ruzanna (1923–1989).[6] Sergei Iosifovich Parajanov, their youngest child, was born on January 9, 1924. As a businessman engaged in trading valuables — what the newly established Soviet state called "speculation" — Iosif frequently ran afoul of the authorities in Stalin-era Georgia and spent time in jail. Parajanov described the family's difficult circumstances in his autobiographical script *Confession* (*Ispoved'*) and elsewhere.[7] In one interview, he told an improbably colorful tale of a visit by the authorities: "My mother took off her diamond earrings and made me swallow them. I wasn't allowed to go out, to go to school — nothing until those diamond earrings passed from my body. When my father saw them, he hit me over the head and said, 'What a strange child! The diamonds were light blue and now they are yellow!'"[8] His mother Siran was a gifted pianist, and like her he developed a lifelong interest in music. As Parajanov often acknowledged, in his childhood he was fascinated by the antiques in his father's shop and managed to acquire a substantial knowledge of them. Later in life this would help him bring in income when he could not find work as a director, but as with his father it would occasionally get him into trouble with the authorities.

His parents enrolled him in a Russian school and his first language thus became Russian, though he also spoke Georgian and, to a lesser extent, Armenian. Aside from a stint in a toy factory and a brief, ill-considered spell as a student in the Construction Department of the Tbilisi Institute of Railway Transport in 1942, Parajanov's interests gravitated early on toward the fine arts. A talented singer, he studied voice at the Tbilisi State Conservatory and performed a large number of concerts for soldiers during the war. Afterward, he applied successfully to the highly competitive VGIK (All-Union State Institute of Cinematography) and matriculated in the fall of 1945.[9]

Education at the VGIK

Parajanov's mentor at the VGIK, the Ukrainian director Igor Savchenko (1906–1950), was one of the more accomplished filmmakers of his day. Admittedly, one could argue that Savchenko never developed the clearly defined artistic identity of older directors such as Eisenstein, Vertov, Pudovkin, or Dovzhenko. This was due at least in part to the timing of his artistic maturation: the early to mid-1930s, when Socialist Realism was already taking shape as an aesthetic policy. By way of context, the epoch-making All-Union Congress of Soviet Writers was held in August 1934, only a couple months after the release of Savchenko's first feature, *The Accordion* (*Garmon'*, Mezhrabpomfilm 1934). During this time Boris Shumyatsky, as the new head of Soyuzkino, was engaged in a concerted effort to create a "cinema of the millions," a Soviet mass entertainment cinema to rival Hollywood in its commercial appeal, while serving simultaneously as a tool for ideological dissemination.[10] Because Shumyatsky dismissed the experimentation of directors such as Lev Kuleshov and Sergei Eisenstein as "formalism," Savchenko was necessarily bound to more conventional narrative forms and stylistic norms than what his older colleagues were able to explore during the silent and early sound era.

The Accordion stands out as one of the first Soviet musical comedies alongside Grigori Alexandrov's *The Jolly Fellows* (*Veselye rebiata*, Mosfilm 1934). Based on Alexander Zharov's popular narrative poem of the same title, the plot of

The Accordion concerns a talented musician who is elected secretary of a collective farm's Komsomol cell and decides that he must stop playing music because of his new role. When a pair of *kulak* hooligans distract the other youths on the farm with liquor and reactionary folk songs, he resolves to take up his accordion again and win back his comrades with uplifting and ideologically sound entertainment. What with its combination of comedy, musical numbers, and message-making, the film might seem the very kind of entertainment that Shumyatsky had in mind. Yet Stalin openly disliked it, complaining of "long-windedness" and "far-fetched psychologism."[11] Nonetheless, it remains Savchenko's most appealing work and a landmark in Soviet sound film, thanks to its dialogue in verse, playful use of sound, rapid cutting and montage effects, and a wealth of painterly images almost certainly inspired by Dovzhenko. Parajanov himself later attempted to emulate the lyrical visual style of Savchenko's musical numbers in his own collective farm musical, *The Top Guy* (*Pervyi paren'*, Dovzhenko Film Studio 1958) as well as in the pastoral sequences of *Ukrainian Rhapsody* (*Ukrainskaia rapsodiia*, Dovzhenko Film Studio 1961).[12] On a thematic level, one can find similar messages about healthy and ideologically sound entertainment in both *The Top Guy* and *The Flower on the Stone* (*Tsvetok na kamne*, Dovzhenko Film Studio 1962).

Although Savchenko's subsequent output was uneven, other important works by him include one of the first Soviet children's films, *The Ballad of Cossack Golota* (*Duma pro kazaka Golotu*, Soyuzdetfilm 1937), the historical epic *Bohdan Khmelnytsky* (Kyiv Film Studio 1939), the Stalinist war film *The Third Blow* (*Tretii udar*, Kyiv Film Studio 1948), and the biography *Taras Shevchenko* (Kyiv Film Studio 1951, completed posthumously). His overall directorial style is somewhat difficult to pin down even taking into account the range of subjects and genres in which he worked, but the critic Rostislav Yurenev emphasizes his Romanticism and his predilection for epic materials.[13] In many respects the historical epic *Bohdan Khmelnytsky* resembles Eisenstein's *Alexander Nevsky* (Mosfilm 1938), especially the monumental, painterly compositions, the declamatory acting style, and the prominent role that vocal music plays on the soundtrack. *The Third Blow* was one of the notorious "fictional-documentary films" (*khudozhestvenno-dokumental'nye fil'my*) made in the late Stalin era, which included Mikhail Chiaureli's *The Fall of Berlin* (*Padenie Berlina*, Mosfilm 1949) and Vladimir Petrov's two-part *The Battle of Stalingrad* (*Stalingradskaia bitva*, Mosfilm 1949–1950). Savchenko's contribution to this cycle juxtaposes scenes of Stalin outlining his shrewd military tactics against the Germans with scenes of ordinary soldiers fighting on the ground during the struggle to retake the Crimean Peninsula. Compared to Chiaureli's notorious *The Vow* (*Kliatva*, Tbilisi Film Studio 1946) or *The Fall of*

Berlin, Savchenko's film is relatively restrained in its mythmaking; it also benefits from memorable battle scenes and strong black-and-white cinematography.

Savchenko left an indelible impression on the students in his workshop, who besides Parajanov included Lev Kulidzhanov and Grigori Melik-Avakian (two other Tbilisi Armenians), Marlen Khutsiev (a Georgian from Tbilisi), Alexander Alov, Vladimir Naumov, Yuri Ozerov, Felix Mironer, Henry Gabay, Nikolai Figurovsky, and Latif Faiziev. Alov and Naumov characterized their teacher as a "cheerful, mischievous, witty person" with powerful charisma, as if surrounded by a "high voltage field." They also stressed how he encouraged the students' artistic independence.[14] In that respect, Savchenko's temperament may have shaped Parajanov's directorial persona as much or more than any stylistic influence per se.

Another area where Savchenko stood apart was his deliberate integration of theory with practice. In the summer of 1947, he assigned his entire class to work as assistant directors on *The Third Blow*. Faiziev, Mironer, and Khutsiev noted that this was actually a first for the VGIK and not part of the standard curriculum at that time.[15] The film's large-scale battle scenes were very different from the more intimate approach — and the necessarily lower budgets — that most of Savchenko's students would later adopt for their early films, but one might see Yuri Ozerov's monumental war epic *Liberation* (*Osvobozhdenie*, Mosfilm 1968–1971) as an outgrowth of that experience.

Parajanov's first run-in with the law occurred in the summer of 1948. According to documents from his 1973 trial, he and a small coterie of young men in Tbilisi were arrested and charged with homosexuality because of their association with Nikolai Mikava, a noted writer, officer in the MGB (Ministerstvo gosudarstvennoi bezopasnosti, or Ministry of State Security), and head of the Georgian Society of Cultural Liaisons with Foreign Countries (GOKS). Parajanov was convicted that October, but was released on appeal in December the same year.[16] In an interview with Patrick Cazals, Parajanov later acknowledged the nature of the charges but appeared to deny any sexual involvement with Mikava, stating: "The Devil only knows whom among them he had intimate relations with."[17] While this scandal in Tbilisi did not result in his expulsion from the VGIK, nor did it appear to have much of an immediate impact on his early career as a film director, it remained a point of vulnerability with the Soviet authorities, who used it eventually as a pretext for his second arrest and imprisonment in the 1970s.

The second film for which Savchenko engaged his students was *Taras Shevchenko*, a biography of the great Ukrainian national poet and painter. The protracted censorship battle associated with that film exacted a terrible personal

toll on Savchenko.[18] It is widely believed that the resulting stress led to his untimely death at the age of 44 in 1950. Savchenko's students (mainly Alov and
Naumov) completed the film for its release in 1951. After this Parajanov served as
an assistant director on a third film, Vladimir Braun's *Maximka* (Kyiv Film Studio 1952). Adapted from the book *Sea Stories* by the popular nineteenth-century
Russian writer Konstantin Staniukovich, the film concerns a young African boy
who is rescued from an American slave ship and adopted by a crew of Russian
sailors.

Back in Moscow, Parajanov fell in love with and married a beautiful young
Tatar woman, Nigyar Seraeva, who worked as a salesperson at TsUM (the
Central Department Store). The exact circumstances are not entirely clear, but
on February 13, 1951, not long after the wedding, she was killed, possibly by
her brothers for Parajanov's failure to pay a bride-price. According to Natalia
Fokina, her body was found with multiple stab wounds near railroad tracks;
other accounts suggest that she died as a result of being thrown directly on the
tracks. Parajanov occasionally returned to Moscow to visit her grave and leave
flowers. Later in life he rarely talked about this event, but it obviously affected
him deeply. A photo of Nigyar is on display at the Parajanov Museum.[19]

Despite this devastating setback, Parajanov managed to complete his diploma project, *A Moldovan Fairy Tale* (*Moldavskaia skazka*, VGIK 1952), based
on the 1946 fairy-tale poem *Andriesh* by the Moldovan writer Emilian Bukov.
Parajanov later reworked the same story for his feature film debut. The actual
diploma film does not appear to have survived, but the feature film version at
least gives some idea of the basic storyline, if little of the original's unique flavor.
According to Rostislav Yurenev, for the diploma film Parajanov constructed a
"large puppet" to represent the character of Andriesh and "filmed the puppet
on location, achieving a remarkable naturalness of movement and a combination of live nature with theatrical illusion."[20] In his 1966 essay "Perpetual
Motion," written after the worldwide success of *Shadows of Forgotten Ancestors*
(*Teni zabytykh predkov*, Dovzhenko Film Studio 1964), Parajanov himself said of
A Moldovan Fairy Tale: "The poetics of this work came to me almost at once. I
heard songs about a shepherd who had lost his flock—the symbol of love and
success—in Georgia, Armenia, and afterward in the Carpathians. I was attempting to build an expressive system originating directly from folk poetry and
mythology."[21] Thus, in Parajanov's account, his diploma film's use of national
folk culture pointed toward his mature aesthetics in a way that his subsequent
Ukrainian feature films before *Shadows* did not. The deliberate play between the
naturalistic qualities of cinema and the artificiality of theater that Yurenev observed in the film would also become a core element of Parajanov's mature style.

At any rate, Alexander Dovzhenko, who replaced Savchenko as their teacher and evaluated the students' diploma films, was impressed with Parajanov's work and invited him to sign on at the Kyiv Film Studio, where he joined his fellow students Alov, Naumov, Mironer, Gabay, and Melik-Avakian as assistants.

Early Years in Kyiv

In 1955, the same year as the release of his debut feature *Andriesh*, Parajanov married Svetlana Shcherbatiuk in Kyiv. The daughter of a diplomat who had served at the Ukrainian consulate in Canada, Svetlana was strikingly beautiful, poised, and well educated; she had learned English during her stay in Ottawa and continued to teach it years later. Their marriage was beset with problems arising from various factors: age difference (at the time of their marriage, she was 17 and he was 31); Parajanov's notoriously difficult temper; Svetlana's own independent-mindedness (Parajanov was apparently looking for a more subservient or "decorative" wife, as Shcherbatiuk and several of Parajanov's friends have commented); and ongoing financial difficulties due to Parajanov's impulsive habits and his lack of regular work. In November of 1958 they had one son, Suren—named after Parajanov's closest friend, the cinematographer Suren Shakhbazian. The couple divorced in March 1962, though they remained in regular contact up to Parajanov's death.

Parajanov's initial financial difficulties and his more general problems establishing a career in Kyiv may have been due in part to behavioral patterns that he exhibited early on. Among other things, he was fond of impersonating or making derisory remarks about higher-ups. According to his colleague Henry Gabay, Parajanov's clownish behavior did not sit well with the authorities and, in general, did not fit in the culture of that studio: "Kyiv directors such as Levchuk and Shvachko were pompous and stout, stressing their closeness to the highest circles of command. For them Parajanov was simply a buffoon."[22] Parajanov also tended to be outspoken in his criticisms of individual authority figures and of the system as a whole, firing off sharply worded letters and telegrams. Later in his career, when he became a bona fide public persona, he also used public speeches and interviews as platforms for airing his complaints, earning him a lifelong reputation among the authorities as a troublemaker.

Probably the earliest surviving example of such a critique was an open letter, dated 1956 or (according to the scholar Yuri Morozov) no later than 1957 and addressed to a whole array of individuals and institutions: David Kopitsa, the director of the Dovzhenko Film Studio; the head of the studio's Partburo (Party Bureau); the chairman of the Creative Section of the studio; the editorial staff of the Ukrainian-language newspaper *For Soviet Film* (*Za radians'kyi fil'm*); the minister of culture of the Ukrainian SSR; the minister of culture of the USSR; the Central Committee of the Communist Party of the USSR and the Central Committee of the Communist Party of Ukraine; and, lastly, the editorial staff of the newspaper *Soviet Culture* (*Sovetskaia kul'tura*).[23]

The bulk of the letter detailed Parajanov's fruitless efforts at producing a script, the rather unpromisingly titled *Fire of a Young Heart* (*Ogon' iunogo serdtsa*). Parajanov complained that he had met with various obstructions, despite the script's approval by the Script Department and even by the Ministry of Culture of the USSR for inclusion in the Dovzhenko Film Studio's 1957–1958 thematic plan. He laid most of the blame on Kopitsa, the studio head, whom he accused of unnecessarily delaying and ultimately scuttling the project. Subsequent comments in the letter pointed to a larger problem, as Gabay suggests above: that on the whole Parajanov was not taken seriously by officials at the studio. Parajanov writes: "I most emphatically reject the accusation directed against me, that instead of real work I am engaging in play-acting and refusing to join a team. In the capacity of what, allow me to be curious. An assistant? I won't agree to such work, and not out of some whim, but because I already did enough of it. Permit me to give the certificate to those who aren't up on things."[24] This, along with the allusion in the letter to his "exceptionally grave material situation," betrays a great deal of frustration from his previous experiences working in the studio. Parajanov's readiness to appeal to the highest levels of authority and to seek newspaper publicity from the outset was likely perceived as rash for a not-yet-established director. Nevertheless, shortly afterward he was allowed to direct his first solo feature, *The Top Guy*. So it is entirely possible that in this instance, the authorities took his complaints seriously and made some attempt to address them.

Context: The Cinema of the Thaw

The time frame of Parajanov's education at the VGIK and his apprenticeship in the Soviet film industry—from 1945 to the mid-1950s—bears significance in more than one respect. First, it marks him generationally as a director of the Thaw. As Josephine Woll has pointed out, the complicated nature of the film production process meant that the changes experienced after Stalin's death in other art forms such as literature happened at a slower rate in the film industry. Such changes included the loosening of crippling bureaucratic and ideological restrictions, improvements in the material and technical base, and ultimately an increase in feature film production.[25] Coming out of the lean years of the late

Stalin era, when only a handful of films were made each year and then only by established directors, the Thaw generation's full entry into the film industry was thus delayed a few years. Parajanov, for example, worked as an assistant director for about four years before he was able to direct his own features. Once they finished their apprenticeship, these young directors typically teamed up in pairs for their feature film debuts. Parajanov co-directed *Andriesh* (Kyiv Film Studio 1955) with Yakov Bazelian; other such collaborations included Alexander Alov and Vladimir Naumov on *Restless Youth* (*Trevozhnaia molodost'*, Kyiv Film Studio 1954), Felix Mironer and Marlen Khutsiev on *Spring on Zarechnaia Street* (*Vesna na Zarechnoi ulitse*, Odessa Film Studio 1956) and Lev Kulidzhanov and Yakov Segel on *It Started Like This . . . (Eto nachinalos' tak . . . ,* Gorky Film Studio 1956). Some directors, most notably Alov and Naumov, chose to continue working as a team for subsequent projects.

One of the main contributions of the Thaw directors was a supposedly more "authentic" and "unvarnished" representation of reality.[26] Alov and Naumov's *Pavel Korchagin* (Kyiv Film Studio 1956), an adaptation of Nikolai Ostrovsky's novel *How Steel Was Tempered*, attempted to capture the emotional fervor of the years immediately after the Revolution, at the same time depicting a reality that was "squalid, disease-ridden and plagued with hunger."[27] Mironer and Khutsiev's *Spring on Zarechnaia Street* is arguably more influential in this regard. Clearly inspired by Italian Neorealism and older Soviet *bytovoi* films,[28] the film touches upon everyday problems such as the difficulty of finding good housing. The narrative focuses mainly on personal problems, though it does contain the requisite tour of the steel factory where Sasha works. The teacher, far from being the conventional wise leader, is inexperienced and emotionally immature compared to some of her students. The resolution of the main conflict—a complicated love relationship between the teacher and her student—remains deliberately open-ended. Stylistically, the film is more relaxed than the "monumental" films of the Stalin era; it uses a more natural, less theatrical acting style and looser, less rigidly formalized visual compositions, with an emphasis on typicality and authenticity of detail in the mise-en-scène. Mironer and Khutsiev's film was a significant popular success, earning 30.12 million admissions and coming in ninth place for box office admissions that year.[29] Kulidzhanov and Segel's *The House I Live In* (*Dom, v kotorom ia zhivu*, Gorky Studio 1957), while perhaps more overtly melodramatic than *Spring on Zarechnaia Street*, is notable for its evenhanded treatment of adultery and for the way it uses the families living in a single apartment building to represent a cross section of Soviet society.

Parajanov's earliest films, in contrast, are not concerned with quotidian realism or, for that matter, with any kind of systematic rejection of Stalin-era aesthetics. Partly this is because unlike some of his colleagues, he had not yet developed a strong artistic identity with which he could mark himself apart from the older generation of directors. *Andriesh* has little to distinguish it from the fairy-tale films of Alexander Ptushko and Alexander Rou. *The Top Guy* shows a certain degree of irreverence in the way it handles the narrative conventions of the *kolkhoz* (collective farm) musical, but one hesitates to call it daring. Certainly, it is a far cry from the supposed "unvarnished truth" of his colleagues. *Ukrainian Rhapsody* and *The Flower on the Stone*, on the other hand, clearly invoke one of the most striking stylistic innovations of the Thaw—Sergei Urusevsky's virtuosic mobile camerawork for Mikhail Kalatozov's films *The Cranes Are Flying* (*Letiat zhuravli*, Mosfilm 1957) and *The Letter Never Sent* (*Neotpravlennoe pis'mo*, Mosfilm 1959). However, the scripts that Parajanov had to work with for those two films were more formulaic and the productions were neither as well-budgeted nor as technically polished as the Kalatozov/Urusevsky collaborations. Parajanov's early features are for the most part of lesser consequence than the best Soviet films of that era, although they contain elements that prefigure his mature style. The next section will look at the individual films more closely and trace their stylistic development.

Andriesh (1955)

The feature-length version of *Andriesh* (Kyiv Film Studio 1955) is a straight-forward example of the Soviet fairy-tale film genre. In the film, the young shepherd Andriesh is charged with guarding the village's flock of sheep. There Andriesh meets Voinovan, a *bogatyr* (hero) who gives the young boy his magic wooden flute (Fig. 1.1). Black Storm, a wicked sorcerer who despises the flute's joyous music, descends upon the village in human form, hypnotizes and kidnaps Voinovan's beloved Liana (Fig. 1.2), sets the village aflame, and steals its flock. Andriesh undertakes a journey to confront Black Storm and meets various individuals who help him, while Voinovan amasses an army of Haiduks (mercenary soldiers) with sun-tempered maces to battle the sorcerer.

The film's visual design is clearly inspired by the illustrations for the 1946 Russian-language edition of Emilian Bukov's narrative poem on which it is based.[30] Although the credits list Bukov as one of the script's authors, the feature-film version of *Andriesh* diverges substantially from its source. In the poem's opening chapter, Andriesh's inseparable companion is a talking ewe named Miora. When Andriesh inquires why she is sad despite her idyllic life, she warns him that the sorcerer Black Storm is planning to steal her along with the

Figure 1.1. Voinovan gives Andriesh his enchanted flute (*Andriesh*).

rest of the flock. (Not surprisingly, the character of Miora is missing from the film altogether.) Liana, the beloved of the hero Fet-Frumos (Voinovan in the film), is kidnapped by a seven-headed dragon, whereas in the film Black Storm spirits her away. In general, Fet-Frumos plays more of a marginal role in the poem's narrative than Voinovan does in the film. As a consequence, the film's dialogue and voice-over narration have been reworked completely. Still, the film retains several episodes from the original poem, such as Andriesh's encounters with Pakala, the oak tree Strezha, and the giant Strymba-Lemna.

Despite these changes, *Andriesh* employs more or less traditional fairy-tale motifs and an overall narrative structure of the type outlined by the folklorist Vladimir Propp in his classic study *The Morphology of the Folktale*. Its visual style also hews closely to the conventions of Soviet fairy-tale films of that era. As the scholar Miron Chernenko succinctly puts it, Parajanov and Bazelian's film is like "half-baked Artur [*sic*] Arturovich Rou."[31] However, while Chernenko compares *Andriesh* to *Vasilisa the Fair* (*Vasilisa prekrasnaia*, Soiuzdetfilm 1939), it has less in common with that particular film, with its lively, grotesque characterizations and its at times bizarrely stylized production design, than with Alexander

Figure 1.2. The wizard Black Storm hypnotizes Liana (*Andriesh*).

Rou's more restrained *May Night, or the Drowned Maiden* (*Maiskaia noch, ili Utoplennitsa*, Gorky Film Studio 1952). As with *May Night*, the skies in *Andriesh* invariably contain dramatic cloud formations or flaming sunsets, and storks invariably nest on the thatched roofs. Ptushko's films of the same era, particularly *Sadko* (Mosfilm 1952), likewise share static, painterly compositions, clouded skies, golden sunsets, frequent use of low angles to film actors, and a declamatory acting style.

Andriesh also contains the obligatory folk dance number that one finds in so many Soviet films with "regional" subject matter, though here it suffers more than usual from a stage-bound feel. The use of regional color and painterly compositions in Soviet cinema is a trend that one can trace back at least as far as Dovzhenko's poetic masterpieces of the silent era, but for *Andriesh* the influence of its immediate generic predecessors — Rou's and Ptushko's films — is much stronger. Indeed, Rou's glossy take on Ukrainian folk culture in *May Night* — colorful, immaculate folk costumes and carefully choreographed song-and-dance numbers — represents precisely the homogenized approach to folk culture that Parajanov and other directors of the Ukrainian poetic school would later rebel against, though Rou's film and many other such works of the late

Stalin era still retain undeniable charm and continue to appeal to post-Soviet audiences.

Chernenko's "half-baked" remark about *Andriesh* is certainly appropriate, for Parajanov and Bazelian's direction lacks the assured touch of those films and the musical numbers in general are not as carefully integrated into the story. But despite its limitations, the film is still enjoyable to watch and it benefits from a solid leading performance by the Moldovan child actor Kostia Russu. The cinematography is also picturesque, if not as polished as the best Soviet films produced during that era, and it contains some effective individual compositions and tracking shots. If any part of the film displays the seeds of Parajanov's future style, it might be the segment toward the beginning that depicts Andriesh walking past villagers at work spinning wool and grinding corn. Their oddly static poses, especially the portrait-shot of a woman holding a sheep in her arms, perhaps point to the tableau aesthetic that he would later develop. In his review in the newspaper *Vechirnyi Kyiv* (*Evening Kyiv*), the critic L. Viktorov praised the performance of Kostia Russu but felt that the adult actors were generally not as successful due to an underdeveloped script. He also praised the musical score, Suren Shakhbazian's cinematography, and the film's "multicolored national costumes, chosen with great taste," though he complained that the set design was "sloppily realized" — especially Black Storm's cave. However, some of Viktorov's criticisms — such as the episodic nature of the script and an insufficient portrayal of "Andriesh's connection with the people" — seem to arise from imposing certain narrative and ideological expectations on what was, after all, a simple fairy tale.[32] The film opened on four screens in Kyiv on June 20, 1955, but played for only one week before disappearing.[33] Later that summer, in the leading Soviet film journal *Iskusstvo kino* (*The Art of Film*), the critic Mikhail Beliavsky singled out *Andriesh* as a particularly bad example of what he considered the widespread "drabness and mediocrity" in Soviet film production during that era. He wrote: "It did not become the poetic, sublime, and moral fairy tale that it could have been, and it did not do so only because creative fantasy, invention, thought, and daring were not introduced in the realization of [its] fairy-tale images. The film was accomplished in a somehow utilitarian and soulless manner."[34] Perhaps due to the perceived failure of *Andriesh*, Parajanov did not receive any further assignments until 1957, as noted earlier.

The Top Guy (1958)

In *The Top Guy* (*Pervyi paren'*, Dovzhenko Film Studio 1958), Yukhim "Yushka" Zhurba is a young mechanic at a Ukrainian collective farm called "Victory"

Figure 1.3. Yushka wins Odarka's affections with his soccer-playing skills (*The Top Guy*). Courtesy of the Oleksandr Dovzhenko National Centre.

and is in love with the Komsomol secretary Odarka. Immature and prone to acting out, he mistakenly assumes that Odarka is instead in love with Danila, a returning soldier. Yukhim and a group of other young men with too much time on their hands stir up trouble on the farm. When the Komsomol starts up a soccer team in order to provide a healthy recreational outlet for the collective farm's youth, Yushka decides that showing off his skills as a goalie to Odarka is the best way to win her attention (Fig. 1.3).

The opening musical medley of *The Top Guy* features images of smiling and singing *kolkhozniks* energetically shoveling wheat, and tractors riding across bounteous wheat fields set against the backdrop of dramatically clouded skies. Soviet viewers would have picked up immediately on the allusion to Ivan Pyriev's *Cossacks of the Kuban* (*Kubanskie kazaki*, Mosfilm 1949). Less directly, it also recalls the harvest number in Savchenko's *The Accordion*, the point of origin for the *kolkhoz* musical. Thus *The Top Guy* functions as an affectionate homage to (or parody of) the *kolkhoz* musical genre as a whole. Miron Chernenko further notes the resemblance both in plot function and physical appearance of its characters to Pyriev's regular cast.[35] To be more specific, not only does

Liudmila Sosiura, who plays Odarka, vaguely resemble Pyriev's favorite lead actress Marina Ladynina, she even raises pigs, evoking Ladynina's character in *The Swineherd-Girl and the Shepherd* (*Svinarka i pastukh*, Mosfilm 1941). The jovial grandfatherly Kirill Pavlovich recalls Anton Petrovich (Vladimir Volodin) in *Cossacks of the Kuban*. Moreover, Ivan Matveev, the actor who plays Kirill Pavlovich, previously appeared as Senka in *The Rich Bride* (*Bogataia nevesta*, Ukrainfilm 1937). Sidor Sidorovich (Nikolai Shutko), the effete salesman at the village's department store, seems almost more interested in lavishing his beloved Frosenka with fancy dresses than in romancing her; he similarly recalls the barber in *The Rich Bride*. There is even an elderly watchman with a propensity for chasing after people with a shotgun, obviously borrowed from the latter film as well.

However, this is 1958 and the ideological underpinnings of the *kolkhoz* musical genre have become more relaxed in the wake of the Thaw. The main coupling of Odarka and Yushka and the plot's emphasis on soccer are transparent bids for the burgeoning Soviet youth audience of the postwar era. The attractive lead actor Grigori Karpov plays a roguish antihero. (He would later appear in *The Flower on the Stone* in an almost identical role.) Life on the collective farm is idyllic and bountiful as one would expect in such a film, but it is relatively down-to-earth compared to *Cossacks of the Kuban*. The district fair in Pyriev's film is an absurd orgy of luscious fruits, rich fabrics, and consumer goods such as record players and baby grand pianos, whereas the fair in *The Top Guy* is far more modest in scale and ultimately more plausible.

In *The Rich Bride* characters compete to be the most productive—indeed, their worth is defined by their productivity—but the characters in *The Top Guy* seem more concerned with play than work. Oksana, the local Komsomol leader, is capricious, subject to the whims of a young woman's heart. From the very beginning she is clearly attracted to the rebellious streak in Yushka, and she is less concerned with reforming him and bringing him into the fold of the Party than with concocting schemes to get him to visit her workplace. Pretending that the power has gone out, she deliberately removes nuts from a switchbox and hides them in the medicine cabinet so that Yushka will have to come and replace them. In an earlier time, such actions might have been labeled as "wrecking," and the perpetrator ostracized or worse. While Yushka is depicted as a loner and something of a delinquent, he does not undergo a significant change of character in the course of the film; his behavioral problems are solved mostly by creating an appropriate outlet for his energies through soccer. (The importance of healthy recreational activities is a regularly recurring theme in Soviet films of that era.)

Parajanov indulges his fascination with folk culture by including Ukrainian

Figure 1.4. A villager pays her respects to a god of the fields (*The Top Guy*). Courtesy of the Oleksandr Dovzhenko National Centre.

folk-inspired choral music on the soundtrack. In one scene, a character pays her respects to the statue of a god of the fields and invites it to her wedding (Fig. 1.4). Perhaps aware of the script's limitations, he also attempts to add interest through all sorts of playful gimmicks. When Yushka watches with jealousy as Odarka and Danila ride together on a bicycle, he is photographed in front of a statue of a deer, thus placing a pair of cuckold's horns behind his head. In another scene, a boy drops a bunch of apples that he has stuffed under his shirt and the shot is repeated in reverse, making them magically fly back up under his shirt. Later, the soundtrack includes a woman's choir singing a folk-inspired song that criticizes Yukhim's behavior and characterizes him as a "hooligan"; irritated, he turns off the loudspeaker and cuts off the music, subverting our initial perception of the music as non-diegetic. Such gags contribute to the genial and playful tone of the film as a whole, but at times they seem forced and are not always organic to the story. While Parajanov's direction is competent and the film contains a number of nicely composed shots, it lacks the sureness of tone, uncluttered simplicity, and occasional delicate touches that give Pyriev's musicals their enduring charm. Compared to Alexei Mishurin's

The Youthful Years (*Gody molodye*, Dovzhenko Film Studio 1958), another highly popular youth-oriented musical produced around the same time at the same studio, *The Top Guy* comes off as less polished but more spirited and exuberant.

Arguably, the film's awkwardness has to do in part with the uncomfortable match between the underlying ideology of the traditional Stalin-era *kolkhoz* musical and the genre's ongoing function as mass entertainment in the Soviet Union. By the time Parajanov made his film, the genre had lost its ideological raison d'être, though not its popular appeal as entertainment. *The Top Guy* was, one should remember, released *after* key Thaw films such as *The Cranes Are Flying* and Eldar Riazanov's *Carnival Night* (*Karnaval'naia noch*, Mosfilm 1956). What remained was a set of established narrative and stylistic conventions that Parajanov was obligated to build from. His "unprincipled eclecticism," to use Kalantar's phrase,[36] and his lack of focus meant that undigested visual and narrative clichés bumped up against weakly motivated comic gags and the occasional fresh directorial touch.

One question that arises from today's perspective is the possible presence of homoerotic jokes. In the scene where Kirill Pavlovich observes the youth training for various sports, at one point he looks down at the ground and says, "Boys! What on earth is this?" Two men stand up and it becomes clear that they are wrestling. A nearby police officer replies, "I'm here. Everything's in order!" Most viewers would read this gag innocently: Kirill Pavlovich thinks that the two men offscreen are merely scuffling on the ground. However, later in the film two young men in the announcer's booth play a waltz over the PA system and dance together. That shot is followed almost immediately by a long tracking shot of young men with powerfully built physiques bathing outdoors. One hesitates to read too much significance into such moments—for instance, this was hardly the first Soviet film to idealize the male body—but considering that Parajanov deliberately introduced more overtly homoerotic elements into his later films, the possibility at least should be raised here as well.

The film received a sympathetic advance write-up in *Sovetskii ekran* (*Soviet Screen*), which emphasized how the characters resembled people one might meet in real life, especially the character of Yushka.[37] Alexander Kiknadze, the reviewer in *Sovetskii sport* (*Soviet sport*), was not so easily convinced. The title of Kiknadze's review characterized the film as a "pumpkin" (*tykva*, a Russian colloquialism for a bad film), which Kiknadze later underscored by writing: "They released a film that, instead of smiles, provokes sad reflections on the fate of the sports-comedy film genre." In particular, Kiknadze described the film as an "artless collection of manufactured clichés" and deplored the "negative hero" and his unconvincing transformation.[38] In an article about the state of

Ukrainian screenwriting, the noted playwright and scenarist Alexander Levada suggested that at least part of the film's shortcomings arose from its script:

> The script department at the Kyiv studio took the screenwriters P. Lubensky and G. Bezorudko through twelve versions of the comedy script *The Top Guy*, and the result turned out unencouraging. Although there are several funny episodes in the comedy, and although the director S. Parajanov made even a stork dance to music in the film, its artistic level can hardly be considered satisfactory. The setting in which the film's events unfold is up-to-date, the kolkhoz girls are also up-to-date, but the guys (and there is a large group of them in the film) are literally dug up for laughs from an archive at least thirty years old.[39]

Ironically, after this Parajanov directed a script by Levada entitled *Ukrainian Rhapsody*, itself no model of freshness and originality.

But if one is to accept the data provided by the Russian film scholar Sergei Kudriavtsev, regardless of *The Top Guy*'s artistic merits it was by far the greatest popular success of Parajanov's career, at 21.7 million domestic admissions in the USSR as a whole. In Kyiv, the film ran for nearly three weeks after its July 25, 1959, theatrical release.[40] To be sure, 1959 was the Dovzhenko Studio's strongest year ever in terms of box office performance; its top grossing film was Viktor Ivchenko's *An Extraordinary Event* (ChP — *Chrezvychainoe proisshestvie*, 1958, Soviet-wide release 1959), at 47.4 million admissions. *The Top Guy* thus placed only seventh among the studio's releases that year, though it still earned more admissions than many of the studio's top-grossing films of the 1970s and 1980s. By way of contrast, Parajanov's *The Flower on the Stone* (1962) sold 5.2 million admissions, *Shadows of Forgotten Ancestors* (1964, Soviet-wide release 1965) 6.5 million, *The Color of Pomegranates* (*Tsvet granata*, Armenfilm 1969, Soviet-wide release 1970) 1.07 million, and *The Legend of the Surami Fortress* (*Legenda Suramskoi kreposti*, Georgia Film Studio 1984, Soviet-wide release 1986) a mere 400,000.[41]

Three Documentary Films

Natalia Uzhvy (1959), *Dumka* (*Derzhavna zasluzhena akademichna kapela URSR "Dumka,"* 1960), and *Golden Hands* (*Zolotye ruki*, 1960) were documentary films commissioned for Ukrainian television and produced at the Dovzhenko Film Studio.[42] They may be minor works in the director's canon, but the subjects unquestionably held personal appeal for him. In his 1966 essay "Perpetual Motion," Parajanov himself acknowledged the creative inspiration he found working on them: "The material on which the films *The Flower on the Stone* and *Dumka* were made is profoundly memorable for me. Folk carving, embroidery, and relief work. The ancient songs of Ukraine. I wanted to convey the world of these songs in all its primitive charm. I wanted to convey the folk "vision" without museum greasepaint [*bez muzeinogo grima*] — to return all these stunning embroideries, reliefs, tiles, to [their] creative source, to combine them in a single spiritual act."[43] Clearly, instead of *The Flower on the Stone* Parajanov meant to refer to *Golden Hands*; for it is in that short film where, faced with the practical problem of displaying a large quantity of folk art in a visually interesting manner, he worked out some of the basic techniques of his mature style.

Natalia Uzhvy celebrates the achievements of the noted Ukrainian stage and film actress, juxtaposing footage of Natalia Uzhvy in the present day with clips from her film roles. The grand dame stands on a bank overlooking the Dnieper, lays flowers on the eternal flame of the Unknown Soldier in Kyiv, plants trees, and finally attends a gala in her honor. The film clips include Savchenko's *Bohdan Khmelnytsky* and *Taras Shevchenko*, Mark Donskoi's *The Rainbow* (*Raduga*, Kyiv Film Studio 1943), and Grigori Kozintsev and Leonid Trauberg's *The Vyborg Side* (*Vyborgskaia storona*, Lenfilm 1938). The section containing reenactments of famous stage roles is similar in style to the montage sequence in *Ukrainian Rhapsody* that depicts Oksana performing various operatic roles in rapid succession — an early example of Parajanov reusing visual ideas that he liked from one project to the next.

Dumka consists of a filmed a cappella performance by Dumka, the State Merited Academic Choir of the Ukrainian SSR. For the individual songs, which include folk tunes, patriotic hymns, and virtuoso choral showpieces, Parajanov provides trite visualizations: sculptures of revolutionary heroes breaking their chains ("Eternal Revolutionary"), crashing waves, rippling ponds, and drooping willow branches ("The Water Flows"), and springtime cherry blossoms ("The Nightingale").

From today's standpoint, the most interesting by far of the three shorts is *Golden Hands*, co-directed by Parajanov, Alexander Nikolenko, and Alexei Pankratiev. Despite the shared directorial credits, of the three shorts it points most clearly toward Parajanov's mature style. The greater degree of creative inspiration displayed in this film is probably due in part to Parajanov's avowed passion for folk art, the film's subject matter. While living in Ukraine he liked to frequent the Museum of Ukrainian Folk Art located at the Caves Monastery complex, admiring the costumes, embroidery, ceramics, and paintings on display there. He was also fascinated by the museum complex's large collection of Scythian gold, especially the famous gold pectoral discovered by an archeologist in 1971, and wrote a brief treatment for a documentary film devoted to that piece.[44]

The phrase "golden hands" is derived from a Russian and Ukrainian idiom meaning "nimble fingers" or "skilled with one's hands." The film surveys a broad range of artworks in various media and genres; many of them are still on display at the museum. Folk art, the film suggests, derives its inspiration from the tribulations and joys of people's lives, as well as the beauty of nature. The first section of the film offers a brief overview of Ukrainian folk art from the distant past (Kievan Rus) to the prerevolutionary era, demonstrating a great variety of techniques for arranging art objects before the camera. In one segment, a smaller wooden bowl and then wooden utensils magically appear inside a larger bowl via jump cuts. In another shot, decorated ceramic tiles appear one by one over bricks until the screen is filled, looking forward to a similar use of antique photographs in Parajanov's short *Arabesques on the Theme of Pirosmani* (*Arabeski na temu Pirosmani*, Georgia Documentary Film Studio 1985).

In one particularly striking point-of-view shot, a hand picks up a small oil lamp and carries it offscreen right. The camera pans right and tracks forward to a painted wooden chest; the lid is raised. A close-up of richly embroidered fabrics dissolves into a series of similar fabrics, accompanied by a folk chorus on the soundtrack. The camera then tilts up from a hand in the process of embroidering to show the elderly woman who is doing the work. Besides reflecting the film's title, the emphasis on hands in this sequence anticipates the scenes of manual labor in *Shadows of Forgotten Ancestors* and in *The Color of Pomegranates*.

A later sequence displays a series of rugs that contain elaborate decorative motifs and miniature scenes with human figures. This use of straight cuts to reveal a series of decorative motifs is, of course, one of the most frequently recurring stylistic traits of Parajanov's mature works. Such techniques and visual motifs are not necessarily unusual in themselves; they arise logically out of the practical need to present a series of objects or decorative motifs, the underlying theme of labor and creativity in the film, and a desire to shape the material in a visually interesting manner. It is unlikely that *Golden Hands* was perceived as particularly experimental when it was first released. Rather, what makes these techniques noteworthy in Parajanov's mature films is the extent to which they will supplant narrative flow within what are supposed to be feature-length *narrative* films.

The first half of *Golden Hands* concludes with dramatized scenes depicting a poor woodcarver in Western Ukraine selling his handicrafts to a local church for a pittance and the famed artist Ivan Honchar creating his satirical clay figurines, arousing the ire of the authorities as a result. The second half of the film shifts to artists working in the present day, including the ceramicist Mikhail Kozlenko, the painter Katerina Bilokur, and the decorative artist Maria Primachenko. One episode in this section contains a series of rugs unrolling one atop the other before the camera, showing off a rich variety of patterns, a device that Parajanov reuses in the later documentary *Hakob Hovnatanyan* (Yerevan Newsreel-Documentary Film Studio 1967). At the same time, the film is very much bound by ideological conventions of the era, closing as it does on a "folk" tapestry depicting beautiful and vigorous Ukrainian peasant women looking toward the bright future, to say nothing of a handcrafted "folk" portrait of Lenin. Nonetheless, the film's enthusiasm for folk art shines through, as does its attempt to create a new cinematic idiom that conveys the charm and originality of the works on display.

Ukrainian Rhapsody (1961)

In the wartime melodrama *Ukrainian Rhapsody* (*Ukrainskaia rapsodiia*, Dovzhenko Film Studio 1961), the young singer Oksana travels to Paris (Fig. 1.5) and wins a major vocal competition. On the train back to Ukraine she reflects on the events that have shaped her life so far: a rich childhood in the Ukrainian countryside that inspired her artistic sensibility, her love for Anton, the couple's separation

Figure 1.5. Oksana on the streets of "Paris" (*Ukrainian Rhapsody*). Courtesy of the Oleksandr Dovzhenko National Centre.

during World War II, and her decision to abandon her singing temporarily and work as a nurse in order to support the war effort. During a parallel train ride back to Ukraine, Anton recalls his capture as a POW by German soldiers, his escape and period of refuge with a kindhearted German organist, and his subsequent detention by Allied forces.

Parajanov's second solo feature is based on a 1958 screenplay by the aforementioned Alexander Levada, the Ukrainian playwright, poet, and essayist, best known for the philosophical tragedy *Faust and Death* (1960). According to Leonid Osyka, Parajanov joked about the finished film, "In *Ukrainian Rhapsody* there are sixteen episodes by Levada, sixteen episodes by me. If you separate them out, there will be one film by Levada, one film by Parajanov."[45] Compared to Parajanov's earlier works, it was a relatively ambitious production that included location shooting in Kaliningrad (Königsberg) for the German scenes. Lviv substituted — not terribly convincingly — for the "Western European city," unidentified in the screenplay, but clearly meant to suggest Paris in the finished film. Parajanov also managed to attract some established talent in the cast: Natalia Uzhvy played the role of Nadia Petrovna, Oksana's music teacher; and Stepan Shkurat, best known for his performances in various Dovzhenko films and in Georgi and Sergei Vasiliev's *Chapaev* (Lenfilm 1934), played Oksana's grandfather. The then-popular songwriter and composer Platon Maiboroda wrote the film's appropriately lush and melodramatic score. This was also the first film in which Parajanov worked with the editor Maria ("Masha") Ponomarenko, who would become his closest artistic collaborator, working on all of his subsequent feature films.

In the same way that *Andriesh* was a typical example of the fairy-tale film and *The Top Guy* was conceived as a latter-day *kolkhoz* musical with added sports film elements, *Ukrainian Rhapsody* bears standard hallmarks of the melodrama. These include the touching story of young lovers separated by war, dramatic meetings and departures at train stations and boat docks, and swells of music on the soundtrack to emphasize every emotional twist, but also specifically melodramatic visual tropes. The latter include faces framed in rain-streaked windows, the image of Oksana's sheet music falling onto the snowy ground when she helps a patient into an ambulance and thereby abandons her art, and the image of the blinded soldier standing up and fervently declaring, "I see!" when she describes the ballet to him. Thus, not only is the film a melodrama in its subject matter, but Parajanov is also consciously deploying the narrative and stylistic clichés of the genre. The critic Miron Chernenko shares a similar view of the film (discussed later).

In some respects Levada's screenplay shares thematic concerns with other

"Thaw" narratives. The sympathetic portrayal of Anton as a POW recalls Mikhail Sholokhov's novel *The Destiny of a Man* and Sergei Bondarchuk's award-winning film adaptation of the same title (*Sud'ba cheloveka*, Mosfilm 1959). In a similar vein, the sympathetic treatment of Heinrich, an ordinary German, is not unlike that of Alov and Naumov's controversial *Peace to Him Who Enters* (*Mir vkhodiashchemu*, Mosfilm 1961), which earned accusations of pacifism and "slander of the Soviet Army."[46] Another striking aspect of Parajanov's finished film is its handling of religious piety: earlier in the film, before Anton takes refuge in the ruined cathedral, individuals stand inside it meditatively and cross themselves. Instead of Bach's organ music as indicated in the screenplay, Rudi, a boy soprano, sings *Ave Maria*. However, these gestures are counterbalanced by a simplistically stereotyped view of the West. During the competition an obviously "bourgeois" American, dressed in a white coat and tails, says in English with a clear American accent: "Well, darling, God will be with you," to his lavishly dressed companion, an American competitor. And the American army major who receives Anton after the German surrender expresses little sympathy for his plight as an escaped prisoner-of-war.

One of the main themes of Levada's screenplay, which Parajanov no doubt found appealing, was its affirmation of the value of art. Oksana's statement while practicing in the conservatory articulates the film's main dilemma: "Hitler's troops are already near Moscow . . . near Leningrad . . . All of Ukraine is in flames and is suffering. And here we are doing vocal exercises. They're not what's needed now." Her teacher Nadia Petrovna replies: "If you believe in victory, they're needed."[47]

Another important theme of the screenplay—one that also likely appealed to Parajanov—is its celebration of the Ukrainian land and folk culture and their formative impact on Oksana as an artist. An episode from Levada's original literary scenario represents inspiration from nature in a ludicrously literal manner:

> On such a stone [a granite boulder] sits Oksana, braiding a wreath [of flowers] and listening to a nightingale, enraptured.
>
> Just as the feathered soloist stops singing, Oksana suddenly, craftily mimics it, repeating an interval from its song.
>
> The nightingale warbles still more insistently.
>
> Oksana, waiting a beat, once more repeats one of the nightingale's trills.[48]

Thankfully, that scene did not make it into the film.

One of the more cloying aspects of Levada's screenplay is its third-person voice-over narration. Like the authorial commentary in *The Top Guy*, it tends to be embarrassingly obvious in its point-making. When Oksana receives the medal at the competition, the narrator rhapsodizes: "What did you think about, Oksana, on this, probably the most beautiful day of your life? Why even here, in a foreign country, does the melody of the steppes, of that silly instrument of the shepherds, from which all the symphonic orchestras of the world have turned away, continually revive in your heart?"[49] The finished film instead uses first-person voice-overs by Oksana and Anton, a shift that encourages greater identification with the protagonists and is more subtle and interesting from a dramatic standpoint.

Throughout the film Parajanov consciously expands his cinematic vocabulary. The narrative structure, which relies heavily on flashbacks, is far more complex than anything attempted in his first two features. While the basic structure itself is part of Levada's original screenplay, the director makes effective use of dual train rides as a visual bridge for the flashbacks. Moreover, he uses the couple's voice-over narration to frame the flashbacks in a sophisticated manner: the extended sequence of their initial romance functions as a shared memory that opens with a voice-over by Anton and closes with a voice-over by Oksana that serves as a bridge to Oksana's own personal memories. The competition sequence includes some showy tracking shots through the lobby of the theater (albeit with camera shadows visible) and the arty, self-conscious device of having the gauze curtain draped in front of the competitors lower as the camera backs away from the singer and raise as the camera tracks in. At the same time, parts of the film remain mired in shopworn imagery. Parajanov may have intended the idyllic images of the Ukrainian countryside (particularly the sunflower imagery) as an explicit homage to Dovzhenko, but as much as anything else they adhere to the pictorial conventions of late Stalin-era films: picture-postcard images of windmills, radiant sunsets, storks nesting on thatched roofs, groups of smiling villagers wearing traditional costumes and performing perfectly choreographed song-and-dance numbers, and so on.

The ambitious invasion sequence is clearly influenced by the opening battle montage of Dovzhenko's *Shchors* (Kyiv Film Studio 1939), what with its stylized crowd scenes and shots of individuals affected by the war (Fig. 1.6), visual metaphors such as a soldier's helmet falling into a field of wheat, and some striking compositions framed around windmills. One shot is also clearly an homage to the Odessa Steps sequence in Eisenstein's *The Battleship Potemkin* (*Bronenosets Potemkin*, Sovkino 1925): when a group of peasant women are fleeing in the woods, a mother is left behind, clutching her child to her chest. Shot by the soldier, she falls backwards to the ground, continuing to clutch the child; the camera cranes down to ground level as she falls. A young girl, probably

Figure 1.6. Dovzhenko-inspired imagery in the invasion sequence (*Ukrainian Rhapsody*). Courtesy of the Oleksandr Dovzhenko National Centre.

her daughter, runs off. On the whole, the sequence's use of montage falls flat because the graphic and rhythmic connections and contrasts between the shots are not distinctive enough. Movement within the frame is frequently staged too far in the background to have the necessary impact. A good example of this is the aforementioned shot depicting the mother's death; Eisenstein's earlier staging of a similar action in *The Battleship Potemkin* is far more effective because it is photographed at a closer distance and because Eisenstein's editing, which cuts between different angles and draws out the falling movement temporally, creates a strong visceral response in the viewer.

The most memorable moment in *Ukrainian Rhapsody* is undoubtedly Anton's dream, which recalls Boris's dying vision in *The Cranes Are Flying* and looks forward to the more overtly surrealistic imagery of *Shadows of Forgotten Ancestors*. The soundtrack consists of choral music, perhaps a traditional Ukrainian tune. Bare branches, hanging in the foreground, wave gently back and forth. Shifting colored lights fill the screen. These images are superimposed over a bed of ice and rock; a pick swings down, breaking into the ice. The camera pans left and zooms back; Anton swings the pick, attempting to dig something out. This is followed by: a brief shot of splashing water; a close, heavily diffused shot of a traditional Ukrainian floral wreath, twinkling as if buried in the ice; and a medium-long shot of Anton bending over and picking up the wreath out of the ice, ribbons dangling from it. The choral music bursts into full volume as the multicolored ribbons stream in the wind against an empty sky. The sequence's lyricism and expressive power make it stand out among Parajanov's early films as a whole.

Ukrainian Rhapsody opened in Kyiv on September 28, 1961, and ran for nearly a month, suggesting at least a moderately successful theatrical release there.[50] The film received little critical attention at the time, but *Iskusstvo kino* did publish a letter by a certain Tatiana Senchenko, a "worker at a cotton plant" in Kherson, who complained about Olga Petrenko's "very bad" acting in the main role of Oksana. Senchenko went on to criticize Parajanov's direction, arguing that his decision to have the heroine stroll by herself through the streets of the "foreign city" was mainly "for showing exotic damsels [*devits*] in slacks and ultra-modern artists," and that his predilection for "cloyingly pretty" landscapes interfered with the flow of the story. Senchenko concluded: "It is time to direct attention to the pictures released by the Dovzhenko studio. This film studio should be proud that it bears the name of a great artist, but it frequently compromises it."[51]

The Flower on the Stone (1960–1962)

The overtly propagandistic, anti-religious plot of *The Flower on the Stone* (*Tsvetok na kamne*, Dovzhenko Film Studio 1960–1962) does not look like promising Parajanov material: when a new Komsomol mine and mining community is established in the Donbas region, a member of a Pentecostal cult sends his daughter Christina to recruit new believers (Fig. 1.7). Arsen Zagorny, an upstanding Komsomol member and a talented violinist, falls in love with Christina and crosses paths with Zabroda, the leader of the local cell of the cult. Additional problems crop up in the form of Grigori Griva—a local boy prone to hooliganism and drink—and his buddy Chmykh, a dissolute accordion player. Grigori learns to mend his ways thanks to the guidance of Pavel Fedorovich Varchenko, the wise and patient director of the mine, and Liuda, the Komsomol organizer with whom he falls in love. The film's title refers to fossilized plants visible on pieces of coal.

An actual viewing of the film only confirms one's initial doubts, though as with most of Parajanov's previous works it contains some memorable visual touches. Not all the shortcomings in *The Flower on the Stone* are Parajanov's fault.

Figure 1.7. Christina and her father (*The Flower on the Stone*). Courtesy of the Oleksandr Dovzhenko National Centre.

In fact, he stepped in to finish the film, originally titled *No One Has Loved Like That* (*Tak eshche nikto ne liubil*), after much of the footage had already been shot. The first director, Anatoli Slesarenko, had been jailed for his role in the death of the lead actress Inna Kiriliuk-Burduchenko, who died on August 15, 1960, from severe burns while filming a scene in which she entered a burning shack. According to a newspaper account at the time, Slesarenko had ordered the actress to shoot repeated takes despite the growing danger from the fire.[52] The Dovzhenko Film Studio later decided to complete the film and Parajanov, who needed work, accepted the challenge of shooting new footage and assembling the whole into a finished form.

In general, the film seems like two separate stories welded together: Christina's rescue from the Pentecostal cult, and Grisha's romance with Liuda and his awakening into consciousness. At minimum Slesarenko shot all the footage containing Burduchenko in the role of Christina, the troubled daughter of the Pentecostal sectarian. As crude antireligious propaganda, that footage would not have made a good film even before tragedy derailed the production. Likely

Figure 1.8. Peter the Great marvels at a lump of coal (*The Flower on the Stone*). Courtesy of the Oleksandr Dovzhenko National Centre.

contributions by Parajanov included: much of the surrounding narrative with Grisha Griva (Grigori Karpov) and his romance with Liuda; the montage sequence devoted to the day of Lenin's death; and the fantasy sequence depicting the introduction of coal to the court of Peter the Great (Fig. 1.8). The latter two sequences in particular smack of padding, and their playful, jocular approach clashes with the somber mood of the film as a whole. Afterward Parajanov himself dismissed the resulting film as "the turd on the stone" [*govno na kamne*], punning on the film's title.[53]

As with *Ukrainian Rhapsody*, the screenwriter was a prominent member of the Soviet literary establishment. The titles of Vadim Sobko's works provide a good idea of their main thrust: the poetry anthology *Tractor Days* (1932), the short story collections *The Assemblers* (1931) and *People of Scaffolding* (1933), and a trilogy of novels about World War II entitled *The Path of the Star* (1943–1947).[54] Besides drawing a deliberate parallel between drunkenness and religious fanaticism, the screenplay for *The Flower on the Stone* features the classic Socialist Realism stock character of the Wise Leader: Varchenko, the mine's director.

He patiently counsels Liuda, the dedicated but inexperienced Komsomol organizer, and provides Grisha, the skilled but emotionally immature and alcoholic
shaft sinker, with the necessary guidance to get his life in order and realize his
full potential as a worker. The film also resurrects the old debate about what
is appropriate entertainment for workers: the accordion (popular culture) or
the violin (high culture). Here, it equates the accordion with the drunkenness,
duplicity, and bourgeois ideology of the character Chmykh. In contrast, Arsen,
a cultivated Komsomol member, plays the violin. In a similar vein, at one point
Varchenko gives Grisha an edifying novel to read: Stendhal's *The Red and the
Black.*

Certainly no one would judge the film as completed by Parajanov to be a
success, but it shows his continuing development as a director. While the plot
is routine propaganda, in places the narrative structure uses flashbacks in a
sophisticated manner. The cinematography creates a menacing atmosphere
through chiaroscuro lighting, the use of wide-angle lenses, and virtuoso camera
movements such as rapid lateral tracking shots and spinning. The soundtrack
likewise contains several imaginative touches. When Christina runs away from
Arsen after his confession of love, the soundtrack expressionistically combines
the sound of wind with a muffled echo of his earlier declaration to her. Perhaps
less motivated but equally striking is the way Arsen's violin solo merges with
Ukrainian folk-inspired choral music when he is shown playing. Despite its
flaws, *The Flower on the Stone* marks an advance over Parajanov's previous films
in terms of stylistic polish and direction of actors, though one must keep in mind
that much of the film was not his.

At the same time, *The Flower on the Stone* contains surely the most bizarre
and gratuitous moment in all of Parajanov's films: the ersatz-Vertov montage
sequence associated with the anniversary of Lenin's death. The sequence begins normally enough with the sound of a factory whistle announcing a halt
in production, the image of a train coming to a stop, close-ups of the somber
faces of miners, and kaleidoscopic images of the mining works. The latter compositions perhaps allude to Dziga Vertov's *Enthusiasm: A Symphony of the Donbas*
(*Entuziazm: Simfoniia Donbassa,* Ukrainfilm 1930). But then the sequence lurches
into the realm of absurdity with images of a doctor removing his mask and
a train filmed from underneath. This is accompanied on the soundtrack by
strains of Tchaikovsky's First Piano Concerto and an infant's cry. The sequence
ends, inexplicably, with a series of electrical poles photographed from different
angles. While Parajanov appears to strive for the visual dynamism of Vertov,
the sequence sorely lacks the conceptual unity and rhetorical power of its model.

The question arises whether the montage sequence was a sincere but misplaced and misguided homage, or whether Parajanov was in some way ridiculing the material he was stuck with. Miron Chernenko suggests that he deliberately inserted elements of parody, possibly even "open insult" into *The Top Guy*.[55] He also argues that Parajanov "constructs" *Ukrainian Rhapsody* "from ready-made blocks; while enlarging the banalities, he even compromises them on the run."[56] The latter film, in his view, also has a certain parodic quality. One could perhaps extend this interpretation to *The Flower on the Stone*, and it is not difficult to imagine Parajanov, faced with the absurd task of completing the film, turning the whole exercise into a private game.

Karen Kalantar, however, takes issue with Chernenko's line of argument: "The point is that now almost any film of the Forties and Fifties seems a parody to us. But a parody of what?—that is the question. [. . .] There can be only one answer: a parody of real life, and our notions at that time about life, of our ideologically blinkered consciousness and our perverted tastes. We are laughing at ourselves, though it is by no means a cheerful laugh. In order to understand what kind of people we were, we had to travel a long road in forty years."[57] Kalantar further takes pains to emphasize that Parajanov was educated and lived in the same environment as everyone else. He is probably correct to suggest that in many respects Parajanov's thinking remained within the bounds of conventional ideology at that time. Like many Soviet intellectuals, at various points in his life he expressed admiration for Lenin, at least in public. But in defense of Chernenko, the notion that Parajanov would deliberately introduce elements of parody into his early films or subvert the material he was forced to work with is hardly out of keeping with his overall personality, his prankish behavior at the Dovzhenko Film Studio, or his subsequent, more formally radical artistic practices. For example, several of his collages from the late 1980s play ironically with Soviet symbols and mythology in a manner similar to Vitaly Komar and Alexander Melamid's Sots Art. Thus, one could argue that parody was just another trait already present in a rudimentary form in his early period, and which he subsequently refined in his mature works.

The Flower on the Stone premiered in Kyiv on September 1, 1962, the Kyiv Day of Cinema. It screened together with Viktor Ivchenko's *Ivanna* (Dovzhenko Film Studio 1959), Inna Kiriliuk-Burduchenko's first starring feature. Its regular theatrical run in Kyiv began on January 24, 1963, and lasted a respectable three weeks. Regardless, *The Flower on the Stone* earned the most negative reviews of Parajanov's career so far, which is saying something considering the reception of his previous films. In the magazine *Science and Religion* (*Nauka i religiia*), the critic Yuri Martynenko complained about the film's "unconvincing" character psychology and its depiction of the fundamentalist sect, to say nothing of the "harping expressive means" used in scenes such as Arsen's confession of love to Christina, in which her raised hands are made to resemble the electric poles in the landscape. Another scene that he singled out for criticism was Zabroda's sudden, unmotivated marriage proposal to Christina and her father's equally sudden appearance from nowhere to bless the union. Martynenko concluded, "If one imagines one's ideological adversaries in such an oversimplified manner and makes them into fools, then the struggle against religion begins to resemble giveaway checkers."[58] Worse yet, in the leading Soviet newspaper *Izvestiia* (*News*), the critic Natella Lordkipanidze singled the film out for attack in an article decrying the overall mediocre level of film production at the Dovzhenko Film Studio during that era. The article opened: "We have not seen a film the likes of *The Flower on the Stone* for a long time, and let us hope we will not see one." Besides pointing out the film's basic incoherence, she claimed that the studio had insisted on completing the film despite the objections of the Main Administration at Goskino in Moscow.[59] Reading between the lines, one suspects that the article was partly intended by Moscow to distance itself from the film.

At this point in his career Parajanov had scored one solid box office hit, *The Top Guy*, but none of his films had achieved any degree of critical success. This was especially true compared to his VGIK classmates Khutsiev, Alov, Naumov, and Kulidzhanov. Indeed, every one of his feature films had been cited in prominent Soviet publications as poster children for mediocre filmmaking, especially that supposedly found at the Dovzhenko Film Studio. This only could have hurt his standing at the studio, such as it was. He was almost forty years old and, according to friends who knew him at the time, acutely aware of his failure to realize his full artistic potential. There may well be some truth to the Ukrainian director Alexander Muratov's recollection that Parajanov was known as the "worst director at the studio,"[60] but certainly he would have remained just one among many Soviet directors consigned to oblivion if he had produced only the early films and more works like them.

2

Shadows of Forgotten Ancestors

Ukrainian Revival

Judging solely by the films Parajanov had made so far, no one could have predicted what would happen when he was given his next assignment. At the urging of Mykhailo Kotsiubynsky's daughter, the Dovzhenko Film Studio agreed to produce an adaptation of the Ukrainian writer's masterpiece *Shadows of Forgotten Ancestors* to commemorate the centenary of his birth. Renata Korol, a member of the studio's Script-Editorial Board, gave the project to Ivan Chendei, who accepted it and agreed to postpone adapting his own novel, *The Bridge*.[1] As a noted writer from the Transcarpathian region of Western Ukraine, Chendei was uniquely suited to adapt Kotsiubynsky's novella, which was set among the Hutsuls, a people living in that region.[2] Initially Korol offered the script to Ivan Kavaleridze, one of the studio's oldest and most well-established directors, but he declined due to a prior commitment. She then offered the project to Parajanov, with whom she had worked as the script editor on previous films, so she was well aware of his long-standing interest in folk culture.[3] It was the creative opportunity that Parajanov had long needed: an adaptation of a genuinely great literary work that resonated with his artistic sensibilities and challenged him to rise to its level. The resulting film brought Parajanov his first international success, largely set the stylistic and thematic agenda of the poetic school of Ukrainian cinema that followed in its wake, and thrust him into the fraught arena of Ukrainian cultural politics.

Mykhailo Kotsiubynsky's Novella

Mykhailo Kotsiubynsky (1864–1913) was a complex figure whose work resonated on multiple levels.[4] He appealed to the Soviets because of his political and social commitments; as someone educated during the late 1870s and early 1880s in a theological seminary—institutions that the literary scholar Bohdan Rubchak characterizes as "hornets' nests of clandestine revolutionary political activity" — Kotsiubynsky participated in various student protests and secret organizations that resulted in periodic surveillance by the Tsarist police throughout his life.[5] Afterward, he continued to express sympathy for the oppressed classes and hatred for the world of the Tsarist bureaucracy, though he was forced to support himself and his family as a clerk in that very bureaucracy. His subsequent membership in *Prosvita* (*Enlightenment*), an organization that supported activities such as developing Ukrainian-language libraries and schools, which were illegal at the time, no doubt helped cement his appeal during the 1960s among intellectuals concerned with promoting Ukrainian language and culture. This would bear significant consequences when Parajanov's film was released. At the same time, as Rubchak points out, Kotsiubynsky was an intensely private individual whose writings often pit the solitary "dreamer" or "poet" against the collective. His writings are also noteworthy from a purely aesthetic standpoint, given Kotsiubynsky's "painterly" attention to color in terms of character psychology and the "musical" effects of his language.[6] Parajanov was attracted to the rich aesthetic dimensions of Kotsiubynsky's prose in general and tried to engage it cinematically both in *Shadows of Forgotten Ancestors* (*Teni zabytykh predkov*, Dovzhenko Film Studio 1964) and in a subsequent, unrealized adaptation of the short story "Intermezzo" (discussed in chapter 5).

The 1911 novella *Shadows of Forgotten Ancestors* arose from Kotsiubynsky's encounter with the Hutsuls during a trip to the Carpathians the previous year. The Hutsuls live mainly in the Ivano-Frankivsk region of Western Ukraine, with some populations also found in the neighboring countries of Slovakia, Romania, and Poland. Traditionally subsisting on forestry and animal husbandry, they have maintained a markedly pagan world view, at least up to the Soviet era. Their belief in sorcery, devils, and forest spirits such as wood nymphs has lain beneath a thin veneer of Christianity. Among Ukrainians it is widely thought that Hutsul traditions reflect older beliefs in Ukraine as a whole. The Hutsuls are also noted for their keen artistic sensibility as expressed through folk music, intricate woodcarvings, and beautifully embroidered traditional costumes. Accordingly, the novella contains a vivid ethnographic component, with its skillful weaving of Hutsul beliefs and customs into the fabric of the narrative. Kotsiubynsky draws extensively upon the Hutsul oral tradition through everyday vocabulary, legends, jokes, and *kolomyikas* (song settings of rhymed quatrains).

Ivan Paliichuk, the main character of the novella, is a young boy who displays a keen sensitivity to nature and who comes from a family marked by tragedy. Most of his siblings have died prematurely, and his father is killed in a feud with the head of the Huteniuk family. As a child Ivan falls deeply in love with Marichka, a daughter of the Huteniuks, but as they grow older they realize that their parents will never permit them to marry. When Ivan goes out to work in the pasture one summer, Marichka drowns in the river. After several years of grieving, Ivan marries the earthy Palahna, but the couple is unable to bear children. Palahna turns to a sorcerer for help and has an affair with him, setting the stage for a fateful confrontation between Ivan and the sorcerer, and a final meeting with Marichka's spirit transformed into a wood nymph.

Beyond the novella's ethnographic authenticity as a representation of Hutsul folk beliefs and legends, the Soviets tended to emphasize its depiction of the poverty and backwardness of Hutsul society, one example of this being the blood feud between the Paliichuks and Huteniuks that sets the events of the story in motion and casts a fateful shadow over Ivan and Marichka's innocent love. Commenting on Ivan Chendei's script in their resolution dated March 13, 1963, the Script-Editorial Board of Goskino of Ukraine not only pointed out that Kotsiubynsky's name was "included in the UNESCO calendar 'Great People and Historical Events 1963–1964,'" but they also emphasized the "democratic,"[7] proto-socialist aspect of the novella: "Its ideo-philosophical contents consist of showing man's struggle for real happiness and great human love, and of the affirmation of the inexhaustible creative forces of the people. The characters of Ivan and Marichka are the embodiment of true human beauty and poetry. The world of private property is set against the world of true happiness."[8]

However, Kotsiubynsky's novella works on much more than just a socio-historical level. Rubchak identifies four levels of representation within the novella: the "realistic-mimetic"; the "realistic-legendary" (i.e., Hutsul legends and rituals, or what Rubchak refers to as "public myth"); the "legendary ritual" (i.e., elemental and cosmic archetypes); and the "personal-mythical" (i.e., "Ivan's poetic reveries").[9] In that respect, *Shadows of Forgotten Ancestors* displays fundamental themes recurring in Kotsiubynsky's work as a whole, such as the solitary dreamer versus the collective, but it does so in a uniquely multivalent manner. Indeed, that very multivalence of Kotsiubynsky's original novella and the attempt by Parajanov, Chendei, Illienko and the rest of the film's creative team to represent these dimensions in the finished film partly explains the film's complicated — though largely enthusiastic — reception after it was finished.

The Film's Production

The initial reception of Chendei's script reflected an underlying uncertainty about how best to frame Kotsiubynsky's work for Soviet audiences. In their aforementioned resolution, the Script-Editorial Board of Goskino of Ukraine praised both the initial script's attempt to create a coherent plot from the novella and the way it incorporated nature and the daily life of the Hutsuls. However, they recommended that Chendei "strengthen the public-social aspect, more precisely, the anti-religious orientation."[10]

A subsequent draft reworked by Parajanov displays his characteristically free approach to literary adaptations, employing voice-over narration and opening with generalized imagery depicting the difficult living conditions of the Hutsuls and the destructive blood feud that drives the narrative. Nonetheless, it reproduces several scenes from the novella almost verbatim.[11] A new resolution from the Script-Editorial Board at the Main Administration of Goskino USSR (Moscow) noted the removal of "arbitrary additions to the description of relations between the Huteniuk and Paliichuk families and to Yura's [the sorcerer's] character." But it also criticized the latest draft for not devoting enough attention to "the working existence of the Hutsuls," and noted that the love between Ivan and Marichka, as depicted, demonstrated "a gravitation toward a dramatic and tragic tonality."[12] Such comments suggest how, to a certain extent, not only the script but Kotsiubynsky's novella itself did not entirely fit within the bounds of conventional Soviet ideology. Nonetheless, the finished film was well regarded on the whole by Soviet authorities and did not encounter anything like the difficulties with censors that would plague *The Color of Pomegranates*.

Shooting lasted from September 1963 until August 1964 and included expeditions to the Carpathians from September 1963 to January 1964 and again from June to August 1964. Locations included Verkhovyna, the crew's base; Bystrytsa for the scenes related to Marichka's drowning; Sokolivtsa for the scenes between Palahna and Yura the Sorcerer; and Kryvorivna for the murder of Ivan's father. The lengthy shoot can be explained partly by exceptional difficulties that the crew encountered: shooting was delayed a total of 34 days due to bad weather and the production was halted altogether from March 9 to June 20, 1964, due to the lead actor Ivan Mykolaichuk's preexisting obligations for the Taras Shevchenko biography *The Dream* (*Son*, Dovzhenko Film Studio 1964) and the illness of Vladimir Denisenko, that film's director. Personal conflicts among the crew, especially between Parajanov and Illienko (described below) also played a significant role in the delays.[13]

Filmmaking is of course a collaborative effort, and the film benefitted from a strong creative team on the whole. The graphic artist Georgi Yakutovich, who served as an artistic consultant and as one of two lead production designers, drew a number of striking sketches that helped set the visual mood for the film and even provided direct models for some of the shot compositions. Yakutovich also illustrated a 1966 edition of Kotsiubynsky's novella with woodcuts to capitalize on the success of the film; his style in general is strongly influenced by Hutsul folk art.[14] Miroslav Skoryk's original score, a Bartok-like composition that combines lively folk-based themes and rhythms with modernistic dissonance, complements the traditional folk songs used in the film and provides an effective emotional counterpoint to the images. The score was all the more remarkable in that Skoryk was only in his mid-twenties at the time and had just completed graduate studies at the Moscow Conservatory before working on the film.[15]

But Yuri Illienko, the cinematographer, was clearly the most significant collaborator on the film after Parajanov. It would not be unfair to say that the film's stunning cinematography was ultimately one of the main factors behind its success, and Illienko subsequently became an important director in his own right. While still a student at the VGIK, Illienko had shot Yakov Segel's *Farewell, Doves!* (*Proshchaite, golubi!*, Yalta Film Studio 1960) and subsequently Artur Voitetsky's *Somewhere There Is a Son* (*Gde-to est' syn*, Yalta Film Studio 1961). Vladimir Lugovsky, the assistant director for *Shadows of Forgotten Ancestors*, had also worked on Voitetsky's film and recalls that Illienko was talented but difficult to work with. The frequent retakes he required "for both creative and technical reasons" resulted in Voitetsky's film going over budget and alienating the veteran actor Nikolai Simonov.[16] Lugovsky writes: "the studio management demanded several times that the director replace the cinematographer with someone more experienced, but A. Voitetsky categorically refused—he believed in the young Illienko, and he was not mistaken in the result. Parajanov also trusted him."[17]

By his own account, Illienko came to *Shadows of Forgotten Ancestors* with very strong ideas about what he wanted to express through camerawork:

> . . . whatever is behind my back, is this also a world? A world in the philosophical sense, a world in the sense of space and time, and of everyday living, and probably most importantly in the emotional sense? [. . .] I always wanted to absorb everything around me. And I began to experiment with a hand-held camera striving in some way to imitate a whirlpool which draws everything into it.[18]

Given Illienko's independent artistic ambitions, it is not surprising that soon after shooting began, tensions erupted between him and Parajanov. Illienko threatened to leave and take his wife, the lead actress Larisa Kadochnikova, with him. In a memorandum dated October 3, 1963, Vasili Tsvirkunov, the director of the Dovzhenko Film Studio, condemned both Parajanov for his poor treatment of subordinates and Illienko for his failure to work productively with the film's director. He further assigned Parajanov's closest friend, Suren Shakh-bazian, to replace Illienko as the director of photography.[19] Some individuals interviewed have claimed that much of the conflict centered on Parajanov's preference at this point for tableau-style compositions versus Illienko's inter-est in Urusevsky-style camera pyrotechnics. There may well be some validity to such claims, since Illienko has subsequently stated that Parajanov did not really "direct" films, that he merely arranged objects in front of a camera.[20] For Illienko, camera movement is clearly an essential component of film language. Nonetheless, Parajanov and Illienko resolved their differences and Illienko was reinstated.

Despite the conflicts and delays, which nearly derailed the production, the authorities for the most part received the finished film warmly. When the studio's Artistic Council screened a rough cut of the film on September 4, 1964, a couple of participants even compared it to the work of Eisenstein and Dovzhenko.[21] In their resolution dated September 21, the Script-Editorial Board at Goskino of Ukraine praised the film for "conveying the poetic quality and philosophical depth of M. Kotsiubynsky's tale through the language of cinema" and called it "a brilliant creative success of the Dovzhenko studio." They felt that the "ethnographic material" was "organically woven into the narrative fabric" and praised the use of "laconic" intertitles. They further characterized Illienko's camerawork as a "whole cascade of camera techniques, introduced into the film not for the sake of formalistic stunts, but in the name of the beauty and poetry that lie at the foundation of this romantic legend." Significantly, they recommended releasing the film only in Ukrainian: "Unfortunately, the rich folkloric material used in the film almost does not lend itself to translation into Russian."[22] Subsequently, Parajanov would claim that he had to struggle to re-tain the film's original soundtrack. However, it is clear that from the start there were other individuals within the Ukrainian film bureaucracy who supported the idea of releasing the film Union-wide with a Ukrainian soundtrack. Based on the surviving documentation in the Goskino files, it does not appear that Moscow strongly resisted the idea. *Shadows of Forgotten Ancestors* became one of the first (and very few) non-Russian Soviet films to be released Union-wide in its original language — that is, with added Russian explanatory titles but without redubbed dialogue or voice-over translation.

Shadows of Forgotten Ancestors as Poetic Cinema

In terms of English-language scholarship, *Shadows of Forgotten Ancestors* has been relatively well-served compared to Parajanov's other features; this is no doubt due both to the wider availability of the film over the years compared to, say, *The Color of Pomegranates*, and to its reputation among many critics as his greatest work. In his analysis of the film, David A. Cook emphasizes how the film's experiments with sound, color, and camerawork serve "to destabilize the viewer perceptually, and therefore psychologically, in order to present a tale that operates not at the level of narrative but of myth, a tale that is an archetype of life itself: youth passes from innocence to experience to solitude and death in a recurring cycle, eons upon eons."[23] Bohdan Nebesio argues that the film's images are tied to either "the consciousness or the subconsciousness of the characters," particularly Ivan.[24] While it is undeniably productive to analyze the film in terms of myth and narration, neither approach wholly accounts for the film's rich variety of techniques and modes of expression. To give just one example, Nebesio sees the wedding sequence preceding Ivan's encounter with Palahna, with its exuberantly spinning camera, as an example of omniscient narration since "the camera [. . .] has the power to foresee the upcoming events" (i.e., Ivan's sexual attraction and marriage to Palahna). However, the sequence is better understood as a poetic rather than a narrative device, since it is primarily a *lyrical* expression of a mood and does not relate clearly to the main action of the plot. The poetic effects of *Shadows of Forgotten Ancestors* are dispersed throughout the film and do not rely on pretexts such as dreams for motivation, in contrast to a film like Andrei Tarkovsky's *Ivan's Childhood* (*Ivanovo detstvo*, Mosfilm 1962). Going further, one could argue that *Shadows of Forgotten Ancestors*, along with Mikhail Kalatozov's *I Am Cuba* (*Ia — Kuba*, Mosfilm 1964), represented the most thoroughgoing experiment in poetic cinema in Soviet feature films since the creative zenith of filmmakers such as Eisenstein, Pudovkin, Vertov, and Dovzhenko in the 1920s and early 1930s.

Watching the film, one is struck by its extraordinary stylistic range. The funeral of Ivan's father provides a good sample of the variety of techniques one can find even in a single sequence, demonstrating heightened attention to the sensuous qualities of language (in this case, film language) — a characteristic that is frequently used to distinguish poetry from prose. The sequence opens with a shot of black-and-white banners decorated with religious iconography being

Figure 2.1. The funeral of Ivan's father, opening shot (*Shadows of Forgotten Ancestors*).

laid out against a snow-covered wooden roof (Fig. 2.1). The next several shots
consist of precisely composed, painterly tableaux of villagers participating in the
funeral preparations (Fig. 2.2). These compositions are static, self-contained,
and do not construct a clearly defined space in which the funeral preparations
as a whole occur. Some of the characters even gaze directly into the camera.
While the details within the individual images more or less fit in the context of
the scene, they do not construct a clear chain of action and, strictly speaking,
the shots do not move the narrative forward. They seem to exist outside of
time. The series of self-contained tableaux would become a primary technique
in Parajanov's films from *The Color of Pomegranates* on, but here it already plays
a significant role.

The tableaux of villagers are followed by a close-up of Ivan watching as a
nail is hammered into his father's coffin in the foreground (Fig. 2.3). In contrast with the tableaux, this shot uses a telephoto lens with a markedly shallow
depth of field to focus attention on Ivan's face. The film then cuts directly to his
mother in medium close-up, wailing, clasping her hands and lurching forward.

Figure 2.2. Frontal tableau of a funeral participant (*Shadows of Forgotten Ancestors*).

Little else around her is in focus, but one can make out some of the banners from the first shot in the sequence, now carried as part of the procession. This shot is especially noteworthy for the viscerally unsettling use of an extreme focal length lens in combination with handheld panning.

Only now does the film use an establishing shot to provide a general sense of the space in which the funeral procession occurs. In a lengthy and complex shot that incorporates both handheld camerawork and tracking, the full procession appears in long shot as the camera cranes up from a low angle in the snow (Fig. 2.4). Ivan's mother follows directly behind the coffin, wailing, while Ivan holds a black lamb in his arms. He puts the lamb down and walks down the hill into the bushes; the camera pans right to follow him. There he meets up with Marichka, and the camera tracks laterally to follow them as they converse. Ivan suddenly looks up at the funeral procession and the camera swish-pans left to follow his perspective. The latter half of the shot challenges cinematic norms by photographing Ivan and Marichka through bushes (Fig. 2.5). The dizzying combination of telephoto lens, handheld camera, and characters photographed

Figure 2.3. Ivan observes the funeral preparations (*Shadows of Forgotten Ancestors*).

through bushes fits organically with the theme of a semi-pagan people whose fates are bound up inextricably with nature.

The sequence closes with a startling trick of spatial dislocation of the kind noted by David A. Cook. At the end of the previously described shot, Ivan looks up suddenly and the camera swish-pans left, following his line of sight. This cuts abruptly to a close shot of the banners from the procession. By this point, the viewer probably assumes that Ivan has not wandered very far, since the combination of tracking and telephoto lens in the previous shot makes it difficult to gauge exactly how far the camera and the characters have moved. The final shot of this sequence reveals that Ivan is now a considerable distance from the procession, dozens of yards or more. This spatial dislocation, however, is not merely a stylistic gimmick; it concretely represents the idea that Ivan has been distracted from the tragedy of his father's death by his growing attraction for Marichka. More broadly, it also reflects the notion that falling in love somehow takes one outside the time and space of everyday existence. These themes are reinforced in the subsequent episode of the film, "Ivan and Marichka."

Figure 2.4. The funeral procession (*Shadows of Forgotten Ancestors*).

So far this analysis has covered only the visual track of this sequence. The soundtrack is equally rich in its range of materials and techniques, which include selectively heightened sound effects, the distinctive Hutsul dialect and oral traditions, folk music, and the expressive use of silence. The first several tableau shots are accompanied by the sounds of women keening for the loss of Petro, Ivan's father. Their cries do not directly correspond to any of the images onscreen but contribute to the atmosphere and texture of the episode. They also serve as a kind of Greek chorus of villagers commenting on the action; this innovative device recurs periodically over the course of the film, most notably during Ivan's period of mourning. The shot of the full funeral procession begins practically in silence, with only the sound of feet treading through the snow until Ivan's mother begins to wail again and pound on her husband's coffin. The *trembita* (alpenhorn) players in the procession halt and call out on their horns again as Ivan wanders away to talk with Marichka. During the conversation between Ivan and Marichka, the sounds from the funeral procession drop out until the end of the shot, when the *trembitas* suddenly call out again and catch

Figure 2.5. Ivan and Marichka have run off into the trees (*Shadows of Forgotten Ancestors*).

Ivan's attention. At this point the wailing of Ivan's mother also resumes, suggesting that the soundtrack reflects Ivan's subjectivity in the same manner as the aforementioned spatial dislocation in the visual track of the sequence.

Indeed, no small part of the film's impact derives from its inventive and expressive use of sound, which was undoubtedly one of the reasons why it was recommended early on that the film retain its original Ukrainian-language soundtrack. There is simply no way the wailing of Ivan's mother, for instance, could be redone in another language, and the unique timbre of Hutsul voices is every bit as important as what the characters are saying. Certain sounds, especially the invisible axe and the *trembitas*, recur as leitmotifs, becoming a significant part of the film's overall poetic structure.

At the same time, silence is also used to great effect. The most notable example of this occurs after Ivan and Palahna's Christmas dinner and the visitation by caroling children dressed as angels. An inebriated Ivan lies down in bed and goes to sleep while Palahna continues to sit up. This shot is accompanied by the sound of ringing bells, presumably from the children who just visited, but the sound also has an aura of the supernatural. The next shot, depicting the food and vodka that Ivan has left in the window for Marichka's spirit, is silent. Ivan lies on his back in bed, his head tossing slightly as if dreaming, accompanied again by the sound of ringing bells. The next several shots, a series of jump cuts showing Marichka's spirit pressing her hands against the windowpanes, are silent altogether. The peculiar combination of silence, static compositions, and jump cuts looks forward to Sayat-Nova's dream in *The Color of Pomegranates*.

More generally, one of the most distinctive aspects of the film is its use of Hutsul folk music on the soundtrack in addition to Skoryk's folk-inspired orchestral compositions. Traditional instruments heard in the film include the fiddle, *tsymbaly* (hammer dulcimer), *duda* (bagpipe), the *sopilka* and *fiyarka/floyarka* (wooden flutes), and, most famously, the *trembita*. Marichka's songs in the early episode entitled "Ivan and Marichka" come directly from Kotsiubynsky's novella and reflect her preternatural talent as a singer in the original story. During Ivan and Palahna's wedding the soundtrack employs a folk song ("I have but one daughter, her name is Nastechka") about marrying off one's daughter, which bears a straightforward relationship to the narrative. In other scenes, the songs have a more indirect relationship to the action onscreen. For example, during the "Christmas" episode the soundtrack contains an amusing song mourning the death of a kid goat, while costumed celebrants dance inside the courtyard of Ivan's house and Yura the sorcerer accosts Palahna outside.

The most obvious feature that marks the film as poetic cinema is its extensive use of recurring symbolic motifs to provide an overarching thematic structure. Thus the grip of death seizes Ivan both at the beginning of the film — when his fallen brother Oleksa grasps his jacket — and at the end when Marichka, in the form of a wood nymph, grasps his arm one last time. In the sequence titled "Solitude" (or "Alone"), Ivan has a vision of Christ that includes the obviously symbolic shot of hands petting a young lamb; shortly afterward, Ivan picks up a lamb and dances around with it, signifying his renewed embrace of faith and life. This motif is inverted during the Christmas episode later in the film, when Ivan picks up a calf and carries it in his arms, saying to Palahna: "Where is my child? Where are my goats?" Related visual motifs appear in Parajanov's later films as well.

A third set of symbolic motifs have to do with sexual desire. When Ivan and Marichka are frolicking in the nude as children, Ivan suddenly rips off the cross around her neck; the two stand frozen for a moment and stare at each other, reflecting the sudden, barely comprehended awakening of adult feelings between them. Ivan gathers some red berries off the forest floor and holds them out in his open palm. When they are older, the consummation of their relationship (and Marichka's impregnation) is symbolized by Ivan bringing a handful of wild strawberries to Marichka's lips. Later, the motifs of the necklace and red berries are ingeniously combined in a single image: after Ivan and Palahna's wedding, Ivan rips off her necklace — a string of coral beads — and holds it out on his palm, spilling some of the reddish beads on the floor.

The association between fruit and sexual desire is further developed in the lyrical sequence that serves as a transition between Ivan's mourning and his courtship of Palahna. It is effected by a passage of pure cinematic lyricism. First, a black-and-white shot depicts Ivan climbing high up into a tree to pick the last apple. This is followed by color footage of the previously described wedding between richly costumed, unidentified Hutsul villagers, photographed through branches using a very long telephoto lens. Between dizzying swish pans and almost invisible cuts the camera picks out faces of the participants, details of costumes, and musical instruments. Some of the cuts are punctuated by celebratory shots from a pistol. The delicate spring coloring, dappled light, and blurred movements suggest an Impressionist painting. The ensuing sequence of Ivan and Palahna's courtship — or rather, raw seduction — closes with a shot of Ivan at the base of the tree seen previously. He now holds an apple, completing the line of action begun earlier in the shot of him climbing the tree. The shots of Ivan climbing the apple tree and fetching a piece of fruit thus provide a deliberate frame for the section as a whole, working on a symbolic rather than a narrative level.

Another important component of Parajanov's poetic cinema is the use of repeated compositions to create visual rhymes. When Ivan is preparing for his wedding with Palahna, a group of elderly women bathe him inside a large wooden building with a high ceiling, most likely the village bathhouse. Near the end of the film, when Ivan's corpse is washed in preparation for his funeral, an identical camera setup and nearly identical composition are used, the main difference being that now Ivan's body is stretched out on a wooden plank.

Finally, one of Parajanov's unique contributions to poetic cinema is his devotion to decorative motifs and handcrafted art objects. Such objects in his films are not simply functional props but have autonomous value. Indeed, the beauty of an object often becomes the main point of a shot. In general, *Shadows of Forgotten Ancestors* strives to convey the richness of Hutsul material culture: the church paraphernalia at the beginning of the film, the costumes paraded one by one before the camera at the beginning of the Christmas episode, and the breathtaking shot during Ivan and Palahna's wedding night in which the ground-level camera setup shows off the richly embroidered, multicolored fabric of Palahna's apron and shoes. Parajanov's subsequent films foreground material culture to the extent that it sometimes overwhelms the dramatic trajectory.

The cumulative effect of such strategies is the de-emphasis of narrative movement in favor of the pictorial, lyrical, and metaphoric aspects of cinema. After *Shadows of Forgotten Ancestors*, narratives with simple outlines — or narratives already widely known to the audience, such as myths and literary adaptations — would become Parajanov's preferred vehicle since they allowed him a great deal of latitude for visual digressions and improvisations. More complicated narratives would have demanded more attention to the mechanics of storytelling in order for the plot to remain comprehensible.

This is not to suggest that Parajanov somehow neglects the conventional virtues of mise-en-scène; Ivan and Palahna's wedding illustrates the extent to which he has consolidated his skills as a director. The interior of the house first appears in a highly formalized composition: on the right side is a door with a black-and-white striped runner on the floor, leading to the foreground. The left side of the frame is masked off by a black object with two decorated cloths hanging in the upper part (Fig. 2.6). As Ivan enters through the door, the two cloths are lifted away and the object is revealed as a wooden chest lid, which an old woman is lowering. The light catches the decorative carvings in the wood. The lowering of the lid further reveals a new space on the left side of the frame: a group of women sitting on a bench, with shelves full of dishes against the wall in the background. The elderly woman sitting at the bench holds up a necklace of crosses to admire it, at the same time displaying it for the camera. As the old woman disappears offscreen to the left, one of the women on the bench gets up and ties a cloth around Ivan's eyes. A second woman helps her escort Ivan to the chest in the left foreground and seats him upon it, his back facing us. Two men carry in a yoke through the front door and bow toward Ivan.

The second shot is taken from the opposite angle, with Ivan facing us as he sits on the bench. It is now revealed that Palahna has been sitting behind him, also with a cloth tied over her eyes and wearing the necklace that the old woman took out of the chest earlier. Two women escort Palahna to the chest and seat her alongside Ivan. The two men with the yoke appear from offscreen left and place it around the newly married couple (Fig. 2.7). Everyone quickly departs to the right foreground, leaving Ivan and Palahna by themselves. Thus Parajanov is not only playing with foreground versus background and onscreen versus offscreen space in a sophisticated manner, he clearly understands the potential of mise-en-scène to conceal and reveal information to viewers as a

Figure 2.6. Ivan and Palahna's wedding: the open chest lid conceals the interior space (*Shadows of Forgotten Ancestors*).

scene unfolds. The calculated naiveté of Parajanov's later films belies the full mastery of craft that enabled him to reach that stage.

Reflecting on his experiences shooting the film, Parajanov displayed a complicated relationship with the Hutsuls in the 1966 essay "Perpetual Motion." On the one hand, he characterized them as a people who have an intimate relationship with nature and who "perceive their world as freshly as a child."[25] One could view this as a projection of his own private nostalgia for childhood or of his avowed artistic aim to imagine the world as freshly as a child. One could even view it as an inadvertent expression of colonialist ideology toward a marginalized and exotic Other on the Soviet Empire's periphery. On the other hand, Parajanov acknowledged that the Hutsuls actively negotiated their own boundaries in representing their culture, allowing him to take some artistic liberties with their rituals while still insisting on their own standards of accuracy and pointing out when details were out of place. Parajanov further recalled: "We brought them to the studio in order to record them playing *trembitas*, and

Figure 2.7. Ivan and Palahna yoked together at their wedding (*Shadows of Forgotten Ancestors*).

they refused to play until they were dressed in their own clothing and had attached flesh flowers to their *trembitas*."[26]

The essay is also striking for Parajanov's frank criticism of the superficial
manner in which an older film, Viktor Ivanov's *Oleksa Dovbush* (Dovzhenko
Film Studio 1959), shoehorned Hutsul culture into Soviet ideology. Examples
that he cited included having the Hutsuls greet each other with "Hello" rather
than "Glory to Jesus" and dressing Oleksa Dovbush in a red shirt to symbolize
his "revolutionary" spirit.[27] Actually, Parajanov's comments are on the mark:
in Ivanov's film, the elements of traditional Hutsul culture serve primarily as
exotic local color in what is an entirely conventional Soviet historical adventure
film. With refreshing frankness, Parajanov further criticized the authorities of
the Stalin era for engaging in a campaign to destroy homemade Hutsul religious
icons, which he characterized as "religious *lubki*."[28] While not overtly religious
himself, he often displayed a sympathetic attitude toward religion in his films
and was certainly fascinated with the aesthetic dimensions of religious art and
rituals.

The Reception of *Shadows of Forgotten Ancestors*

In the spring of 1965 *Shadows of Forgotten Ancestors* began a highly successful tour of the international film festival circuit, followed by overseas theatrical engagements. At the Mar Del Plata festival in Argentina the film received an award for Best Production and honorable mention "for color photography and special effects."[29] Andrew Sarris, who was reviewing the festival for *Variety*, characterized the film as "technically admirable if dramatically incomprehensible."[30] Reviewing the film at Venice (under the mistaken title of *In the Shadow of the Past*), Gene Moskowitz of *Variety* called it "visually resplendent" and "a youthfully excessive, but filmically beguiling film in spite of its way out techniques."[31]

The film also attracted positive critical attention in a number of major Soviet publications. In an early review for *Literaturnaia gazeta* (*Literary News*), Mykola Bazhan characterized it as "a true work of art," adding that this was "something that can be said very rarely, unfortunately, about the films of the Kiev film studio."[32] In particular, he praised the film's use of color, which he felt displayed a kind of "polyphony." Against potential accusations of "folklorism" in the film Bazhan countered: "The profound humanist contents of Kotsiubynsky's tale have not been lost, neither in the varied landscapes nor amongst the colorful clothing, nor beneath the masks of folk games."

Writing for the newspaper *Komsomol'skaia Pravda* (*Komsomol Truth*), Vladimir Turbin praised Parajanov's direction of actors, the production design, and the cinematography, especially the "remarkable" use of color. Still, Turbin was not wholly uncritical; among other things, he complained about the filmmakers' attempt to "historicize" the mythic story by introducing superfluous details such as a portrait of the Austrian Emperor Franz Josef.[33] In a subsequent essay published in *Molodaia gvardiia* (*Young Guard*), Turbin also tied the film to the broader issue of nationality politics in the Soviet Union. According to him, it signaled the appearance of "youth, full of intellectual courage" and the erasure of the "hidden division of artists working 'in the center' and working 'on the periphery.'" He further noted that among young intellectuals "the problem of further development, further formation of national origin in our social life is rising more insistently, more bravely." Focusing on the example of Slavic cultures in the Soviet Union, he declared that the "national perception of the world" is "alive and will survive" and "cannot level off or disappear," although it may transform "into new, contemporary forms."[34] It is striking how Turbin used the film as a vehicle to advance a particular view about nationality: that national differences are something more or less eternal; instead of withering away in the future, they would simply change form. In Turbin's conception, the Soviet Union was thus an "assembly of people of different nations" who, while united, do not lose their distinct national identities in the process of becoming the new Soviet man. Incidentally, "national models," and "a national picture of the world" were common tropes in Soviet thought that continued to appear decades later in the work of intellectuals such as Georgi Gachev.[35] Turbin's account of the film thus frames it primarily within orthodox Soviet discourses about nationality not unlike the Karaganov essay mentioned in the Introduction. Elsewhere in the essay, Turbin perceptively identified the energy of *Shadows of Forgotten Ancestors* with the then-burgeoning youth culture in the Soviet Union, a comment that seems to anticipate the controversies to come.

Fittingly, two other reviewers — the poet Ivan Drach and the literary critic Ivan Dziuba — were leading members of the *shestydesiatnyki*, or the Sixties generation of writers in Ukraine. Other members of this group included the poets Vasyl Symonenko, Lina Kostenko, Mykola Vinhranovsky, and the literary critic Ivan Svitlychny. As Kenneth C. Farmer and Orest Subtelny have argued, one of the main concerns of this generation was to speak out against the injustices of the Stalin era and the oppressive cultural atmosphere that lingered in Ukraine to a certain extent. Coming of age during the Thaw, this group shared with contemporary Russian intellectuals such as Yevgeny Yevtushenko and Aleksandr Solzhenitsyn a youthful sense of political engagement. One crucial difference between the Ukrainian *shestydesiatnyki* and their Russian-speaking counterparts was their concern with the status of Ukrainians as a nationality within the Soviet Union, especially the status of the Ukrainian language. However, their agenda was not exclusively political; as Farmer points out, the *shestydesiatnyki* were also devoted, perhaps even primarily so, to artistic innovation.[36] One can easily see why *Shadows of Forgotten Ancestors*, with its combination of "national" subject matter and innovative artistic form, could have such a powerful impact on young Ukrainian writers like Dziuba and Drach, to say nothing of filmmakers like Leonid Osyka and Yuri Illienko.

Drach's review in the annual publication *Ekran* (*Screen*) describes the appearance of *Shadows of Forgotten Ancestors* as "an explosion shattering many canons into bits, stirring up many circulating tastes and notions." He added, "And thus I want to believe that it is no chance occurrence, but the brilliant beginning of a new phase in Ukrainian cinema."[37] In addition to praising the film's handling of the ethnographic material, Drach described how the filmmakers successfully expanded on Kotsiubynsky's story in episodes such as Oleksa's death under a falling tree at the beginning of the film, Ivan's solitude after Marichka's death, and the lyrical wedding sequence mentioned above. He also singled out the soundtrack for opening up new creative possibilities, citing as one example the offscreen comments by villagers during Ivan's period of mourning.

Dziuba's essay entitled "A Day of Searching," which was published in *Iskusstvo kino*, posited that *Shadows of Forgotten Ancestors* embodied the ideal of a "national" film: "The film, with its deep and, I would say, its 'intensive' courageous national character, stands in opposition both to pseudo-national masquerade profanations, provincial conservatism and the sweet harmonies of sentimental farmers, and to sexless, a-national, sickly creations. The themes of the national psyche and the aesthetics of the picture develop fundamental themes of human life. Which is why it would be extremely worthless to pass-portize [*pasportizirovat'*] individual 'national moments' or 'national features': the essence itself is national, life itself is national, the truth itself of national disposi-tions and fates."[38] In his analysis of the film, Dziuba quotes from the dialogue in Ukrainian rather than translating it into Russian. This is not necessarily unusual — Turbin does it as well in his review — but it is nonetheless in keeping with Dziuba's overall conception of the film as a distinctly "national" work of art. It is an effective rhetorical gesture that draws attention to the differences between Ukrainian and Russian, emphasizing the linguistic boundary between both the two languages and the two nationalities. Here it is also worth noting Dziuba's association of national identity with traditional gender roles, a notion that would resurface in a negative sense later in Parajanov's career.

One should bear in mind that Dziuba's estimation of the film as signaling the rebirth of Ukrainian national cinema, and by extension, Ukrainian culture as a whole, does not necessarily reflect nationalism in the secessionist or "bour-geois nationalist" sense, to invoke a common Soviet formulation of that era. Rather, his analysis fits more or less within the program laid out in his essay *Internationalism or Russification?*, in which he critiqued existing Soviet nationali-ties policies through a putative framework of Marxism-Leninism. According to Dziuba, the actual policies of the era, among them the de facto preference given to the Russian language in education, were effectively a form of Russian great-power chauvinism. Using the writings of Lenin and other theorists such as Anatoly Lunacharsky as a starting point, Dziuba went so far as to question whether the ultimate disappearance of national distinctions, as envisioned by many Marxist theorists, was even feasible or desirable, since he viewed nation-ality as a basic fact of all human existence, not unlike how Turbin and other Soviet intellectuals of that period viewed it. However, at the same time Dziuba made a point of acknowledging the legitimacy of socialism and Soviet rule.

Ironically, Parajanov had in fact invented some of the purportedly "authentic" rituals performed in the film with the collaboration of Hutsul villagers. One example is the yoking together of Ivan and Palahna during the wedding sequence, which Parajanov himself mentions in his essay "Perpetual Motion." This does not invalidate Dziuba's or other Ukrainian intellectuals' enthusiasm for the film so much as it points up the inherent constructedness of nationality in general. To borrow Hobsbawm and Ranger's terms, all "traditions" are "invented" ones. The nationalist's identification and valorization of the "pure" and "authentic" is necessarily a willful and selective process.

Dziuba's association with *Shadows of Forgotten Ancestors* did not end with this essay in *Iskusstvo kino*. A few months later that same year, by making the film the focus of a public protest, he attempted not only to draw attention to the arrests taking place at that time, but also to link the film more directly to the political cause laid out shortly afterward in *Internationalism or Russification?* The protest took place on September 4, 1965, at the Ukraina Theater in Kyiv during a premiere screening of the film in conjunction with the sixth annual Kyiv Day of Cinema festival. Parajanov and other crew members made a special appearance at the screening. Afterward F. Braichenko, the manager of the theater, sent a report to Sviatoslav Ivanov, the chair of Goskino (Derzhkino) of Ukraine, in which he described the protest in detail. According to him, when Parajanov took the floor he "began to settle scores with the studio management" and criticized the delay in the film's release, claiming that he had to fight against dubbing the film into Russian.[39] Without warning Ivan Dziuba seized the microphone and addressed the audience; Braichenko quoted his speech thus: "Comrades! The reaction of 1937 [i.e., the purges] has advanced. At this moment arrests of Ukrainian intellectuals — writers, poets, and artists — are being carried out in Ukraine. Thus, a group of people has been arrested in the cities of Kyiv and Lviv . . . The mothers of Ukraine are weeping and moaning for their sons. Shame on the authorities! Whoever is with us, stand as a sign of protest!" In Braichenko's account, the theater management turned on the PA system and played music to return the situation to normal, and members of the audience expressed their "indignation that these people should be punished for their anti-Soviet speeches."[40] In contrast, the dissident Leonid Plyushch, in his memoirs entitled *History's Carnival*, recalled that Parajanov spoke in Dziuba's defense when the theater manager attempted to take the microphone away and that members of the audience also voiced their support for Dziuba.[41] Another individual who spoke out was Vasyl Stus, though in a 1990 interview Vyacheslav Chornovil claimed that he and Dziuba had planned the protest in secret, and that Stus joined them "spontaneously."[42] Regardless, the protest appears to have taken Parajanov — and the authorities — completely by surprise.

News of the protest later made its way up to Moscow. Nikolai Mikhailov, the chair of the Press Committee of the Council of Ministers of the USSR (Komiteta po pechati pri Sovete Ministrov SSSR), submitted a classified report dated January 15, 1966, to the Central Committee of the Communist Party. The report mainly covered ideological issues in contemporary culture and the activities of Soviet artistic intelligentsia. In the section on Soviet youth it described Dziuba's protest at the premiere, as well as Parajanov's complaints about the purported difficulties he encountered releasing the film with its original Ukrainian soundtrack. However, it did not mention Parajanov specifically by name, referring to him instead as "one of the film's creators."[43]

Despite the film's controversial premiere, it opened a few days later for an exclusive run in Kyiv at the Ukraina Theater through October 13. In the second half of the month it went into wider release before playing in second-run theaters in early November.[44] As mentioned in the previous chapter, in the Soviet Union as a whole it ultimately earned about 6.5 million admissions, a respectable figure considering its specialized appeal as an art film. Parajanov and Illienko also received nominations for the Lenin Prize from the Union of Cinematographers of the USSR in June 1967.[45]

Arguably, the film's greatest coup was its smash run in France under the title *Les Chevaux de feu* (*The Horses of Fire*). Distributed by Rank, the film opened on March 25, 1966, on three screens simultaneously in Paris. The ad copy described it as "A film like you've *never* seen!"[46] This premiere engagement lasted until May 13, after which the film ran continuously at various theaters in Paris until September 23 — just short of six full months.[47] Not surprisingly, it received ample coverage in the French press. *Les Lettres Françaises* published an abridged translation of Parajanov's essay "Perpetual motion" in its March 24 issue to accompany the film's opening.[48] Samuel Lachize of *L'Humanité* emphasized its unique style and characterized it as "a museum of folk arts and traditions transformed into a Chagall painting."[49] Jean De Baroncelli of *Le Monde* called the film a "pure poem." While acknowledging that it might seem "perhaps marred by an excessive formalism," he considered such minor flaws "in large measure inherent to an art that has not yet set itself apart from Socialist Realism."[50] In *Cahiers du cinéma* Sylvain Godet consciously evoked Russian Formalist criticism, opening with a quote by Viktor Shklovsky: "The life of a poetic work stretches from vision to recognition, from poetry to prose, from the concrete to the abstract." Godet elaborated: "Parajanov is not creating prosaic or poetic objects; they are becoming it [i.e., poetry] and, thanks to the perpetual passage of a 'cinema of prose' to a 'cinema of poetry,' the film tells us the story of this transformation itself."[51] The film's profound impact on French intellectuals helps explain why, nearly a decade after the film's release, so many of them joined together to protest Parajanov's arrest and imprisonment and repeatedly lobbied the Soviet government for his release.

Shadows of Forgotten Ancestors and Ukrainian Politics

If the September 1965 protest apparently did not harm the film itself in the eyes of the authorities during the first few years after its release, Parajanov personally became embroiled in Ukrainian politics and paid a heavy price for years afterward. Here some context is necessary. After Khrushchev's ouster in 1964, the Soviet authorities initiated a general crackdown against intellectuals, apparently based on the perception by many Communist Party leaders, especially in Russia and Ukraine, that Khrushchev had tolerated too much open dissent in the name of the Thaw and de-Stalinization, the chief literary example of this excessive tolerance being Solzhenitsyn's *A Day in the Life of Ivan Denisovich*. The most notorious manifestation of this crackdown was the September 1965 arrest and subsequent trial (in February 1966) of the writers Andrei Sinyavsky and Yuli Daniel, who had published pseudonymous works in the West.[52] In July 1967, Yuri Andropov, the chair of the KGB (Komitet gosudarstvennoi bezopasnosti or Committee for State Security), established the Fifth Directorate within the organization to deal with internal political issues such as censorship and dissent.

If anything the crackdown was most severe in Ukraine, where around the same time (late August and early September of 1965) some twenty individuals from both literary and scientific fields were arrested in secret and charged with offenses such as "agitation or propaganda conducted for the purpose of undermining or weakening Soviet rule."[53] In this set of criminal cases, the charges typically entailed the dissemination of "bourgeois nationalist" propaganda and advocating Ukrainian secession — which, as many dissidents pointed out, was a right supposedly guaranteed by the Soviet constitution. Some of the individuals charged had in fact called for secession, but many intellectuals — most prominently, Dziuba — were instead attempting to critique Soviet policies toward Ukraine within a putative framework of Marxism-Leninism. At the same time, Ukrainian dissidents in the 1960s did not limit their platform solely to nationality policies; they often invoked broader human rights issues such as freedom of political expression, freedom of religion, and due process in the judicial system. Many of the arrested dissidents received closed trials, evidently in violation of established Ukrainian and Soviet law, which limited the use of closed trials to exceptional circumstances: cases involving state secrets, defendants under sixteen years of age, or charges related to sexual perversion and other "intimate aspects of [the] life of persons who take part in the trial."[54] Michael Browne notes that only three defendants were tried "nominally" in public; sixteen were tried *in camera* and one was deported without trial.[55]

Why did *Shadows* attract the attention it did within the Soviet Union? And why the protest at this particular film? First was the subject matter and setting. The Hutsuls have often been regarded as a colorful tribe with peculiar costumes, folksongs, crafts, and superstitions, while at the same time being viewed as a kind of ur-Ukrainian. This is partly because the image of Ukraine as rural locale is central to Ukrainian national identity. Within Soviet discourse, it was also connected to the idea of "folk-genius," or richness in indigenous cultural capital. Second was the issue of language: the Hutsul dialect, which could at times be difficult to understand even for urban speakers of Ukrainian, became a special signifier of the film's Ukrainian-ness. Ordinarily, for Soviet films such linguistic distinctions got lost in the process of dubbing; films in non-Russian languages were dubbed into Russian or given even more intrusive Russian voice-over summaries for distribution outside the republic of origin. On the surface, this was nothing unusual since in the Soviet Union, much like in Italy, dialogue was generally post-synchronized from the start in domestic productions and imported films were also dubbed as a matter of routine. But given the significant role that nationality occupied in Soviet political discourse, dubbing could also be seen as a literal homogenization, even suppression, one might say, of the voice of non-Russian peoples. Because Goskino allowed Parajanov's film to retain its original soundtrack, audiences throughout the Soviet Union— including many primarily Russian-speaking Ukrainians—were confronted with a film whose language they could only partly understand at best.

In general, language has been closely intertwined with the problem of national identity in Ukraine.[56] During the Tsarist era, this included the central impact of the poet Taras Shevchenko on the emerging Ukrainian national consciousness, and the blanket prohibition against Ukrainian-language theater, publications, and education by Tsar Alexander II's regime in 1876. The legacy of the Stalin era was mixed at best. More progressive policies such as *korenizatsiia* (literally, "nativization," which entailed the preferential recruitment of a republic's titular nationality into the Party and state apparatus within non-Russian republics) and the promotion of Ukrainian-language education in the 1920s hardly balanced out against the special ruthlessness of collectivization in Ukraine and the engineered famine of 1932–1933. Khrushchev's educational reforms of the late 1950s partly reversed the gains made in Ukrainization by permitting Russian speakers to avoid taking Ukrainian language classes altogether if they chose. Important complicating factors were the large, well-established Russian-language speaking populations in areas such as the Crimean peninsula (ceded to Ukraine in 1954) and eastern Ukrainian districts such as Kharkiv and Dnipropetrovsk, as well as a wave of Russian immigration into the republic during the 1960s. Even in Kyiv, a substantial portion of the population spoke Russian on an everyday basis. Thus, by the mid-1960s, the situation in Ukraine was markedly different from republics such as Georgia and Armenia, where not only did a larger percentage of their populations as a whole speak Georgian or Armenian as their first language, but ethnic Armenians and Georgians were less likely to speak Russian as a second language than their Ukrainian counterparts. In that respect, one can understand why many Ukrainian intellectuals during that era expressed concerns about the fate of the Ukrainian language.

Any discussion of Ukrainian politics during this period must also include the complex figure of Petro Shelest, who served as the first secretary of the Communist Party from 1963 to 1972. He played a central role both in the ongoing debate about nationality in Ukraine and in Parajanov's individual fate. During his tenure he vigorously promoted Ukraine's economic and political interests, and he tolerated — within narrow limits — expressions of nationalism among the Ukrainian intelligentsia and Party cadres. Privately, Shelest defended intellectuals such as Ivan Drach. Although he disagreed with the premises of Dziuba's *Internationalization or Russification?*, his son Vitaly later claimed that he read the book closely and discussed it with him at length.[57] His relatively moderate stance in this area increasingly put him at odds with Moscow, which expected more overt fealty. By the mid-1960s, key Politburo members such as Brezhnev and Mikhail Suslov (the Central Committee's leader on ideological issues) pressed Shelest about the republic's efforts at Ukrainization and about various "manifestations of nationalism."[58] At times Shelest also acted as a hardliner, presiding over the 1965–1966 wave of arrests in Ukraine, which admittedly may have been due in part to pressure from Moscow. In July 1968 he warned against "reformism and revision, whenever and in whatever form they may appear," and was reportedly one of the main advocates for the Soviet-led invasion of Czechoslovakia the following month.[59]

Parajanov, the Armenian "Ukrainian Nationalist"

The protest at the screening of *Shadows of Forgotten Ancestors* thus drew Parajanov into a highly fraught political field: the central authorities in Moscow, the Ukrainian Party apparatus including Shelest, the Ukrainian cultural intelligentsia, and nationalist dissidents (with significant, but not complete overlap between the latter two factions). Parajanov himself occupied an unusual position within the Ukrainian cultural intelligentsia as an ethnic outsider but a core member. Far from being resentful of Dziuba's co-option of the screening for his political cause, Parajanov befriended him and also became active in subsequent protests against the arrests.

While Parajanov's friends almost invariably insist that he was not interested in politics per se, this needs to be qualified. He was certainly disturbed by the events of that period and, like many intellectuals, felt compelled to speak out about them. First, in late October 1965, along with six other signatories—Vitaly Kyreiko, Platon Maiboroda, Leonid Serpilin, Lina Kostenko, Ivan Drach, and Oleh Antonov—Parajanov wrote to the Central Committees of Ukraine and the Soviet Union inquiring about the fate of several individuals who had been arrested, among them the literary critic Ivan Svitlychny. They also pleaded for open trials, arguing that the secrecy under which the process had been conducted violated existing Soviet laws.[60] In April 1968, Parajanov, together with 138 other signatories, submitted another petition (since known as the "Appeal of the 139") to Brezhnev, Alexei Kosygin (chair of the Council of Ministers), and Nikolai Podgorny (chair of the Presidium of the Supreme Soviet of the Soviet Union). This letter criticized how the 1965–1966 wave of political trials—in particular the trial against journalist Vyacheslav Chornovil in April 1966—had been conducted *in camera* and without due process, declaring them to be an "intensified restoration of Stalinism" and "a form of suppression of those who do not conform in their thinking and a form of suppression of the civic activity and social criticism which is absolutely essential to the health of any society."[61] In both letters, Parajanov was listed prominently as the first signatory.

Given Parajanov's lifelong craving for attention, it is likely that the controversy surrounding *Shadows of Forgotten Ancestors* and his public role in the subsequent protests were not altogether displeasing. Vladimir Lugovsky recalls that Parajanov once joked, "Today there's a meeting of Ukrainian nationalists at my place. [. . .] I'm obliged to receive them! I'm like a father to them . . . For them I'm the head Ukrainian nationalist!"[62] However, to view Parajanov exclusively as "apolitical" and driven to seek personal notoriety minimizes the courage he demonstrated as the only filmmaker in Ukraine to sign the petitions. Over the next several years a large number of the signatories on the "Appeal of the 139" were subsequently reprimanded, dismissed from their positions, had their homes and belongings searched, or were even arrested—as was the case with Parajanov.

Still, Ukrainian support for Parajanov and *Shadows of Forgotten Ancestors* was by no means unanimous. In his 1970 essay "Chronicle of Resistance," Valentyn Moroz bitterly decried the destruction of the Ukrainian cultural heritage under the Soviet regime, writing at length about the theft of religious art from the church of the Hutsul village of Kosmach, which was established in 1740 thanks to a large donation by Oleksa Dovbush. It was later reconsecrated as a Uniate church and finally turned into a museum in 1959. Moroz claimed that the church's iconostasis had been borrowed by the Dovzhenko Film Studio for the shoot, but the borrowed items were not returned in spite of a detailed inventory and "a promise to return the iconostasis in five months." According to Moroz, the people of Kosmach "were told that the iconostasis had been turned over to the museum of Ukrainian art in Kyiv."[63] He maintained that Parajanov also stole a number of artworks from Kosmach, the Sahaydacha museum in Kosiv, and from other individuals and locations.[64] Moroz wrote: "The word 'parajanov' has become synonymous with the word 'thief' ('You're from Kyiv? Tell Parajanov to return my antique waistband.')."[65] As part of his broader argument about the Russification of Ukrainian culture, he then accused Parajanov, along with other "non-Ukrainian" artists such as Dovzhenko's wife Yulia Solntseva, of exploiting the riches of Ukrainian culture for their own artistic ends without ultimately understanding its culture.[66] Here Moroz explicitly highlighted Parajanov's Armenian origin and took pains to point out that Armenian cultural artifacts would not have been abused in the same way. He even drew into question the significance of Parajanov's contributions to the film, suggesting that Parajanov was merely a "talented impresario who successfully recruited the necessary people": that is, the Ukrainians Yakutovich, Illienko, and Skoryk.[67]

Alexei Korotyukov, a Ukrainian writer and journalist who immigrated to the United States in September 1974, reiterated the accusations of theft in a 1975 interview and further claimed that Parajanov gave many of these objects away to guests in his apartment, including visitors "from foreign countries." He concluded: "One can say that *Shadows of Forgotten Ancestors* was made at a dear price — the rape of a Nation's culture." Korotyukov added that Parajanov was hardly alone in this respect, that Tarkovsky also supposedly "plundered churches" while working on *Andrei Rublev* (Mosfilm 1966).[68] Given Parajanov's well-known weakness for beautiful art objects, such reports are not altogether implausible. At the same time, one should take into account that Moroz, at least, was clearly using such narratives of cultural theft to advance his own nationalist agenda. Furthermore, as discussed in chapter 6, the authorities later investigated these accusations against Parajanov in conjunction with his 1973 arrest but ultimately did not pursue charges in court.

The Ukrainian Poetic School

Besides Parajanov as its Armenian figurehead, other members of the Ukrainian poetic school included directors such as Yuri Illienko and Leonid Osyka, the poet and screenwriter Ivan Drach, and the iconic actor Ivan Mykolaichuk, who also co-wrote scripts and later became a director in his own right. These younger artists shared a thematic focus on Ukrainian history and identity, a pronounced tendency to use myth, ritual, symbols, and metaphors, and an interest in expanding the boundaries of cinematic language. Parajanov himself was a gracious supporter of the younger generation's work; in 1971, he published an essay in *Sovetskii ekran* (*Soviet Screen*) praising some of their recent films in the hope of drawing wider attention to them within the Soviet Union as a whole.[69]

The majority of these films are set in the past or in rural locales, a trope that the filmmakers often use to explore the impact of imperialism on Ukrainian history and identity. As one might expect, the films' basic cultural materials are also closely connected to Ukrainian national origins. However, it would be reductionist to argue that the films are simply fodder for a nationalist movement; rather, they often examine the problem of Ukrainian identity in a surprisingly complex manner. This is especially true of those based on scripts written by Ivan Drach.

Yuri Illienko (1936–2010) was easily the most interesting of these directors in terms of style, although his output as a whole was uneven in quality. His brilliant debut, *A Well for the Thirsty* (*Rodnik dlia zhazhdushchikh*, Dovzhenko Film Studio 1966), based on a poetic script by Drach, was surely one of the most daring formal experiments ever produced in Soviet cinema. Virtually plotless and lacking dialogue for large portions of its running time, the film concerns an old man who lives alone since his wife has passed away and his sons have departed. The village where he lives is surrounded by parched soil, but the water from his well sustains the villagers and, years ago, the soldiers passing through during the war. He envisions a beautiful young woman, presumably his wife at a younger age (played by Larisa Kadochnikova), carrying pails of water. The densely textured film uses repeated visual and audio motifs to create a structure akin to a musical composition. Continuing the experiments with film stock that he began on *Shadows of Forgotten Ancestors*, Illienko uses special high-contrast stock, at times pushed even further so that the stark black-and-white imagery looks like an engraving or ink drawing. The sound track is a complex audio collage of recited poetry, song fragments, cries, and sound effects such as ringing bells; no doubt it served as a major source of inspiration for Parajanov's subsequent use of sound in *The Color of Pomegranates*. In its deeply ambivalent representation of "Ukraine," the film is thematically linked with Osyka's *A Stone Cross* (*Kamennyi krest*, Dovzhenko Film Studio 1968), discussed below.

The sharply divided reception for *A Well for the Thirsty* during a January 26, 1966, Artistic Council meeting encapsulates the resistance that the Ukrainian poetic school encountered almost from the start. As one of the invited attendees, Parajanov spoke more extensively than any other individual at the meeting, acknowledging some minor flaws in the film but nonetheless calling it "an absolute masterpiece of cinema."[70] He also underscored its relationship to the nascent poetic school as a whole: "Indeed, perhaps at our studio there will be some kind of division so that poetic cinematography, which I have been seeking since my first days of residence at this studio and have found in the themes of the film *Ivan's Childhood*, will be developed further. The entire artistic heritage of Dovzhenko, the contemporary poetry of Ukrainian poets — Kostenko, Drach — all have a bearing on this film."[71]

Several other creative personnel from the studio likewise supported the film and defended the principle of artistic experimentation. But a significant contingent of both regular Artistic Council members and invited attendees implied that the film fell short of the aims of Socialist Realism. They accused it of lacking sufficient humanity, being inaccessible to a broad audience — a charge difficult to refute — and having an overly mournful, elegiac tone. The production designer Vulf Agronov stated, "It seems to me that it was made by a complete egoist. It was made, undoubtedly, by a talented director, but the kind of person who doesn't love people." The director Abram Naroditsky said, "I don't feel that the requiem is a good genre for film art." The director Viktor Ivanov appeared to direct his comments at the poetic school as a whole, arguing that "much of our searching is not forward-looking but, on the contrary, backward-looking."[72] In response, Parajanov directly confronted some of the individual critics and accused the whole faction of being "afraid of art."[73] To be sure, he may have been on the defensive at that time in part because his own film, *Kyiv Frescoes* (*Kievskie freski*, Dovzhenko Film Studio 1965–1966), had already run into serious trouble (discussed in the next chapter). Illienko's and the poetic school's troubles hardly ended there. In a June 1966 decree of the Central Committee of the Communist Party of Ukraine, entitled "On Serious Individual Defects in the Organization of Film Production at the Kyiv Dovzhenko Film Studio," the authorities accused Illienko's film of manifesting "ideological deviations."[74] Whatever their underlying objections, the film remained banned for over twenty years.

Illienko's second feature, *The Eve of Ivan Kupalo* (*Vecher nakanune Ivana Kupala*, Dovzhenko Film Studio 1968) is an ambitious adaptation of Gogol's story of the same name. On the most immediate level, the film's style and imagery attempt to recreate the phantasmagorical world of Gogol's prose in cinematic terms through jump cuts and other forms of trick editing, exaggerated Ukrainian decorative motifs, and distortions of scale and perspective. Beyond that, Illienko tries to make the film into a meditation on Ukrainian history; at one point, Pidorka is caught up in the Mongol invasion of the thirteenth century and subsequently witnesses Catherine the Great and Potemkin's legendary tour of facade-villages in the Ukrainian countryside. Ultimately, the film seems overburdened with trick effects and was coolly received by Soviet critics, but it remains memorable for its extraordinary wealth of surrealistic imagery.

Illienko's greatest commercial and critical success was by far *White Bird with a Black Spot* (*Belaia ptitsa s chernoi otmetinoi*, Dovzhenko Film Studio 1970), which won the Golden Prize at the Moscow Film Festival in 1971 and drew 10.5 million admissions in the Soviet Union as a whole. Co-written by Illienko and its star Ivan Mykolaichuk, the film concerns an impoverished Hutsul family whose loyalties are divided between the Soviets and the Romanians during World War II. It deploys a straightforward narrative and pointedly orthodox representations of negative figures such as the band of Ukrainian nationalist insurgents and the priest. But it also contains many of Illienko's characteristic stylistic touches, including jump cuts, 360-degree tracking shots, and telephoto camerawork that strongly recalls *Shadows of Forgotten Ancestors*.

Another major figure of this movement is Leonid Osyka (1940–2001). His first feature, *Love Awaits Him Who Returns* (*Kto vernetsia — doliubit*, Dozhenko Film Studio 1966), is an overtly poetic film dedicated to the "memory of the poet-soldier" and prominently featuring the war poetry of Vladimir Bulaenko and Semen Gudzenko on the soundtrack. In it, a young soldier goes off to war, is wounded on the battlefield, and has a series of encounters with a young war widow, a fellow artist, and a group of Gypsies who are eventually slaughtered by the Germans. A stylistically eclectic work, it contains a number of visually striking shots that use a telephoto lens to flatten perspective and to emphasize the graphic qualities of the image. Some episodes, most notably that of the soldier getting ready for departure while his mother prepares him milk and bread, also employ a tableau aesthetic.

Osyka's most highly regarded feature is *A Stone Cross* based on a script by Ivan Drach and adapted from the writings of Vasyl Stefanyk.[75] In this film, an old man in Western Ukraine tires of working his barren plot of land and decides to emigrate with his family to Canada. On the eve of his departure, he catches a thief on his farm and plans to kill him, but succumbs to compassion while his neighbors stand fast in their implacable code of honor. As a memorial to his life in his homeland, he leaves behind a stone cross on the hill. Especially noteworthy is the farewell party, which takes up about half of the eighty-minute film. In a series of long takes, the camera circles around the villagers, following the old man while he approaches various individuals, speaks, and offers to drink toasts with them. The overall texture of the film is deliberately spare compared to the kaleidoscopic quality of *Shadows of Forgotten Ancestors* or *The Eve of Ivan Kupalo*, and it depends more heavily on dramatic dialogue than *A Well for the Thirsty*. Still, a great deal of the film's sense is carried by its expressive imagery, including intense close-ups of the villagers' time-ravaged faces and heavily flattened, almost abstract images of the countryside.

The Lost Letter (*Propavshaia gramota*, Dovzhenko Film Studio 1972) is another Gogol adaptation written by Drach, but this time directed by Boris Ivchenko. Like *The Eve of Ivan Kupalo*, it uses a painterly and phantasmagorical style to represent Gogol's prose, though it is less frenetic and ultimately more accessible than Illienko's film. Nonetheless, *The Lost Letter* was shelved for some fifteen years; Ivchenko has maintained that it was due to the film's representation of center-periphery relations in the episode when the Cossacks visit the Empress Catherine the Great at Peterhof.[76]

At the same time, the poetic school's rural and folkloric conception of Ukrainian identity hardly represents the diverse experiences of Ukraine as a whole; it is very far from the cosmopolitanism of Odessa, whose own film studio produced some of the leading films of the Thaw era and became home to the singular talent of Kira Muratova. In spite of their manifest artistic achievement, the films of the Ukrainian poetic school often encountered difficulties with the film and Party administrators, receiving only limited distribution or, in the case of *A Well for the Thirsty*, winding up banned altogether. As Joshua First points out, the school's inherently specialized arthouse appeal also lost favor with Goskino in Moscow under the more profit-oriented Filipp Yermash.[77] For Parajanov, the situation was much worse; after *Shadows of Forgotten Ancestors*, he was unable to complete any further film projects in Ukraine and was finally forced to leave the republic permanently in the early Seventies.

Despite whatever problems Parajanov may have had with Ukrainian authorities at this time, *Shadows of Forgotten Ancestors* still appeared to maintain a high reputation among Party officials in the Soviet Union as a whole, at least for a few years after its release. In February 1968 Vasili Shauro, the head of the Cultural Section of the Central Committee, issued a report entitled "On the Contemporary State of Soviet Filmmaking," in which he attacked several recent films on ideological grounds as part of a broader critique of Goskino's operations as a whole. Significantly, this report came at a time when a number of films had already been banned or shelved, including Illienko's *A Well for the Thirsty*,

Tarkovsky's *Andrei Rublev*, and Andrei Konchalovsky's *Asya's Happiness* (*Istoriia Asi Kliachinoi, kotoraia liubila, da ne vyshla zamuzh*, Mosfilm 1966). Yet even after the protest associated with the film in Kyiv and Parajanov's own signing of petitions against the arrests of Ukrainian intellectuals — to say nothing of the controversy surrounding his subsequent, aborted project *Kyiv Frescoes*— Shauro still singled out *Shadows of Forgotten Ancestors* for praise alongside films such as Sergei Bond-archuk's *War and Peace* (*Voina i mir*, Mosfilm 1965–1967), Rezo Chkheidze's *The Father of a Soldier* (*Otets soldata*, Georgia Film Studio 1964), and Sergei Yutkevich's *Lenin in Poland* (*Lenin v Pol'she*, Mosfilm 1965).[78] Shauro and the other officials in the Central Committee could not have been unaware of the events in Ukraine and Parajanov's role in them. This suggests that to some extent, Soviet officials may have tried to separate the film itself from the controversy surrounding it and its maker. On the whole, *Shadows of Forgotten Ancestors* was duly recognized both by Soviet critics and the authorities at the time of its release as a major achievement for its innovative film style, its fresh treatment of "ethnographic" subject matter, and the universality of its underlying themes.

But the path of poetic cinema, as its practitioners learned, proved increas-ingly treacherous during the ideological retrenchment of the late 1960s and early 1970s. *White Bird With a Black Spot*, the sole other unambiguous success of the Ukrainian poetic school, was even more careful to avoid stylistic excess than *Shadows of Forgotten Ancestors* and offered a pointedly orthodox interpreta-tion of Western Ukraine's experiences during the Great Patriotic War. As the school's practitioners learned, if a film pushed stylistic boundaries too far, failed to offer an easily understood positive message, or critiqued center-periphery relations even indirectly, it risked being deliberately under-distributed, shelved, or banned outright. Despite his reputation, or perhaps because of it, Parajanov would prove more vulnerable than most of his colleagues.

3

Kyiv Frescoes

The Film That Might Have Been

*K*yiv Frescoes (*Kievskie freski*, Dovzhenko Film Studio 1965–1966), the aborted project that Parajanov had planned as his follow-up to *Shadows of Forgotten Ancestors*, represented a major turning point in his career. It marks the first systematic articulation of his mature tableau style associated with *The Color of Pomegranates*, but it is also of great interest for its unusual perspective on contemporary life in Kyiv. Work on *Kyiv Frescoes* lasted a little over one year, from late 1964 or early 1965 to early 1966. Although Parajanov never received approval to begin shooting it due to conflicts with the authorities, he did manage to complete a literary scenario, shooting script, and screen tests. He then edited the screen tests into a self-contained thirteen-minute short with a soundtrack. Through these surviving materials, this chapter provides a detailed reconstruction of the film Parajanov never shot. It will also look at the reasons behind the project's ultimate cancellation, which represented an intensification of his conflicts with the Soviet filmmaking authorities over his vision of poetic cinema within a broader environment of ideological retrenchment in the Soviet Union as a whole.

The Literary Scenario

Like any number of Soviet films produced in the mid-1960s, *Kyiv Frescoes* served the ostensible purpose of commemorating the twentieth anniversary of the Great Patriotic War. But rather than depicting the war directly, Parajanov's script examines contemporary life in Kyiv using the celebrations of May 9, 1965 (the anniversary of the city's liberation from the Germans) as its focal point. The story could hardly be simpler: an unnamed film director—referred to simply as "the Man" (*Chelovek*) but obviously Parajanov himself—pays a "Longshoreman" (*Gruzchik*) to deliver a basket of flowers to a retired general. Somehow he inadvertently gives the incorrect address to the Longshoreman, who delivers the basket instead to a "Woman," a war widow working as a custodian at the Bohdan and Varvara Khanenko Museum of Arts in Kyiv, home of a famed portrait of the Infanta Margarita by Diego Velázquez.[1] The Longshoreman ends up spending the night at the Woman's apartment. In the final episode of the script, the Infanta Margarita steps out of the painting to pay her respects to the widow who has devoted her life to the upkeep of the museum. A group of soldiers, who are visiting the museum in conjunction with anniversary celebrations, tiptoe past the napping Woman and pause to admire the beauty of the Velázquez painting.

Parajanov's goals for the film were in fact much broader and more ambitious than a simple commemoration of the war. Against the background of the ongoing anniversary celebrations, the script presents, to use Cora Tsereteli's apt term, "kaleidoscopic" impressions of contemporary life in Kyiv.[2] The fragmentary episodes provide glimpses of people from all walks of life, from the working class to the cultural intelligentsia and the military elite. While it depicts the filmmaker as only one character, hints crop up throughout that the entire story is in some way filtered through his imagination. This self-reflexive, autobiographical aspect of the script, which incorporates dreams and fantasy, is undoubtedly inspired by Federico Fellini's *8½* (1963). Awarded the first prize at the 1963 Moscow Film Festival, Fellini's film was widely viewed and discussed among filmmakers and critics in the Soviet Union at that time. Other clues regarding Parajanov's intentions appear in the somewhat rambling remarks he made at a subsequent Artistic Council meeting that evaluated the shooting script: "This is a film about kindness, humaneness, concern for people. The flowers go to the wrong address, where they are needed, but in the home where the flowers were sent other things are needed." He then summed up the social vision behind his particular mode of poetic cinema as follows: "When the romantic fuses with the everyday, the everyday with the private, the epic with the details, the sum total amounts to film-poetry."[3]

The script underwent so many stages of revision—due in no small part to Parajanov's protracted battle with the authorities—that it is difficult to speak of a definitive version. The text published in the December 1990 issue of *Iskusstvo kino* represents, according to E. Levin, the literary scenario (*literaturnyi stsenarii*) that Parajanov officially submitted to the studio for approval.[4] That version had already been revised from his first draft, which Levin claims "was impossible to submit to the studio in the prescribed manner." Levin characterizes that initial draft rather exuberantly as "outwardly chaotic, incoherent, rhythmic, film-imagistic [*kinoizobrazitel'nuiu*] prose: more precisely, a romantic ballad for the screen, set forth in metaphors that are subtle, whimsical, often difficult to catch or — better to say — a lyrical, wistful film-poem suffused with light," and so on.[5] Such language hardly seems out of place given what appears in subsequent, supposedly tamed-down drafts.

The script opens with the legend: "I have conceived the film as CINEFRESCOES [*kinofreski*]." Thus, at the outset Parajanov suggests that the film will be a departure from conventional film narrative; the episodes will be relatively self-contained, the visual style of the film influenced by the fine arts. He then supplies the following definitions for the term "fresco," citing the Great Soviet Encyclopedia:

> Fresco (Ital. fresco): Primary meaning — fresh.
> Fresco: enables the creation of monumental works that are organically linked with architecture and time.
> Fresco: the palette of a fresco is quite restrained, giving a noble simplicity.
> The method of executing frescoes has changed with their development.[6]

From the outset, the wording is cannily chosen to inform the reader of the character of the future film: a public work of art that is at the same time formally innovative. Implicitly, it defends innovation as necessary to the development of any art form, including film. In that respect, it fits closely with Parajanov's comments on poetic cinema above.

The opening paragraph of the prologue indicates that while the film is closely tied to the director's perceptions and thought processes, its scope is actually much broader:

> Light is burning in an apartment . . . In the nighttime silence tires are still making noise on the wet asphalt of the boulevard . . .
> The silhouettes of a poplar, Shchors, Vladimir [Volodymyr] are outlined in the darkness . . .
> In "the apartment where light was burning" the camera slowly glides past dilapidated *parsunas*[7] [icon-style portraits] of hetmans, antique copperware . . . hand-worked glass [*gutnomu steklu*] . . . it stops on a sleeping man . . .
> "The Man" opened his eyes . . . he listens attentively to the silence of the city . . .[8]

Thus, in his typically condensed manner Parajanov evokes a broad range of Ukrainian experience, from historical figures to traditional and contemporary folk art (the hand-worked glass). The Man is subsequently awakened in the middle of the night by three soldiers who drop by his apartment to ask for hot water and matches. He invites them inside and urges them to make themselves at home before he goes back to sleep.

The remainder of the script is divided into ten "frescoes," not unlike Parajanov's later use of the term "miniatures" to describe the individual chapters in the original script for *The Color of Pomegranates*. Each "fresco," while taking place in a relatively constricted moment of time, does not necessarily consist of a single image or tableau, as one would expect from Parajanov's choice of terminology; they incorporate various juxtaposed details, actions, and locales, suggesting at times a monumental and complex composition too vast to be taken in at a single glance.

In Fresco No. 1, the Man awakens in the morning to discover the soldiers thoughtfully washing and polishing his floor.

> "The Man" awoke with a chill . . .
> It smelled of *kirza* [oilcloth] . . .[9]
> Somewhere water was running . . .
> In the doorway stood three pairs of boots . . . and on the rigid boot tops,
> foot wrappings were drying out . . .
> Bare feet moved rapidly back and forth over the wet floor . . .
> It smelled of *kirza* . . .
> Water was running . . .
> Bare feet moved rapidly . . .[10]

After the soldiers have left, the Man finds that, as he requested, they have turned off the gas and shut the door behind them. They have also left a single apple out of the fruit he offered them the night before. Thus the script emphasizes the basic kindness and decency of ordinary people. On a stylistic level, the scene demonstrates how Parajanov constructs scenes out of finely observed fragmentary details and sensual impressions. The use of repetitions further give the film a sense of rhythm.

Fresco No. 2 is by far the longest section of the script, taking up nearly half its length. Suggesting a virtuoso display of montage, it juxtaposes the ceremony in Victory Square, which consists mainly of soldiers marching in formation and artillery salutes, with seemingly random details observed throughout the city or imagined by the Man. Since Parajanov's actual apartment at that time directly overlooked Victory Square, it is likely that at least part of the celebration was to be filmed from his own balcony, reproducing his literal point of view. Although the section is too long to reproduce in its entirety, the opening portion gives a sense of how it is structured:

> . . . A parquet floor, polished until it gleams . . .
>
> . . . Soldiers' boots walk knowingly on their tiptoes . . .
>
> . . . The parquet floor creaks a little . . .
>
> . . . Boots walk . . .
>
> . . . Taking aim at Kyiv — a hand turns an artillery drum . . .
>
> SALVO (fireworks) . . .
>
> . . . Boots march on tiptoes . . .
>
> SALVO.
>
> . . . The art museum . . . the Infanta [Margarita] by Velázquez . . .
>
> Zurbarán . . .
>
> Goya . . .
>
> Morales . . .
>
> Soldiers tiptoe past them . . .
>
> SALVO.
>
> A wheelchair . . .
>
> A pot of flowers with white crowns . . .
>
> A string bag with cannonball-like oranges . . .
>
> The invalid presses on the pedals . . . flies past the stoplight . . . enters alone on the empty Victory Square . . .
>
> SALVO.
>
> . . . The Shchors monument . . . A group of generals stand in line . . .
>
> . . . The photographer focuses off his knee . . .
>
> . . . Wives straighten up their husbands' overcoats, blow away bits of lint . . .
>
> . . . Mirrored giants — refrigerated trucks — speed up the highway . . .
>
> . . . Wheelchairs bustle . . .
>
> SALVO.
>
> Twenty military cargo trucks with soldiers drive up to the columns of the circus . . .
>
> . . . Twenty military cargo trucks are unloaded . . .
>
> . . . Twenty companies one after the other make their way toward the entrance among the columns . . . they disappear . . .
>
> . . . Only one block of soldiers broke out . . . split off . . . scattered . . .
>
> . . . The soldiers ran . . . overtaking the streetcars . . . crossing the asphalt . . .
>
> SALVO.

. . . An old Pobeda car came to a sudden stop . . .

The "Woman-driver" opened the hood . . . stuck her head inside to check the gears . . .

. . . The flowing stream of soldiers came to a sudden halt . . .

. . . The open door of the café "Express."

The soldiers are standing once again, are once again closing ranks into a square . . . They march . . . disappear among the columns of the circus.

SALVO.

"The Man" ran into a flower shop . . . it smelled damp.

"The Woman-decorator" [*zhenshchina-dekorator*] offers him a basket that looks like a salad à la carte . . . she assures him that the arrangement has a center, pointing to a red flower.

"The Man" doesn't like the basket.

He has to pay up front in order to have a basket made to his taste.

SALVO.

. . . A hand opens a plywood chest . . . takes out newspapers . . . blows off naphthalene . . . uncovers a "general's uniform" . . .

The uniform bent . . . began to jingle with the medals, decorations . . . stars . . . [11]

The twenty shots fired in commemoration of the twentieth anniversary structure the entire montage sequence, both marking changes in location and linking them together in time. At first glance some of the fragmentary images are difficult to place within the overall narrative, though some—particularly the image of the tiptoeing soldiers—are developed more fully later in the script. The device of synchronizing cuts to sharp sounds would later reappear in *The Color of Pomegranates*, albeit to very different effect; there, cuts are occasionally marked by sounds such as a tolling bell.

The images in the sequence are organized primarily around the script's two main themes, war and art. They also share something of the vision of the city expressed by artists such as James Joyce in *Ulysses* (particularly the long central chapter that follows different characters throughout Dublin), Andrei Bely in the novel *Petersburg*, and Dziga Vertov in *The Man With a Movie Camera* (*Chelovek s kinoapparatom*, VUFKU 1929). In other words, here the technique of montage represents the experience of the city as simultaneity, as loose juxtapositions of people and details from different walks of life. In that respect, Parajanov's vision of Kyiv is typically Modernist.

Fresco No. 3 offers a glimpse of the Man's (i.e., the director's) private life. On an impulse, he visits his ex-wife's apartment on Pyrohovska Street late at night and asks for their old baby carriage, which he has decided to give to a neighborhood police officer whose wife has just given birth. The fact that the Man's wife is not seen at all but is represented as only a voice behind a door implies family troubles, a reading that is reinforced in Fresco No. 9, in which the Man's son gets caught in the middle of a fight with other boys and lights trash cans on fire during a visit to a city park.

Frescoes 4, 5, and 6 comprise a triptych depicting the interconnected dreams of the filmmaker, the Woman, and the Longshoreman, respectively. The script indicates that the first two episodes are to be accompanied by a Bach fugue on the soundtrack. All three begin with parallel images of the sleeping city, followed by shots of the individual dreamers. In Fresco No. 4, the Man dreams that "flowers are floating along an empty street." The Longshoreman approaches his window in expectation of the flowers' arrival, but his hope is frustrated when they fall and are carried away by water flowing down the street. He is left only with a handful of dirt and roots:

> ... Earth ... roots ... glass is broken ... Glass floats without a sound ... along the asphalt, and water, running water carries the pieces away ... And the winds ... they catch the white lace of the curtains, with two big hands they sail, sail, sail over the sleeping city ... .[12]

The image of lace curtains fluttering in the wind represents the underlying psychological connection between the three sleeping individuals.

Fresco No. 5, the Woman's dream, contains pointed allusions to the siege of Kyiv during World War II: namely, pasting strips of gauze on windowpanes to protect the glass during bombing raids and burying cultural artifacts (in this case, Velázquez's portrait of the Infanta Margarita) in order to hide them from the German troops. The association that the script develops between the curtains, the widow's bridal veil, and the gauze strips is particularly affecting:

> ... The wind caused the curtain to flutter ... .
> ... The City was sleeping ...
> ... "The Woman" was also sleeping ...
> ... The curtain touched her and she became entangled in a bridal veil.
> ... then in lace ...
> ... then in gauze ...
> ... The gauze was cut up into ribbons ...
> ... The ribbons were dyed in ink ...
> ... The ribbons were glued onto windows ...

Fresco No. 6, the Longshoreman's dream, likewise alludes to the bombing of Kyiv during the war: the extinguishing of lights, required for safety reasons during air raids, and the symbolically loaded image of spilled milk flowing down gutters (the Longshoreman first dreams of carrying a crate of milk). In his dream, the curtains fluttering in the breeze transform into a surrealistic vision of the air raid:

> And in the courtyard where "He" was carrying flowers, where underwear and sheets were hanging, naked young women, awakened by the cry, were running wild in the night, snatching up the underwear . . . rushed about among the broken clotheslines and snapping clothespins.

The dream ends abruptly as the Longshoreman wakes up in the morning, in the Woman's apartment. The widow has already left; he finds only a note reading, "I went to get some milk." Thus the three central frescoes (numbers 4, 5, and 6) make up the film's thematic fulcrum: the characters' interconnected dreams represent the collective memory of the war that binds together all the inhabitants of the city.

Early the next morning, in Fresco No. 7, the Man stands on the balcony of his apartment overlooking Victory Square. He watches equestrian exercises, during which the four white horses become agitated when they see a black stallion led into the back of a truck heading to the slaughterhouse. This incident is juxtaposed comically with the image of an older, heavily decorated "General" and his elderly mother waiting in front of the Aeroflot cashier and trying to hail a taxi to the airfield. The General ends up hitching a ride in the back of a cargo vehicle full of apples, while his mother walks off with a young boy who is heading to the zoo to feed the animals.

Fresco No. 8 revisits the General and his mother. The General drives a white Volga on the highway to Lubny, racing past a bus, passing in front of it, and forcing it to stop so that he can help his mother onto it.

In Fresco No. 9, the Man takes his son to kindergarten, where children tease the boy because of the divorce: "One daddy brings him here, and another daddy takes him home!" A fight breaks out and the son runs off, crying, setting refuse containers on fire along the way. The Man runs to catch up with him, but the son stops only when he hears the whistle of a policeman, whereupon he hides behind his father. This is directly juxtaposed with a scene at the Khanenko Museum of Arts: the hand of an unidentified individual "opens a *cassone* (a chest from fifth-century Spain) and places a bottle of milk in the corner," custodians clean the museum and its artifacts, and the Woman dozes underneath the painting of the Infanta Margarita.[13] Here the image of custodians polishing the floor echoes that of the floor-washing at the beginning of the script. In addition, the bottle of milk recalls — and contrasts with — the bombed milk crates in the Longshoreman's dream.

The action of Fresco No. 10 immediately follows this last scene, opening with a fantasy that expresses the director's feelings of compassion and respect for the Woman. The Infanta Margarita steps out of the painting, polishes the floor as if "dancing the Galliard," and bows to the sleeping Woman. The inspired closing passage depicts a group of soldiers visiting the museum. They tiptoe respectfully past the sleeping Woman and listen to an art historian describe Velázquez's portrait of the Infanta Margarita:

> — Stand in a circle . . . the "Infanta Margarita," Velázquez, Spain . . . Attention please . . . The heartfelt beauty of the young Infanta . . . her sunny color . . . the execution of her silken hair is conveyed with great realistic force . . . Her eyes reflect the emotional world of her youthful existence . . . The Infanta looks across the ages . . . as a symbol of beauty and rapture . . .[14]

The art historian's comments thus make explicit what Parajanov's script has amply suggested earlier. The script concludes:

> . . . The solders are reflected in the glass over the masterpiece, scrutinizing themselves, straightening their hair . . . adjusting their belts . . . puffing out their chests . . . they take turns . . . nudging each other . . . then they slowly turn their heads . . .
>
> . . . A window is opened wide . . . two barefooted girls sharply wring out rags and wash off the dust from the windowpanes . . .
>
> . . . The wind causes their silhouettes to sway . . . they are entangled in the spring branches of chestnut trees . . .
>
> . . . Water streams over the glass . . . in it is reflected
>
> . . . Spring
>
> . . . The Infanta . . .
>
> . . . Red columns . . .
>
> . . . Kobzar . . .[15]

Through these impressionistic and evocative details snatched from everyday life, Parajanov evokes not only the ongoing impact of the war, but Kyiv as a locale, the character of its inhabitants, and even Ukrainian history in the broadest sense. The script's dense, associative montage and its free use of dreams and self-reflexive gestures not only place it squarely within Ukrainian poetic cinema but also make a conscious nod toward European art cinema.

Parajanov's vision in the script is profoundly humanistic; through close observation of the characters' individual gestures, he both affirms the basic generosity and kindness of people on an everyday level and celebrates art as a reflection of their inner beauty and their capacity for good. While he acknowledges the sacrifices that war entailed, for him war is not the natural state of human existence. War is transient, but art is eternal. In that respect, the most expressive image of the script is the juxtaposition of soldiers marching in formation and salvos fired into the air with the serene beauty of the Infanta Margarita. This is echoed in the image of a group of soldiers touring the museum and stopping in front of the painting, using the reflection in the protective glass covering the painting to adjust their uniforms. While humans still possess the capacity for violence, Parajanov views it as an immature state, as represented by the playground fight in Fresco No. 9. To be sure, parts of the script ultimately work better than others; in particular, the Longshoreman's dream of a deaf-mute accosting a girl during the air raid seems forced and mawkish compared to the obliqueness and subtlety of many other images. However, on the whole it remains a vivid and touching work, the strongest of Parajanov's unrealized scripts after *Confession*.

The initial reception of the literary scenario was, on the whole, sympathetic. In the April 5, 1965, resolution summarizing the March 25 meeting of the Dovzhenko Studio's Script-Editorial Board, the Board praised the film both for its formal qualities—among them, its originality of conception, "the concentrated quality of the composition," and "unexpected montage conflicts that give birth to a brilliant associative vision"—and for its profound treatment of the impact of World War II upon contemporary life in Ukraine. In particular, they described the script as "striking for its generous collection of vivid, unusual details that reveal sides and aspects of city life to us that are at times invisible to the naked, unaided eye" and stated that "the poetic quality of the narrative is magnificently combined with journalistic acuteness." They also praised the script's balance between "a general symbolic image of the war" and "the most subtle psychological scenes."[16]

The Board's two main criticisms focused on the "haphazard" arrangement of the individual frescoes and the protagonist's lack of a clear personal connection with the war. In fact, the full transcript of the March 25 meeting reveals that there was some debate about who was actually the main character. Most people attending the meeting argued that the Man should be understood as the main character, but a few insisted that it was the Longshoreman instead. Some members also recommended that Parajanov flesh out the dialogue in the shooting script, since the literary scenario was largely lacking in it.[17] One sign of troubles to come was that the "appallingly vulgar bourgeois world" mentioned in the resolution was in fact the home of an army general. The script's unflattering representation of military commanders would become an increasingly bitter point of contention as the project moved forward.

The Shooting Script

The draft of the shooting script dated May 30, 1965, is probably the version that Parajanov initially submitted to the studio. At this point the officially listed crew included Alexander Antipenko (director of photography), E. Sarenko (production designer), Lidia Baikova (costumes), Valentin Silvestrov (composer), S. Sergienko (sound operator), Maria Ponomarenko (film editor), and Alexander Sizonenko (script editor). It is especially worth noting the presence of Antipenko, who was supposed to have made his professional debut with this project. He first met Parajanov while working as a still photographer on *The Flower on the Stone*. As a student in the cinematography program at the VGIK, he fulfilled his practicum as an assistant on *Shadows of Forgotten Ancestors*. Because Antipenko had not yet completed his degree, Vasili Tsvirkunov, the head of the Dovzhenko Film Studio, expressed reservations about Parajanov's choice. Antipenko has claimed that Parajanov chose him precisely because of his inexperience, which enabled him to experiment freely without preestablished conceptions and habits.[18] Regular crew members carried over from *Shadows of Forgotten Ancestors* included Baikova, Ponomarenko, Sergienko, and Sizonenko.

The shooting script is substantially similar to the literary scenario, but there are some telling differences. The prologue has been expanded, emphasizing the script's self-reflexive quality even further; no doubt Parajanov did this in part to answer criticisms that the character of the film director was not developed enough.

> FADE IN
> A hand in a white glove opened a case . . .
> Optics [optical instruments] on black velvet began to shine . . .
> Filters of various specifications and sizes.
> A hand draws out tulle . . . white . . . black . . .
> The wheels of a dolly roll . . .
> The flaps of a camera open out. An "Ukraina."
>
> A complex cascade of wheels . . . The hand in the white glove loads the camera . . .
> The camera doors slam shut . . . "Ukraina"

The handle on the tripod revolves.
The camera glides . . .
Against a background of black velvet . . . three white faces . . .
The cinematographer . . .
The production designer . . .
The director . . .

Hands in white gloves cover them up with black velvet . . .

The cinematographer . . .
The production designer . . .
The director . . . disappear under the black canopy . . .

The camera glides . . . comes to a stop . . .
The hand in the white glove removes the lens cover . . .
The movie camera lens fills the entire screen . . .
The lights of Kyiv are reflected in the halo of the lens . . .
The lights go out . . . the city's quarters go dark . . .
Darkness comes . . . A pause . . .
The lights from lighting equipment flick on . . .
Great and small, filling the scene with light . . .

A title appears:

KYIV FRESCOES[19]

The subsequent section repeats the opening of the literary scenario, only in this draft Parajanov specifies that the Man's apartment is a soundstage, and that a clapper is held up in front of the camera to mark the beginnings of shots.

This passage marks the origin of an important current that runs throughout Parajanov's subsequent films: a self-conscious examination of film *as a medium*. In addition to *8½*, the most obvious point of reference here is Vertov's *The Man With a Movie Camera*, although the main body of Parajanov's screenplay is fictional—a crucial difference between his and Vertov's work. Nonetheless, here Parajanov's self-reflexivity shares common goals with Vertov: to underscore the authenticity of what we see and ultimately to achieve greater realism. This motif reappears in the closing section of the shooting script, when the three production heads are reflected in the glass that protects the painting of the Infanta Margarita.

Another noteworthy scene added to this draft of the shooting script appears between Frescoes 3 and 4, after the Man gives the police officer the baby carriage and before his dream. Walking the streets at night, the Man witnesses a soldier in a Panama hat flirting with a young woman pricing hats in the display window of a department store. This image inspires a brief reverie:

FADE IN
Wires buzzed on two high-voltage poles passing through the cemetery . . .

Under a pole stood an ashugh, he sang Sayat-Nova . . .
On a fresh grave lay a hat . . .
"THE MAN" stood near the grave . . .
Pause . . .
The wind picks up . . .
The wind lifts the hat off the grave . . .
The wind lifts the hat off "THE MAN"
The hats snatched up by the wind were carried off into infinity . . .
"THE MAN" — it seems funny to him, running off in hopes of catching his hat . . .
Escaping in the wind, the hats are suddenly united, turning into a soccer ball . . .
The poles and crosses disappear.
"THE MAN" disappears . . .
Just the wind [which] blows before it boys chasing after the ball . . .
Excited white steeds neigh, harnessed to a lacquer phaeton . . .
A man with a sacrificial lamb . . .
It whines in his arms . . .
A BOY — "THE MAN" — stops abruptly . . .
. . . approaches the phaeton . . .
The wind blows the boys toward the horizon . . .
And the horizon engulfs them . . .
A hand presses on a lever . . .
Creaking, the lacquer canopy of the phaeton raises . . .
Pause . . .
. . . "THE MAN" approaches the grave . . . He has a hat in his hands . . .
He beats the dust off it . . . puts on the hat . . .

Pause.
The wires buzzed . . . the ashugh began to sing Sayat-Nova.
"THE MAN" took off the hat and placed it by the head of the grave . . .
pinned it down with a stone.
The hat struggled in the wind, wishing to escape to the steppe.
FADE OUT[20]

This graveyard episode clearly evokes the private fantasy world of Fellini's *8½*, only with an Armenian accent. Significant details include the *ashugh* singing Sayat-Nova and the animal sacrifice. Besides indicating rather clearly what Parajanov already had in mind for his next project, the explicit reference to his ethnic identity makes the autobiographical aspect of the shooting script unmistakable and sets the character of the Man apart from the predominantly Ukrainian location and characters. Another innovative aspect of film's planned style that emerges in the shooting script is Parajanov's insistence on conveying much of the narrative information visually. Not only is there relatively little dialogue, but he specifically notates "pantomime" in a number of scenes next to the action.

As would become apparent, Parajanov's desire to create an art film stood fundamentally at odds with what the authorities expected from films about the Great Patriotic War. In a memo dated June 29, 1965, the Main Administration of Goskino USSR wrote to Sviatoslav Ivanov, the head of Goskino of Ukraine, acknowledging the script's stylistic accomplishment with the kind of language that only a Soviet committee could invent: "The associative quality of an overwhelming number of episodes and their interesting pictorial and plastic realization makes the script brilliant in its visual-emotional perception and frequently symbolic."[21]

Tellingly, the Main Administration proceeded to criticize the shooting script for lacking enough concrete ties to the Great Patriotic War: "Touching upon such a crucial theme as that of the Great Patriotic War—and this is determined by the choice of characters (the general, soldiers, the woman who lost her husband in the war, etc.) and the time of the action (the anniversary of the liberation of Kyiv)—the author should have introduced, albeit in an associative form, episodes into the script that would speak about the heroism of the Soviet people, about the great feat accomplished by them. Unfortunately, this is not in the script so far. And to not talk about it means to say nothing about the Great Patriotic War." They also complained about the "utter lack of the living human word in the script" and the "excessive encodedness of a number of episodes," which made it too difficult for the average spectator to understand.[22] So while they gave Goskino of Ukraine permission to launch the film into production, it was clear that Moscow harbored significant reservations.

Another draft of the shooting script, most likely written after the one discussed above, lists Ivan Drach as a script editor. It is likely that Drach was brought in to help Parajanov shape the project into something more acceptable to the authorities, while still working in the mode of poetic cinema. The script's new prologue apparently attempted to address the complaint that the script did not have enough to do with World War II by adding a series of striking, almost surreal images that are not connected to the main plot, but that do connect directly with the war. In the opening scene, set in Peterhof, ten German sappers take electric saws to the fountain's famed statue of Samson:

> The saws touch the bronze "Samson," who is tearing apart the lion.
>
> The sappers in black are reflected like ghosts in the gold of the sculpture.
> One after another the saws were turned on and sank their teeth into the body of the Giant.
> Bronze shavings shot forth.[23]

The script then cuts to images from a zoo, echoing the metaphorical violence of the statue's destruction.

> With a roar, living lions hurled themselves against the bars in the zoo.
> Baring their teeth, panthers threw themselves against the bars . . .
> The Giant gave a start and broke into pieces.

The surrealistic scene that immediately follows this is set far away in Ukraine, along the Dnieper river:

> Bridegrooms [were] up to their necks in the water, and bullets pierced their chests . . .
> The youths fell, and out from their soldiers' blouses bloody bridal veils flew up into the sky.
> And girls in white wedding gowns walked along a bank of the Dnieper, peering into the waters of the river . . .
> . . . and in the dead, shot-up waters arose a soldier in full dress uniform, with wide-open eyes looking up to the sky.
> The soldier swam upstream.
> And the girls went on and on, and their lips mechanically, scarcely audibly, articulated a single word:
> —SWIM! SWIM! SWIM! [*vydubai*— in Ukrainian]
> Dead soldiers floated toward the soldier in the red waters of the Dnieper, and the soldier pushed though them like an icebreaker.
> And German fraüleins moved toward the girls in white.
> They wept black tears and chewed the lipstick off their lips.
> Silence comes abruptly . . .

The opening credits then appear over footage of women mourning from Dovzhenko's wartime documentaries, as the script indicates.

The image of bloodied bridal veils flying up to the sky suggests that

Parajanov was planning to deploy the kind of surreal trick effect that abounds in *The Color of Pomegranates*. While disconnected from the main plot, the scenes in this new prologue do resonate with it on a purely thematic level. Specifically, the image of the Samson statue sawed apart by German soldiers foreshadows that of the painting of the Infanta Margarita buried in a crate for protection during the evacuation of Kyiv. Similarly, the scene of young brides observing soldiers who have been shot in the river points to the Woman's identity as a war widow in the main body of the script. However, given the authorities' response to other aspects of the project one can easily imagine that this new, poetic prologue would have failed to alleviate their concerns.

The Screen Tests

The film was subsequently launched into production. In October 1965 Parajanov shot screen tests, which he edited into a self-contained thirteen-minute short complete with a soundtrack — in effect a sketch of visual ideas for the future film. Many of the shots are filmed on a bare soundstage, giving them a more abstract quality than the actual scenes likely would have had on location or on a fully dressed set. As screen tests, they also necessarily lack the full narrative logic reflected in the shooting script. Nonetheless, the contents of many shots correspond more or less to passages in the shooting script. For our purposes, it is especially revealing how Parajanov used the screen texts to explore the parameters of his new directorial style. Indeed, many of the distinctive features of *The Color of Pomegranates* appear already fully fledged in *Kyiv Frescoes*.

Frontally staged tableaux

While *Shadows of Forgotten Ancestors* did employ a number of tableau shots along with its celebrated camera movements, in *Kyiv Frescoes* the static camera dominates. Admittedly, the shooting script indicates a number of camera movements — the celebrations on Victory Square call for a helicopter shot, for instance — and by definition the screen tests would have precluded expensive tracking shots. Still, the screen tests reveal the extent to which Parajanov was consciously developing his tableau aesthetic with this film. Here the camera's perspective is not so much a single point of view or a window on the world, but a frame within which all the objects in the shot are arranged. Characters often stare directly into the camera or otherwise break the fourth wall of dramatic illusion that most narrative films strive to maintain (Fig. 3.1). One effect of this rupture is to turn individual shots into self-contained tableaux or portraits, rather than links in a chain of action.

Figure 3.1. Breaking the fourth wall (*Kyiv Frescoes*). Courtesy of the Oleksandr Dovzhenko National Centre.

The picture frame as a compositional device and decorative motif

Another way in which Parajanov emphasizes the film image as graphic art is to incorporate actual picture frames into the compositions. One shot of a dead soldier (presumably, the war widow's husband) lying on his back with a gun resting on his chest is bordered by a large gilded frame, thus drawing our attention to the film frame *as a frame*. Later, a young boy tosses paper airplanes through a gilded frame that swings like a pendulum. Likewise, empty picture frames are repeatedly displayed in the short film *Hakob Hovnatanyan* and a section of gilded frame is even used for purely decorative effect in *The Color of Pomegranates*, most notably during Sayat-Nova's dream. Another visual motif carried over from the screen tests into *The Color of Pomegranates* is of characters standing inside frames laid flat on the ground. In *Kyiv Frescoes* the figures are a church patriarch and the director's son, whereas in *The Color of Pomegranates* it is King Erekle II.

Still-life compositions

In Parajanov's mature style objects take on a life of their own, often emphasizing their formal qualities at the expense of narrative flow. In *Kyiv Frescoes* specifically, everyday objects such as a pedal-operated Singer sewing machine or an antique iron are arranged as elements of still-life compositions. At the same time that such objects assert their presence, the *absence* of human figures is reinforced through details such as the pair of empty shoes arranged on the sewing machine pedal. This looks forward to the empty shoes during the bath sequence in *The Color of Pomegranates* and similar visual motifs in Parajanov's later films.

Tripartite compositions within individual shots

In one scene from the screen tests, three solders remove their foot wrappings and boots before washing the wooden floor of the Man's apartment. The nearly identical movement of all three actors anticipates the scene in *The Color of Pomegranates* in which three monks have their feet washed before they are picked up by other monks and carried over to vats of grapes, or when three separate sacrifices of rams are performed simultaneously under the arches of the fountain at Haghpat. Besides creating strikingly formalized visual compositions, this stylistic device emphasizes the aesthetic qualities of movement over dramatic functionalism.

Abstraction of the mise-en-scène

Starting with *Kyiv Frescoes*, Parajanov often pares down the number of elements present within a shot to the point of abstraction. What might seem on the surface a question of exigency in *Kyiv Frescoes*— the use of a bare soundstage — later became a stylistic mannerism in itself, particularly in *Hakob Hovnatanyan* and *The Color of Pomegranates*. Thus, in *The Color of Pomegranates* the same soundstage, with minor alterations in décor, serves variously as the location for the scenes of Sayat-Nova as a child observing wool-dyeing and carpet-weaving, the brief shot portraying the competition between the young Sayat-Nova and other *ashughs*, and Princess Ana's apartment. Only the minimum number of details necessary to evoke a particular milieu are used; characters or objects are often posed against neutral or white backgrounds. Among other things, this results in a deliberately flattened image (Fig. 3.2). Individual shots also tend to display a limited palette of colors.

Pantomime and other experiments with actors' movement

Parajanov was hardly the first film director to subordinate the movement of actors to the overall composition — Eisenstein's *Ivan the Terrible* parts 1 and 2 (*Ivan*

Figure 3.2. The Man (the film director) in a flattened composition (*Kyiv Frescoes*).

Groznyi, Mosfilm 1945–1946) come immediately to mind as a possible influence. But *Kyiv Frescoes* is nonetheless striking for the way it uses the movement of actors as just one of several malleable elements within the overall texture of the film. The hieratic gestures and slow, fluid movements of actors, like the stylized tripartite compositions mentioned above, emphasize the aesthetic qualities of movement. Perhaps the best examples of this in *Kyiv Frescoes* are the graceful pantomimes symbolizing the frustrated relationship between the Man and what appears to be his ex-wife (based on the written script). Her pose with the wedding ring and her rueful gaze at the camera specifically anticipate the play of rings between Sayat-Nova and Princess Ana in *The Color of Pomegranates* (Fig. 3.3).

Editing

It is more difficult to speak about this aspect of Parajanov's style in *Kyiv Frescoes*, insofar as the actual film was never shot. However, it is worth noting the self-contained nature of many shots from the screen tests, as is notoriously true with Parajanov's subsequent films. One gesture that does seem deliberately

Figure 3.3. The Man's wife poses with her wedding ring (*Kyiv Frescoes*). Courtesy of the Oleksandr Dovzhenko National Centre.

thought-out in the screen tests is the series of objects (such as the three *parsunas*) linked by straight cuts. As mentioned previously, in Fresco No. 2 of the literary scenario, the salvos fired by soldiers marching in Victory Square serve as punctuations between the fragmentary, seemingly random images of life in contemporary Kyiv and give a clear indication of how he planned to use cutting in that episode.

❀

Kyiv Frescoes set the stage for Parajanov's subsequent films on a more general thematic level as well. On the surface, *Kyiv Frescoes* and *The Color of Pomegranates* could hardly be more different in terms of subject matter: the former represents the legacy of World War II and its impact on everyday life in contemporary Kyiv, while the latter is ostensibly the biography of an eighteenth-century poet. Nonetheless, together with the overtly autobiographical script *Confession*, they exhibit an overriding concern with the place of the artist in society and attempt to situate the artist's perceptions within the world at large. In that respect,

Parajanov's film shares a common thematic concern not only with Dziga Vertov, but also Fellini's *8½*, Tarkovsky's *Andrei Rublev*, and Pasolini's short "La
Ricotta" in the omnibus film *Ro.Go.Pa.G* (1963).

Private associations also abound in *Kyiv Frescoes*. Svetlana Shcherbatiuk, who
had divorced Parajanov a few years before the film was made, recalled being
convinced that he was alluding to their marriage when she first saw the screen
tests, and it is not difficult to see why.[24] The role of the war widow was to be
played by the well-known Latvian actress Vija Artmane; as made up in the
screen tests, she bears a strong physical resemblance to the director's ex-wife.
In one scene, the Longshoreman runs a golden hair through his mouth, perhaps
in recollection of the night spent with the museum custodian. This image later
reappears in the autobiographical script for *Confession*, where the film director,
once again named simply "the Man," finds a golden hair of his ex-wife Svetlana
ten years after the divorce.[25] At another point in the screen tests, the soundtrack
uses the popular Debussy prelude "The Girl with the Flaxen Hair" to accompany an erotically tinged dream in which golden tresses are pulled underneath
the Longshoreman's head while he is sleeping. In the script, the director runs
across a policeman who announces that his wife just gave birth to a baby boy. In
a typically Parajanovian gesture of impulsive generosity, the director promptly
pays a call to his ex-wife's apartment; an unseen figure pushes out an empty
baby carriage for him to give to the policeman.[26] Parajanov's real-life son was
already several years old by time the script was written, making the unused baby
carriage fit within an autobiographical framework. A similarly empty baby carriage appears in the screen tests during the pantomimed scene of the Man with
his ex-wife. Lastly, Parajanov cast his own son Suren in the role of the director's
son in the screen tests.

Many at the studio were in a state of shock after viewing the screen tests.
One particularly scandalous aspect was the appearance of a nude female model,
a detail not indicated in the shooting script (Fig. 3.4). At this time, full-frontal
nudity was extremely rare in Soviet cinema; *Andrei Rublev*, one of the few films to
use it, would be shelved until the early 1970s. Parajanov's radical formal experiments also aroused much concern. Even Sviatoslav Ivanov, the head of Goskino
of Ukraine, who was normally very supportive of Parajanov and remained so up
to the time of the latter's arrest, was sharply critical of the screen tests, perhaps
fearing that his credibility with Moscow was on the line if he simply signed off
on the production. In a memo dated October 21, 1965, Ivanov complained that
the film was "marked" by "a distorted, somewhat pathological perception of
reality, a longing to affirm human solitude, to show delirium, spiritual hopeless-
ness." He continued:

Figure 3.4. The presence of a nude model aroused controversy (*Kyiv Frescoes*). Courtesy of the Oleksandr Dovzhenko National Centre.

Having permitted the conducting of screen tests, the State Committee on Cinematography of the Ukrainian SSR requested maximal clarification of the artistic conception of the future film from Parajanov, from the entire shooting team, and also from the directorship of the Dovzhenko Film Studio. The screen tests had to demonstrate the preparedness of the director and the creative team to embody on the screen those human ideals, that image of the modern city and its workers, which, as S. Parajanov demonstrated, he cannot express on paper, but which he will confirm on the screen. However, the tests, to the point, are almost unconnected to the script materials and are almost, to be frank, denials of any kind of thought, of a realistic image. Gifted actors and a talented cinematographer are engaged in the tests, but the inclination toward purely formal effects weighs on everything.[27]

Nonetheless, the screen tests were eventually sent to Moscow for evaluation. In a letter to Ivanov and Tsvirkunov dated December 2, 1965, Yuri Yegorov, the head of the Main Administration, merely confirmed what Ivanov had said earlier, though in more diplomatic terms. He acknowledged that the film, "having in essence an experimental character, attests to an interesting quest for a distinctive graphic language of filmmaking, in which the plastic expressiveness of pantomime, painting, music, and the execution of details are organically blended." Despite this, he complained that the screen tests "do not have a straightforward relationship to the plot of the film." In conclusion, he recommended that the studio "assign a man of letters" to revise the shooting script with Parajanov and that the director "should be granted the possibility to carry out new screen tests, engaging actors in scenes that take place in the script."[28]

In fact, many shots in the screen tests do refer to specific scenes in the shooting script: the soldiers removing their boots, tiptoeing about the apartment and washing the floor; the widow in her wedding dress, gluing strips of her cut-up wedding veil to a window; and the pantomime with the Man and his ex-wife, the dismantled piano, the baby carriage, and the wedding ring. (The specific actions of the latter pantomime may be different, but the basic idea had already been indicated in the script.) It seems likely that the radically stylized staging may have distracted the authorities from the scenes' manifest content.

In spite of these complaints, and perhaps to gauge better the public response to Parajanov's proposed approach to the film, the edited screen tests were shown as part of a retrospective of Parajanov's work at the Kyiv House of Cinema, with screenings of his early Ukrainian features and documentary shorts, starting on December 3, 1965, and culminating on January 14, 1966, with a screening of *The Flower on the Stone* and *Kyiv Frescoes*.[29] Interestingly enough, *Shadows of Forgotten Ancestors* was not included in the program, perhaps because it was already fresh (too fresh?) in the minds of Kyiv film professionals.

In response to Moscow's demand for a "man of letters" to work with Parajanov on the script, the novelist and screenwriter Pavlo Zahrebelny (1924–2009) was brought in to shape the unruly material into something more logically organized and ideologically sound. Zahrebelny was an obvious choice not only because of his overall stature in the Ukrainian literary scene, but because his writings on World War II, especially the novel *Ballad of an Immortal* (1957), made him uniquely qualified to bring the screenplay's treatment of the war closer in line with official ideology.[30] Zahrebelny later worked with Parajanov on *Intermezzo*, another of Parajanov's Ukrainian projects that was never filmed.

On February 5, the studio's Script-Editorial Board met one last time to discuss the new set of revisions. Leonid Osyka, one of the younger members of the poetic school faction, acknowledged that the script was now put together more logically and that "the complex associations of the author became comprehensible," but he criticized the dialogue, saying, "all the characters speak with some kind of identical inexpressive language."[31] He recommended trimming the dialogue down to what was strictly necessary, but on the whole he felt that the script could go forward into the development stage. G. Zeldovich mostly agreed with Osyka, adding: "Already now in the literary version I sense the contours of the future film, a film standing on the positions of Socialist Realism, a film that will teach people to love one another, to regard each other and the collective with confidence; the authors of the film are teaching us not to forget the heroic past of our country, not to see the environment from an oversimplified perspective."

A few of the attendees were more critical. One said, "The script evokes a somewhat divided feeling: on the one hand, very brilliant expressive solutions; and on the other hand, as it were, quotes from bad popular-science films. This, of course, reduces the significance of the material." The same person also complained that the script was "overburdened with visions of the artist and the other characters," but he still recommended it for approval. Another said that the script seemed "eclectic" because of the latest draft's shift in focus from the vision of a single character (i.e., the film director) to several characters. She also expressed dissatisfaction with some of the added plot elements: "The widow's daughter showed up, and the scene in the evening when the mother asks the daughter to leave and doesn't allow her inside surprises with its vulgarity. It's like a second-rate quote from a trite film." She concluded her remarks by saying, "In a word, the script's plot still requires certain corrections."

Parajanov responded to their remarks by stating that he thought Zahrebelny had done a "great job" on the script so far and accepted his proposed changes. He went on to say:

> Of course, to logically link a poetically associative image track is a very complex and difficult task. And it's natural that some things didn't turn out. Thus Zahrebelny, for example, removed the relationships between the heroes and family tragedy that are hardly advisable and interesting. This should still be seriously thought through. The historical associations are really not necessary in the script — after all, the plot is laconic, like a chamber play.
>
> Today, I can't make everyday [*bytovoi*] cinema — I need a complex associative image track, a film that is complex in its thought, and all the time I have been looking agonizingly for the meaning and form of this work. Obviously, the shooting script will be discussed in more detail. I will work on the development stage with such a demanding artist as the cinematographer [Suren] Shakhbazian. We will try to make all the components of the shooting script carefully adjusted and described in detail.[32]

So while Parajanov at least verbally agreed with the notion that the plot outline needed to be clarified, he nonetheless made it clear that he intended to continue working in the same "complex associative" (in other words, poetic) vein. One suspects that this in itself became an underlying cause of concern for the authorities. In his concluding remarks, the film's script editor Alexander Sizonenko asserted that Zahrebelny's revisions had indeed "removed the alarm and doubts that the previous version aroused" by giving the work a stronger plot outline and "logically link[ing] individual uncoordinated episodes and pieces." In his view, the revised script was ready "for development into a shooting script."[33] Regardless, the project was cancelled not long afterward. Seeing that his options in Kyiv were limited, Parajanov accepted an invitation by the Armenfilm studio in Yerevan to make what became *The Color of Pomegranates*.

Official concerns about the aesthetics and ideological underpinnings of *Kyiv Frescoes* may have been sufficient in themselves to sink the project, but they were undoubtedly exacerbated by external political events that happened to coincide with the time frame of the project. It is worth recalling that the arrests of Ukrainian intellectuals and the protest at the screening of *Shadows of Forgotten Ancestors* took place in late August–early September of 1965, less than a month after Yegorov's August 7 letter to Ivanov criticizing how the screenplay represented World War II. In October of the same year, around the time that Parajanov completed the screen tests, he and six other signatories wrote the aforementioned letter to the Central Committees of Ukraine and the Soviet Union inquiring about the fate of several individuals who had recently been arrested, among them the literary critic and translator Ivan Svitlychny. Outside of Ukraine, the trial of Sinyavsky and Daniel took place in February 1966—shortly before *Kyiv Frescoes* was cancelled. This was at the start of the period when a number of high-profile Soviet films were banned or shelved, including Illienko's *A Well for the Thirsty* (1965–1966), Tarkovsky's *Andrei Rublev* (1966), Konchalovsky's *Asya's Happiness* (1966), Alexander Alov and Vladimir Naumov's *A Nasty Joke* (*Skvernyi anekdot*, Mosfilm 1966), and Alexander Askoldov's *The Commissar* (*Komissar*, Mosfilm 1967). Thus, one might count *Kyiv Frescoes* as another victim of this broader crackdown in the film industry, reflecting the general ideological retrenchment of the Brezhnev era.

In retrospect, *Kyiv Frescoes* illustrates the dilemma that Parajanov faced as an experimental (or rather, poetic) filmmaker working within the Soviet system. On the one hand, projects on "significant" topics such as the twentieth anniversary of Kyiv's liberation from the Germans were actively encouraged by the authorities and helped ensure generous logistical support. On the other hand, the close ideological scrutiny that accompanied these same topics gave filmmakers like Parajanov little leeway to pursue aesthetic innovations. It is not surprising, then, that Parajanov's attempt to apply his mode of poetic cinema to this particular subject was plagued with pitfalls from the start. One could also argue in retrospect that his decision to show off the most radical aspects of his new style in the screen tests was a serious tactical error that hastened the demise of the project. Nonetheless, in the process of making *Kyiv Frescoes* he was at least able to work out many of the techniques and specific visual concepts that appear in all their mastery in *The Color of Pomegranates*.

4

The Color of Pomegranates

The Making and Unmaking of a Film

However exotic *Shadows of Forgotten Ancestors* must have seemed to Soviet viewers when it was first released, it nonetheless represented a clear synthesis of three major stylistic paths in Soviet cinema: Kalatozov and Urusevsky's virtuoso camerawork, Dovzhenko's poetic tableau imagery, and Tarkovsky's surreal dream sequences. As an adaptation of Mykhailo Kotsiubynsky's novella, *Shadows* also used a relatively straightforward, folklore-based narrative to anchor its visual flights of fancy.

The Color of Pomegranates (*Tsvet granata*, Armenfilm 1969) in contrast, seduces us with ravishingly composed tableaux that are often startling and cryptic, in effect throwing down a gauntlet before the viewer. It is a film-poem about a poet, Sayat-Nova (ca. 1712–1795), who famously wrote:

> Not everyone can drink of my water, it is of another water.
> Not everyone can read my writing, it is of a different script.
> Do not think my substance sand: it is a crag of solid rock.
> As like a torrent that never dries, do not [try to] wear it down![1]

Parajanov no doubt kept these same verses in mind as he worked on his own film, among the most challenging feature films ever produced in the Soviet Union. Yet if *The Color of Pomegranates* were merely a beautiful but forbidding puzzle, it could not sustain its fascination and resonance with so many viewers over the decades since its first, limited release in Armenia. The film has survived

114

the indignities of being made deliberately inaccessible by the Soviet authorities and being reedited against Parajanov's wishes, to emerge as the most widely seen of all Armenian films, even a source of inspiration for music videos on MTV. For the adventurous, it can open up an entire world.

This chapter examines the complicated history behind the film's production, censorship, and reception in the Soviet Union. Primarily, *The Color of Pomegranates* became the site of a protracted battle between Parajanov, the Armenian film bureaucracy, and the central authorities in Moscow. This battle was not just over the representation of Sayat-Nova as a cultural figure, but over the proper role of artistic experimentation within the official policy of Socialist Realism. This chapter also offers an extended reading of what is by far Parajanov's most complex work.

For the Soviets, the difficulty with the film was not so much a lack of familiarity with the poetry and life story of Sayat-Nova, the Armenian *ashugh* (troubadour poet) on whom the film was based. Starting in the early 1960s and culminating in 1963, the various cultural organs of the Soviet state celebrated the 250th anniversary of Sayat-Nova's birth to such an extent that it even earned a remark in the *New York Times*.[2] Never shy of publicity, Parajanov himself also spoke eloquently about his project on several occasions and described his overall conception in an interview for the almanac *Ekran*: "The film won't be traditionally biographical, as in tracing the life of the poet year after year, consecutively. We want to show the world in which the *ashugh* [Sayat-Nova] lived, the sources that nourished his poetry, and for that reason national architecture, folk art, nature, daily life, and music will play a large role in the film's pictorial decisions. We are recounting the epoch, the people, their passions and thoughts through the conventional, but unusually precise language of things. Handicrafts, clothing, rugs, ornaments, fabrics, the furniture in their living quarters — these are the elements. From these the material look of the epoch arises."[3] The unnamed author of the article went on to explain how the film was to consist of "cinematic miniatures," that it would be "poetic" rather than "historical" or "biographical," that it would lack dialogue and would instead use recordings of songs by contemporary *ashughs*, and that its use of color would have a "dramaturgical function" recalling Eisenstein's theoretical writings. The author also pointed out that Parajanov was a Tbilisi Armenian like Sayat-Nova, suggesting an underlying autobiographical connection with the subject of his film. In another contemporary article by Levon Grigorian, one of the film's assistant directors, Parajanov further emphasized that he intended the film "to reveal the culture of the three peoples of Transcaucasia."[4]

Parajanov's comments *in Ekran* necessarily leave out the film's subversive playfulness and its sensuality, but they nonetheless illustrate that he had a clear notion of what he was trying to accomplish through his aesthetics, and how he attempted to convey this to potential viewers. However, reading about such an approach on paper and experiencing it on the screen are two different matters. It is not difficult to understand why the authorities were bewildered, even shocked by Parajanov's deliberately archaic, radically stylized cinematic language, which encompasses such disparate influences as the visual style of medieval Armenian and Persian miniatures, the editing and narrative style of early filmmakers such as Georges Méliès, Pier Paolo Pasolini's fascination with the material culture of the ancient past and his tendency to stage shots as portraits or tableaux, and the decidedly modernistic technique of jump cuts. For good measure, Parajanov tosses in an abundance of oblique, metaphoric imagery and private jokes, some of them gleefully obscene if one digs just a little below the surface.

Considering all this, it is remarkable that Parajanov made *The Color of Pomegranates* not as a small, privately funded experimental film along the lines of Jean Cocteau's *The Blood of a Poet* (1930), Kenneth Anger's *Inauguration of the Pleasure Dome* (1954), or Stan Brackhage's *Dog Star Man* (1962–1964),[5] but as a relatively ambitious studio production that drew upon significant resources from the Soviet state. Like any other Soviet filmmaker during that time, he had no choice but to work within the system, though that same system arguably had certain advantages compared to the West. Parajanov would not have gotten very far with such a script in a Hollywood studio. He succeeded at pushing the film through to completion precisely because it was not about just himself or a single poet, but about the creative spirit and historical fate of the peoples of Transcaucasia. Despite significant practical constraints and conflicts with the Soviet authorities — some admittedly caused by his own difficult personality and erratic work habits — he succeeded in producing a work of extraordinary beauty and power.

The Context of the Production

By 1966 the atmosphere at the Dovzhenko Film Studio in Kyiv had chilled considerably, casting doubts on Parajanov's future career as a filmmaker there. Fortunately, he received an invitation to produce a film in Armenia; Vahagn Mkrtchian, the director of the Armenfilm (Hayfilm) Studio, later brought the official agreement with him to the All-Union Film Festival, which took place in Kyiv that year.[6] Studio officials at Armenfilm were eager to work with Parajanov due to his status as an award winner at international festivals with *Shadows of Forgotten Ancestors.* The success of that film had improved the standing of the Dovzhenko Film Studio with Goskino USSR, and the management at Armenfilm likely believed that a similar international success would greatly help their studio, which at the time faced difficult circumstances.[7]

In a memo to the Central Committee of the Communist Party of Armenia dated April 15, 1966, Alexei Romanov, the chair of Goskino, criticized the Armenfilm studio on several counts. While recognizing the studio's artistic potential as displayed in recent films such as Frunze Dovlatian's *Hello, It's Me!* (*Zdravstvui, eto ia!*, Armenfilm 1965), he complained that for the coming jubilee year marking the 50th anniversary of the October Revolution, it had not developed enough projects "containing serious life problems, reflecting the past or the present of the Soviet Republic of Armenia." He went on to describe the studio's organizational problems at length, which included frequent delays in planning and production. He concluded: "In our opinion, the most serious measures should be taken for the improvement of all units that hinder the normal life of the collective and its creative growth."[8] Consequently, the three different studio heads[9] in charge during the film's lengthy production process (approximately three years) gave Parajanov a certain degree of latitude with both the kind of film he was allowed to make and with his working conditions.

Sayat-Nova as a Historical Figure

In order to understand the rich implications behind Parajanov's choice of subject matter, it is necessary to examine Sayat-Nova both as a historical figure and within Soviet ideology. Not a great deal is known for certain about Sayat-Nova's life, including the exact year of his birth, though it is most commonly given as 1712.[10] His father Karapet came from Aleppo and his mother Sara came from the Havlabar district in Tiflis (Tbilisi), located directly across the river from the historic town center and the sulfur baths. Sayat-Nova himself was possibly born and educated in Sanahin, a monastery in the Lori region of present-day northern Armenia. His given name was Arutin, a variant of Harutyun ("Resurrection"). While his family name is often listed as Sayadyan, the scholar Charles Dowsett, author of the most exhaustively researched study on Sayat-Nova in English, argues that it is quite possible that his family did not have a surname at all, considering his origins and the conventions of the period.[11] Tradition has it that Sayat-Nova and his family were weavers by trade, a detail reflected in the film. Dowsett points out that his "most fluent script was Georgian" and argues that it may have been his mother tongue, though Sayat-Nova evidently considered himself Armenian and maintained close ties to the Armenian Church.[12] By the time he was about eighteen, Sayat-Nova had established his reputation as an *ashugh*. His three main musical instruments were the *tar* (a long-necked lute), the *kamancha* (a bowed string instrument with a globe-shaped body), and the *chonguri* (a Georgian long-necked lute). Varieties of these instruments are played throughout the Caucasus and Iran. While numerous theories exist about the meaning of his pen name, the one most commonly accepted is a derivation from the Persian *sayyâd-i navâ*, or "hunter of song."[13]

The *ashugh* tradition of Transcaucasia is noteworthy for the very direct way in which it reflects the pervasive influence of Islamic — especially Persian — culture upon the region. The word *ashugh* derives from the Arabic word *ashiq*, or "lover." Although *ashughs* composed in vernacular languages, their songs typically employed the poetic conventions of classical Arabic, Persian, and Turkish poetry. These featured included the traditional subject of love, the *ghazal* form of rhymed couplets and strict metrical patterns, the device of the poet "signing" his work by incorporating his name into the last stanza, and highly conventionalized stock imagery: slender waists like cypresses, weeping tears of blood, the mole on the beloved's cheek, lips like candy, the nightingale and the rose, and so on. The fourteenth-century Persian poet Hafiz, whose work is widely translated into English, offers a good frame of reference for the conventions of the *ghazal* genre as a whole.[14] In point of fact, Sayat-Nova even makes direct allusions to Persian literature: one of his most popular songs, "In This World I'll Not Sigh" ("Ashkharumes akh chim kashi"), evokes Rakhsh, the mighty steed of Rostam, the hero of Ferdowsi's eleventh-century epic *Shahnameh*. Other songs allude to the tragic love of Layla and Majnun, immortalized in Nezami Ganjavi's late twelfth-century narrative poem. However, Dowsett argues that Sayat-Nova probably did not read Persian and may have absorbed the conventions and imagery through Turkish, Azerbaijani, or Georgian poetry instead.[15]

It is important to keep in mind that these traits are hardly unique to Sayat-Nova. Another celebrated Armenian *ashugh* (and painter) of the preceding generation, Naghash Hovnatan (1661–1722), similarly employed imagery from Persian poetry and used his own name in the last stanza.[16] Not unlike Sayat-Nova, Hovnatan moved to Tbilisi in some time after 1700 to serve as court poet; they were probably not the only Armenian *ashughs* to do so during that era. So while Sayat-Nova's talents may have been unique, his artistic identity very much reflected the common cultural milieu of Transcaucasia.[17]

Sayat-Nova's surviving 1765 manuscript of his own poems is a fascinating document of how the cultures of Transcaucasia were once intertwined to an extent that is virtually a distant memory today. The poet's extant works include 128 poems in Azerbaijani, 63 in Armenian, and 35 in Georgian. As

Dowsett points out, at that time Azerbaijani Turkish was the "social, commercial and also artistic *lingua franca* of the Caucasus," which explains why Sayat-Nova wrote such a large number in that language.[18] However, he wrote out the Azerbaijani poems using Georgian, and to a lesser extent Armenian, script. Similarly, he often used the Georgian script in his Armenian poems, and in one poem even alternated Georgian and Armenian letters. The poems' liberal borrowing of vocabulary from each of the other languages (as well as Persian) and use of dense multilingual puns make them difficult to decipher today, even for native speakers.

According to tradition, Sayat-Nova served as a court poet to Erekle (or Irakli) II, who was at that time the king of Kakheti in Georgia. He eventually lost favor and was banished from the court in 1759; popular legend holds that this was due to his love for the king's sister, Princess Ana (sometimes spelled Anna). But in fact, based on the available evidence, he appears instead to have served one of Erekle II's sons, either Giorgi XIII or more likely Vakhtang in the court at Telavi. King Erekle II ruled only Kakheti at that time and did not assume joint rule of Kartli-Kakheti until the death of his father, Teimuraz II, in 1762, after Sayat-Nova had already left the court. It is likely, however, that Sayat-Nova would have performed for Erekle in Telavi and he did refer to the king occasionally in his poems.[19] For example, his Georgian language poem "The Garden is Full of Nightingales" ("Baghi bulbulit avsila") closes with the line, "The emperor of Sayat-Nova is the royal-falcon prince Irakli."[20]

Around the time of his banishment, Sayat-Nova stopped composing poetry and joined the priesthood in the Armenian Church. Although it is not reflected in Parajanov's film, he took a wife named Marmar and worked as "a married priest (*k'ahanay*) in Anzal on the shores of the Caspian, in the province of Gilan."[21] He may have had up to four children, including an eldest son named Melik'set'/Melko, a second son named Ioane/Ivan, and possibly a third son named Grigor. In 1765 he copied down his poems in his *Tetrak* (*Notebook*), around which time he had apparently relocated to Kakho Karavansaray.[22] His wife Marmar passed away in 1768, and shortly after this he became a monk at Haghpat.

Although there are conflicting accounts surrounding his death and even the actual date, he is generally believed to have been killed during the Persian army's siege of Tbilisi in 1795; legend has it that he died defending one of the city's cathedrals. By way of context, in 1783 Erekle II signed the Treaty of Georgievsk with Catherine the Great, placing Kartli-Kakheti under Russian protection. This move alarmed Iran and the Ottoman Empire, though Iran took no direct action at the time because of internal power struggles. Agha Muhammad

Khan, the de facto leader of the Qajar tribe and a eunuch since childhood, rose to power in Iran and quickly earned notoriety for his ruthlessness. Determined to reassert control over all of Transcaucasia, he demanded that Erekle II acknowledge Persian suzerainty. When the Georgian king refused, Agha Muhammad Khan invaded in September 1795, culminating in the Battle of Krtsanisi and the sack of Tbilisi. Thousands of the city's residents were killed on the spot or captured and taken as slaves.[23] Agha Muhammad Khan also sacked the monasteries in the region, including Haghpat and Sanahin, which fell within the border of the Kartli-Kakheti kingdom at that time. Dowsett argues that this would account for Sayat-Nova's presence in Tbilisi during the siege.[24]

Almost 30 years after Sayat-Nova's death, Georgian Crown Prince Teimuraz requested that Sayat-Nova's son Ioane write down another copy of his father's poems. This manuscript is the main source for Sayat-Nova's Georgian-language poems, which were not included in the *Tetrak*. Today Sayat-Nova's tomb stands next to the entrance of the Saint George (*Surb Gevorg*) Cathedral, Tbilisi's main Armenian church, located in the old city center.

❈

Parajanov's intensified interest in Sayat-Nova and Armenian culture in general dated at least as far back as the jubilee year of 1963, when he painted a portrait of himself wearing a Ukrainian embroidered shirt and seated against a stone wall in the Haghpat Monastery; this painting is on display in the Sergei Parajanov Museum in Yerevan. In the unfilmed script for *Kyiv Frescoes*, he also made a passing reference to Sayat-Nova in relation to his own Armenian identity, as mentioned in the previous chapter. Even so, working on *The Color of Pomegranates* awakened a deeper connection with Armenian culture than he had ever demonstrated up to that point. A product of Tbilisi's cosmopolitan cultural environment and educated in a Russian-language school, he spoke primarily in Russian and was, if anything, a bit of a "Georgiaphile," as Mikhail Arakelian and the architect (and close friend) Victor Jorbenadze have claimed.[25]

Regardless, Parajanov was overwhelmed by the beauty and rich history of both Armenia's and Georgia's ancient churches and monastic complexes, some of which dated back almost as far as the adoption of Christianity in the region, the beginning of the fourth century. Arakelian, a member of the film's production design team, also provided the director with a difficult-to-find book on Armenian miniatures and introduced him to the work of modern Armenian artists such as Vardges Sureniants (1860–1921).[26] Indeed, Sureniants' brilliant gift for texture and decorative motifs as found in paintings such as *Ara the Fair and Semiramis* (1899) and his 1899 illustrations for Alexander Pushkin's narrative poem *The Fountain of Bakhchisaray* most likely inspired Parajanov's later scripts on the same two works. An Armenian translation of Pushkin's poem with reproductions of Sureniants's illustrations was published in 1964, and Parajanov was almost certainly familiar with it.[27]

Parajanov saw himself, like Sayat-Nova, as a poet of all of Transcaucasia, and indeed he was. No other filmmaker has better captured the rich sense of cultural intermingling and conflict between cultures in that region: the populations of Armenians, Georgians, Azerbaijanis, and Kurds, the religious traditions of Christians, Muslims, and Jews, and the pervasive cultural influences of the Persian, Turkish, and Russian Empires. In that respect, Sayat-Nova represented the director's ideal subject. One could argue further that *The Color of Pomegranates* is not just about the poet, but also about Parajanov's own relationship to this region, how his immersion in it shaped his imagination as an artist. When a male voice intones at the beginning of the film, "I am he whose life and soul are torment," one might even assume that this verse refers as much to Parajanov himself as to its original author. Sayat-Nova provided the solid foundation for Parajanov's fantastic edifice: through the poet's life story, the filmmaker was able to engage history and culture in the most profound and sustained manner of his career.

Sayat-Nova in Soviet Ideology

From the standpoint of official Soviet ideology, Sayat-Nova was more than just a great national poet. As Parajanov scholar Karen Kalantar points out, "Sayat-Nova, who wrote in the Armenian, Georgian, and Azerbaijani languages, embodied the idea of the friendship of peoples [*druzhba narodov*]."[28] As a result, the Soviets openly encouraged cultural projects of various kinds related to the poet. In 1960, just a few years before the actual Sayat-Nova jubilee, the Yerevan television studio produced a feature-length, black-and-white film entitled *Sayat-Nova*, directed by Kim Arzumanian and starring Hrair Muradian. Despite its severely constrained budget, the film takes some care to evoke the rich flavor of Old Tiflis, with its distinctive wooden balconies and lively markets. As one might expect, Arzumanian's film emphasizes the multicultural roots of the *ashugh* tradition by depicting Georgian and Azerbaijani characters alongside the Armenians. One of Sayat-Nova's *ashugh* friends is a Georgian named "Shalva" who exclaims stereotypically Georgian phrases such as *"Gamarjoba, genatsvale!"* ("Hello, my dear friend!") But more than anything else, the film's performance style and mise-en-scène suggest a stage melodrama. Given the rigid conventionalism of Soviet biographical films and this film in particular, it is not difficult to see why Parajanov might have been moved to attempt a more stylistically innovative approach to the same subject.

Further activity around the jubilee included a 1963 documentary short directed by Gurgen Balasanian for the Yerevan Chronicle-Documentary Film Studio, with a script by the noted Sayat-Nova biographer Paruir Sevak. More prominently, around that time the city of Yerevan named one of its major boulevards after Sayat-Nova. That period also witnessed a flurry of publishing: new editions of Sayat-Nova's poems, biographies, scholarly essays about the poet, and even a novel.[29] The 1963 Russian-language anthology of Sayat-Nova's poems, which Parajanov himself very likely used while writing his script, pointedly devoted separate sections to the Armenian, Georgian, and Azerbaijani poems, thereby emphasizing the poet's status as a multilingual and multinational figure.[30]

To be sure, the Sayat-Nova jubilee was hardly unique. Soviet cultural policy, insofar as it was shaped by Soviet ideology as a whole, viewed art forms such as poetry as markers of development within a national culture. Accordingly, every major Soviet nationality had to have at least one great national poet, to be celebrated in jubilees and immortalized on celluloid.[31] Examples of this include Igor Savchenko's *Taras Shevchenko*; Eldar Kuliev's *Nizami* (Mosfilm and Azerbaijanfilm 1982); Tengiz Abuladze's adaptation of Vazha-Pshavela poems entitled *The Entreaty* (*Mol'ba*, Georgia Film Studio 1967); and Boris Kimiagarov's popular adventure films *The Legend of Rostam* (*Skazanie o Rustame*, Tajikfilm 1971) and *Rostam and Sohrab* (*Rustam i Sukhrab*, Tajikfilm 1971), both based on the hero of Ferdowsi's *Shahnameh*.

Actually, the Georgian poet and literary scholar Ioseb Grishashvili's introductory essay to the aforementioned Russian edition of Sayat-Nova's poems provides a good example of an orthodox Soviet representation of the poet as a historical figure. In Grishashvili's account, Sayat-Nova's name "is a synonym of friendship, a banner of internationalism and brotherhood between the peoples of Transcaucasia."[32] Grishashvili also fashioned Sayat-Nova as a classic "poet-patriot": "*ashughs* participated directly in the campaigns of Erekle II against foreign invaders. Sayat-Nova himself took part in them and marched in the front lines of the king's warriors."[33] At the same time, Grishashvili's Sayat-Nova was a "great poet humanist" and a "servant of the people," who wrote in "plain colloquial language" so that his songs "were accessible and clear to all his contemporaries."[34] Grishashvili further emphasized the extent to which motifs in Sayat-Nova's poetry arose from the concrete social and historical circumstances in which he lived; for example, he tried to connect the "motifs of loneliness, sorrow, and abnegation" in Sayat-Nova's work to a broader condemnation of feudal society.[35] Summing up the poet's achievement, Grishashvili wrote: "Sayat-Nova was the first to introduce the songs of the *ashughs* of the Caucasus into the course of national development, and it played an important role in the development and drawing together [*sblizhenie*] of the national cultures of the peoples of Transcaucasia."[36] Thus, if one is to accept Grishashvili's account, the historical figure of Sayat-Nova satisfied practically every imaginable ideological criterion of the period in which Grishashvili was writing.

Parajanov's conception of Sayat-Nova actually was not as different from the official Soviet view of the poet as one might suppose. The literary scenario opens with the following epigram by the Russian Symbolist poet Valery Briusov, who translated some of Sayat-Nova's verse: "Sayat-Nova is one of those first-rate poets who, by force of his genius already ceases to be the property of an individual people, but becomes a favorite of all humanity."[37] Thus, from the outset Parajanov emphasizes the universal — as opposed to narrowly national — significance of the poet. While the literary scenario hardly depicts Sayat-Nova fighting on the front lines in the manner of a true poet-patriot, it does allude to the poet's despair at the region's occupation by the Persian Empire — symbolized by Muslims with hennaed beards and palms winding a turban around Erekle II's head — and his martyrdom during the sack of Tbilisi.

Especially significant in this regard is Parajanov's poetic conceit of a mason capturing Sayat-Nova's voice for eternity in resonator-vases and burying them in the walls of a church. This is meant to represent how, after his death, Sayat-Nova has become a voice of the people. The idea comes through with particular force in the finished film's finale, when the poet sings and a multitude of different voices echo back — a brilliant example of the composer Tigran Mansurian's densely textured constructions for the film's soundtrack. So for all his legendary intransigency, Parajanov clearly attempted, in his own peculiar way, to construct a version of Sayat-Nova that had at least some points of correspondence with official ideology.

The Literary Scenario and the Screen Tests

Parajanov completed the literary scenario in the fall of 1966 and submitted it to the studio no later than December of that year.[38] In a memo dated December 21, Vahagn Mkrtchian, the director of the Armenfilm Studio, and L. A. Karagyozian, the acting editor-in-chief of the studio's Script-Editorial Board, expressed their support for Parajanov's decision to write the scenario as a "film poem" and to focus on "revealing the source roots of Sayat-Nova's poetry and his ties to the era," rather than recounting a straightforward biography. They also attempted to justify the scenario on ideological grounds, emphasizing how it depicted Sayat-Nova's connection with "the sufferings and aspirations of the people," and the "friendship of the three peoples of Transcaucasia."[39] Goskino of Armenia then approved the scenario and forwarded it to the Main Script-Editorial Board of Goskino USSR, but Moscow expressed decidedly mixed feelings about the project. Two expert readers from the old guard of Soviet filmmaking submitted reports to Moscow's Script-Editorial Board: the director Sergei Yutkevich and the screenwriter Mikhail Bleiman. Yutkevich admired Parajanov's poetic approach and his gift for striking imagery, but recommended that he work with an established "playwright-poet" to strengthen its underlying dramaturgy and engagement with history.[40] Bleiman was far less enthusiastic, complaining of the scenario's "subjectivity" and that much of it was "incomprehensible and unclear" because Parajanov had failed to establish basic biographical facts for the potential viewer. He warned that the film risked "failure" if Parajanov allowed himself to become "carried away with that capricious, associative course that gives rise to the life and poetry of Sayat-Nova and leave aside the object of the associations — reality."[41] The Script-Editorial Board's subsequent resolution reiterated these concerns and further recommended that Goskino of Armenia take the film "under special control" since the scenario was "constructed on the basis of the vast and diverse artistic heritage of a remarkable national poet."[42] This last comment may be read in more than one way. In one respect, it suggests that Moscow wanted to allow the local authorities in Armenia a certain degree of autonomy to avoid the appearance of treading on their national culture. It also suggests that Moscow viewed the project as problematic and sought closer ideological scrutiny of it at the local level.

❀

The cast included a fascinating mix of professionals and non-professionals selected for their looks. It is especially worth noting how Parajanov cast the roles across ethnic lines. For Erekle II he chose the Armenian painter Onik (Hovhannes) Minasian, boasting to various Georgian filmmakers during a trip to Tbilisi that Minasian looked better than the Georgian actor "with bovine eyes" who played the same role in Rezo Chkheidze's *Maia Tzqneteli* (Georgia Film Studio 1959).[43] The venerable Georgian actors Medea Japaridze and Spartak Bagashvili played Sayat-Nova's mother and father. (Parajanov had used Bagashvili before as Yura the sorcerer in *Shadows of Forgotten Ancestors*.) Vilen Galustian, who played the critical role of Sayat-Nova as a monk, was a

Figure 4.1. Sofiko Chiaureli as the poet Sayat-Nova (*The Color of Pomegranates*). Courtesy of the Sergei Parajanov Museum.

dancer at the Yerevan Opera and Ballet whom Parajanov cast because of his very close physical resemblance to portraits of the poet. Given the director's interest in movement and pantomime, it is not difficult to see why casting a dancer in the role might also have appealed to him. Non-professionals from the crew and from the various shooting locations were chosen for smaller parts. But the most significant presence in the film by far was the Georgian actress Sofiko Chiaureli, who crossed not only ethnic but gender boundaries, appearing in no less than five roles: Sayat-Nova as a young poet (Fig. 4.1), his beloved Princess Ana, the Mime, the Nun in White Lace, and the Angel of Resurrection (also commonly called the Poet's Muse). The gifted actress easily met the challenge with her inspired use of pantomime and facial expressions, bringing emotional conviction to the multiple roles that she performed and doing much to help Parajanov's vision succeed onscreen.

For all intents and purposes, the shooting script was identical to the literary scenario. In his final report, production manager Alexander Melik-Sargsyan noted that the studio management had moved the film ahead into the preparatory stage despite complaints by director of photography Suren Shakhbazian and production designer Stepan Andranikian about the lack of a fully developed shooting script. Given an eight-day deadline by the studio's deputy director, Parajanov had submitted a typescript of the literary scenario hastily cut and pasted onto cardboard.[44] This shooting script is in fact preserved at the Parajanov Museum.

As was the case with *Kyiv Frescoes*, Parajanov used the screen tests as an opportunity to showcase his planned visual style for the film. Even more than the finished film, the screen tests use the plain background of the soundstage and the highly formalized arrangements of costumed actors and props to create a flattened visual perspective reminiscent of Armenian miniatures. According to Karen Kalantar, their screening before the studio's Artistic Council turned into "a notable event in the cultural life of Yerevan," which included the presence of the painter Martiros Saryan, one of the country's foremost cultural figures.[45] Saryan's support for the film carried a great deal of weight, though Laert Vagarshian, who had replaced Mkrtchian as the studio head of Armenfilm, later recalled that not everyone at the screening liked Parajanov's proposed approach.[46] In a new memo evaluating the screen tests, the Goskino Script-Editorial Board in Moscow noted the "undoubted artistic interest" of the screen tests and praised their "pictorial quality," "good taste," and their "striving for expressive and laconic metaphorical solutions." At the same time, they reminded Parajanov of the need "to avoid the excessive hieroglyphic and encoded qualities of his pictorial system" and of the film's basic task to introduce the figure of Sayat-Nova to "the broad mass of Soviet spectators" in a "clear and distinct form." They also recommended "that the authors think through the intonational key of the film more clearly," since it showed signs of turning out "religious-passionate and elegiac."[47] This would not be the only time the authorities expressed discomfort with the film's religious imagery, though ultimately little was cut from the film in that regard.

Hakob Hovnatanyan: Sketches for a Masterwork

In 1967, shortly before Parajanov began the actual shooting phase of *The Color of Pomegranates*, he directed the ten-minute documentary film *Hakob Hovnatanyan* for the Yerevan Newsreel-Documentary Film Studio.[48] Hakob Hovnatanyan (1806–1881) was a revered Tbilisi-Armenian portrait artist from a family of painters whose roots traced back to the painter and *ashugh* Naghash Hovnatan, mentioned previously. Hakob Hovnatanyan's paintings stand out for their strong characterization of the individual sitters and the delicacy with which he handled details in costuming. The portraits are also of great cultural value as visual records of the prosperous Armenian community in Tbilisi, which, as mentioned earlier, made up more than half the city's population through much of the nineteenth century. Today the most significant collection of Hovnatanyan's works is housed at the National Gallery of Armenia.

On a practical level, the documentary functioned as a trial run for the style that Parajanov would elaborate in his feature film, especially the distinctive use of still-life compositions and jump cuts. It also served as a diploma work for the young sound operator Yuri Sayadyan, whom Parajanov had in mind for *The Color of Pomegranates*. But *Hakob Hovnatanyan* deserves far greater recognition in its own right as a charming, artistically harmonious evocation of Old Tiflis culture and as a relatively accessible introduction to the poetics and themes of *The Color of Pomegranates*.

The film opens with a series of still-life arrangements composed out of miscellaneous objects from the past: a length of lace, an imperial decree written in Russian, paper monetary notes and coins, billiard balls, playing cards, and so on. These objects point to the increasing political and economic influence of the Russian Empire in the nineteenth century and the corresponding influx of European material culture. For Parajanov such objects also serve as literal connections to the past, which he engages through his creative imagination and brings into active dialogue with the present. While this is a crucial idea behind all of Parajanov's major works, it is especially evident here and in the later documentary short *Arabesques on the Theme of Pirosmani*.

In the second section, Parajanov depicts the raw materials of Hovnatanyan's — and his own — art. Among them: a series of richly decorated fabrics, some of which the director will reuse in *The Color of Pomegranates*; trimmings from a costume similar to what one of Hovnatanyan's sitters might have worn; a bare studio with a wooden window frame; patches of pure color from Hovnatanyan's own canvases; an empty gilded picture frame; and pink roses arranged in a vase on the studio's "windowsill." Thus, in his typically laconic manner Parajanov invites us to reflect not just on the relationship between painted representations and reality, but between film and painting, and beyond that, film and reality. Tellingly, much of this section is accompanied by the sound of a stringed instrument being tuned, anticipating the sound of the *kamancha* in *The Color of Pomegranates* during the scenes of the poet's youth.

Rather than introducing us to the paintings in their entirety, Parajanov prefers to start by focusing on the sitters' hands, which reveal the variety of poses employed, the different objects they hold, and especially the finely rendered sleeves that show off Hovnatanyan's skill as a painter. Parajanov's whimsical use of sound comes to the fore in the sections devoted to female and male portraits, which are accompanied by a female voice — possibly that of the famed Armenian singer Lusine Zakaryan — performing the hymn "Amen, the Father is Holy" ("Amen hayr surb") and a martial drumbeat, respectively. The sound mix becomes more elaborate in the section devoted to childhood, as if recorded live from everyday life in Old Tiflis. The sounds of a piano and young boys conversing in French, presumably with their French nanny, are juxtaposed with portraits of young boys and close-ups of women's chests adorned with crosses or pearls — the maternal breast from a child's point of view. The film then depicts a series of architectural details from the historic city center, among them its distinctive wooden balconies.

The play between past and present, representation and reality becomes still more complex in the rest of the film. A young couple — two portraits linked through montage — go on a romantic carriage ride, represented by a lone white glove arranged on a black carriage seat in motion. A male hand — the first live human element up to this point — grinds the crank on an antique barrel organ, a remnant of the city's vibrant street life. The same barrel organ becomes the focal element in a couple of whimsical compositions using a young man, an old man, and an umbrella. In the final section of the film, the carriage arrives at Tbilisi's Armenian Pantheon, where the coexistence of past and present is developed further: horses grazing contentedly, young boys playing among the gravestones, the empty carriage standing before electrical power lines, and the onion domes of a nineteenth-century Russian Orthodox church. The church is photographed with an aerial cable car in the background. Finally, accompanied by music played on *duduks* (an Armenian double reed instrument), the film closes on the thirteenth-century Georgian Church of Metekhi, with the modern equestrian statue of Vakhtang Gorgasali standing in the foreground. These juxtapositions demonstrate a playful interplay between past and present, a key element of the city's identity and one that shaped Parajanov as an artist. As a study for the film he was about to shoot, it also reveals the painstaking care and far-ranging thought behind his new aesthetic.

Production

The production of *The Color of Pomegranates* proved remarkably complicated, due in no small part to Parajanov's vision of Sayat-Nova as an explicitly Transcaucasian figure. Several scenes were shot on a soundstage at the Armenfilm Studio, among them the wool-dyeing, the scenes in Princess Ana's chamber, and the dance of the mimes. A large portion of the film was shot in the mountainous Lori region of northern Armenia; locations there included the aforementioned

Sanahin Monastery for the scenes depicting Sayat-Nova's education; Haghpat, where he lived for a time after becoming a monk; and Akhtala for the scene depicting the desecration of the fresco of the Virgin Mary. Locations in the Kakheti region of Georgia included the Alaverdi Cathedral (the poet's childhood vision of Saint George and the poet's death) and the Dzveli Shuamta Monastery (King Erekle's hunt). The episode of Sayat-Nova and Princess Ana visiting a tomb was shot in the walled Old City of Baku and nearby locations such as the Nardaran Castle. Shooting at these locations presented a whole range of logistical challenges for the production crew and inevitably caused shooting to run over schedule, though they were essential to convey the palpable sense of the past that Parajanov sought.

The footage of nude female bathers, only a small portion of which ended up in the finished film, was shot on a soundstage at the Dovzhenko Film Studio in Kyiv. Parajanov also requested permission to use the editing facilities at Kyiv rather than those in Yerevan, presumably so that his editor of choice, Maria Ponomarenko, could avoid travel. Another likely motive, suggested by Valery Fomin, was that it gave Parajanov greater independence from the Armenian film administrators.[49] Most exceptionally, Vazgen I, the Catholicos of the Armenian Church, granted the crew permission to transport many rare religious artifacts from the treasury at Etchmiadzin to the Lori region for use as props. This is an example of the kinds of privileges that filmmakers could claim in the state-controlled Soviet film industry. By way of contrast, it is difficult to imagine an Italian filmmaker transporting rare treasures from the Vatican up to the mountains in northern Italy.

Some of Parajanov's requests were indeed capricious. From the outset his script called for a llama, which Vagarshian recalled had to be "delivered to Yerevan with tremendous difficulty and effort," since the city zoo lacked them.[50] It is remarkable that Parajanov would insist so strongly on an animal that, as Levon Abrahamian has pointed out, was not only utterly alien to Sayat-Nova's world but also functioned mainly as a sexual symbol in his vision of the film.[51] Actually, this was very much in keeping with his compulsion to test the limits of what he could get away with, both in terms of censorship norms and, off the set, broader social mores.

The film's shooting plan was further complicated by the aforementioned organizational problems at the studio, external factors such as frigid weather in Haghpat, and, not least, the difficult personality of Parajanov himself. The production and censorship files from Goskino USSR contain a long series of sharply worded telegrams by Parajanov complaining about his treatment by the Armenfilm Studio, despite Vagarshian's clear attempts to accommodate his requests and to allow him a broad degree of creative freedom. The first surviving telegram was sent on August 17, 1967, after the first scheduled day of shooting(!):

> When sad circumstances forced me to arrive in Yerevan I was thirty nine[.] Now I'm forty two[.] August sixteenth after a prolongation the first shooting day was set that didn't take place because Gegechkori the main actor submitted by me is not confirmed by someone for the main role[.] 16 August the second director went on prof-leave[.] Production manager Melik Sargsyan who is a pensioner of the KGB ruined work is threatening to go on vacation[.] Cinematographer Shakhbazian has been testing defective film stock from Shostka for six months[.] He has turned the creative process into Nikfi[.][52] It's hot[.] Peaches cost two rubles[.] I'm suffocating from intrigues and stifling rooms with cockroaches[.] I insist on closing the picture send me to Kyiv immediately with subsequent voluntary departure from film[.] Kyiv Frescoes and the repression of Tarkovsky are enough for me—
> Parajanov[53]

After receiving a number of such telegrams over the course of several months, Vladimir Baskakov, the deputy chair of Goskino, finally sent a telegram in April 1968 to Gevorg Hairian, the chair of Goskino of Armenia, ordering the Armenfilm Studio to cease interfering in Parajanov's work.[54] At the same time, Parajanov's constant complaints hardly could have endeared him to Moscow.

Vagarshian further recalls that Parajanov himself disappeared unexpectedly on that first day of shooting. The production manager Melik-Sargsyan finally located him in Rustavi, a city located in Georgia near Tbilisi, and brought him back. Vagarshian comments, "[H]e didn't begin shooting because there was nothing to surmount. Everything was ready, everyone was ready to work. Therefore he made all the strings out of tune so that he could tune them again in his own way."[55] In a similar vein, Stepan Andranikian recalls that Parajanov needed to stir up the atmosphere in some way to spark his imagination, and thus would periodically declare at the start of a shoot that he couldn't work and was leaving. Fifteen or twenty minutes later, someone would go talk to him and he would begin working normally.[56]

Parajanov's weakness for valuable objects also created problems during the production. Mikhail Arakelian, who was responsible for acquiring the many authentic historical artifacts used in the film, recalls that before shooting began, Parajanov took a rare carpet from the collection of props. Arakelian confronted him and demanded that he return it lest the assistant responsible for its security wind up in legal trouble.[57] Andranikian likewise recalled that Parajanov, in an impulsive show of generosity, gave some objects to friends visiting from Tbilisi while the film was in production. (Throughout his life, Parajanov loved to bestow lavish gifts upon guests and friends.) Arakelian had to retrieve the items afterward; the visitors understood the situation and naturally obliged.[58]

Due to inclement weather and various operational problems, shooting fell at least two months behind schedule; principal photography was not finished until July 22, 1968. Baskakov reprimanded both Vagarshian and Hairian and docked Parajanov's pay 20 percent.[59] Incidentally, this was a standard sanction for failure to fulfill the production plan. Like other aspects of the Soviet economy, the film industry operated according to predetermined production plans, both in terms of annual output as a whole and on the level of individual films. Filmmakers were expected to produce a given amount of footage within a given time frame, and failure to meet the plan could result in sanctions for the crew and responsible administrators.

Censorship

One must acknowledge up front that, to a certain extent, the film comes down to us in a compromised form. Parajanov originally wanted it to maintain a more direct connection to Sayat-Nova throughout, which was necessary to anchor his flights of fancy. This was reflected not only in his original title for the film — *Sayat-Nova* — but also in the original script's chapter titles, which explicitly indicated the contents of each scene. By labeling most of the chapters as "miniatures," he sought to cue potential viewers from the outset that the underlying narrative principle was a series of loosely connected episodes inspired by the illustrative qualities of medieval Armenian and Persian miniature painting. The chapter titles also make it clear that parts of the film are meant to represent the world as perceived through Sayat-Nova's imagination, a notion that also appears at various points in the main body of the script.

Ironically, Parajanov's attempt to make the film's intentions explicit to viewers wound up as one of the main casualties in the censorship process. Gevorg Hairian instructed him to remove all direct references to Sayat-Nova from the film based on comments by the Armenian Communist Party apparatus and various members of the creative intelligentsia.[60] Presumably Hairian and others had decided this on the grounds that the film was not really "about" Sayat-Nova since Parajanov took liberties with the poet's biography and indulged his private fancies. The film's title consequently changed from *Sayat-Nova* to *Ashkharums* and eventually to *Nran Guyne* (*The Color of Pomegranates*), the actual title under which it premiered in Armenia. The studio also engaged the popular novelist and short story writer Hrant Matevosyan to write entirely new chapter titles. One example of this is the chapter in the script entitled "Miniature that shows how the poet Sayat-Nova, in love with Princess Ana, withdraws to the monastery for life."[61] In the Armenian release version it became "How am I to protect my wax-built castles of love from your red-hot fires?"[62] In that respect, the Armenian release version arguably became even more cryptic than Parajanov originally wanted. At the same time, Matevosyan's new chapter titles are vividly written and do closely reflect each chapter's underlying emotional thrust. For Armenian viewers already familiar with Sayat-Nova's biography, the more poetically indirect titles likely would not have posed the same barrier to understanding as they would have to other viewers in the former Soviet Union and abroad.

Apart from the change in chapter titles and the removal of all intertitles quoting from Sayat-Nova's poetry, the seventy-seven-minute Armenian release version was not cut as badly as one might expect. While various memos in the film's censorship file complained about its excess of religious imagery, it still abounds in the finished film. And while several shots containing nudity were ultimately discarded from the bathing sequence and elsewhere, the woman's nude torso that does remain in the bathing sequence was nonetheless an extremely rare occurrence in Soviet cinema of the period. Alexei Romanov's biggest complaints after seeing the finished film were that the film failed to teach Soviet audiences about "the real life journey of the great poet of Transcaucasia and about his place in the development of Armenian national culture" and that Parajanov's "striving for purely formal, decorative effects" resulted in an incoherent work.[63] The implication here was that Parajanov had created a "formalist" film rather than something "accessible and clear," to borrow Grishashvili's characterization of Sayat-Nova's poems. Romanov did, however, agree to let Goskino of Armenia and the Armenfilm Studio continue to work on the film "with the aim of molding a picture [out of it]" and stated that he would consider releasing the film after the necessary changes were made.[64]

❋

The film premiered in Armenia in October 1969 at the Moscow Theater in Yerevan. Romanov refused to allow distribution of the film outside of Armenia but it was not officially banned or shelved, in contrast to works such as Andrei Tarkovsky's *Andrei Rublev* (1966–1972) or Andrei Konchalovsky's *Asya's Happiness* (1966). Thus, while it was not available commercially in the USSR as a whole, professionals such as film critics could still screen it upon request in Moscow, as

Mikayel Stamboltsyan recalled doing on a number of occasions while working at Goskino.[65]

The seventy-one-minute version later prepared by Sergei Yutkevich for Soviet-wide distribution replaced Matevosyan's Armenian-language titles with new Russian-language titles and reintroduced several quotes from Sayat-Nova's poetry. While Parajanov himself had quoted some of these verses in the original literary scenario, others were newly selected by Yutkevich. In addition, Yutkevich cut a few minutes' worth of footage, moved some footage to different sections altogether, and divided the chapters differently in places. One chapter title ("Chapter 7: Encounter with the Angel of Death: The poet buries his love") reflects an outright misreading of the film, as discussed below. Still, one should acknowledge that Yutkevich had served as one of the script's readers for the Main Script-Editorial Board in Moscow and thus was closely familiar with Parajanov's original Russian-language literary scenario. By reediting the film, he sought to overcome the impasse between Armenia and Moscow and thus gain a wider release for the film, which he had admired from the start.[66]

The table of chapter titles below provides a general sense of how each of the three versions — Parajanov's original literary scenario, the Armenian release version, and the Yutkevich version — are structured. In the literary scenario, the titles in all capital letters indicate subsections or the setting of a particular scene, in the terse style of the chapter headings for *Shadows of Forgotten Ancestors*.

Analysis

This analysis of *The Color of Pomegranates* is based primarily (but not exclusively) on the Armenian release version, often called the "director's cut."[67] Although it already bears the marks of censorship, it is nonetheless closer to Parajanov's original vision than the version reedited by Sergei Yutkevich. The analysis also draws comparisons throughout to the initial literary scenario, which clarifies many points that became obscured in the process of editing the Armenian release version.

The prologue cues the viewer to read the film from the start as poetic cinema, introducing both the film's major themes and the parameters of Parajanov's film language through a series of highly condensed images. It begins with an Armenian manuscript lying open, accompanied by a male voice reciting a line from one of Sayat-Nova's Azerbaijani poems, only translated into Armenian: "I am he whose life and soul are torment."[68] Given Parajanov's avowed personal identification with Sayat-Nova, one is invited to apply it to him as well. Over the course of the prologue, the phrase is repeated like an invocation. These

Table 1: Comparison of Chapter Divisions in the Script, Armenian Release Version, and Yutkevich Version of *The Color of Pomegranates*

Parajanov's original script	Armenian Release version (titles by Hrant Matevosyan)	Yutkevich version (titles by Yutkevich)
[Prologue]		
Miniature in which a lament is played by the peoples of Transcaucasia in memory of Sayat-Nova		
MATAGH [Armenian for "sacrificial offering."] Episode not filmed; different from the sacrifice sequence in finished film.		
Miniature in which the world of mystery and beauty is revealed to the young boy Arutin.	How many more have come before me, have tentatively, tentatively known this amazing world and then extinguished, expired ahead of me.	Chapter 1: The Poet's Childhood.
Miniature in which play the amusements, passions and childish imagination of the future poet.	From the colors and aromas of this world, my childhood made the poet's lyre and offered it to me.	
MAIDAN		
Miniature in which we see Arutin Sayadyan as a young *ashugh* in the court of King Irakli [Erekle] II. The *ashugh* creates his pseudonym—Sayat-Nova.		
EREKLES ABANO [Georgian: "Erekle's bath"]		
		Chapter 2: The Poet's Youth.
Miniature in which Sayat-Nova still doesn't realize that he loves the princess, and only in the name of Majnun does he sing of the beauty of Layla.	We were searching for ourselves in each other.	

Parajanov's original script	Armenian Release version (titles by Hrant Matevosyan)	Yutkevich version (titles by Yutkevich)
THE PRINCESS TATS LACE		
PRAYER SERVICE AND HUNT IN THE MOUN- TAINS OF SAMTAVISI	In this healthy and beautiful life only I have been given suffering. Why is it given? We were searching for a place of refuge for our love, but instead the road led us to the land of the dead. [Continuation of previous chapter in script.]	Chapter 3: The Poet in the Prince's Court: prayer before the hunt.
Two pantomimes, as if allegories or symbols, in which the poet Sayat-Nova sees the hard times of the country in connection with the Persian invasion of Nadir-Shah in the territory of Georgia — Armenia. [Episode not filmed.]		
SAYAT-NOVA'S DREAM [Episode not filmed.]		
Miniature [which] shows how the poet Sayat-Nova, in love with Princess Ana, retires to the monastery for life.	How am I to protect my wax-built castles of love from your red-hot fires?	
YAR [Armenian for "Beloved."]		
HAGHPAT	Go then and find your refuge of selfless love. I will go and search the monasteries one by one.	Chapter 4: The Poet Enters the Monastery.
Miniature that shows how a night full of asceticism and mysticism unexpectedly falls upon the poet.	As a crowd of naïve victims, we come from this world to you, my Lord, as an offering . . .	

Parajanov's original script	Armenian Release version (titles by Hrant Matevosyan)	Yutkevich version (titles by Yutkevich)
How Sayat-Nova, the sacristan of Haghpat, found in the women's monastery the very best shroud for the body of Ghazaros, and saw a nun who resembled the princess . . .	I asked for a shroud to wrap the dead body; instead, they showed the frenzied convulsions of their living bodies. Where can I find selfless love?	
HRIPSIME		
Miniature that shows and tells how Sayat-Nova, still a young monk but exhausted by life in the monastery, decides to enter once more into his youth and childhood.	In the sunny valley of distant years live my longings, my loves and my childhood.	Chapter 5: The Poet's Dream: He returns to his childhood and mourns the death of his parents.
GIZH MART [Georgian: "Mad March"]		
SPRING	I saw everything clear and strangely blunt, and I understood that life had abandoned me.	
Miniature in which Sayat-Nova, already an old man, is spoiling for a duel with a young *ashugh*, but on the road to Tbilisi he sees the sorrow of the people . . . and remains with the people . . .		Chapter 6: The Poet's Old Age: The poet leaves the monastery.
	I hear calls of homecoming and hope, but I am weary. Who has spread all this sorrow upon this old and tired earth? [Continuation of previous chapter in the script.]	Chapter 7: Encounter With the Angel of Death: The poet buries his love.
Miniature in which it is shown how the poet died.	The bread you gave was beautiful, but the soil is more than beautiful. Let me go and turn to earth. I am weary, I am weary.	Chapter 8: The Poet's Death.

spoken words are accompanied by the melody of another Sayat-Nova song, "Ashkhares me panjara e" ("The World is a Window"). It is performed by an ensemble of *duduks*, an instrument much admired for its plaintive timbre. But from the very start, Tigran Mansurian's musical score alerts us to how the film will use traditional Armenian musical culture in a free and creative manner. Normally, such a melody would be performed by two or more *duduks*, with the secondary instruments providing a drone. Here, Mansurian layers the melody contrapuntally, in the style of a fugue. The music continues over the entire prologue. Shots of the manuscript alternate with several symbolically loaded images.

1. Three pomegranates whose juice seeps out from underneath, the red stain spreading out over white linen. During the course of the film Parajanov repeatedly deploys this symbolically rich fruit, cultivated throughout the Caucasus and the Middle East, to conjure up an entire range of associations: life and death, fertility, temptation, and bloodshed. The pomegranate's unique sweet-sour-bitter flavor suggests the complex tenor of life itself. The image of seeping juice also introduces a general motif of spilling or overflowing liquid that reappears in many guises and is loosely associated with abundance, eroticism, and creativity.

2. A dagger with pomegranate juice spreading out beneath it (Fig. 4.2). This perhaps symbolizes the martyrdom of Sayat-Nova and, more broadly, the tragic history of the peoples of Transcaucasia.

3. A male foot slowly crushing grapes on a stone surface covered with Armenian inscriptions. On one level, this image condenses two elements from Sayat-Nova's life in the monastery: making wine and carving stone inscriptions. It also functions as a visual metaphor: poetry is the making of wine from words. The image of wine further carries a wealth of connotations, especially from the Bible and the Persian literary tradition, both of which informed Sayat-Nova's poetry. But for Transcaucasia, wine has still deeper cultural roots; recent archeological and linguistic research indicates that it is among the earliest known sites of wine production.[69]

4. Two loaves of bread in a curved baton shape common to Transcaucasia, with two trout lying in between. A third fish appears as if by magic via a jump cut; this cinematic trickery evokes Christ's miracle of the loaves and fish. The third fish convulses and gasps for air, literally embodying the notion of torment.

5. A *kamancha*, beautifully inlaid with mother-of-pearl. This musical instrument not only functions as a metonym for Sayat-Nova's art but exists as a work of art in its own right, its lavishly decorated surface just one expression of the

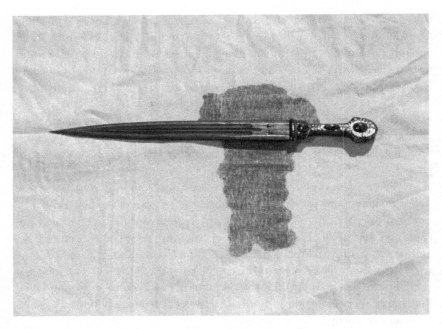

Figure 4.2. The dagger, a recurring visual motif (*The Color of Pomegranates*).

creative spirit of an entire people. In the same composition, lying next to the *kamancha* on white brocaded silk, a finely engraved metal vase holds a white rose on a stem stripped of leaves. Taken as a whole, the image refers to the doomed love of Sayat-Nova and Princess Ana; the very same objects will reappear during the sequence depicting the idealistic beginning of their romance.

6. A tangle of thorns against a stark black background. Rather obviously, it evokes further Christian symbolism and more generally the notion of torment, while creating a strong graphic contrast with the previous shots.

To sum up the stylistic traits seen so far, Parajanov cultivates a carefully restricted, symbolically charged color palette—primarily the colors red, gold, black, and white. He often uses neutral or indistinct backgrounds in order to isolate objects and to emphasize both their abstract qualities and their concrete presence as real objects. The movement of actors is deliberately stylized and slowed down, as if characters are performing rituals before the camera. Many compositions are inspired by genre painting—Armenian and Persian miniatures, the still lifes of Pirosmani, and to a lesser extent Renaissance painting. But despite the static, painterly nature of the tableaux, they often incorporate subtle forms of movement within the frame, thus retaining a fundamentally cinematic quality. Parajanov's main cinematic frame of reference is likewise archaic: the "magical" trick cuts and frontal tableaux evoke the early cinema of Méliès in particular. Finally, insofar as he conceives of film in poetic terms, Parajanov employs symbols, metaphors, repetition, and rhyme as basic tools of his craft. By "rhyme" I mean primarily visual or audio motifs that are echoed across the film, giving it a definite underlying structure. One example of such a rhyme in the prologue is the recurring visual pattern established by juxtaposing the shot of bleeding pomegranates with that of the bleeding dagger.

As the above analysis of the prologue suggests, one of the most remarkable and underappreciated aspects of the film is its rigorously constructed soundtrack, whose qualities unfortunately are not always represented well on the available prints. The film's almost complete avoidance of synchronized speech sets it apart from *Shadows of Forgotten Ancestors*, although it is possible that Parajanov had wanted to move in that direction with *Kyiv Frescoes*. The soundtrack for *The Color of Pomegranates* is not a conventional mix of dialogue, sound effects, and music. Rather, it is in itself a fully integrated musical composition employing sound effects, newly composed musical passages, performances of Sayat-Nova's songs, other folk songs, field recordings of church liturgy and hymns, and even deliberately placed passages of silence. The composer Tigran Mansurian constructed the soundtrack out of tape recordings, including audio recorded both out in the field and in the studio, with the help of the film's sound engineer Yuri Sayadyan.[70] Once in the studio, Mansurian cut and mixed this material freely, sometimes using abrupt audio splices and repeated tape fragments. In that respect, his work on the film is a kind of audio-collage akin to *musique concrète*, and he himself has acknowledged a debt to Pierre Schaeffer and Pierre Henry. Parajanov had a few specific requirements, such as the inclusion of the Georgian hymn "Shen khar venakhi" during the scene of the royal hunt; otherwise he allowed Mansurian to work with a great deal of freedom.[71] Given Parajanov's interest in representing the multicultural dimension of Transcaucasia and his general interest in the authentic textures of speech, it is likely that he also had some input regarding the inclusion of materials in multiple languages on the soundtrack. Mansurian's resulting soundtrack was without precedent in Soviet cinema, excepting perhaps Dziga Vertov's first sound film, *Enthusiasm*. It remains one of the more adventurous uses of sound in any feature film, something that often gets lost in the focus on the film's stunning visual style.

Major Themes

As Parajanov himself mentioned in the interview in *Ekran*, the main goal of the film is to "show the world in which [Sayat-Nova] lived, the sources that nourished his poetry." In Parajanov's view, Sayat-Nova not only derived his inspiration from the people, he ultimately became the voice of that people through his beloved songs. At the same time, the film serves more broadly as a celebration of the music, architecture, folk art, and customs of the peoples of Transcaucasia, but with a particular focus on Armenia as befits Sayat-Nova's origins and biographical circumstances.

The idea of Sayat-Nova drawing inspiration for his poetry and music from his immediate surroundings is realized in an amusingly literal fashion in the chapter depicting his childhood. After a frontal tableau of the young Arutin holding a yellow rose, the film cuts abruptly to the image of feet tramping in a circle to wash an intricately patterned carpet. As if viewing the scene from the ground-level perspective of a child, the camera catches an impressionistic glimpse of silver anklets and the brightly colored hems of the young women's skirts. The jangling sound of a musical instrument (most likely a *tar*) playfully mimics the jangling of the anklets. However, Parajanov is not content to let this footage simply play out; he interrupts it with a jump cut, giving the viewer a visual jolt. This is followed by an overhead shot of the young Arutin, now in a scarlet-colored shirt, tramping about on carpets as women wash them on a domed rooftop.

The jangling music ends abruptly as the film cuts to a shot of Arutin standing before a loom, his arms outstretched and his fingers plucking yarn like the strings of an instrument. A female face (his mother?) is barely visible through the rows of yarn stretched behind him. A persistent ticking sound suggests the action of a loom or a weaver snipping yarn, at the same time recalling a metronome. From the reverse side, two women weave rugs while Arutin carries a skein of dark blue yarn and sits down, raising the skein above his head. The sound of water dripping into a metal drum or tub leads us still deeper into the world of the boy's imagination, as he thinks of the wool being dyed (Fig. 4.3). The exaggerated sound of skeins dripping water and plopping onto metal trays resembles that of a drum. Thus Parajanov represents, in purely cinematic terms, how the young Arutin already displays a basic trait of poets — the ability to transform concrete sensory impressions into something new via metaphorical thinking.

The most direct image of Sayat-Nova becoming the voice of the people appears after Sayat-Nova's death, in which the resonator jars that the mason

Figure 4.3. The young Arutin observes wool-dyeing (*The Color of Pomegranates*). Courtesy of the Sergei Parajanov Museum.

buries in the wall echo back the poet's song in a multitude of voices. Another, deeply moving example — whose intent has become somewhat obscured due to the film's censorship history — is the interconnected series of episodes pertaining to motherhood and loss, which are found in the chapter dealing with the poet's old age and his departure from the monastery. In a deliberately elliptical manner, the film introduces the historical context of invasions that plagued the region during that era. Along the way to Tbilisi (as indicated in the script), Sayat-Nova stops at the Church of the Holy Virgin of Akhtala.[72] Dipping into the font with a small brass bowl, Sayat-Nova discovers that it is now dry. He imagines a "Turkish" warrior, with a bronze-painted face, shooting an arrow at the image of the Virgin Mary, thus causing her face to fall away and the font to run dry. (The script mentions "Turkish arrows" specifically.) If such a detail seems odd given the Persian Empire's control over the region during that era, it is important to keep in mind that a significant percentage of the Persian military in that region was of Turkic origin, as was the Qajar dynasty itself. On the whole, the Muslim population in the region was a mix of ethnic Persians, Turkic peoples, and Kurds. Furthermore, during the Turkish-Persian wars of the sixteenth and seventeenth centuries, control of the region shifted between the two empires multiple times, much to the misery of the local population. Thus Parajanov's fantasy is in its own way more or less plausibly grounded in history.

In order to understand Parajanov's full intent behind this and the subsequent sections, it is necessary to refer to the outtakes for this sequence. One discarded shot was of the face of Sayat-Nova's mother (Medea Japaridze) replacing that of the Virgin Mary: her face surrounded by arrows, she peers through a hole in a decorated backdrop, recalling Georges Méliès's *A Trip to the Moon* (1902), in which women's faces poke through a painted backdrop depicting stars.

After the Akhtala episode in the script, Sayat-Nova arrives at another church and encounters a group of grieving sons and daughters bearing the corpse of their mother, whose face reminds him of the Holy Virgin of Akhtala. (In the film, Japaridze plays this role as well.)[73] At the graveside he leads them in mourning, whispering, "My wounds are bleeding afresh!" and "O Woe! Mother is no longer in the sublunary choir!" The sons and daughters echo him. In the finished film, the soundtrack instead contains a full solo performance of one of Sayat-Nova's finest songs, "The World is a Window" ("Ashkhares me panjara e"). Evidently, by the time shooting began Parajanov had already decided to use "The World is a Window," based on the presence of the ubiquitous stained-glass window as a prop. Nonetheless, Parajanov retains the notion that the poet is leading the sons and daughters in mourning, and that his song serves as a vehicle for them to express their grief (Fig. 4.4). In the final shot of this sequence, the sons and daughters stand around their mother's corpse and recite collectively, "The World is a Window," one of the few instances of synchronized speech in the entire film.

The third apparition of the maternal face is of Sayat-Nova's own mother raising a skein of black yarn over her head. The same black yarn falls over the shoulder of Sayat-Nova's father and wraps around his hands as he holds a pair of red candles. The son, wearing golden angel's wings, likewise holds up a skein of black yarn; an overabundance of the yarn rests at his feet. This leads to a whimsical, deliberately unfinished parody of an Armenian miniature with a pair of angels knitting socks from the black yarn, their halos not yet in place. This is followed by the completed composition: the father, son, and mother holding up skeins of black yarn for the two angels as they knit, all with golden halos placed behind their heads. Thus, in these subtly interconnected episodes Parajanov draws a conscious link between three kinds of motherhood: personal, collective (i.e., of the people), and divine.

As the presence of the "Turkish" warrior indicates, another important

Figure 4.4. Sayat-Nova leads people in mourning (*The Color of Pomegranates*). Courtesy of the Sergei Parajanov Museum.

thematic thread that runs throughout the film is the historical and cultural influence of Persia—and the Orient in general—throughout the Caucasus. During the chapter depicting Sayat-Nova's childhood in Tbilisi, the young Arutin plays on the roof of one of the city's Turkish-style sulfur baths. He peers down to observe a male and female bather, respectively. In the script, Parajanov makes it clear that Arutin is observing King Erekle II and Princess Ana. A subsequent "miniature" in the script portrays King Erekle's sadness under the domination of the Persian Empire. In that regard the *hamam* (Turkish bath), complete with a Tatar bath attendant washing the king, is an especially vivid and symbolically resonant setting. However, as a consequence of the censors' requirement to remove all direct biographical references, the finished film instead presents the two as unidentified bathers and frames the episode mainly within the context of the young boy's sensual awakening. Another trace of this plot element remaining in the finished film is in the episode of King Erekle II preparing to hunt. Not only does the king wear a Persian-style crown—a historically accurate detail—but several images in this sequence deliberately evoke Persian miniatures of royal hunts.

The young Sayat-Nova's Persian-style costumes recall male figures in Qajar-era painting. The cultural link to Persia is further underscored by his henna-tinted palms. However, as mentioned earlier Sofiko Chiaureli plays not only Sayat-Nova, but also his beloved; this inspired touch of androgyny likewise derives from Persian miniature paintings, which often depict the amorous couple with virtually identical facial features. In the aforementioned interview in *Ekran*, Parajanov specifically cites Qajar-era painting as an influence in that regard.[74] However, the convention hardly originates in the Qajar era; it is famously present in Safavid miniatures as well.

The episode of Sayat-Nova's death serves not only as the culmination of the Persian/Oriental strand in the film, it also illustrates how Parajanov is able to accumulate great resonance in his imagery through the film's underlying poetic structure. In the script Parajanov indicates the location as the Saint George Cathedral in Tbilisi, where Sayat-Nova's tomb is actually located.[75] In the film Sayat-Nova sits with his book before a white cathedral, holding in his right hand a skull adorned with a medieval helmet. One may recall that this object appeared previously in the episode depicting Sayat-Nova in Princess Ana's chambers. Having written about death in the poetry of his youth, now Sayat-Nova must confront it for real. Accompanied by a series of shots depicting details from the white walls of the church, the tolling bell on the soundtrack gives way to silence. An arm covered in medieval armor (mail and vambraces) has thrust a dagger into the white wall; blood drips from the metaphorical wound (Fig. 4.5). This segment climaxes with images of a dagger lying next to three crushed pomegranates and a field of crosses against a black background. These stunning and emotionally charged compositions encompass Sayat-Nova's individual martyrdom, the Persian invasion of 1795, and more broadly, the tragic history of an entire region.

Another important theme running through the film is the struggle between asceticism and sensuality. Indeed, the film embodies this opposition through its very style: one the one hand it is constructed largely from a series of tableaux using a restricted color range and a limited degree of movement within the frame; on the other hand it displays a great deal of surface tactility and employs a densely layered soundtrack. In the childhood scenes this dynamic is established already in the episode portraying the young Arutin's monastic education, which is followed immediately by the scenes depicting his sensual discovery of the world. In the episode where Arutin observes weaving and wool-dyeing, one is struck by the vivid colors of the wool, the rising steam from the kettles, and the splashing of water on the trays. Similarly, the bathing sequence shows not only

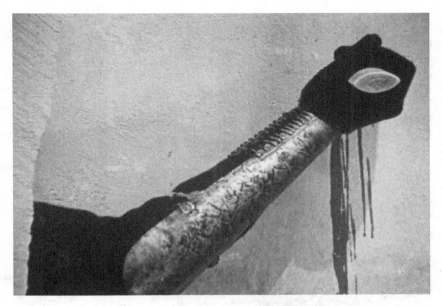

Figure 4.5. The invasion and the poet's death represented metaphorically (*The Color of Pomegranates*). Courtesy of the Sergei Parajanov Museum.

Arutin gazing at male and female nude bodies, but also water flowing down the surface of one of the cupolas as he gazes toward the camera.

When Sayat-Nova enters the monastery as an adult, he hopes for a retreat from all worldly things but even there finds an abundance of sensuality and desire. In one strikingly formalized composition, Sayat-Nova stands to the side holding an open book while his fellow monks noisily suck the juice from pomegranates. Even the making of sunflower seed oil becomes a sensual affair: monks run their hands through the seeds, the finished oil spilling over as it is poured into a metal pitcher. At the end of that section, Sayat-Nova succumbs to temptations of the flesh as he dips a bowl into one of the wine-jars buried in the ground and drinks heartily from it, wine spilling down the front of his cassock.

In Parajanov's vision, this struggle lies at the very foundation of Sayat-Nova's poetry. During the episode depicting Sayat-Nova's death, Sofiko Chiaureli's final incarnation is as a pale, androgynous youth with a rooster perched on his shoulder. In the credits for the finished film, he is called the "Angel of Resurrection." In the *Ekran* interview, he is called the "youth in white" and "poetry in the dreams of Sayat-Nova."[76] In the original script, Parajanov describes him

Figure 4.6. The Youth pours wine on the poet's chest (*The Color of Pomegranates*).

thus: "A youth is covered in grapevines . . . And a wreath of grapes adorns his brow . . . But there are no berries on the clusters of grapes, and with a chirp a bird dashes about anxiously . . . it is searching for a kernel."[77] This grape and wine imagery would seem to indicate that the figure, at least initially, was inspired by traditional representations of the androgyne Dionysus. In the finished film, the symbolism has become more complicated—the Youth instead wears a wreath of oak leaves and white roses. But his androgyny, the abstract vine patterns on his robe and the pair of vines rising on the wall behind him in one shot all point to a lingering connection with Dionysus, even if now the Youth has become more of an abstract figure, in line with the notion of "poetry in the dreams of Sayat-Nova." He steps forward to stand in the foreground, the pair of vines climbing the wall behind him and positioned so as to resemble wings. In the background, the blind Angel of Death once again carries a piece of folded lavash to Sayat Nova, who accepts it and sniffs at it longingly before extending it to the Youth. Gazing at the camera, the expressionless Youth pours a jar of wine over Sayat-Nova's chest. The poet thrusts his chest forward as if to savor this one last experience of the worldly senses (Fig. 4.6).

This sensuality at the film's core also crops up repeatedly in the form of bawdy humor and visual puns. The most obvious example of this is the figure of the llama, which signifies base sexual desire. Since llamas are not native to the region, one suspects that Parajanov chose it over other domesticated animals such as sheep because of its graceful bearing and naturally long eyelashes. In the script, its meaning is made plain by directly juxtaposing a group of young men accosting a llama with the romance of Sayat-Nova and Princess Ana. In the finished film, after Sayat-Nova departs from Ana's chambers he is shown standing on the ground below a wooden balcony; a trio of *ashughs* ascend the stairs while he steps backwards and grasps the harness of a llama standing to his left. During Sayat-Nova's dream, the llama also appears in a tableau depicting Sayat-Nova as a monk. Ana wears her hunting outfit and points her pistol in the air. The llama rests between them, happily munching hay. On the upper level stand Sayat-Nova as a young boy and an angel with stag horns for wings, the latter holding a golden ball. Between them lies King Erekle, nude except for a cloth draped over his waist, recalling the bathing scene. The Angel and the boy Arutin toss the golden ball back and forth, but when Ana fires her pistol in the air the boy collapses, as if dead, next to Erekle. (This refers back to a visual gag during the royal hunt sequence, when the princess similarly fires her gun into the air and one of the attendants in the procession collapses, apparently felled by the bullet.) A white lace robe magically rises up from Sayat-Nova's feet to cover his black robe. While the tableau as a whole remains difficult to decipher, it condenses a series of visual motifs from earlier into a complex set of associations related to bisexuality and the opposition between childhood and adulthood, and purity and profanity (Fig. 4.7).

Much of the film's thematic richness and emotional resonance derive from its dual vision as a film about Sayat-Nova and as a coded autobiography of its author. During an interview for Mikhail Vartanov's documentary *The Color of the Armenian Land* (*Haykakan hogi guyne*, Yerevan Newsreel-Documentary Studio 1969), shot during the same period as *The Color of Pomegranates*, Parajanov emphasized the interrelationship of the autobiographical and the broader historical layers of the film: "If I were to show my creative portrait and the beauty of Armenia, its depth and Biblical beauty, I would like to show the film Sayat-Nova." He further explained how he, like Sayat-Nova—indeed, like "any Armenian boy in Tbilisi"—spent his childhood among the same sulfur baths and churches, synagogues and mosques in the center of city. Watching *The Color of Pomegranates* from today's perspective, one is further tempted to speculate that the awakening of erotic desires that the young Sayat-Nova experiences while spying upon the nude King Erekle II and Princess Ana in the sulfur baths has an element of bisexuality that parallels the director's own life.

Figure 4.7. Sayat-Nova's dream (*The Color of Pomegranates*). Courtesy of the Sergei Parajanov Museum.

In the episode of Sayat-Nova's dream, the images associated with his childhood reveal the underlying depth of feeling that Parajanov brings to this aspect of the film and that ultimately lends it universal resonance. At one point the adult Sayat-Nova rocks back and forth like a metronome alongside his old teacher at Sanahin. The boy Arutin then leads the adult Sayat-Nova back to his childhood home, now in ruins. There the boy is surrounded by an abundance of lavash that poignantly evokes the notion of childhood as a lost paradise of plenitude, warmth, and parental love. Arutin tramps around gaily while his parents play musical instruments. Father, mother, and son tease a large pile of wool, representing their life of toil as carpet weavers.

The soundtrack here alternates between fragments of two songs by Komitas, performed by the same singer.[78] "Kele Kele" ("Walk, Walk") is a folk song that compares the beloved to a quail; "Im Hayrenyats Hogi Vardan" ("Vardan, Soul of My Fatherland") is a hymn about the heroic Armenian sacrifice at the battle of Avarayr (451 AD). During that battle, Vardan Mamikonian and his troops fought against the Sassanid Persians for religious independence. Although the Armenians were badly outnumbered and ultimately lost the battle, the Armenian Church was preserved. The hymn is commonly sung on

Vardanants (May 26), one of the holiest days in the Armenian calendar. Thus, this sequence provides an excellent example of how Mansurian's soundtrack, working in counterpoint to the images, enriches the film's meaning as a whole. Here the music extends beyond the expected historical framework and connects Sayat-Nova's life to a more encompassing idea of Armenian identity, whether through the common roots of folk music or through shared historical trauma.

Immediately after this, three musicians decked with garlands are shown standing in a grave — two playing *zurnas* (reed instruments) and one playing a *dhol* (drum). (This type of musical ensemble is commonly seen in Transcaucasia during weddings, funerals, and other special occasions.) Now Sayat-Nova's father, mother, and a third woman stand before *khachkars* (intricately carved stone stelae with cross designs), cloaked in white and carrying funerary wreaths, a mound of wool lying at their feet. In counterpoint to the specifically Armenian image of *khachkars*, the soundtrack includes the keening of Georgian women, saying approximately, "Your mother should have died, my child! Woe to your mother!"[79] Standing next to a *khachkar* with the three musicians and bobbing slightly to the rhythm of the music, Sayat-Nova's father lifts the white gauze hanging over the *khachkar* and reaches out to touch the stone surface.

The wind picks up as a group of women clutch loaves of bread and stand before the walls of a church, cypress trees swaying behind them. The metal cupola of a church flies in the air past them. (This detail was inspired by Parajanov's childhood memory of a strong gale blowing the cupola off of a church in Tbilisi.) Now clutching loaves of bread, Sayat-Nova's father and mother stand before *khachkars* as the wind blows everything away, including the wool piled at their feet. A group of monks chisel *khachkars* into the wall of an Armenian church while one man lowers his head and another turns to face the camera, pounding his chest with grief. The church cupola, torn off by the wind, lifts up and dashes against the rocks below. The last shot in the sequence returns to Haghpat, in wintertime; Sayat-Nova feels blindly at the walls in a niche, as if sleepwalking, and steps out into the snow.

This chapter as a whole stands out as among the most poignant and perfectly realized in all of Parajanov's work. Through a series of poetic images that speak with great emotional directness — cradle and grave; child, parents, and man; bread, wool, and wind — Parajanov conveys how a man, reaching the middle of his life, reflects on the loss of his one great love and the death of his parents.[80] He is forced to confront his own mortality and the ultimate impermanence of this world.

A further autobiographical subtext crops up through visual motifs that Parajanov reused from the aborted project *Kyiv Frescoes*. The pantomime with rings from the screen tests to that film, which represents the Man's failed marital relationship, here has become the interplay of rings between Sayat-Nova and Princess Ana during their initial romance. Similarly, the golden hair of the museum docent—and, more explicitly, of the Man's ex-wife in the script—now appears on Princess Ana in the dream sequence. The empty baby stroller, which likewise represented the failed relationship of the Man and his ex-wife, has transformed into a more complex symbol: the empty cradle that appears throughout Sayat-Nova's dream. In the tableau that parodies the Nativity, in which Princess Ana is substituted for the Virgin Mary as she prepares for childbirth, the empty cradle that Sayat-Nova holds up suggests the ultimately barren relationship between the poet and the princess. Elsewhere in the sequence, the same cradle is associated with nostalgia for lost childhood.

As is evident so far, architecture and other facets of material culture play a critical thematic role within the film. Parajanov does not merely use locations such as Sanahin and Haghpat as settings for dramatic action, he engages them in playful and creative ways that draw attention to their aesthetic qualities and not just their functionality. In one striking composition the young Arutin lies with his arms outstretched on the roof of the Sanahin Monastery, surrounded by open books whose pages are drying out under the sun. Toward the end of the film, in the section devoted to Sayat-Nova's old age, a group of bare-chested men stand on the roof of the thirteenth-century Saghmosavank Monastery, using scythes to mow the tufts of grass that have grown on it.

Handcrafted objects are in some ways as important as human characters, and they each carry unique histories. The sequence depicting the burial preparations for the Catholicos Ghazaros illustrates the complex ways such objects function within the film's aesthetic system as a whole. On the surface, it treats us to the beauty of Armenian liturgical music and ecclesiastical paraphernalia such as mitres, an intricately carved staff, a chalice, and liturgical fans. But beyond their intrinsic aesthetic value, these treasures of Etchmiadzin represent, in metaphoric terms, the long succession of catholicoi in the Armenian Church.

In a similar vein, at the beginning of the sequence depicting Erekle II's hunt, the soundtrack contains the famous Georgian hymn "Thou Art a Vineyard" ("Shen khar venakhi"). One of the oldest and most popular Georgian polyphonic hymns, it compares the Virgin Mary to a vineyard "newly in bloom." Ana stands before one of the masterpieces of medieval Georgian art—the lavishly detailed Khakuli icon triptych (eighth to twelfth century). Sayat-Nova himself stands before another iconostasis panel; this image is followed by a pectoral cross set with rubies.[81] As is often the case in the film, the choice of these particular images and music does not necessarily imply that they are somehow connected to the historical figure of Sayat-Nova. Rather, Parajanov is celebrating the artistic genius of the peoples of Transcaucasia and here the splendor of medieval Georgia in particular.

The bathing sequence contains a series of exquisitely composed still-life shots evoking the lavish culture of the royal baths: wooden bath shoes inlaid with mother-of-pearl, colorful pieces of cloth, arrangements of food recalling paintings by the Georgian folk artist Pirosmani, ornately patterned robes and shoes, and metal pitchers. The din on the soundtrack ironically emphasizes the absence of human figures in these shots. Indeed, this play of presence and absence is highly characteristic of Parajanov's mature style. One could argue further that these objects not only function within the dramatic world of the story and stand in for the characters associated with them, they acquire a life of their own. If *The Color of Pomegranates* represents in part a long vanished, alien past gazing back at us on the screen, these objects also gaze back at us as the sole remaining witnesses of that past.

Outtakes

Fortunately, most or all of the outtakes for *The Color of Pomegranates* appear to survive. In October 2006, over four hours of footage, including both screen tests and outtakes, were broadcast on the film program Fuori Orario on RAI 3 in Italy. Unfortunately, the shots were also arranged in more or less random order, but the broadcast enabled the public to see this rare and undeniably fascinating footage for the first time. The documentary filmmaker Levon Grigorian, who served as an assistant director on the film, also used some of the same outtakes in his half-hour documentary *Memories about "Sayat-Nova"* (*Vospominaniia o "Sayat-Nove,"* Armenfilm 2006). This section will describe some of the more noteworthy episodes in greater detail and place them within the context of the film as a whole.

An alternate opening to the Sanahin episode depicts the young Arutin arranging bunches of yellow flowers around the outline of a human figure carved on a gravestone, representing his early affinity for art and beauty. A rainstorm compels him to leave behind his creation, which gets washed away in a growing stream of water. Presumably, this scene was to continue with the images of rain flowing down the interior walls of the monastery in the finished film.

Other footage from the poet's childhood expands upon the episode at the Surb Gevorg Cathedral. In Arutin's imagination, everything around him disappears except for the Armenian cathedral, the Georgian cathedral (Sioni), and the mosque; stylized white miniature models of these three buildings appear on the ground. Saint George comes riding through on horseback, dwarfing the models, and invites the young Arutin to jump up and ride behind him on his horse.

A significant amount of discarded footage relates to the bathing sequence. One group of shots depicts various women in the nude or with cloths wrapped around them, lying or sitting on dark-colored blankets atop a wooden floor streaming with water, recalling the floor-washing imagery from *Kyiv Frescoes*. Metal pitchers and trays sit at their side and occupy otherwise empty blankets. The overhead angle of most of the shots and the women's stylized poses emphasize the flatness and strong graphic design of the compositions, bringing to mind paintings by Matisse. Another shot (most likely filmed at Sanahin) depicts a nude woman, perhaps the young Princess Ana, standing on a metal tray with scalloped edges that alludes to Botticelli's painting *The Birth of Venus*. A pair of female attendants dressed in long robes and head-coverings wash the woman with scrubbing mitts. An alternate take shows the woman with a cloth draped around her waist. Thus Parajanov initially envisioned a much more prominent place for the beauty of the female body than is the case with the finished film. However, it is unlikely that most of the shots, with their full frontal nudity, would have passed the censors regardless of their painterly merits.

Another sequence set at the baths depicts King Erekle wrapped in a red cloth printed with an elaborate paisley design, standing proudly next to his throne, a pomegranate in his left hand. Two attendants stand to his right, wrapped in white cloths with identical paisley patterns and bearing trays of fruit. Erekle holds out the pomegranate, squeezes it and gazes down at it thoughtfully, and in one shot sniffs at it longingly. The most amusing shot in this sequence depicts the king's attendants sitting together on rug-covered platforms, rocking their heads gently back and forth and tossing pomegranates on the floor as if in a game of lawn bowling.

In the chapters pertaining to Sayat-Nova as a monk, one discarded scene depicts him bathing as part of his induction to the Haghpat Monastery. Although he wears a cloth in front, when he turns his back to the camera his nude buttocks are visible. All the while, another monk peers down from the grassy roof (Fig. 4.8). This composition, according to Levon Abrahamian, was inspired by a medieval Armenian miniature depicting Christ's baptism. In addition to that possible artistic allusion, the shot deliberately echoes the bathing episode from Sayat-Nova's childhood. Abrahamian, who performed the role of the monk peering down, recalls that Parajanov decided not to use the shot because the homoerotic content was too obvious.[82]

By far the most striking footage dropped from this section of the film is

Figure 4.8. A discarded scene of Sayat-Nova bathing (*The Color of Pomegranates*). Courtesy of the Sergei Parajanov Museum.

the scene that Parajanov jokingly called "Sayat-Nova's Night Pollution" (i.e., nocturnal emission), which according to the script would have been part of the longer dream sequence. It appears to have been filmed in its entirety, though he ultimately decided against including it. Based on the surviving footage, it is possible to present a tentative reconstruction. In the sanctuary of the church, Sayat-Nova pulls back an altar curtain to reveal the iconostasis and altar; the setting is populated by three angels dressed in lace, wearing stag antlers on their backs for wings and lit candles on the antler points. One of the angels hands Sayat-Nova a large chalice, which he carries off. As Sayat-Nova walks through the darkened monastery, he encounters more angels. One of them gives him a llama, which he leads into a corridor. Framed in a doorway, he kneels beside the llama and milks it, filling up the chalice. A vision of Princess Ana dressed in black with a piece of black fur on her chest is now standing in the doorway. Sayat-Nova approaches her from behind and hurls the milk at her. It splashes against a glass pane in the doorway behind the princess and runs down the glass, obscuring Sayat-Nova. As he smears his hands over the glass pane behind her, she tears away the piece of black wool on her chest to reveal another piece of wool, this time specked with white. While the sequence is certainly memorable, it was cut either for reasons of length or because the sexual symbolism was too obvious.

Additional footage connected to the dream sequence develops the empty cradle motif, which presumably represents the barren nature of Sayat-Nova and Ana's relationship. In a series of shots various figures pose on the same set papered with antique book pages: blackamoors, young maidens, musicians, and twirling cherubs. Visually, the shots are all linked by the rocking of the gilded cradle. The culmination of this series of images would have been the parody of the Nativity mentioned earlier, in which all of these figures appear together within a single composition. There is also more extensive footage of Sayat-Nova pursuing the cupola that has been torn from the church, as it blows past various groups of people and through a graveyard full of *khachkars*.

With regard to the poet's old age, a significant amount of discarded footage pertains to the poet's visit to Akhtala, where he finds the font dry and the Virgin Mary defaced by an invader's arrow. Besides the aforementioned shot in which the mother's face replaces that of the Virgin Mary, another series of shots create a stunning trick effect in which the Virgin's face falls from the fresco into a pool of water below. Her face appears to be falling directly toward the camera until it hits the surface of the water and ripples spread out from it. Considering the prodigious visual artistry in this and so many other outtakes, the footage deserves to be restored and shown alongside the film.

Critical Reception

Relatively few Soviet critics reviewed *The Color of Pomegranates* after its 1969 release in Armenia and its very limited Soviet-wide distribution the following year. Sabir Rizaev published a substantial essay on it in *Literaturnaia Armeniia* (*Literary Armenia*), in which he bemoaned the lack of critical dialogue about the film. Among other things, he argued that the film's change of title and the prefatory text declaring that the film depicted a "collective image of an Armenian medieval poet" both indicated that the film ultimately "never succeeded at revealing the real Sayat-Nova."[83] Rizaev further hinted at the film's problematic treatment of gender: "But the main thing is that the spiritual anguish of man in medieval Armenia, as the literature, the astonishing miniatures, and the national architecture all attest, is full of poetic passion, which was always remarkably transparent, enviously strict, and emphatically manly [*muzhestvennyi*]."[84] In contrast, he characterized the passions of the film's hero as "luxurious," a quality which he argued was alien to the era.[85] On the positive side, he singled out the film's painterly visual style and described certain shots as "poetry in composition and light," invoking the praise of the painter Martiros Saryan. He further asserted that regardless of one's response to the film, exposure to its "exceptional artistic culture" would "enrich" viewers and encourage them to "relate to the beautiful with greater care." In conclusion, he wrote: "To know how to instill such a thing in people means to be in the ranks of outstanding creators. And with this facet of his talent Sergei Parajanov has entered the sphere of truly great cinema."[86]

Mikhail Bleiman, who as mentioned earlier had served as one of the script readers for the Main Script-Editorial Board in Moscow, was notably less sympathetic in his essay "Archaists or Innovators?" published in *Iskusstvo kino*.[87] As one of the Soviet film industry's most well-established scriptwriters, his opinion carried a great deal of weight with the authorities. In the essay, he argued for the existence of an "anonymous" school of Soviet filmmakers without "territorial links" — that is, across republics — whose point of origin he posited as Parajanov's *Shadows of Forgotten Ancestors*. (In other words, the poetic school.) Common features that Bleiman identified were "laconism," heavy use of allegories or parables, a visual style influenced by the fine arts with a tendency toward static images, and a "predilection for ethnographic, exotic-historical material."[88] The sum total of these features contributed to the impression of "archaism," as Bleiman called it.

For Bleiman, these films tended to "deny the experience accumulated by cinema" and return it to an "illustrative" quality.[89] While he did not think that this in itself was necessarily problematic, he argued that the filmmakers in question were ultimately unable to remain within a strict framework of allegory or parable because of their own "baggage" as contemporary artists. Thus, in his view, the metaphors or allegories in *The Color of Pomegranates* at times became "arbitrary and not always comprehensible." As a result Parajanov's film, like other works of the poetic school, suffered from a "lack of compositional unity."[90] He summed up: "The film *The Color of Pomegranates*, for all its indisputable talent, has plunged the 'school' into a critical state. In this film, as is natural, the rigorous allegorical quality of the parable was exploded from within by the unrestricted and arbitrary subjectivism of the metaphor. And it was not a denial of principles, but their logical end."[91] While Bleiman's criticisms of *The Color of Pomegranates* are not without merit, he clearly intended to attack the ideological foundations of the poetic school by further arguing that such films "disavow realism" and fall back on "archaic thinking." His choice of loaded terms such as "subjectivism," "disavow[ing] realism," and "archaic thinking" make it clear that he viewed the poetic school and Parajanov in particular as alien to the core tenets of Socialist Realism.

For all of the blood and toil behind *The Color of Pomegranates*, and despite Parajanov's thoroughgoing attempt to connect the private world of the artist with the broader history and culture of the people, his most ambitious film had emerged bruised from conflicts with the authorities in both Armenia and, more damagingly, in Moscow. In addition to limiting its overall distribution within the Soviet Union as a whole, Goskino refused to allow the film to be shown abroad. Only in the mid-1970s, while Parajanov sat in prison, did it appear in the West in the form of a bootleg print.

5

Silent Years

Unproduced Scripts, 1967–1973

During this period Parajanov wrote some of his most significant scripts, among them *The Demon (Demon)*, *Confession (Ispoved')*, and *The Slumbering Palace (Dremliushchii dvorets)*. Three projects — *Intermezzo, Inga,* and *A Miracle in Odense (Chudo v Odense)* — went into preproduction. He was unable to realize them because of conflicts with the authorities that came to a head with his December 1973 arrest and subsequent imprisonment on politically motivated charges of homosexuality. This chapter describes the most significant projects undertaken during this period and their place within his work as a whole. It also offers a detailed account of his increasing conflicts with the authorities leading up to the 1973 arrest.

Confession

From a literary standpoint, the autobiographical *Confession* is Parajanov's richest script. In it he weaves enigmatic, often subtly ironic character observations with memories and dreamlike reveries akin to Fellini's *8½*. The loose, associative structure — not unlike what he had attempted in *Kyiv Frescoes* — makes the script difficult to follow at times, and the significance of some images is not always clear, but it achieves undeniable emotional power.

Most sources date the original version of the script to 1969, relying on

Parajanov's own, likely embellished account: "In 1969 I had double pneumonia. I was dying in a hospital and asked the doctor to prolong my life at least six more days. In these few days I wrote the script."[1] Despite his claims, the Parajanov Museum in Yerevan possesses an incomplete typescript draft marked "Yerevan — 1967." This would date the earliest surviving draft instead to when he was working on *The Color of Pomegranates* and *Hakob Hovnatanyan*, further emphasizing how this particular period was not only one of newfound artistic mastery and confidence, but of self-discovery. This draft lacks the auction passage, described below, that opens later versions and begins instead at the section entitled "Tbilisi, April 1941."

The published script opens with a brief prologue in which Parajanov returns after a long absence to Tbilisi in 1966. He visits the Old Veri District Cemetery, his ancestors' resting place, already shut down for conversion into a park of culture and rest. The visit sparks recollections that form the main body of the script. The first section comprises a surreal auction in which Parajanov himself — here named the Man as in *Kyiv Frescoes* — sits alone with the auctioneer in a decaying hangar, buying up objects from his past. Some of these include: a Singer sewing machine, a favorite object that turns up in several of his films; his mother's "flared fur coat [*shuba-klyosh*] from dyed French desman with a surplice collar"; "a white donkey from Etchmiadzin and a purple policeman"; "a blank white canvas in a gilded frame and a young nurse in a white smock with fresh, bared breasts"; Madame Germaine's "extremely rare" French accent; and the "belly of a piano [which], stood upright, resembles a harp." In the next scene, the Man strolls down the streets of Tbilisi with his parade of auction purchases. Parajanov writes: "This procession seemed neither funny nor strange in the middle of the daytime city, bathed in sunshine."[2] Besides underscoring the script's surreal tone, this suggests that Parajanov views Tbilisi as a city in which surreal juxtapositions seem an everyday occurrence.

The next major section focuses on childhood impressions of his first encounter with death, namely his cousin Vera succumbing to tuberculosis and the subsequent funeral. The episode opens with a tragicomic depiction of his aunt Anichka struggling in vain against two omens of death: a hen that crows like a rooster and a cherry tree that blossoms in the middle of the winter. Like much of *Confession*, this passage surely counts among Parajanov's best work thanks to its evocative and emotionally compelling details:

> Aunt Anichka, a woman with a goiter, in a black sateen dress, overtook the black brood hen that crowed like a rooster.

A black stain, over which black down fluttered and flew up, remained on the white snow.

Then aunt Anichka grabbed an axe.

The neighbors stood on the balconies and demanded that she chop down the cherry tree. The cherry tree that bore white blossoms in the winter.

Aunt Anichka's husband, Uncle Vaso, a chain-smoking tailor, attempted to snatch the axe away from her. Galvanized basins toppled over, issuing strange sounds. Anichka cursed, wept, choked up with tears, and broke loose from the tailor Vaso's hands.

Vera, the tailor's youngest daughter, looked out from behind the smoke-stained curtain.

Vera was constantly being taken away to Abastuman.[3] She rarely went to school. Vera was tall, beautiful, taller than anyone in the class, with deep blue shadows under her eyes. Vera, in flat patent leather shoes, with a knapsack behind her back, would appear on the street, and the anxious gaze of Anichka, Vera's mother, would follow her. The children in school stubbornly spread a cock-and-bull story that Vera had eaten a dog.[4] In class Vera sat at a single desk.[5] A large black rep ribbon emphasized her paleness and beauty.[6]

Here and elsewhere in the script, Parajanov employs elements of magical realism, especially the literal representation of superstitions and folk beliefs, to portray the collision between urban, modernized Tbilisi and the beliefs of an older cultural system.

The next two sections continue Parajanov's dreams and memories of childhood. First comes the death of aunt Siran, who sewed shirts for him as a child; this section includes the overtly dreamlike, Felliniesque image of Siran sitting in her coffin and sewing a shirt. His mother's fur coat then sparks recollections about his family's experiences during the Stalin years. His father, who was relatively well off as the owner of an antiques commission shop, was jailed more than once by the authorities and their home was frequently searched (Fig. 5.1). His mother, anxious to avoid public displays of wealth, "only wore the coat twice: the first time when it snowed in Tbilisi, and the second at my father's funeral."[7]

Years, later, the Man returns to Tbilisi for his father's funeral. His father's grave is not located with their ancestors at the Old Veri district cemetery but instead at Saburtalo, a windy plateau that was the site of much new construction in Tbilisi. Both his hat and that of his father, which he had placed on the grave, are blown away by the wind, an image that recalls a similar scene from

Figure 5.1. *Search of the Premises* (1988). Collage-sketch for *Confession*. Courtesy of the Sergei Parajanov Museum.

the shooting script of *Kyiv Frescoes*. Moving back in time to his childhood, the Man visits his jailed father at the Metekhi castle, which had been converted into a prison during the Tsarist era. His father gives him a toy horse made from masticated bread crumbs.

Now awakening from his dream, the Man finds a golden hair in his mouth — that of his ex-wife, some ten years after their divorce. In a flashback, the Man and his newlywed wife ride on the train to Tbilisi where his mother welcomes Svetlana into the household. While playing the piano and singing *Ave Maria*, Svetlana loses her wedding ring in the piano — an omen of their future divorce. This image also recalls the screen tests for *Kyiv Frescoes*, specifically the panto-mime with wedding rings staged next to the open body of a piano.

In another humorous episode evoking the lively, now vanished culture of Old Tbilisi, Parajanov describes the funeral of a *kurtan* — a pad made from string, straw, and a piece of rug. (Kurds typically wore *kurtans* on their backs in order to carry heavy items.) When three Kurds place the *kurtan* on a stretcher to have it buried, a fight breaks out between them and the police cart them away. Parajanov further links Tbilisi's colorful past with the city of the present by setting this episode outside of Laghidze, a famous soft drink establishment that dates back to the late nineteenth century. Today, he writes, "The grandsons and great-grandsons of the 'kurtan' wear light nylon raincoats and Dacron, they eat *khachapuri* and wash it down with rose water, like everyone in Tbilisi."[8] Another specter from the past is the ninety-year-old Madame Germaine from France, who sells moth-eaten artifacts from the belle époque to collectors and to the Georgia Film Studio for period dramas. Now that she has nothing left, Parajanov offers to buy up her impeccable French pronunciation during the same auction that opened the script.

Shifting focus to his ancestral land of Armenia, he recounts a 1966 trip to Bjni, where he has dinner at the home of a priest.[9] He is moved by the simplic-ity of everyday life there, and spiritual longings awaken within him. He writes of the dinner: "For the first time in my life — consecrated food. Everyday food, but . . . gaining a biblical sacrament."[10] Ironically, the priest drinks Borjomi mineral water (i.e., from Georgia) even though Bjni is known for its own mineral water. This kind of wry observation often enlivens Parajanov's scripts about contemporary life, making it all the more a pity that he was unable to realize any of them. What begins as a seemingly realistic episode at the priest's house takes on an increasingly surreal tone as it progresses. The priest gnaws and then swallows whole bones at the dinner table. Three men enter, each displaying a different color painted on his palm. Parajanov imagines that they are grave-diggers who have come for him.

In the final section, he takes an airplane from Etchmiadzin back to Tbilisi. Visiting the Old Veri cemetery, he witnesses bulldozers destroying his family's tombs. The ghosts of his ancestors leave the cemetery to pull one last prank on the city's living residents, placing an armoire on the funicular line: "And in total silence, an empty armoire with an open door arrives at the top of the funicular line and comes to a halt."[11] This enigmatic image beautifully encapsulates both the conflict between modernization and tradition and the lingering traces of the past.

In the Epilogue, Parajanov — "the Man seeking the truth" — has died, but the strange and fantastical world of his childhood memories lives on. His mother asks the Armenian priest performing the funeral service to re-sanctify her marriage, claiming that she had only divorced her husband Iosif to save the house and fur coat, presumably when he was jailed. The priest refuses. Parajanov writes: "On the holiday of Surp-Sarkis [Saint Sargis] the Man's mother brought a white cockerel, which she had purchased from a Tatar woman in Shulaver, to the cathedral for sacrifice. According to custom, before the ritual the sacrificial cockerel is supposed to crow. The rooster that Madame Parajanov bought from the Tatar woman in Shulaver laid a pink egg in the cathedral. Amazed and concerned by what had happened, Madame Parajanov consulted the Filatov Clinic in Odessa with a request for an eye operation."[12]

This last passage represents the culmination of multiple themes underlying the script and Parajanov's work as a whole. First, like the armoire on the funicular, it extends the magical realist view of Tbilisi culture into the present day. Secondly, as Cora Tsereteli points out in her notes, the Georgian village of Shulaver is located near the borders of Armenia and Azerbaijan.[13] In that regard, the location signifies Transcaucasia as a multiethnic region, a point further emphasized by the Tatar woman who sells his mother the cockerel. Lastly, as with the black hen crowing like a rooster, the image of a rooster laying a pink egg reflects the theme of androgyny or crossing gender boundaries that recurs frequently in Parajanov's films after *Shadows of Forgotten Ancestors*. The richness of invention, densely layered imagery, and autobiographical resonance that run throughout *Confession* make the ultimate failure of his lifetime dream to realize this project all the more regrettable.

Ara the Fair

Another important script from this period is *Ara the Fair* (*Ara prekrasnyi* in Russian; *Ara Geghets'ik* in Armenian). Written in 1968 (according to the Sergei Parajanov Museum), it is based on an ancient Armenian legend relating to the historical kingdom of Urartu, which lasted from approximately 860 to 585 BC and was centered in the region around Lake Van in present-day Turkey. Parajanov's script is inspired by the 1946 verse drama by Nairi Zarian in its Russian translation by Maria Petrovykh, and even uses some of that work's dialogue verbatim.[14]

Ara, the king of Urartu, is renowned for his handsomeness. Shamiram (Sammuramat, also commonly known as Semiramis), the beautiful but arrogant and treacherous queen of Assyria, falls in love with him when he arrives with his caravan in Nineveh. When Shamiram declares his gifts a "tribute," Ara takes offense and leaves her court. Deciding that she wants Ara all for herself, she has her husband King Ninos beheaded. However, Ara refuses to abandon Nuard, his wife, for Shamiram and is drawn into battle with Assyria. Shamiram orders him brought to her alive. When Ara is felled by an arrow, Shamiram brings his body to Nineveh in the vain hope of resurrecting him.

Besides the dramatic appeal of the legend itself, Parajanov was no doubt attracted to the opportunity to recreate the pagan world of ancient Mesopotamia. In the beginning of the script, he establishes a strong visual impression of the court at Nineveh:

> Nineveh — the capital of Assyria.
> A greenhouse on the roof of the royal palace . . .
> Philodendrons, coconut palms, and a fern under umbrellas made from bull
> bladders . . .
> The king and queen's throne in the image of crowned, winged bulls.
> Large fans swing back and forth . . . and rust-colored herds of monkeys
> jump in fright.
> Shamiram cries out with a monkey's cry . . .
> Shamiram tosses rust-colored dates and olives to the monkeys . . .
> Shamiram is in an olive-colored tunic of fine leather.
> . . . Shamiram with an olive-colored face . . .
> . . . Shamiram with big, olive-colored eyes . . .
> . . . Shamiram with a cascade of olive-colored hair . . .[15]

In a parallel passage he introduces the caravan of Ara and a set of visual motifs associated with the kingdom of Urartu:

> Urartu!
> The lilac-colored organs of the cliffs . . . Lilac-colored haze . . .
> The lilac-colored waterfalls of the lilac-colored mountains . . .
> The caravan of King Ara, nicknamed the Fair . . .

Lilac-colored camels bearing gifts for the Assyrian queen . . .
The king's troops are armored in metal and sheepskin . . .
Herds of bulls, sheep . . . herds of gazelles . . . with bells tied to their horns
and tails . . .
The herds are crowned with garlands of blossoming pomegranate . . .
Bales made from hand-woven rugs . . .
Bales with arms and adornments for kings . . .[16]

Clearly, Parajanov is attempting to create a systematic dramaturgy of color. He also sets up an interesting contrast between agricultural and pastoral societies through these images.

On the whole, the script contains far more dramatic dialogue and is more conventional from a narrative standpoint than the subsequent scripts *The Slumbering Palace* or *The Demon*; thus it would seem a more likely candidate for successful adaptation. Tsereteli claims that the script ultimately was not produced because Goskino of Armenia was skittish about dealing with Parajanov after its protracted conflict with Goskino USSR over *The Color of Pomegranates*.[17] Another probable factor was the project's expense. *The Color of Pomegranates* had already been unusually costly for an Armenian feature film and did not bring in the returns they had hoped because of the impasse with Moscow. *Ara the Fair* would have required constructing sets for the sumptuous Assyrian and Urartian courts, to say nothing of large numbers of extras and costumes. Given Parajanov's tenuous position at that time, it is unlikely that the Armenian authorities would have received much material support from Moscow for the project, even if they had agreed to produce it.

The Slumbering Palace

The unfilmed 1969 script *The Slumbering Palace* (*Dremliushchii dvorets*) is a loose adaptation of Alexander Pushkin's 1824 narrative poem *The Fountain of Bakhchisaray*. Set in Crimea, Pushkin's poem depicts a Tatar king, Khan Giray, whose harem includes women captured in military conquests. Maria, a beautiful young Polish princess who pines for her lost family and homeland, has captured the Khan's imagination. Disturbed by her grief, the Khan allows her to live apart from the rest of the harem. Zarema, another wife who was brought from Georgia, has converted to Islam and was the Khan's favorite before Maria's arrival. Out of jealousy, Zarema threatens to kill Maria if she continues to steal Khan Giray's heart. Later we learn only that Maria has passed away and that Zarema has been drowned in punishment, implying that the latter has carried out her threat.

The poem ends with the narrator visiting the abandoned palace in the present and seeing the apparition of a young woman, perhaps Maria or Zarema. The poem's imagery is redolent with Orientalist motifs, including a capricious and despotic ruler, harem intrigues, eunuchs, and the Orient as a place of luxurious lassitude and untamed passions. It is not difficult to see why the poem appealed to Parajanov, with its vivid narrative and exotic trappings. As mentioned earlier, it was also likely inspired by the Armenian artist Vardges Sureniants's exquisitely detailed illustrations for the 1899 Russian edition of the poem.

The legendary "Fountain of Tears" in fact has a concrete historical basis: it was commissioned in 1764 by Khan Qırım Giray, who ruled Crimea from 1758 to 1764. He dedicated it to a woman named Dilara, about whom nothing is known. The legend that inspired Pushkin's version holds that Dilara was a Polish noblewoman named Maria Potocka. The fountain is believed to have been located originally next to Dilara's mausoleum, though in 1783 it was moved to what is now called the Fountain Court inside the palace.[18]

Parajanov's script opens with a section entitled "Chronicle of the Times," which suggests a series of establishing shots of the Bakhchisaray palace and its interior features, finally closing in on the burial vault of Khan Giray's wife. The main theme here is of the palace as an unchanging entity. The second section, entitled "Chronicle of the Eighteenth to Twentieth Centuries," shifts the focus from place and architecture to historical artifacts and *objets d'art* that are undergoing restoration. As with *Hakob Hovnatanyan* and *The Color of Pomegranates*, Parajanov does not simply admire such objects for their craftsmanship or their historical and aesthetic value. Rather, they represent a material link between past and present, and serve as vehicles for us to imagine the past and bring it back to life. In addition to expected objects such as "chain mail, a helmet, and couters of Selim-Giray [*sic*] in a kerosene solution" and "an armchair of Catherine II," Parajanov slyly tosses in the image of "a jeweler fastening turquoise to a chastity belt."[19]

The next section, entitled "Bakhchisaray Palace," depicts the location in the present day, mobbed with buses and tourists. Pushkin himself materializes in a frock coat and top hat, an element of deliberate fantasy not unlike the Infanta Margarita stepping out from the painting in *Kyiv Frescoes*:

> The morning resembles dusk . . .
> In the amorous Khan's palace the electric light bulbs went on . . .
> Pushkin looked at the electric light . . .
> In his hands Pushkin held a wet red peach . . .
> The wind tugged at the hem of his frock coat . . .

Pushkin wrapped his collar tighter around himself and stood under the downpour . . .

In the harem, the museum curator put pails on the rugs . . .

Water dripped from the ceiling . . . Water dripped in the Empress's apartments, in the mosque, in the restorers' workshop. Water dripped in the Fountain of Tears . . .[20]

The sudden downpour and dripping water recall the rainstorm and waterlogged manuscripts at the Sanahin Monastery in *The Color of Pomegranates*. This and other passages in the script are also noteworthy for their playful intermingling of past and present, a theme that recurs periodically throughout Parajanov's films. The closest points of comparison are perhaps the documentary shorts *Hakob Hovnatanyan* and *Arabesques on the Theme of Pirosmani*.

A subsequent image of Pushkin burying the peach pit in the ground segues to a brief flashback of him with Ekaterina Andreevna Karamzina — the historian Nikolai Karamzin's second wife, with whom he was infatuated. Parajanov concocts this episode inside a Saint Petersburg bookshop as the supposed source of inspiration for Pushkin's poem. When some books fall from an upper shelf, Ekaterina Karamzina catches one and reads aloud from it the phrase "the Fountain of Tears." This cuts to Catherine the Great visiting Khan Giray's palace. Field Marshal Alexander Suvorov issues a decree to save the fountain from destruction; soldiers dismantle it and move it into the courtyard. Shifting back to the present, the script depicts tourists photographing the location. Afterward, the ghost of Pushkin appears mysteriously in the developed photographs.

It is only with the section entitled "Selim-Giray" that the actual narrative of the Pushkin poem begins. Yet even here Parajanov liberally intersperses quotes and paraphrases from Pushkin with his own eccentric details. In the section entitled "The Eunuch," eunuchs drug stallions with opium smoke in order to facilitate their castration. One eunuch blacksmith rivets shut a chastity belt on a Tatar girl. Parajanov also expands the story of Maria's life in Poland before her capture by the Tatars.

The fundamental problem that any filmmaker attempting to adapt Pushkin's poem must confront is the deliberate ambiguity surrounding Maria's death, as mentioned earlier. Not surprisingly, for dramatic effect Parajanov chooses to implicate Zarema more explicitly. He further sets Zarema's confrontation with Maria during the Shia religious holiday of Ashura in the section of the script entitled "The Passion." This most likely would have aroused criticism from both Muslims and the Soviet authorities, though it would have been visually striking:

Shahsey-Vahsey[21]

The Tatars lit fires . . .

A Mullah threw fire from a minaret.

Warriors stripped down to the skin.

Women tore up black cloth and placed gold at the remains of Ali . . .

They brought fire to the mosque . . .

Warriors sharpened scimitars on a stone . . .

They put stones in bulls' bladders . . .

And someone was the first to cry out—

Shahsey-Vahsey!

And in an instant the bull bladders were battered against the backs of Tatars.

A scimitar split open a brow . . .

The Mohammedan moon was carved on their backs . . .

The moon bled profusely . . .

Shahsey-Vahsey!

The holiday of Ali!

Women tore up black cloth and placed it at the remains of Ali!

Selim-Giray, having bared his chest, beats himself with whips . . .

Giray's warriors repeat the rite . . .

In a gilded cage hens took wing, roosters took wing!

Leopards snarled . . . The mullah cried out . . . And the women thrashed themselves against the rocks.

Shahsey-Vahsey!

The holiday of Ali!

Giray's wives tugged at their chests and the eunuch, stripped down to the skin, beat himself with stones.[22]

As suggested by the use of repeated words and phrases in the script, Parajanov consciously associates cinematic repetition with ritual. One can find parallels to this in *The Color of Pomegranates* (the triple sacrifice of rams) and *The Legend of the Surami Fortress* (Vardo's prayers and sacrificial offerings). It is not just that repetition is a fundamental component of ritual itself; rather, the films strive to represent the incantations and hieratic movement typically associated with ritual, and to capture the timelessness or altered perception of time that is often part of the ritual process.

Returning more closely to Pushkin's narrative, the script then depicts Maria's funeral, Zarema pushed over a cliff in retribution, and Selim-Giray weeping over Maria's grave. The Epilogue, in contrast, is dense with freely imaginative, associative imagery. The image of tourists consuming fruit resonates on multiple levels; first, the theme of bloodshed and sacrifice in Pushkin's poem (and amplified by Parajanov in the "Shahsey-Vahsey" episode) is echoed ironically by the image of the tourists splashed with red juice from eating grapes. That, together with the comparison of the white sides of the buses with movie screens, suggests that Parajanov is also commenting self-reflexively on the consumption of the tragic tale by the movie-going public. The images of "gilt edge" and "blue broadcloth," combined with the closing lines quoted from Pushkin, further draw attention to Pushkin's poem itself as a literary artifact. At the same time, they echo the earlier episode with Ekaterina Karamzina in the bookshop, Parajanov's imagined source of inspiration for the poem.[23]

Tsereteli characterizes the ending as "not completely written out [and] sketchy in places."[24] One could argue instead that the script was more or less finished and that Parajanov deliberately made the ending laconic and fragmentary since it recapitulates motifs that have already been expressed earlier. Certainly, in its present state it would not be out of keeping with Parajanov's style during that period. For all its fragmentary quality, the final section beautifully ties together the work as a whole. Still, the script in this form mostly likely would have made only a medium-length film like *Kyiv Frescoes*, as opposed to a full-length feature.

During this time Parajanov began to correspond regularly with Viktor Shklovsky, who had taken an interest in his work; Shklovsky read and commented on some of his scripts, and even offered to collaborate on subsequent projects. In a letter dated December 15, 1969, Shklovsky wrote: "The script is interesting, motley, and written in such a way that it seems difficult for any studio to pass it. The alternation of the chronicle and Pushkin's theme and the combination of different styles will certainly lead immediately to serious objections."[25] Given what had happened to *Kyiv Frescoes* and *The Color of Pomegranates*, it is not difficult to see why Shklovsky felt that Parajanov's provocative take on a classic work of Russian literature would never pass muster with the censors.

But perhaps even more problematic than Parajanov's poetic approach was his very choice of subject matter, as Shklovsky argued: "The theme of Crimea is the sole national theme closed to us, because there are no Crimean Tatars in Ukraine . . . The Fountain of Tears weeps for Crimea's past — a cruel past, treacherous, but tragically terminated. The script will not pass."[26] Here Shklovsky is referring to the wholesale deportation of the Crimean Tatars during World War II. Of course, Pushkin's poem was not banned and the Soviets continued to publish editions of it, including in the form of children's books.

Moreover, they continued to stage Boris Asafiev's ballet based on the poem and to reprint music from it; excerpts from the ballet were even filmed for the dance anthology *Russian Ballet Masters* directed by Gerbert Rappaport (*Mastera russkogo baleta,* Lenfilm 1953). The real problem, as Shklovsky most likely perceived it, was that the concrete historical dimension of Parajanov's script—particularly the present-day scenes of the palace as a tourist destination—inevitably raised the question of the Crimean Tatars' historical fate.[27] Thus *The Slumbering Palace* proved yet another example of the complications Parajanov encountered when attempting to work in his preferred mode of poetic cinema using historical or quasi-ethnographic subjects.

Intermezzo

No projects were forthcoming at the Dovzhenko Film Studio, and less than a year later Parajanov's frustration began to show more openly. On July 14, 1970, he submitted a written application to Sviatoslav Ivanov, the chair of Goskino of Ukraine, in which he declared: "For six years I haven't been making films in Ukraine!!! I request that you immediately and unconditionally transfer me to the Main Administration of Moscow, from where I will be assigned to a permanent residence and work."[28] Parajanov's pleas were evidently heard, because around that time Petro Shelest, the first secretary of the Communist Party of Ukraine, summoned him for a meeting and the two discussed the possibility of making a film about contemporary Ukrainian farmers, provisionally entitled *The Earth . . . Again the Earth!* The title and subject matter suggest that the project was intended as an homage to Dovzhenko. Parajanov conducted location scouting at some Ukrainian collective farms, though a script or other detailed plans for the production have not surfaced. His disparaging reference to the project as a "meaningless little statement" during his fateful December 1971 speech in Minsk indicates that he did not take it seriously, but rather viewed it as something mainly to please Shelest and other authorities.[29]

Parajanov also received the green light on a project he valued far more highly: an adaptation of Mykhailo Kotsiubynsky's 1908 short story "Intermezzo," considered by many critics to be that author's masterpiece. "Intermezzo" is a dense prose work that anticipates the stream-of-consciousness technique in the way it attempts to capture its protagonist's thought process. As the title indicates, Kotsiubynsky deliberately invokes music as an artistic model—not just in terms of its lyrical expression of the protagonist's emotions, but also through his use of repetition to create both a sense of rhythm and an overall structure. The descriptions of nature, especially the fields in the Ukrainian countryside, further point to the influence of painting and the Impressionist school in particular.

The first-person narrative has little in the way of a traditional plot: a writer, unnamed but clearly Kotsiubynsky himself, hoping to escape "the iron hand of the city" and the human misery that continually plagues his consciousness, rides the train out to his country house. The main conceit of the story is of the writer as a musical instrument on whose strings "the woe of others" is played. In that respect, the story is centrally concerned with the artist's engagement with the political realities around him. When he is alone at night in the country house, the protagonist is seemingly haunted by specters of his fellow people. More specifically, he is troubled by the Tsarist repressions in the wake of the 1905 Revolution. At the same time, he acknowledges his own occasional apathy:

> You there, have had your blood run out through a little hole drilled by a sol-
> dier's bullet and you, bare bones, you were covered with white sacks, swung
> at the end of ropes, then thrown into badly covered ditches to be dug up by
> dogs . . . You look at me reproachfully, and you are right. I once read that they
> hanged twelve of you at a time, a whole dozen, and I yawned. Another time I
> reacted to a report about a row of white sacks by eating a ripe plum. I took up a
> fine juicy plum in my fingers . . . and felt a pleasant sweet taste in my mouth . . .
> You see, I do not even blush; my face is as white as yours, for dread has drained
> all my blood. There is not a single drop of hot blood in me even for those living
> corpses among whom you wander like bloody specters. Begone! I am tired.[30]

Surrounded by nature, the earth's bounty, the protagonist eventually finds peace and renewal, but it is only temporary—an intermezzo. When a peasant approaches him in a field and tells of what he has endured as a consequence of participating in a revolt, it reminds the protagonist again of human misery. Kotsiubynsky concludes: "Farewell! I am going among people. My soul is ready, its strings are tensed and tuned. It is playing already."[31]

One can easily see why the story appealed to Parajanov, what with its painterly and musical influences and its thematic focus on the artist's way of perceiving the world, his creative process, and his relationship to society as a whole. Presumably, the story also would have appealed to Soviet authorities because it directly concerns the political engagement of the artist. However, it poses inherent problems for film adaptation since it contains very little in the way of dramatic incident. Only one other character besides the narrator—the peasant he meets in the field—is developed to any extent.

The writer Pavlo Zahrebelny, who had helped out on the script for *Kyiv Frescoes*, was brought in at an early stage to collaborate on *Intermezzo*. The first memos in the Goskino file, which date to May 1971, list him as a coauthor.[32] Parajanov and Zahrebelny's script expands considerably upon the original story, unambiguously representing the narrator as Kotsiubynsky himself and depicting his life in turbulent prerevolutionary Kyiv. Although the Script-Editorial Board of Goskino of Ukraine cites Kotsiubynsky's story "The Name-Day Gift" ("Podarok na imeniny") as an additional source of inspiration for the script in their memo dated May 17, 1971, the surviving drafts do not contain any plot elements or imagery from that story, nor do Kotsiubynsky's other stories appear to be the source of the imagery that was not taken directly from "Intermezzo." In all probability, most of the expanded material was simply invented by Zahrebelny and Parajanov. The shooting script lists the poet Mykola Bazhan as a consultant, so he may have been a source of ideas as well.

At the beginning of the script, the character of the Writer—identified directly in one draft as Kotsiubynsky himself—is under continuous surveillance by the Tsarist secret police. Yet in spite of political repression, social change burgeons everywhere. At the Cathedral of the Transfiguration, the Writer witnesses a rendezvous between a "poet," a "composer," and a "worker." The script later reveals that this worker has written a hymn to the revolution, which will be set to music by the composer and disseminated as an underground song. A legless cripple selling newspapers at the church slips in a pamphlet containing a quote from Lenin. The Writer's children tear out pages from magazines containing images of the Romanovs and the Russo-Japanese War, fold them into paper "pigeons" and drop them from the balcony of his apartment, provoking the ire of a police officer.

Yet Parajanov and Zahrebelny's script is not just about politics; its vivid details evoke the sights and textures of the era as a whole. For example, in the "Madame Dyshel" shop, seagull-shaped hats are sold to capitalize on the success of Chekhov's play. Later, when the writer boards the train for his trip out to the country, Parajanov positively revels in the accessories of the era:

> In the parlor car, upholstered with chintz and mahogany, ladies and gentlemen sat in deep armchairs . . .
>
> The ladies lifted black veils with sparkling dots, removed their hats in the shape of crows, pheasants, guinea fowl . . .
>
> With great solemnity the women drew the long needles that fastened down their hats out of their hair and handed the hats to their traveling companions.

Figure 5.2. Collage-sketch for *Intermezzo* (1973). Courtesy of the Sergei Parajanov Museum.

Cavalier-ensigns each in turn cleaned traveling binoculars with a chamois . . . unscrewed nickel-plated cups from traveling thermoses.

Hats in the shape of crows and pheasants hung on bronze hooks or seemed to hatch eggs in the wicker shelves under the ceiling . . .[33]

This fascination with extravagant hats would later resurface in his short film *Arabesques on the Theme of Pirosmani* and the series of hats he created around the same time, in the mid-1980s.

Besides establishing the historical and cultural context for the story, Parajanov and Zahrebelny attempted to suggest possible real-life sources of inspiration for Kotsiubynsky's work. For example, another of Kotsiubynsky's stories, "He is Coming" (1906), is about a Jewish community's response to the threat of pogroms instigated by the Black Hundreds. Accordingly, in Parajanov and Zahrebelny's screenplay the dreamlike episode entitled "The Lark" ("Zhavoronok") contains a reference to Mendel Beilis, a Ukrainian Jew who was wrongly accused of the ritual murder of Andrei Yushchynsky in 1911 and tried but acquitted in 1913, in a modern-day example of the medieval blood libel. In this respect Parajanov and Zahrebelny obviously have taken a great deal of liberty with chronology, for the original story "Intermezzo" was actually written in 1908 and published in 1909.[34] Another example of Parajanov and Zahrebelny's very free treatment of history is the subplot in the shooting script regarding the young poet who writes a hymn to the revolution: "Eternal revolutionary . . . Spirit . . . Body . . . Burn . . . Combat!" This hymn is immediately recognizable as "The Eternal Revolutionary" ("Vichnyi revoliutsioner") by Ivan Franko and Mykola Lysenko, but that work was in fact composed in 1880, 28 years before Kotsiubynsky wrote the story.

More importantly, Parajanov and Zahrebelny take a decidedly unorthodox interpretation of the aforementioned passage in which the author reflects on his indifference to accounts of people being shot or hanged and put in white sacks. This imagery is not explained directly in Kotsiubynsky's story, no doubt to circumvent censorship, but it is most likely connected with the Tsarist reaction to the 1905 Revolution mentioned earlier. Such an interpretation certainly makes the most sense in connection with the narrator's subsequent conversation with the peasant. Soviet critics also tended to read the story as a whole in terms of Kotsiubynsky's response to those events.[35] However, Parajanov and Zahrebelny oddly re-envision this episode as a reference to the Russo-Japanese war. They also de-emphasize the narrator's apathy compared to Kotsiubynsky's story in the passage quoted above:

[. . .] You see, I don't even blush, my face is as white as yours since the terror has sucked out all of my blood . . . Come closer . . . eat . . . I'm tired . . .

Both processions came closer to the table . . .

They were all reaching for white plates with cold milk soup . . .

Casts and bandages hindered the soldiers . . . They couldn't hold the spoons . . .

They only wiggled their fingers . . .

Kotsiubynsky fed the soldiers . . . He tried to find the mouths . . . of the soldiers . . .

The soldiers' mouths were walled up in casts . . .

The white soup flowed over the plaster chins of the soldiers . . .

A dying Japanese soldier eagerly held up in his plaster hand a white delftware soup tureen and beat the ladling spoon against the empty bottom.

The Japanese soldier stormed:

—Bia . . . Biu . . . bitch! Nyao! . . . Oya . . . Si!

The solder cried fiercely from the pain . . . And beat against the tureen . . . Beat until he knocked out the bottom . . .

The broken delftware tureen emitted a human cry . . .

Kotsiubynsky closely examined his hands, slowly wiggled his fingers, and tried to bend his feet under the blanket.[36]

Considering the political crackdown already underway in the Soviet Union and within Ukraine in particular, it is not difficult to understand why Parajanov and Zahrebelny might shift from an internal conflict between revolutionaries and the Tsarist security force in Kotsiubynsky's story to a war with a foreign enemy. This tactic also had the advantage of minimizing potential parallels between Ukraine's earlier oppression under Tsarist Russia and the current situation under Soviet rule. Their adaptation further attempted to make the story more ideologically palatable by portraying the protagonist's active engagement in the events of the period and foregrounding the story's connection to the imminent revolution.

In a resolution dated May 17, 1971, the Script-Editorial Board of Goskino of Ukraine voiced its support for the script, arguing that Parajanov and Zahrebelny aspired "to focus on the cinematic front of expressiveness, not a formal quest, but first and foremost on the sharp, militant affirmation of the lofty ideological and social significance of art and on the unambiguous, categorical denunciation of so-called 'pure art,' the alienation of the artist from the people."[37] However, this transparent attempt to forestall any official complaints of formalism failed to convince Goskino USSR in Moscow.

Once again the Moscow authorities assigned Mikhail Bleiman as a reader for the script. As if to order, Bleiman wrote a lengthy response in effect recommending that Parajanov no longer be given work in the Soviet film industry. While acknowledging the power of individual images in the script, he wrote: "We need to decide as a matter of principle and definitively whether our cinema can be so generous as to produce pictures with such an individual style as Parajanov's. If not, then we need to say so up front, i.e., to state that Parajanov does not have a place in the system of our cinema." In Bleiman's view, Goskino did not "have the right to decide this question" but needed to refer it to the Union of Cinematographers and the Cultural Section of the Central Committee.[38]

In June, most likely due to behind-the-scenes pressure, Sviatoslav Ivanov removed the film from Goskino of Ukraine's thematic plan. Nonetheless, negotiations continued in Ukraine with the Central Committee of the Communist Party. The scriptwriter and journalist Tamara Shevchenko, Ivanov's widow and a friend of Parajanov, claims that she introduced the director to Petro Shelest's son Vitaly at this time. Vitaly Shelest became a supporter of Parajanov's cause and prevailed upon his father to let the director resume work on his film.[39] Ivanov later requested that Alexei Romanov reinstate the project in the 1972 thematic plan, and Romanov approved on the condition that the script be cleared first with the Central Committee of the Communist Party of Ukraine.[40] Finally the project was cancelled altogether by the spring of 1972, roughly around the time that Shelest was ousted as the first secretary of the Communist Party of Ukraine.

Parajanov's Speech in Minsk

One of the immediate factors behind the cancellation of *Intermezzo* and ultimately behind Parajanov's arrest was no doubt the scandal surrounding a speech that Parajanov delivered in Minsk on December 1, 1971. The film scholar Olga Nechai and the journalist Alla Bobkova had invited Parajanov to screen his film *The Color of Pomegranates* there and to speak before members of a film club and local creative intelligentsia.

After brief introductory remarks Parajanov shifted to his main focus, the creative bankruptcy of much of Soviet cinema during the "stagnation" of the Brezhnev era. He even used the precise term *zastoi*. He declared the recent Lenin Jubilee a "colossal failure," stating that "the least talented people made films about Lenin."[41] Another problem, he felt, was an overly literal and unimaginative approach toward the adaptation of classic literature. Recent films he singled out for criticism included Sergei Bondarchuk's *War and Peace*, Grigori

Kozintsev's *King Lear* (*Korol' Lir*, Lenfilm 1971), Andrei Konchalovsky's *Nest of the Gentry* (*Dvorianskoe gnezdo*, Mosfilm 1970), and Lev Kulidzhanov's *Crime and Punishment* (*Prestuplenie i nakazanie*, Gorky Film Studio 1969). If these particular films are arguably better than he makes them out to be, Parajanov's posture should perhaps be understood as one of defensiveness or even thinly disguised professional jealousy, for his own vision of cinema was proving increasingly difficult to realize.

Parajanov then cited a general "mistrust" of the artist by the authorities, both within the film bureaucracy and in the Communist Party hierarchy. On a personal level, he mentioned that a member of the Central Committee had threatened that he would no longer be allowed to make films. He also made disparaging remarks about various officials, referring to one unnamed member of the Cultural Section of the Central Committee in Armenia as a "floor polisher." He specifically named Alexei Romanov, Irina Kokoreva (the editor-in-chief at the Script-Editorial Department), and Raisa Zuseva (another script editor) as individuals within the central office of Goskino USSR who had opposed *The Color of Pomegranates*.

Throughout the speech, he further complained about the authorities' general lack of understanding on artistic matters. For instance, he joked that Sviatoslav Ivanov (whom he mentioned explicitly by name and patronymic) had criticized him for using an unattractive nude in *Kyiv Frescoes* and had failed to recognize Parajanov's mention of the French sculptor Maillol. Jokes by artists about the supposed artistic ignorance of the authorities were of course commonplace in the Soviet Union and Eastern Bloc countries — they flourish wherever a hierarchical decision-making body rules on the fate of an individual artist's work. But it was rare for a Soviet artist to make such remarks in a public forum. Indeed, the deliberately provocative humor of the speech is typical Parajanov. Among other things, he claimed that he was forbidden to travel to Minsk because of a pending meeting with Shelest but went anyway, that he brought along a stolen print of *The Color of Pomegranates* for the screening, and that he had to deceive the Armenians in order to get that film made. He also made some teasing remarks about prominent individuals who in point of fact supported him and his work, among them the aforementioned Ivanov and the film directors Sergei Bondarchuk, Sergei Gerasimov, and Sergei Yutkevich.

Given all this, it is hardly surprising that the KGB recorded the speech and that the authorities were extremely displeased with it. Yuri Andropov, at that time the chair of the KGB, sent a transcript of the speech along with a cover letter dated January 25, 1972, to the Central Committee in Moscow. In it, Andropov wrote: "Parajanov's speech (transcript attached), which was patently demagogic in character, provoked the indignation of most present."[42] The speech was almost certainly discussed among members of the Politburo, since a handwritten note on the copy housed at the Russian State Archive of Contemporary History (RGANI) indicates that Mikhail Suslov, the Party's hardline head of ideology, passed it on to Pyotr Demichev, the Minister of Culture. In contrast to what Andropov claimed in his memo, Bobkova characterizes the audience response to Parajanov's speech as mostly sympathetic and claims that those objecting to it were in a minority. One person called out, "If you feel that way, why don't you go abroad?" To which Parajanov replied: "I want to remain in my own country."[43]

As a matter of course, the speech was also forwarded to the Central Committee in Ukraine. In a memorandum to Shelest dated December 28, 1971, Pavlo Fedchenko, the head of the Cultural Section of the Central Committee of the Communist Party of Ukraine, complained that Parajanov had "slandered" individual films and "also the general state of Soviet film art." In his view, Parajanov displayed a "lack of respect at times bordering on cynical mockery" toward various "cultural figures" and Soviet officials. He further criticized Ivanov for supporting Parajanov too uncritically.[44] In response, Ivanov wrote a letter to Shelest acknowledging problems with Parajanov's behavior but arguing for his importance to Soviet cinema and warning of an "undesirable reaction by the public, especially the intelligentsia, that will be used by the international press and the radio."[45] Ivanov's letter may well have had some influence on Shelest and the Central Committee, though perhaps not as much as Ivanov had hoped; for while Parajanov was still unable to launch any projects of his own, he was later invited to take over direction on *When a Person Smiled*, which he retitled *Inga* (discussed later in this chapter). Thus he was not yet completely excluded from work. In the longer term, however, the unfavorable attention that the Minsk speech attracted both at the Central Committee in Ukraine and at the Politburo in Moscow surely counted against him and contributed to the decision to have him arrested two years later.

The Demon

While Parajanov was working on *Intermezzo*, he completed yet another script for the Dovzhenko Film Studio — an adaptation of Mikhail Lermontov's 1841 narrative poem *The Demon*. Lermontov himself characterized the work as an "Oriental tale" (*vostochnaia povest'*), which suggests immediately why Parajanov was attracted to it, what with its exotic setting and mythical storyline.[46]

Once again, Parajanov makes a number of significant changes to the original. Lermontov opens his poem by depicting the character of the Demon as he reflects wistfully on the time before the Fall and his separation from God. The main protagonist of Lermontov's original poem is clearly the Demon: condemned to wander the universe alone, he functions as a tragic antihero in the Romantic tradition. Seeking redemption through his love for an earthly woman, the Georgian princess Tamara, the Demon is thwarted when she expires after giving herself up to him and is taken away to heaven as an angel, leaving him once again alone in the universe.

In contrast, Parajanov's script opens with a prologue depicting Lermontov's moment of inspiration for writing the poem: while the poet is standing outdoors in the Caucasus, an eagle feather drifts down from the sky and the canvas on which he was painting falls into the water and floats away. Various legendary figures of the Caucasus such as Prometheus and Medea spark his imagination before he settles on the character of the Demon.

Parajanov's own conception of the Demon as a shadow or phantom is undeniably evocative from a cinematic perspective. He writes: "The phantom retreated over the rocks of mountain crags, and on the rocks of the mountain crags arose smoking footprints . . ."[47] However, in Parajanov's version the dramatic focus is shifted to Tamara. (An alternate title for the project was in fact *Tamara*.) To flesh out her character, Parajanov adds an episode depicting her as a child, taken along by her father Prince Gudal during a hunt. In a clear omen of her future fate, she is struck by a black swan falling from the sky after it has been shot. As an adult, she cries out like a swan at various points and a black bird falls on her bed when her bridegroom is killed by the jealous Demon, signifying the force of destiny upon her. Parajanov also depicts the nuns attempting to persuade Tamara, who is still traumatized by her bridegroom Sinodal's death, to participate in the convent's daily chores such as fruit-gathering and milking buffaloes. The script thus becomes the story of a woman driven mad and ultimately killed by thwarted desires.

The scene in which the Demon declares his desire and subsequently ravishes her surely would not have passed the censors:

> . . . And the spirit touched her breasts . . . the pomegranate between her breasts . . . It seemed to Tamara that she cried out . . . A hand crushed the pomegranate . . . Tamara begged herself to keep silent . . . She begged the shadow to keep silent . . . begged it to fasten the hook on the door . . . Tamara lit the oil lamps . . . The lamps fell . . . Hot oil spilled . . . Tamara once again submissively lay on the bed . . . And once again ran toward the window . . .[48]

But the most striking change from Lermontov's poem is that Parajanov excises almost all the passages describing the Demon's speech and thoughts, particularly the long monologue where he tries to convince Tamara to give herself up to him. Cora Tsereteli persuasively argues that in Parajanov's interpretation, the character of the Demon represents less of a concrete presence than Tamara's "sick imagination, her disease."[49]

According to Tsereteli, Shklovsky acted as "curator" for the script when Parajanov submitted it to Goskino. In a series of letters exchanged between Parajanov and Shklovsky during the summer and fall of 1971, Shklovsky criticized the script for its paucity of dialogue: "Unfortunately, we can't shoot a silent film. People have to speak." He also criticized some of Parajanov's specific imagery: "The black swan isn't necessary. Mauve buffaloes can't live in the mountains. That's Western Georgia. There was already a pomegranate in a Parajanov film." Furthermore, Shklovsky pointed out, "One should sympathize with the Demon, and not with Tamara."[50]

In this case, one would have to agree with Shklovsky that the script displayed basic conceptual problems. Admittedly, Parajanov's reinterpretation of the story is an intriguing reversal of Lermontov's basic conception, and it has no shortage of striking imagery. But in the final analysis, one could argue that Parajanov's approach discards the essential core of Lermontov's poem, what makes it truly memorable as a work of Romantic literature: the conflicted character of the Demon. So while Parajanov's interpretation is provocative and potentially legitimate in its own way, it is weaker from a dramatic standpoint.

Ultimately Goskino rejected the script.[51] In 1987 Parajanov attempted to resurrect the long-shelved project, this time for the Georgia Film Studio, seemingly a more logical home for it given the subject matter. He also developed a script for another "Oriental tale" by Lermontov, the short fairy tale "Ashik Kerib." Only the latter film would ever be completed.

The Gilt Edge

A lesser-known original script that Parajanov also worked on during this time was *The Gilt Edge* (*Zolotoi obrez*). As Tamara Shevchenko notes, it was written in 1972 while Parajanov was hospitalized for a blood clot in his right eye.[52] According to Shevchenko, Parajanov presented her with the prose treatment (*libretto*) to develop into a full screenplay.[53] Set in contemporary Kyiv, the fragmentary, subtly observed narrative focuses on a secondhand bookseller haunted by memories of the German occupation of Kyiv, his shy daughter, and a theater

prompter. Parajanov dedicated the script to the actors Yuri Nikulin, Inna
Churikova, and Vladislav Dvorzhetsky, whom he had in mind to play the bookseller, the daughter "Inna," and the prompter, respectively.

The script opens with the bookseller and his daughter in an amateur performance of the play *Cyrano de Bergerac*. This is followed by various details from the
daily operations of the book shop, including a humorous incident where a group
of children run about town collecting paper for recycling. When the bookseller
sees them carrying off a gilt-edged encyclopedia, he speaks with the school's
director about rescuing some of these discarded books. The theater prompter,
a man "about forty years old . . . with sad blue eyes," invites the bookseller and
his daughter to a sold-out performance of *Cyrano de Bergerac* and takes them
backstage. Although the prompter is married with a child, he and Inna begin a
tentative, apparently unconsummated romance.

The bookstore is later renovated by the city, along with other shops in the
same building, and the bookseller is put on semi-retirement. Inna seeks out
the prompter again, but instead is confronted by his wife. Distraught, she runs
through the city and engages in an act of symbolic protest against her own
repression:

> Inna stood on the bank of the Vydubetsky Monastery.
> She loosened the chain from the boat.
> The liberated boat glided over the water.
> She rowed against the current.
> Naked soldiers swam in the torrent, offering their services, they whistled
> like nightingales . . .
> She passed them.
> She crossed the Dnieper.
> Then she floated in the limpid waters.
> At the bottom of the waters were the Rusanovky Gardens.
> The young crowns of apple trees gleamed like the flashes of nuclei.
> The gardens swelled with water.
> She floated toward a shack, knowing precisely the address of the shacks
> sunken in the water.
> She floated up to the familiar doors and, overcome from the impact of the
> water, opened a door.
> The current of water gushed out from the location . . . The water carried in
> its currents last summer's apples that surfaced . . .
> Apples struck against her chest.
> She clambered onto the roof.

> She looked around at the ocean of water, removed her dress.
> She wringed out her wet dress in the Dnieper.
> The water that had soaked into the dress made a noise as it struck against the silent flood . . .[54]

Inna's fate is not revealed, though it is implied that she has drowned. The script closes on the bookseller, who devotes himself to saving gilt-edged books from being pulped for recycling. These books, like the character of the bookseller, represent valuable aspects of society that are in danger of being discarded in pursuit of the new. While the prose treatment stands apart from Parajanov's other scripts during this period with its more realistic, character-oriented approach, it nonetheless contains familiar images and themes — the glinting of gilt-edged books recalls *The Color of Pomegranates*, while the wry observations of contemporary life and the allusions to World War II point back to the script for *Kyiv Frescoes*.

Inga

Parajanov's last project in Ukraine was the melodrama *Inga*, eventually directed by Boris Ivchenko under the title *When a Person Smiled* (*Kogda chelovek ulybnulsia*, Dovzhenko Film Studio 1974). Viktor Ivchenko, the director originally slated for the project and the father of Boris, had collaborated with the scriptwriter Yuri Parkhomenko on a screenplay adaptation of the novel *The Fourth Turn* by Peter Lebedenko. "The fourth turn" (*chetvertyi razvorot*) is a Russian aviation term for the final adjustment in the plane's course to align itself for landing. The novel's plot concerns the romance between two individuals brought together by an airline accident: Inga, who lost her boyfriend Roman, the pilot; and Alexei, who lost his wife Olga, one of the stewardesses. The project was approved and had reached the preproduction stage, but was postponed after Ivchenko fell gravely ill while location scouting in Rostov-on-Don. He passed away on September 6, 1972.

Once Parajanov was appointed as the director, he rewrote the script significantly to suit his own interests, though in very general terms he retained the same plot outline. The draft of the shooting script dated January 5, 1973, shows how Parajanov tried to adhere to the Party line by depicting pilots, aeronautical scientists, and astronauts as worker-heroes who risk their lives, hence the association throughout with the figure of Icarus. At the same time, he continued to work within his usual poetic, associative style. The script opens with a montage sequence set in northern Ukraine:

The damp, light green, and endless morning meadow of the Chernihiv region beyond the Desna.

Clumps of willows and haycocks are scattered just like Cossack's caps.

The pure, bottomless blue eye of the lake.

A young girl leaves the water, removing from her shoulder, cheek, and legs the white lilies that have wound around her with their dark stalks. On the green grass lie a yellow rake and a polka-dotted dress . . .

A herd of antelope races over the scorched steppe . . .

The roar of planes flying overhead, shaking the ground . . .

The rumbling rhythm of concrete slabs—triangles, trapezoids, polygons, crashing in the forest, the meadow, the unruly water of the river . . .

The rhythm of a die-stamp, breaking off the gigantic emblem of twin wings . . .

Tsiolkovsky, stepping forward from the rostrum of the Mausoleum on May 1, 1935 . . .[55]

Boys on the straw roof of an old threshing barn stretch out a "parachute" sewn from pieces of linen on four cords. They tie on still another with them. A boy, arms outstretched, jumps from the roof and . . . falls, covered by the cloud of white linen . . .

The linen cloud turns into the takeoff of a spaceship.

The face of Gagarin, his smile and his famous words: "We're off!" . . .

A young bearded guy on the facade of a skyscraper is completing the mosaic fresco "Icarus" . . .

Icarus's wings in the golden hair of a bride . . .

Airports with the emblem of twin wings . . .

Mighty engines take off with a roar, the shimmering haze of silver flying off in the shape of a gigantic bird . . .

The ocean of the sky . . .

morning,

day,

night.

Dovzhenko, walking through the endless steppe . . .

A gray burial mound smokes with feather grass . . .[56]

Some of these motifs are developed further in the main body of the script. At one point, characters watch television on the day of Yuri Gagarin's fatal crash, a tragedy that affected all of Soviet society. The character of Roman is also compared to Icarus, particularly by his girlfriend Inga—a symbolic gesture foreshadowing his untimely death.

By this time no stranger to criticism, Parajanov prefaced the script with the following statement:

> The Blossoming Tree of Socialist Realism is many-branched. On it, various fruits sprout, not weighing down and not choking the others: Dovzhenko, and Eisenstein, Platonov and Mayakovsky, Sholokhov and Aitmatov, Kachalov, Petritsky and Saryan, Tarkovsky. In this, most likely, is its strength. Roots. And fruits.
>
> My sole wish is to make a film filled with Beauty and Good, permeated by significant contemporary problems, a feature production that is necessary and useful to people, to the country. Everything for this is in the draft presented to you — it is permeated with Good, in the loftiest sense of the word.

Parajanov's plea for his own branch on the tree of Socialist Realism, however, would prove fruitless. By the end of the month, Boris Pavlenok, the deputy chair of Goskino USSR, sent a telegram to Goskino of Ukraine requesting to see Parajanov's shooting script "with the goal of determining prospects of further work on the film."[57] The deputy chair of Goskino of Ukraine replied in a memo dated February 2 that Parajanov's shooting script had "significantly departed from the literary scenario written by Yu. Parkhomenko and V. Ivchenko" and that it was "under consideration" at the Script-Editorial Board of Goskino of Ukraine.[58] By March 2 Parajanov was removed from the project and Ivchenko's son Boris was named director instead.

Parajanov's position had become untenable in the increasingly repressive atmosphere of Ukraine. An especially ominous sign was the ouster of Petro Shelest as Ukraine's first secretary of the Communist Party in May 1972 and then from his position in the Politburo in April 1973. This period also saw a fresh wave of arrests of Ukrainian intellectuals on charges of nationalism, among them Ivan Dziuba, the literary critic, author of *Internationalism or Russification?*, and close friend of Parajanov. Eventually Parajanov was forced to leave Ukraine altogether, although he still maintained his apartment in Kyiv.

A Miracle in Odense

The very last project Parajanov worked on before his arrest was *A Miracle in Odense*, a film about Hans Christian Andersen. According to Tsereteli, the version published in *Ispoved'* represents an earlier draft before Viktor Shklovsky's collaboration. She characterizes it as a "sketch," which in this case seems apt since several episodes appear to be fully written out and others seem to be missing, giving the whole a fragmentary feel.

The script opens in Odense at the turn of the century, 26 years after Andersen's death. During the New Year's celebration in the city, residents release white doves with cards attached to them and cannons fire from the bastion. Andersen himself materializes and wanders through the city carrying a harp. When the city's children see him, they at once identify him as Old Shut-Eye (Ole Luk-Oie) from Andersen's tale of the same name. Andersen, in the guise of Old Shut-Eye, enters the bedroom of Hjalmar (the boy to whom Old Shut-Eye tells his stories in Andersen's tale) and brings a painting to life by touching it with his magic umbrella. Helping Hjalmar to escape through the window, Andersen wanders with the boy through turn-of-the-century Odense.

The time then shifts back to earlier periods such as 1835 and 1841. Everyday events that Andersen witnesses become the inspiration for future fairytales. A small girl who wants to avoid going to church pretends there is a pea in her shoe, anticipating "The Princess and the Pea." "The Steadfast Tin Soldier" also makes an appearance as a tin soldier washing up on the beach. In the epilogue, Ole Shut-Eye / Andersen and Hjalmar go out on the street and observe a memorial plaque being set in place at Andersen's birth home. Entering the basement, they see Andersen's father and mother working as a cobbler and washerwoman. Hjalmar plays among the sheets hung out to dry. (This particular episode is perhaps meant to recall the scenes of Sayat-Nova's childhood in *The Color of Pomegranates*.) As Andersen continues to walk through the streets of Odense, he leaves golden footprints on the paving stones. The closing image is of Hjalmar standing on the shore of Odense, bidding farewell to Andersen as the latter goes out to sea, leaving behind his golden harp for the boy. Although it is essentially a children's film and lacks the dense symbolism of some of Parajanov's other scripts, it nonetheless displays characteristic themes such as the artist in his historical context and the artist's creative process. It also displays the director's usual obsession with the material culture of a different historical epoch.

According to Tsereteli, Shklovsky agreed once again to collaborate on the script and proceeded to rework it into something "passable." Shklovsky also secured a grant from UNESCO to help finance the film.[59] Tamara Ogorodnikova, who was friends with Parajanov and Andrei Tarkovsky, served as deputy chair of "Ekran," the feature film unit of Gosteleradio in Moscow, and agreed to back the project with the approval of Sergei Lapin, the chair of Gosteleradio. Producing the film in Kyiv at this point was out of the question. Although one of the Baltic States would have provided excellent architectural and natural settings given the film's subject matter, the authorities in Latvia, Lithuania, and Estonia all refused. In the end, only the Armenfilm Studio in Yerevan agreed to take on the project for their 1975–1976 production plan. Parajanov prepared a shooting script, but in November he was compelled to return from Tbilisi to Kyiv since his son Suren had been hospitalized with typhus. Gosteleradio sent the official requisition for the film to Yerevan, arranging for the initial transfer of funds on December 15, 1973, only days before his arrest.

6

Internal Exile

Arrest and Imprisonment, 1973–1982

As new details continue to emerge about Parajanov's 1973 arrest, it has become clear that the Ukrainian KGB, both on its own and likely under direction from Moscow, played the main role. According to one report by the Ukrainian KGB, Parajanov had fallen under scrutiny by the agency since 1962 due to "his meetings and correspondence with foreigners from capitalist countries."[1] Vitaly Nikitchenko, the chair of the KGB in Ukraine, sent a report dated April 4, 1969, to the Central Committee of the Communist Party of Ukraine about problems at the Dovzhenko Film Studio. This report detailed numerous complaints by informants at the studio both about its operations and the behavior of certain individuals, especially Parajanov. It stated: "In the opinion of one of the production managers of the studio, the film director S. I. PARAJANOV has had a negative influence on the fostering of young creative workers. In repeated conversations with his contacts, he has admitted ideologically harmful opinions and expressed thoughts of not returning home in the event of his departure abroad." Specifically, the report alleged that Parajanov, when asked by the Great Soviet Encyclopedia to submit information about his work, wrote a letter in reply that "contained a series of attacks of anti-Soviet character." Among other things, he was said to have written, "Inform your readers that I died in 1968 due to the genocidal policies of the Soviet regime." The KGB report further claimed that he had asked a French exchange student to marry him so that he could emigrate, allegedly saying that "he and the communists don't understand each other."

Parajanov's name came up again in another KGB report, dated December 23, 1971, to the Central Committee of the Communist Party of Ukraine regarding the ongoing controversy over the Kosmach church iconostasis, which had been removed during the production of *Shadows of Forgotten Ancestors* and was eventually transferred to the State Museum of Ukrainian Art in Kyiv for safekeeping. In his report Leonid Cherchenko, the head of the Administrative Department of the Ukrainian KGB and head of the Third Section of the Fifth Directorate, accused various dissidents — especially Valentyn Moroz and Vyacheslav Chornovil — of attempting "to stir up nationalist sentiments among the inhabitants of the village of Kosmach."[2]

Attachments to this report included a letter by Parajanov protesting the ongoing accusations of theft against him and a devastatingly negative report on the director's activities. Cherchenko wrote, "Many of the workers at the studio characterize him as a morally decayed personality who has turned his apartment into a gathering place for all manner of dubious persons engaged in drunkenness, depravity, speculation, and in politically harmful, even anti-Soviet conversations." Besides reiterating the accusation about the letter to the Great Soviet Encyclopedia, he cited Parajanov's ties to nationalist intellectuals, various remarks against communism and the Soviet regime to visitors from foreign countries, and comments expressing his desire to leave the country.

Cherchenko further attempted to implicate Parajanov in the loss of some of the Kosmach church artifacts: "According to operative data, PARAJANOV allegedly bore relation to the fact that part of the objects in question did not reach the museum, and some of them may have been substituted." The vague language used here is worth noting; although state prosecutors later questioned individuals about these church artifacts in conjunction with Parajanov's 1973 arrest, none of the accusations would ultimately hold up.

Cherchenko wrote in summary, "In the opinion of individual colleagues of his, PARAJANOV's treasonous and anti-Soviet pronouncements are the manifestation of political illiteracy, disorderliness, thoughtlessness, striving to achieve popularity by any means, and to attract attention to himself." At the very end of the report he further mentioned Parajanov's signature on a 1966 letter "in defense of certain persons among the intelligentsia who were convicted for anti-Soviet activity" and his alleged treatment in 1964 "at the October hospital in Kyiv in connection with the illness of syphilis."[3] This last detail would crop up again during the trial. One should also note that the KGB issued the

December 1971 report a few weeks after Parajanov's speech in Minsk, although the attached report on Parajanov did not mention the speech specifically. Most likely, this was only because news of it had not yet filtered down to the Ukrainian branch of the KGB.

The question arises: why was Parajanov not arrested until December 1973, two years after this report? First, it is likely that the KGB needed time to craft a credible set of criminal charges against him. According to the artist Olha Petrova, around that time the KGB questioned her and other associates of Parajanov about his mental state, raising the possibility that they were also exploring psychiatric hospitalization as a way to take him out of circulation.[4] But one of the main reasons for the delay appears to have been Parajanov's friendship during this time with the Shelest family, especially the son Vitaly. In a subsequent interview, Vitaly Shelest maintained that his father "saved" Parajanov and that the latter's arrest resulted when his father was removed from power.[5] The sculptor Nikolai Rapai, one of Parajanov's closest friends in Kyiv, has further supported this claim: "If Shelest had remained in place, Parajanov's fate would have turned out differently. [Volodymyr] Shcherbytsky hated him. Once they removed Shelest, they arrested him."[6] To be sure, Parajanov's relationship with Shelest must have been complicated considering his penchant for making provocative remarks and his ongoing friendships with dissidents, but Shelest apparently recognized his value as an artist and had also taken Sviatoslav Ivanov's pleas to heart.

Considering all this, one should understand Parajanov's imprisonment as part of the renewed crackdown in Ukraine that followed the removal of Petro Shelest from the position of first secretary of Ukraine in May 1972, mainly due to accusations of "localism" associated with the publication of his book *Our Soviet Ukraine* (1970). Shelest was later relieved of his position in the Politburo in April 1973. Shelest's political rival, Volodymyr Shcherbytsky, who helped engineer his ouster and ultimately replaced him as first secretary, was part of Brezhnev's Dnipropetrovsk circle and thus could be trusted to emphasize the "second" rather than the "equal" portion of the "second among equals" formula commonly used to describe Ukraine's status within the Soviet Union. Shcherbytsky's government consequently increased Russification and cracked down even harder on Ukrainian dissidents than Shelest's administration ever did.[7] The latest sweep included a large number of individuals who had signed petitions or otherwise had protested against the first wave of arrests, among them Parajanov, Dziuba (see chapter 2), and Leonid Plyushch. Especially relevant are the arrests and other measures of reprisal taken against many signatories of the April 1968 petition known as "The Appeal of the 139" (discussed in chapter 2), protesting the lack of due process in previous trials of Ukrainian dissident intellectuals.

While this new crackdown in fact took place throughout the entire Soviet Union, as with the crackdown of the mid-1960s, it was particularly severe in Ukraine.[8] Historian Orest Subtelny notes: "In Ukraine, the secret police worked under fewer constraints than in Moscow. Isolated from the Moscow-based Western media, the Ukrainian dissidents did not have the relative protection of the 'publicity umbrella' that their prominent Russian and Jewish colleagues have enjoyed. Moreover, the issue of Ukrainian national rights aroused little interest in the West. Meanwhile, the regime's fear of Ukrainian nationalism led to particularly harsh repression in Ukraine. Hence, the reputation of the Kyiv KGB as being the most vicious in the USSR and the disproportionately large number of Ukrainian 'prisoners of conscience.'"[9] One of the single most important factors in this regard was the replacement of Vitaly Nikitchenko as the head of the Ukrainian KGB by Vitaly Fedorchuk in July 1970. Nikitchenko reportedly had maintained a close working relationship with Shelest and was relatively moderate toward dissent. Fedorchuk, in contrast, pursued dissidents with such zeal that Shelest wrote in his diary that Fedorchuk "occupies an obviously extremist position."[10] Alexander Yakovlev, the Politburo member widely considered the architect of glasnost and perestroika and an acquaintance of Shcherbytsky, has stated that he did not feel Shcherbytsky was the "initiator of the campaign to prosecute Parajanov," implying that it may have been a KGB functionary instead.[11]

Alexei Korotyukov, a journalist who had emigrated from Ukraine in September 1974 and had known Parajanov since the mid-1950s, provided a detailed account of the arrest in a 1975 interview for *Cinema-TV-Digest*.[12] His perspective is valuable since the interview took place only a year or so after the arrest and trial. While Korotyukov perhaps inevitably mixes up some facts, a large percentage of his recollections correspond closely with what is known about the case and about Parajanov in general. In 2008 Alexander Korchinsky, a journalist for the Russian-language Ukrainian newspaper *Segodnia* (*Today*), published extensive excerpts from Parajanov's criminal court case file held at the Kyiv District Court.[13] These and the actual court verdict, a copy of which is held at the Parajanov Museum, at least provide a rough sketch of what happened.

Although Parajanov himself apparently was aware that he was now in danger of arrest in Kyiv, he felt it necessary to be with his son, who was gravely ill with typhus as mentioned previously. The putative starting point of the criminal investigation was a vaguely worded letter of complaint by a certain Semyon Petrovich Petrochenko, dated December 8, 1973, which accused Parajanov of "engaging in debauchery with minors, young men, and grown men" and of having turned his home into a "den of debauchery." On December 12, Arte-menko, the investigating officer, reported: "It did not prove possible to secure the deponent. However, the facts set forth in the statement were confirmed."[14] Korchinsky suggests, plausibly, that the initial letter of complaint was fabri-cated by the local authorities to meet a demand from above to have Parajanov arrested.

Wasting no time, the state obtained multiple incriminating statements. One was an affidavit written by Mikhail "Misha" Senin, a talented young Kyiv archi-tect and the adopted son of Ivan Senin, a leading Ukrainian Party member who was the first deputy chair of the Council of Ministers of the USSR and who had served in the Central Committee and the Politburo in Moscow. A close friend of Mikhail Senin and Parajanov has affirmed that Senin in fact had a romantic relationship with Parajanov at some point in the past, although the two were probably no longer together by that time.[15] In his affidavit, evidently extracted under duress, Senin named Vladimir Kondratiev, Ivan Peskovoi, and Valentin Parashchuk as individuals with whom Parajanov had allegedly engaged in sod-omy.[16] Kondratiev was a documentary filmmaker with whom Parajanov had worked in the past. Peskovoi was a married man, Communist Party member, and resident of Kanev; Parajanov allegedly met him in the Ukraina department store during the former's visit to Kyiv.[17] Parashchuk was a student from Lviv who had been staying at Parajanov's apartment. He testified that Parajanov had demanded sexual favors in exchange for housing and that he felt compelled to submit because he had no place else to go in Kyiv. Alexander Vorobiev, a mechanical engineer, further testified to the police that Parajanov had raped him on November 6 while he was passed out drunk at Parajanov's apartment. Lastly, Felix Desiatnik testified to the police on December 13 that on the same day (!) he had submitted to Parajanov's request for sexual favors in exchange for a break in the film industry.[18] The court verdict indicates that Desiatnik's testimony was accompanied by forensic evidence attesting to an act of sodomy.

Around this time, Parajanov left Kyiv for Moscow in order to attend the funeral of the art director Yakov Rivosh (1908–1973), who had passed away suddenly on December 11. In the meantime Senin, evidently distraught over his coerced statement to the police, committed suicide at home in his bathroom on December 16 and left a note whose contents are not known. When Parajanov returned from Moscow, he was brought in for interrogation on December 17 and was booked on December 20. He remained in detention until the trial.

In Korotyukov's view, the authorities had been laying the groundwork for the arrest for some time, citing a series of negative articles about Parajanov "in the Kyiv press." Korotyukov continues: "But the real start of the plan to arrest Parajanov, as far as I can tell, began a year before the arrest, with the arrival from Lviv of a young man with a movie script, who went to Parajanov and asked him for help in establishing himself in the Kyiv film circles."[19] Korotyukov insists that this person, whom he names as "Peter" but who appears to correspond with the student Parashchuk, was a plant by the authorities to keep tabs on the director. The role of Parashchuk in Parajanov's arrest also appears to fit with Svetlana Shcherbatiuk's account, though she does not mention his name and hastens to add that Parajanov later forgave him.[20] Regardless of Parashchuk's actual role, many of Parajanov's friends and acquaintances rightly suspected that his apartment, which had a constant flow of visitors, was under regular KGB surveillance. Furthermore, Shcherbatiuk has pointedly called into question the engineer Vorobiev's accusation of rape:

> I saw him a couple times at Sergei's home. And I saw him again on Surenchik's [Suren's] birthday, November 10th. That's very important! Our son was lying in the hospital, I called Sergei on the telephone, and he asked me to pass on to the physicians and nurses flowers, fruits, and cakes from him. When we met, Sergei was not alone, but with this person. He was tall, around thirty years old, a robust man who couldn't possibly become a rape victim. Sergei's lawyer told me that Vorobiev maintained that he was raped precisely on November 10. How? I saw him that very day, it was already evening, and if something tragic had happened to someone, he wouldn't look so peaceful and cheerful, and of course he wouldn't be helping the rapist carry flowers and fruits! I even said this at the trial, but they didn't attach any significance to it. Everything had been decided beforehand.[21]

One should note that Vorobiev claimed to have been passed out due to drunkenness when the rape occurred. Also, the alleged rape took place a few days earlier than November 10. However, the latter circumstance does not necessarily negate the basic thrust of Shcherbatiuk's argument.

Various sources in the West at the time of Parajanov's imprisonment state that he was initially charged with a variety of offenses in addition to that of homosexuality, particularly trafficking in art objects and "speculation" (i.e., trading in valuables or hard currency for profit). Yevgeni Makashov, the public prosecutor for the case, did in fact allude to "speculation" and dealings in hard currency in a 1990 interview with the journalist Alla Bossart.[22] So while the initial complaint filed against Parajanov dealt solely with accusations related to homosexuality, the state cast a much wider net in the investigation that ensued. Ultimately, the prosecution settled on charges of sodomy and the dissemination of pornography (Articles 122 and 211); the court verdict indicates that the pornography charges arose from "pornographic images in a magazine of foreign manufacture, playing cards of foreign manufacture, and photographs." The verdict also mentioned a ballpoint pen belonging to the documentary film-maker Kondratiev, "of foreign manufacture, in the cap of which was mounted pornographic images."[23] In other words, it was the kind of cheap souvenir pen widely produced in the West during the 1970s.

The trial took place on April 23 and 24, 1974, with a verdict declared on April 25. Korotyukov recalled that Parajanov had requested D. I. Kaminskaya, "a good lawyer" and an "experienced attorney from Moscow." However, she declined to take on the case since she was not given sufficient time to prepare. Ultimately Parajanov was assigned Taras Sheiko, whom Korotyukov characterized as "a weak Kievan lawyer."[24] Whatever Sheiko's merits, the conviction was a foregone conclusion. The trial was closed to the public; many of those attending were friends and relations of Parajanov who testified because they were summoned either by the prosecution or by the defense. Parajanov himself was sentenced to five years in a "corrective labor colony of strict regime." Kondratiev and Peskovoi each received a suspended sentence with three years' probation.[25]

The charges of homosexuality against Parajanov had multiple advantages. First, in order to deflect international criticism, the state could claim that Parajanov's arrest was an ordinary criminal case and not a political one. Second, the charges would injure his public reputation since homosexuality was still very much taboo in Soviet society as a whole. Well in advance of the trial, in the March 1, 1974, issue of the newspaper *Vechirnyi Kyiv*, P. Dolinsky, the first deputy prosecutor of Kyiv, published an article entitled "In the Name of the Law." Among several other criminal trials was a brief but luridly worded reference to Parajanov's case: "S. I. Parajanov — worker at the Dovzhenko feature film studio — led an immoral way of life, wrecked a family, turned his apartment into a den of licentiousness, engaged in sexual depravity, and has now been brought to account according to Article 122 of the Criminal Code of the Ukrainian SSR."[26] In case there are any doubts that the article was planted in the newspaper solely to discredit Parajanov, Fedorchuk admitted precisely that in a March 5, 1975, memo to Shcherbytsky, stating that the article had been published in the newspaper "with the aim of compromising foreign ant-Soviet ideological centers and the prevention of the further spreading of tendentious rumors."[27] Third, while Soviet law generally guaranteed an open trial, sexual perversion was one of the few circumstances permitting a closed trial. Predictably, the state took advantage of this and allowed only a limited number of people directly involved with the case to attend.

Parajanov's arrest and conviction also held great symbolic significance for the Ukrainian (and Soviet) state. Parajanov was a figurehead for the poetic school thanks to the success of *Shadows of Forgotten Ancestors,* his highly visible public persona in Kyiv, and his support of younger Ukrainian artists and intellectuals, including their political activities. Indeed, one cannot help but think that Shcherbytsky had Parajanov specifically in mind when he delivered a lengthy report at the May 16, 1974, Plenum of the Central Committee of the Communist Party of Ukraine, entitled "On the Tasks of Party Organizations of the Republic for the Further Improvement of Ideological Work in Light of the Ruling of the Twenty-Fourth Congress of the CPSU." In the section entitled "To Enhance the Role of Mass Media and Propaganda, Literature and Art," Shcherbytsky began his comments on film production as follows: "As is known, one of the most popular [*massovykh*] forms of art is film. It must be said that the situation in the republic's filmmaking is getting corrected, albeit slowly. For some time the devices [*priemy,* also has a pejorative connotation of "tricks" or "ploys"] of the so-called 'poetic film,' with their emphasis on abstract symbolism with sharply underlined ethnographic ornamental design, were treated by individual filmmakers almost as the leading principles of the development of filmmaking in Ukraine. These views, one might say, have been overcome."[28] The text of the full report was published the following day in the newspaper *Vechirnyi Kyiv,* including the comments about poetic cinema.[29] Many of Parajanov's colleagues have since insisted on a direct connection between Shcherbytsky's remarks and Parajanov's arrest. Such an interpretation is certainly plausible, considering that the speech took place only a month after the conviction. One should note, however, that Alexander Yakovlev questions the extent to which Shcherbytsky was personally aware of the concept of "poetic cinema" and suggests that shortly before the speech Shcherbytsky may have happened across it or it was given to him to put in the report.[30] This seems doubtful given the highly fraught politics of the arts in Ukraine during that era and the fact that squelching political dissidence ranked high on Shcherbytsky's agenda. But it is also unlikely that Shcherbytsky wrote the entire report himself, given its length.

Prison Art

During his imprisonment Parajanov was sent to three separate "strict regime" camps: Gubnik (Vinnytsia oblast) from July 1974 to April 1975, Strizhavka (Vinnytsia oblast) from April 1975 to August 1976, and Perevalsk (Voroshilovgrad oblast) from August 1976 to December 1977.[31] Despite brutal conditions, he managed to maintain regular correspondence with family and friends, much of which has been published over the years in books and journals.[32] He also produced a remarkable number of sketches, collages, dolls, and other artworks using materials that he was able to obtain at the prison camps. Many of these objects are on display at the Parajanov Museum; they offer a fascinating window into his existence in prison among hardened criminals and his evolving ideas as an artist during this period. In a 1989 interview Parajanov recalled: "It's only because I have a clever and cunning character that I managed to survive. I was a scavenger. There's a song in prison, 'A thief will never be a laundryman,' and I became a laundryman. I would paint playing cards in the Persian style for thieves in exchange for packages of tea. I painted a picture of Jesus on the cloth they put over a cadaver. I did a lot of things for those jailbirds and they had respect for me."[33]

Figure 6.1 is a ballpoint pen sketch representing daily life in prison: inmates being inspected for signs of syphilis. Figure 6.2 is a detail from a panel of miniatures depicting episodes in the life of Christ; he created the series after learning of the November 5, 1975, murder of Pier Paolo Pasolini.[34] Parajanov's surviving paintings and sketches in fact date back to the 1950s, and starting in the mid-1960s he was already experimenting with collages and assemblages. Collages and assemblages had also become a component of the creative process for his films, as demonstrated by costume design collages he created for *The Color of Pomegranates*. Thus his prison art represents a logical outgrowth of his artistic output as a whole.

The International Campaign

Once news of Parajanov's arrest reached the West in January of 1974, leading filmmakers circulated a petition for his release. According to Patrick Cazals, signatories included: Agnès Varda, François Truffaut, Jean-Luc Godard, Réné Clément, Jacques Demy, Francesco Rosi, Marco Ferreri, Jacques Tati, Marcel Carné, Jacques Rivette, Luis Buñuel, Louis Malle, Federico Fellini, Joseph Losey, Luchino Visconti, Roberto Rossellini, Michelangelo Antonioni, Pier Paolo Pasolini, Sergio Leone, Bernardo Bertolucci, and Jules Dassin.[35] Various international committees and "collectives" also organized on Parajanov's behalf. One such group was the "Comité contre la répression," which included Alain Corneau, Bertrand Tavernier, Dominique Labourier, and Roger Blin as its members; it staged a dual protest against Parajanov's imprisonment and against the expulsion of Wolf Biermann from East Germany in November of

Figure 6.1. *Syphilis in the Zone: Looking for the Source* (1974–1977). Ballpoint pen on paper. Courtesy of the Sergei Parajanov Museum.

1976.[36] Another collective in Marseilles, which focused solely on Parajanov's case, was founded by Varoujan Azumanian.

Herbert Marshall, a professor at Southern Illinois University who had studied in the VGIK under Eisenstein, had befriended Parajanov during a visit to the Soviet Union in the early 1970s. He circulated a further petition for the director's release and published an article about *The Color of Pomegranates*, which still had not received official distribution in the West, in the British film journal *Sight and Sound*.[37] Marshall also obtained a clandestine print of the film, inserted

Figure 6.2. Detail from *The Gospel According to Pasolini* (1976). Ballpoint pen on paper. Courtesy of the Sergei Parajanov Museum.

his own explanatory intertitles and poems by Sayat-Nova, and screened it at public venues throughout Europe and the United States in order to drum up support for the campaign to release Parajanov and to pressure the Soviet authorities to distribute the film officially. Finally, as part of the November 1977 "Biennale of Dissent" program associated with the Venice Biennale, Antonín J. Liehm organized a panel and edited a collection of documents and essays on Parajanov.[38]

However, the factor that appears to have had the biggest impact on Parajanov's release was the personal intervention of Louis Aragon. That same year Aragon was to be awarded the Order of the Friendship of Peoples by Brezhnev. Aragon's wife, Elsa Triolet, was the sister of Lilya Brik, who had become close friends with Parajanov through her stepson Vasili Vasilevich Katanian, a documentary filmmaker who had known Parajanov since the 1950s. Parajanov also had corresponded regularly with the Katanian family during his imprisonment. Aragon traveled to Moscow to accept the medal but pressured Brezhnev to release Parajanov from prison; this finally appeared to have an effect and Parajanov was released on December 30, 1977.[39]

Return to Tbilisi; A New Arrest

No longer permitted to live in Kyiv, Parajanov returned to his family home in Tbilisi. He was still barred from making films and thus had no regular means to support himself, relying instead on aid from various friends, selling family belongings, and trading privately in antiques. According to Zaven Sargsyan, in 1978 he wrote to the authorities in Armenia seeking permission to make films of *Ara the Fair* (discussed in chapter 5) and the Armenian folk epic *David of Sasun*, but ultimately received no reply because of opposition in Moscow.[40] In 1980, Parajanov conducted an interview with A. Anessian, a French-Armenian reporter visiting Tbilisi. It was published under the title "Paradjanov, cinéaste indésirable," in the January 27 issue of *Le Monde*. In it he spoke frankly about his experiences in prison and his inability to find work as a film director after his release, declaring that he was "already a dead man" and that "this life is worse than death." He also expressed interest in emigrating to France, which he called his "adopted homeland," and even mentioned specific projects on Armenian subjects that he wanted to direct there. Once again dredging up the example of Sergei Bondarchuk's film of *War and Peace*, which he felt "lacks the voice of the people," he decried the state of contemporary art in the Soviet Union: "When I think about the present-day poverty and the mawkishness of official art, be it in music, dance, architecture, or cinema, I want to weep." Eager to attract the sympathy of Western readers, he was also not above stretching the truth a little: "I had already been arrested once before in Ukraine. I was accused of being a Ukrainian nationalist, because I had refused to dub a film [i.e., *Shadows of Forgotten Ancestors*] into Russian — this dubbing would have debased and vulgarized the meaning of the words."[41] (Actually, as indicated previously, the Ukrainian authorities had argued in favor of releasing the film throughout the Soviet Union in the original language and Moscow did not appear to have put up much of a battle, even though it was not standard practice. Parajanov was certainly not arrested because of it.) As one might expect, a Russian translation of the interview wound up in the files of the Central Committee in Moscow about five months later, sent by Alexander Karaganov, the secretary of the Board of Directors of the Union of Cinematographers of the USSR.[42] No doubt the interview raised eyebrows not only for its frankness, but also for the simple fact of Parajanov's unauthorized interview with a foreign journalist.

Parajanov ran afoul of the authorities yet again when he spoke out at an October 31, 1981, Artistic Council meeting for Yuri Liubimov's controversial play *Vladimir Vysotsky* at the Taganka Theatre. Vysotsky, a noted actor and singer-poet (popularly known as "bards" in Russia), had developed a massive cult following in the Soviet Union for his satirical songs, which included a great deal of slang and commonly identified with prisoners and other outsiders. The most notorious of his songs was "The Wolf Hunt" ("Okhota na volkov"), narrated from the wolf's point of view and widely understood as a metaphor for the repressive apparatus of the Soviet state. He recorded a small number of songs officially for Melodiya, the state recording firm, and performed some of them in films, but his work achieved its greatest impact by far through *magnitizdat*, or the private underground circulation of audio cassette recordings. His premature death at the age of 42 in 1980 resonated throughout all of Soviet society.

Liubimov planned to stage the play's premiere on July 25, 1981, the anniversary of Vysotsky's death. In a memo to the Central Committee, KGB chair Yuri Andropov outlined his concerns with the event, which included the show's "tendentious viewpoint" and the existence of an unofficial committee within the theater company planning to "carry out measures dedicated to the memory of the actor" at his gravesite and on stage, which Andropov felt "could arouse unhealthy excitement on the part of Vysotsky admirers," and could "create conditions for possible demonstrations of an antisocial character."[43] The play did receive its premiere on July 25 as planned after Liubimov spoke personally to Andropov, but the theater was tightly cordoned off. Both tickets and passports were required for admittance.[44] Further plans to include the play in the company's regular repertory were held back by official concerns about both the popularity of Vysotsky as a countercultural icon and the play's ideological thrust. Among other things, the authorities felt that the excerpts from *Hamlet* and Tom Stoppard's *Rosencrantz and Guildenstern Are Dead* (one of Vysotsky's best-known roles as an actor was Hamlet) solidified the image of Vysotsky as an oppositional figure. They also objected to the play's use of songs that had circulated without official approval, among them "The Wolf Hunt."[45]

Rehearsals continued for the next several months, with a number of noted cultural figures attending and participating in the theater's Artistic Council meetings in addition to the cast and crew. Among those attending the aforementioned October 31 meeting was Parajanov, who had previously befriended Vysotsky, Liubimov, and others associated with the theater. Other attendees included the composers Rodion Shchedrin and Alfred Schnittke, the poet Bella Akhmadulina, the "bard" Bulat Okudzhava, and the writer Fazil Iskander. Parajanov spoke at length, praising the show's emotional impact. At the same time, he hinted at the presence of a KGB informant during the meeting and acknowledged the possibility that the authorities would force the production to close:

> Let them shut you down! Let them torment you! You can't imagine how good it is for me to do nothing. I've received immortality—the Pope supports me. He sends me diamonds and jewelry. I can even eat caviar every day. I'm not doing anything. Who stands to gain for me not to do anything? I really wanted to compete with you and do something.
>
> What a stunning show! What stunning movement of the actors [*plastika*]! A requiem. I'm equating you with Mozart. Everything you've done and my first encounter with Gubenko[46] on the stage of your theater—it's all a shock for me.
>
> And the main thing is that today took place. And if they have to shut you down, then let them shut you down all the same! I know this absolutely precisely. Don't write any letters, don't beg anyone. You mustn't beg. You mustn't humble yourself! There is Liubimov, and we prefer him to some kind of machinery out there.[47]

People attending the meeting recall being taken aback in particular by Parajanov's patently outlandish claim that the pope was sending him diamonds.

Not surprisingly, the authorities viewed both the interview for *Le Monde* and his comments at the Taganka Theatre as a direct challenge. According to Tsereteli, Moscow sent the text of Parajanov's speech to the KGB in Georgia with instructions to find an excuse to arrest him.[48] The Tbilisi-based photographer Yuri Mechitov, one of Parajanov's closest friends at that time, recalls Parajanov boasting that when he was summoned by the KGB to read over the transcript and confirm its accuracy, he declared that not only was he not going to cross anything out, but the he wanted to "underline" what he had said.[49]

According to Mechitov, at this time Parajanov also sought help from Eteri Gugushvili and Dodo Aleksidze, the directors of the Shota Rustaveli State University of Film and Theater, in order for his nephew Georgi "Garik" Khachaturov to gain admittance to the acting program.[50] A comedy of errors ensued in which another, less talented Armenian student applying to the institute at the same time was mistakenly passed in place of Garik, who received a failing grade initially despite his superior performance. (He auditioned a second time and passed.) Mechitov writes: "Parajanov never tired of repeating, especially in Garik's presence, that his admission cost $5,000 US dollars — a fantastic sum for Soviet ears. That is what Parajanov freely valued a ring that he had given to the rector of the institute as a sign of gratitude. Of course, those of us around Sergei didn't see anything criminal in this — Parajanov loved to give things both with and without cause."[51] Much to the suspicion of Parajanov's friends, around this time a handsome young police officer befriended the director, who boasted about the gift in front of him as well. The police officer later told Parajanov that he was in dire economic straits due to a sick child and asked him for five hundred rubles, which may have been implied as a bribe to keep quiet about Garik. On February 11, 1982, Parajanov met with him inside a car to hand over the money. At that moment another car drove up, catching Parajanov in the act of giving the alleged bribe. He was arrested and taken to Tbilisi's infamous Ortachala prison, where he spent the next several months awaiting trial.

The trial took place over three sessions from September 22 to October 5, 1982, in the Tbilisi House of Arts Workers and then in the district court. As one might expect, it assumed surreal proportions. The ordinarily proud and recalcitrant Parajanov was humbled at the prospect of another prison term and pleaded contritely with the court, assuring them that he respected the Soviet state and that he would not cause further problems. Sofiko Chiaureli spoke out forcefully on his behalf, demanding, "What kind of people are you to put him on trial? Do you know on the whole who Parajanov is?"[52] The outcome of this latest legal circus was his sudden release.

One possible factor behind Parajanov's release was the intervention of the Italian screenwriter Tonino Guerra and his Russian wife Laura. The couple had befriended Parajanov in the late 1970s and were visiting a spa in western Georgia at the same time as Eduard Shevardnadze, the first secretary of the

Communist Party of Georgia. According to them, during a private meeting Shevardnadze listened receptively to Tonino's request that Parajanov be released.[53] Regardless, it is likely that, in the period leading up to the trial, the Soviet authorities carefully weighed their desire to take Parajanov out of circulation against the risk of another embarrassing international campaign. Only now was this most difficult period in his life truly behind him.

7

The Legend of the
Surami Fortress

Thunder Over Georgia

In late November 1982, only weeks after Parajanov's release from jail, Rezo Chkheidze, the head of the Georgia Film Studio, offered him the opportunity to direct a new film: *The Legend of the Surami Fortress* (*Legenda Suramskoi kreposti*, Georgia Film Studio 1984), based on a script by Vazha Gigashvili. The proposal came with the support of Eduard Shevardnadze, the first secretary of the Communist Party of Georgia.[1] Together with the production of Tengiz Abuladze's television film *Repentance* (*Pokaianie*, Georgia Film Studio 1984, released 1986), this gesture marked the beginnings of glasnost in Georgia and in the Soviet Union as a whole.[2] The revered Georgian actor David "Dodo" Abashidze, who plays the roles of Osman-Agha and Simon the Piper in Parajanov's film, was designated as co-director. This credit was widely understood as a formality to help gain approval for the project, though Abashidze and Parajanov were good friends and their working collaboration continued with *Ashik-Kerib* (Georgia Film Studio 1988).

There are multiple variants of the legend surrounding the Surami fortress, but the best-known version by far is the 1860 novella *The Surami Fortress* by Daniel Chonkadze, which has not been translated into English.[3] Literary historian Donald Rayfield characterizes *The Surami Fortress* as the most accomplished Georgian prose narrative of the mid-nineteenth century.[4] (Due to various social and economic factors, modern literary prose genres developed much later than poetry in Georgia). Within the brief work, Chonkadze incorporates a wide range of literary devices such as stories within stories, letters, and lengthy exchanges of dialogue. A bitter critique of serfdom, it also contains an anticlerical theme insofar as the clergy are complicit with the feudal lords in upholding the brutal system.[5]

Chonkadze's narrative is framed with a first-person account of the literary circle he frequented in Tbilisi. Every evening during the summer, they would take turns telling stories. His colleague Niko relates the tale of Durmishkhan and Gulisvardi, young servants of Prince Murkhran-Batoni and Princess Maria Tsereteli in Tbilisi. Durmishkhan was originally from Imereti, but his lord thoughtlessly sold him to Mukhran-Batoni when the latter expressed an interest. Gulisvardi and Durmishkhan discuss marriage, but Durmishkhan insists that they cannot be happy together unless they are free, painting dire scenarios of likely outcomes if they marry while still under servitude. Gulisvardi convinces Princess Tsereteli to free both of them, but Durmishkhan decides to leave her behind with her mistress while he goes to find work and gain economic independence.

On the road Durmishkhan meets Osman-Agha, a Muslim merchant. The "Turk" reveals that he is in fact a Georgian by the name of Nodar. Years ago he had murdered his master out of rage: the prince was responsible for the death of his mother and later the suicide of his beloved, a servant in the same household. Afterward Nodar fled to Turkey, changed his name, and converted to Islam. Osman-Agha adopts Durmishkhan as his son and arranges for him to marry his goddaughter at Surami, along with the gift of half his belongings. However, Durmishkhan loves only wealth; he does nothing to help Osman-Agha when the latter reconverts to Christianity and is subsequently tortured and killed by the Turks for renouncing Islam. Durmishkhan eventually has a son, Zurab, for whom he harbors great ambitions. When Gulisvardi receives a letter from Durmishkhan about his new wife and son, she is devastated and vows revenge. She studies fortune-telling and witchcraft with an older fortune-teller.

Years later, when Zurab has grown into a young man, tensions between the Georgians and Turks are rising and war appears imminent. A fortress is built at Surami, but for some reason its walls will not stand. Gulisvardi, who is now a revered fortune-teller in her own right, is consulted for advice on how to save it. She declares that Zurab must be buried alive within the walls to make them hold up against invaders. He is seized by the crowd and immured against his will. Durmishkhan goes to Tbilisi to confront Gulisvardi, and the two kill each other. Mad with grief, Zurab's mother wanders about. When she stands before the fortress one day, she suddenly comes to her senses, remembers what has happened, then passes away.

In 1922, Ivan Perestiani directed a film adaptation starring Hamo Bek-Nazarov as Durmishkhan and Mikhail Chiaureli as Osman. The two actors would later become foundational directors in Armenian and Georgian cinema, respectively. Perestiani's film begins with a depiction of the author writing the book; images from the novel appear to him in a series of visions. The main body of Perestiani's film more or less follows the outline of Chonkadze's story and re-tains the same anti-feudal and anticlerical thrust. One important change — also employed by Parajanov's film — is that the enraged Nodar/Osman-Aga slays his master soon after his mother dies, and not years later. Perestiani's film also portrays Zurab not as a young man but a child, and he is placed in a wooden cross-shaped frame before being immured. Driven mad, his mother haunts the wall, saying, "How tall my son Zurab has become!" She meets her fate wandering over the edge of a waterfall. The film ends with several iris shots of the ruined fortress from various angles, emphasizing the ultimate futility of the cruel system of feudalism. While the plot may seem melodramatic and convoluted to modern viewers, Perestiani's film is undeniably well crafted, with many strikingly composed shots and excellent use of exterior locations. It is ultimately a superior production by one of the leading directors of early Soviet cinema.[6] Parajanov himself pays homage to Perestiani's final sequence in the credit sequence of his own film, which is interspersed with various black-and-white shots of the fortress. Indeed, one could even interpret the culminating, shattered-mirror image of the fortress as Parajanov's declaration of artistic independence from his forebears as much as a whimsical representation of the collapsing fortress.

The most important change in Parajanov's film is its interpretation of Zu-rab's immurement as a form of patriotic self-sacrifice. This approach derives from a less well-known 1944 novella entitled *The Inflexible* (*Kedukhrelni*; *Nepreklon-nye* in Russian) by the Georgian writer Niko Lortkipanidze. Apart from the plot element of a young man named Zurab who willingly allows himself to be immured, Lortkipanidze's work shares little in common with Chonkadze's novella.[7] Nonetheless, the film quotes Lortkipanidze loosely in one of its title cards: "If the country has a young man who is capable of being bricked alive in the fortress wall, then the country and its people are unconquerable."

In fact, Parajanov's film as a whole emphasizes the theme of patriotism. In the opening sequence, a man blows on a horn to summon people in the countryside. Women step forth offering eggs, which they pile up on the man's cart. The man then mixes eggs and black soil on a board; this is evidently mortar for the fortress under construction at Surami. Zurab will later use a similar mortar

Figure 7.1. Simon the Piper teaches Zurab about Georgian culture (*The Legend of the Surami Fortress*). Courtesy of Yuri Mechitov.

when he walls himself in. In the middle of the film, Zurab as a child is given lessons in Georgian history and myth by Simon the Piper. Using dolls, Simon teaches the boy about famous Georgian figures: Saint Nino, who introduced Christianity to Georgia; Tamara, the Demon's beloved in Lermontov's poem; Parnavaz, who invented the Georgian alphabet; and Amiran, the Georgian name for Prometheus (Fig. 7.1). Of the latter Simon the Piper says: "When he breaks his chains, Georgia will be free." Later in the film, when Gulisvardi (or Vardo) tells the grown-up Zurab that a handsome blonde, blue-eyed, and tall young man must bury himself in the wall for the Surami fortress to stand, Zurab declares passionately, "I understand!"

The immurement sequence opens with a shot of Zurab silhouetted with strong backlighting, creating a distinct halo effect to emphasize his sainthood. Not only are the dolls that Simon the Piper once used to teach Zurab about Georgian cultural heroes suspended over the young man's head while he prepares the mortar to brick himself in, but Simon the Piper himself helps lay the bricks and places a battle helmet on his pupil's head. Gulisvardi then hangs a blue baby's quilt on the wall, calls Zurab her son, and begs for forgiveness, declaring that she did not send him to his death out of revenge. The king orders a young warrior to take up a sword and bow down in reverence before the mother of the martyred Zurab and summons forth a brilliant white light. While this theme of willing sacrifice has been developed systematically in the script, as a result the film loses some of the tragic force that propels both Chonkadze's novel and Perestiani's film.

The anticlerical subtext of the Perestiani film (and Chonkadze's story) is gone altogether; in contrast, Parajanov's film is full of religious imagery. In the episode of Durmishkhan's wedding, the Mother of God appears in a vision to chide Osman-Agha for renouncing Christianity. A young girl in a white robe, who strongly resembles the angel in Pasolini's *The Gospel According to Matthew* (1964), steps forward and declares: "You didn't spare him." In a tableau shot recalling Christian medieval miniature painting, Osman-Agha is depicted standing in the niche of a church wall next to the young girl, a grazing sheep, and a boy holding up a cross made of sticks tied together with hair—an allusion to the cross that Saint Nino created when she introduced Christianity to Georgia. In the next shot, Osman-Agha holds the boy ("the Lamb of God") in his arms; as he turns around, the child is magically transformed via a jump cut into an actual lamb, signifying Osman-Agha's renewed embrace of the Christian faith.

One distinctive touch throughout the film is Parajanov's playful use of Oriental (especially Persian and Turkish) imagery and decorative motifs that, if anything, go beyond what he employed in *The Color of Pomegranates*. In the sequence where Vardo performs fortune-telling for the prince's Muslim guests, the opening shot consists of an ornate still-life arrangement featuring a peacock, hand-painted hookahs, a metalwork pitcher and tray, and small, hand-painted porcelain bowls. The main tableau deliberately recalls Persian miniatures through its decorative style and vivid coloring. Ismail, the male guest, wears an elaborately embroidered jacket and a turban with a rich paisley pattern; a yellow quince is placed behind him as a color accent (Fig. 7.2). In the "Gulan-sharo" chapter, a muezzin is depicted standing on a minaret, chanting a call to prayer in Arabic. Contributing to the exotic atmosphere of the sequence, tightrope walkers, fire-breathers, and male dancers in Oriental garb parade before the camera. This is followed by a scene set in an Oriental bazaar, accompanied by the sound of a male shouting in Azerbaijani Turkish, alternated with Eastern-style singing.

However, the film is not exclusively an Orientalist fantasy; it also makes liberal use of specifically Georgian visual motifs. In other words, it imagines a Georgia that possesses a distinct cultural identity but is nonetheless permeated with Persian and Turkish cultural influences. The most obvious Georgian motif is the set of dolls that Simon the Piper uses to teach the young Zurab about Georgian mythology and history. The open-air shops and vendor stands

Figure 7.2. Decorative Orientalism (*The Legend of the Surami Fortress*).

present throughout the film are also clearly inspired by the street markets of Old Tbilisi. In the chapter entitled "The King and Berikaoba," Parajanov evokes *Berikaoba*, an ancient Georgian spring festival that has its origins in pagan fertility rites. Traditionally, a group of masked celebrants go from house to house performing plays and dancing in exchange for gifts of food. In the film, mummers reenact Saint George's rescue of a princess from the dragon, then dance in a circle and show off motley costumes (Fig. 7.3).

In that regard, the film reflects an ongoing fascination with both the carnivalesque and pantomime in Parajanov's work that dates back to *Shadows of Forgotten Ancestors* and is a major element of his mature films. As discussed more fully later, the Georgian scholar Giorgi Gvakharia suggests that this dimension of Parajanov's work is closely tied to "the very spirit" of Tbilisi, which includes "the variegated colors and textures of the spectacular and carnivalesque."[8] If one thinks more broadly of Parajanov's work within the framework of the carnival tradition, one could go further in arguing that he is well aware of the tradition's subversive potential. For instance, he frequently introduces campy,

Figure 7.3. Costumed dancers during Berikaoba (*The Legend of the Surami Fortress*). Courtesy of Yuri Mechitov.

sexually ambiguous, and homoerotic elements into the film. In the opening sequence, the Georgian king wears a strand of pearls around his neck. When Osman-Agha goes into hiding after killing the lord, he dresses as a woman. And Zurab as a grown man (Levan Uchaneishvili) is at least as much an icon of male beauty as of heroism.

Parajanov's subversion of norms extends to the representational conventions of realism in narrative film. While one can find subversions of cinematic realism in earlier films such as *Hakob Hovnatanyan* and *The Color of Pomegranates*, in *The Legend of the Surami Fortress* he playfully foregrounds it in certain scenes. In one shot from the episode entitled "Gulansharo," a man waves a pair of semaphore flags and another man beats a tall cylindrical drum on the seashore (Fig. 7.4). Modern-day oil tankers are visible in the distant background, but in the middle ground a small mockup of an antique-style ship is suspended midair to appear as if floating in the water. The anachronistic oil tankers may have been an unavoidable result of location shooting on the shore of the Caspian Sea, but they are deliberately worked into the film. The same mockup hovers squarely in the middle of the frame in the next shot, a reverse angle, in which lines of men carry bundles and roll barrels to be loaded on ships.

While the style of *The Legend of the Surami Fortress* is unmistakably of a piece

Figure 7.4. Subverting the conventions of realism (*The Legend of the Surami Fortress*).

with Parajanov's other mature works, the overall approach is more relaxed and less formalized than *The Color of Pomegranates*, which surely counts among the most rigorously formalized feature films ever made. This film makes frequent use of static, precisely composed tableau shots, but Parajanov and the cinematographer Yuri Klimenko also employ pans and tracking shots. One particularly effective touch, which again echoes *The Color of Pomegranates*, is to signal the transformation of the young Gulisvardi (Leila Alibegashvili) into a middle-aged woman (Sofiko Chiaureli) by having the first actress sway back and forth behind a figure cloaked in black. When she comes to a halt, the woman in front — the older Gulisvardi — pulls down the cloak to reveal her face and begins to sway in the same manner. More generally, actors still often face the camera directly and sometimes engage in pantomime, but there is also quite a bit of dramatic dialogue and consequently a far clearer storyline. One suspects that this approach arose in part because it was understood from the outset that he could not make another film as hermetically stylized as *The Color of Pomegranates*, though there is also no need to assume that Parajanov was necessarily planning to make other films exactly the same way.

Production and Censorship

The film's censorship process was not nearly as protracted and contentious as that of *The Color of Pomegranates*, but the production as a whole nonetheless lasted from the beginning of 1983 to the summer of 1984. The initial work and script development stage lasted from March 1, 1983, to July 31; the preparatory period lasted from August 1 to October 27; and the shooting period lasted from October 28, 1983, to February 29, 1984. The primary delays occurred in the editing stage, which lasted from March 1 to June 26, 1984, thus running 18 days over schedule.

Although the town of Surami still has a large fortress, Parajanov ultimately did not use it in the film. Shooting locations in Georgia included the villages of Chailuri (the site of the fortress used in the film) and Garikula (the scenes with the fortune-teller), as well as Uplistsikhe and the David Gareja monastic complex. Locations in Baku, Azerbaijan included the Palace of the Shirvan-shahs. In his production account, the production manager S. Sikharulidze noted that the work on the film was "very complicated" due to its elaborate style: "It required reconstructing an era, and this dictated a careful and exact approach to the determination of the milieu, locations, props, costumes, and the physical types [*tipazh*] [of the extras]."[9] Originally budgeted for 523,015 rubles, the film finally cost 631,100. Much of the excess cost was due to props and costumes, since the studio lacked ready materials fitting the period in question and, in Sikharulidze's words, "especially since the individual approach of the director and the choice of milieu required the purchase of unique and costly props and costumes."[10]

In a memo of February 1, 1983, evaluating Gigashvili's initial script, Goskino of Georgia's Script-Editorial Board members R. Mirianashvili and N. Makharashvili acknowledged its relative de-emphasis of the anti-feudal aspect of Chonkadze's story, but argued that it had the virtue of strong cinematic storytelling: "the contemporary cinematic interpretation of this work brings in vivid characters, sharp dramatic collisions and psychological depth, violent passions, stirring us not only through the social vicissitudes of that time, but also through the complexity, the indefatigability, and the changeability of the human character."[11] In their memo dated February 21, A. V. Bogomolov (editor-in-chief) and A. E. Balikhin (director of the thematic team) of the Script-Editorial Board at the Main Administration in Moscow replied that they felt it was possible to accept the script, but with the following proviso: "In the process of further work on it, we urgently recommend that you eliminate religious motifs as a means of developing the plot and characters from the fabric of the script, and focus particular attention on the development of social conflicts and moral changes in human interrelations."[12]

Even though the censors in Moscow expressed concerns about religious motifs in the script from the outset, there is certainly no shortage of religious imagery in the finished film, as was the case with *The Color of Pomegranates*. Indeed, Bogomolov and Balikhin's recommendation appears to have gone more or less unheeded, based on a subsequent memo by V. F. Zaika (deputy editor-in-chief at the Main Administration) and A. E. Balikhin, dated April 27, 1983: "In connection with the necessity of eliminating religious motifs from the script (which was written about in our Resolution No. 1/169 from 2/21/83), we direct the studio's attention to the treatment of Nodar/Osman-Agha's story as a problem of choosing between a "true" and a "false" religious faith, although the essence of the moral tragedy that this character experiences obviously consists of betraying his homeland, native soil, and national way of life. You are requested to reexamine this story from the angle of revealing in it the real reasons for the tragedy of the hero and to avoid an emphatically naturalistic solution (the execution of Osman-Agha) in work on the film."[13] Again, at least some of Moscow's recommendations went unheeded, considering the symbolic weight and overall tone of the scenes depicting Nodar/Osman-Agha's conversion back to Christianity in the finished film. However, Parajanov hardly could be said to handle Osman-Agha's beheading in a "naturalistic" manner given the playfully stylized treatment of it within his dream.

The censorship file in Moscow does not contain as complete a record of the Main Administration's evaluation of the film at its subsequent stages as does the file on *The Color of Pomegranates*, but the finished film was well-received by the Script-Editorial Board of Goskino of Georgia. In his memo dated May 28, 1984, Editor-in-Chief R. Mirianashvili praises the film's "lofty patriotic significance," at the same time noting its "stylized and palpable image of the medieval Orient."[14] It is worth noting how Mirianashvili strongly emphasizes the patriotic elements of both the script and the finished film. This indicates the extent to which, at least at this particular point in time and in this context, the Soviets tolerated expressions of nationalism by non-Russian republics. For example, in their aforementioned memo Zaika and Balikhin did not object to the script's patriotic Georgian sentiments as much as the religious content. In other words, secular patriotism was not problematic, but the excessive religious imagery and particularly the pitting of Christianity against Islam was.

Of course, in a multinational state that arises out of an empire as did the Soviet Union, there is always the danger that locals can read historical narratives of subjugation or invasion—in this case, by the Turks—as an allegory of the present-day situation. Some Georgians evidently wanted to interpret the narrative this way, as the film's subsequent, controversial reception suggests. It is also important to note that in the same memo Mirianashvili praises the film's "authentic texture" (*dopodlinnaia faktura*), arguably a necessary condition for it to succeed as a patriotic historical narrative. The film's evocation of "authenticity" is in fact a rather complicated matter; for while Parajanov deploys authentic objects and locations that give the film a lush texture and a tangible sense of "pastness," as usual he treats these materials with great freedom. For example, the same pagan ruins are recycled throughout the film with a bare minimum of changes in decor to evoke the prince's court when Gulisvardi tells the guest's fortune, the caravan of Osman-Agha, and Durmishkhan's conjugal bed with his new wife. Parajanov is also not above mischievous fillips at the very notion of authenticity, such as the aforementioned oil tankers juxtaposed against a miniature mockup of an ancient ship.

Critical Reception

Heralded as Parajanov's comeback, *The Legend of the Surami Fortress* garnered awards at international festivals (most notably, at São Paulo and Rotterdam), though it received relatively few reviews in the Soviet press compared to other key films of the perestroika era during its initial release in 1986 and 1987. (It premiered in Georgia in January 1986 and opened in Moscow that April.) In *Sovetskii ekran*, the critic Rostislav Yurenev acknowledged that the story was difficult to follow and suggested that the film may have been weakened by Parajanov's failure to show sufficiently how the threat from invaders necessitated Zurab's sacrifice. (Indeed, this might have been the best solution to make the film's patriotic interpretation of the legend more convincing.) However, Yurenev strongly defended the film's aesthetic achievement as a whole, especially its painterly compositions, "rhythmic contrasts," and "epic" performance style. He concluded: "*The Legend of the Surami Fortress* is complex and difficult to take in, but a work full of real poetry. There are obvious contradictions in it, and it is possible to observe imperfections. But its originality—the sign of real talent—makes the film an outstanding phenomenon."[15]

The film's appearance also sparked two significant essays published in the May 1987 issue of the Soviet film studies journal *Iskusstvo kino*: the review entitled "The Timelessness of Eternity," by the film scholar Miron Chernenko, and the essay entitled "The Novelty of Legend," by the renowned semiotician Jurij Lotman. They turned out to be the most thought-provoking and substantial pieces of criticism on Parajanov published in the Soviet Union up to that time.

Chernenko stresses the film's continuity with the style and some specific imagery of *The Color of Pomegranates*. In general, Chernenko sees the film as a paradoxical combination of the archaic and the modern. For example, he compares the film's "frontal mise-en-scène" and its tendency to line up characters in the foreground to the staging of medieval mystery plays, and compares imagery from other scenes to Persian miniatures.[16] Its method of narration, he argues, does not operate according to the customary rules of "Aristotelian [. . .] dramaturgy," but instead draws upon the fresco, the iconostasis, the medieval miniature, and Cubism (thus yoking together the ancient and the modern once again).

In particular, he notes the director's use of what he calls "plastic epigraphs," the discrete still-life compositions that introduce each section of the film.[17] One example of this is the previously described still life that opens the scene in which Vardo performs fortune-telling for the prince's guests. As Chernenko points out, such "epigraphs" bear a relationship of some sort to the scene that follows, but not always in a straightforward symbolic or metaphorical manner. He also compares the film's use of myth, its flow of "material symbols, metaphors, and signs" to a "sacral performance" or a "mystery play" and characterizes it as a "dialogue of cultures — not even cultures, but their essences and archetypes — carried out without conflicts and confrontations."[18] If one accepts Chernenko's basic premise, then the muting of the legend's tragic dimension that results from Parajanov's reworking of the material is not necessarily a flaw, but rather an innovative aesthetic principle. In conclusion, Chernenko argues that Parajanov's aesthetic not only exceeds the bounds of ordinary cinematic storytelling, but calls for a new kind of spectatorship: "To whom would it have occurred that [*The Color of Pomegranates*] is the real beginning of a cinema for video, for a new kind of [film] rental, for a fundamentally new perception of cinema by the spectator, an intimate, complicit perception? A perception-dialogue. In this sense, *The Legend of the Surami Fortress* belongs not only to the present day, but also to tomorrow, to the future."[19] It is interesting to note that five years earlier, film critic Gilbert Adair had made a similar point in his review of *The Color of Pomegranates* for *Sight and Sound*, calling the film "an essential video text."[20]

Chernenko's and Adair's comments get to the heart of Parajanov's dilemma as a filmmaker. In order to realize his vision, he needed to work within an industry — in this case, state-controlled — that was geared primarily toward the production and distribution of narrative feature films for a mass audience. However, the density of his films as texts and the unconventional ways in which they produced meaning challenged the usual paradigm of film consumption. That is to say, film as something that unfolds in real time and is commonly viewed only once. That paradigm favors clear, linear storytelling. Unlike with a painting or a literary text, the viewer cannot stop to ponder a metaphor or admire a particular detail. Parajanov partially compensated for this basic limitation by his use of extended, static tableaux, but viewers coming with the expectation of an ordinary film narrative are still often confounded. While his films require projection of a good print in 35mm to fully appreciate their sensuous rendering of detail and texture, they also benefit from the video format's ability to pause and review, enabling a more interactive kind of viewing.

Lotman likewise stresses the combination of the archaic and the modern in his essay "The Novelty of Legend," which frames *The Legend of the Surami Fortress* within his scholarly focus on artistic languages from a semiotic perspective. In fact, Lotman had briefly discussed *The Color of Pomegranates* as an example of poetic cinema in his 1973 book *The Semiotics of Cinema and Problems of Film Aesthetics*, so this was not the first time he had taken an interest in Parajanov's work.[21] The first half of the essay examines *The Legend of the Surami Fortress* as a form of illustration, which he characterizes as a "transformational (secondary) art." He cites as examples "program music, paintings on historical subjects, and any kind of theatricalization illustrating a 'primary text.'"[22] According to him, the process involves turning "a single, unbroken verbal text into a chain of images, compositionally divided by breaks, a certain series of freeze frames." He continues: "The connection between separate illustrations is realized in a dual manner: on the one hand, through turning toward the verbal text; on the other hand — by using the stylistic unity of the drawings, their consistency and compositional cohesion, thus forming a peculiarly connected text, a unified narrative-illustration."[23] As with *The Color of Pomegranates*, the visual style of *The Legend of the Surami Fortress* is strongly influenced by illustrative art forms such as medieval miniature painting. In this particular case, the narrative is based on a commonly recounted Georgian legend, so the viewer can effectively supply the first half of the text-illustration formula, especially if he or she is already familiar with the basic legend.

Ordinary cinematic narration, in contrast, employs moving images and also uses montage to construct meaning through shot linkages, as Lotman points out. Parajanov's imagery is notably static, though not completely devoid of movement, and the individual shots tend to be self-contained. As a result, in Lotman's words, "the dependence of the shot's semantic significance on the montage effect is weakened in the film."[24] Thus, this self-containment often extends to the semantic dimension as well.

The second half of Lotman's essay provides an insightful reading of the film's mythic or archetypal imagery. Among other things, he discusses the concepts of "mother" and "father" in relation to the dichotomy of "motherland" (*rodina*) and "people" (*narod*), extending the metaphor to the relationships between characters in the film. He also examines the theme of the double and the film's use of archetypal animal imagery such as the eagle, the sacrificial lamb, and the horse. He sums up as follows: "The mythologism of the film's language manifests itself in yet one more [aspect]: it is panchronic. [. . .] It flows in the recurring time of myth and freely combines signs from different epochs."[25] Having noted at the beginning of the essay that "illustrativeness" (*illiustrativnost'*) as applied to cinema generally has a negative connation, he concludes by reiterating his contention that "the artistic language of *Legend* is new because it is not afraid of archaism. It is profoundly cinematic, for it violates the canons of cinematicness."[26] Parajanov was reportedly flattered that an intellectual on Lotman's plane would devote such considered attention to his work, and he liked to show off the article to his friends.

Arabesques on the Theme of Pirosmani

Parajanov's next project was the delightful twenty-minute short *Arabesques on the Theme of Pirosmani* (*Arabeski na temu Pirosmani*, Georgian Studio of Popular-Science and Documentary Films 1985). The Georgian folk painter Pirosmani (Niko Pirosmanashvili, 1862–1918) has become an archetypal figure in Georgian culture, and images from his paintings permeate the Georgian popular imagination. A self-taught artist who moved to Tbilisi from Kakheti, he painted portraits, genre paintings, animals, and historical subjects in a primitive style, often selling them as decor for local shops. In 1912 the Russian poet Ilya Zdanevich discovered Pirosmani's work during a trip to Tbilisi. Together with the painter Mikhail Larionov, he promoted Pirosmani's paintings in Russia and eventually they were exhibited in Moscow and Saint Petersburg. Pirosmani was known for his fierce pride, but also for his kindness and generosity. Living in abject poverty and finally winding up homeless, he died on the eve of Easter in 1918, in effect a martyr to his art. He has since become viewed as something of a holy innocent, or even a Christ figure in Georgian culture. The largest collection of his works is on display at the Art Museum of Georgia (the Shalva Amiranashvili Museum of Fine Arts) in Tbilisi. Years earlier, Giorgi Shengelaia made a feature film about him, simply titled *Pirosmani* (Georgia Film Studio 1969), which stands among the artistic high points of Georgian cinema.[27]

Like Parajanov's feature films, *Arabesques* is divided into a number of discrete chapters headed by intertitles. The first section, entitled "Tiflis," evokes the atmosphere of Old Tbilisi by focusing on details from one of Pirosmani's paintings. In "The Photographer's Studio," Parajanov evokes the cultural milieu of

Old Tbilisi via period photographic portrait-cards arrayed like playing cards, antique photographic equipment, and actors dressed in period costume, posing as if for portraits. Scratchy old recordings of music on the soundtrack also help evoke the feel of a bygone era. In one series of shots, a woman dons three different hats, adopting slightly different facial expressions with each. Many, if not all, of the film's hats belong to a collection that Parajanov created "in memory of the unplayed roles of Nato Vachnadze," the beautiful Georgian actress of the silent era who often starred in her husband Nikoloz Shengelaia's films. (Their sons are the leading Georgian film directors Giorgi and Eldar Shengelaia.) Most of these extravagant creations are currently on display at the Parajanov Museum in Yerevan.

The section entitled "The Pages of History" contains Pirosmani's diptych of Imam Shamil and Prince Alexander Baryatinsky (the governor of the Caucasian Province during the successful 1859 military assault against Shamil and his rebels in Gunib, Daghestan); a portrait of King Erekle II wearing the distinctive combination of Persian-style headwear of the Qajar era and a Western-style military tunic; and a portrait of Queen Tamar and Shota Rustaveli. The section entitled "Animals" depicts various animal paintings — a favorite subject for Pirosmani — including exotic creatures such as a giraffe. The soundtrack for this sequence contains a bizarre combination of animal cries and atonal music. "Barrenness and Motherhood" uses the painting of a wealthy, childless couple standing next to an impoverished mother and her children to highlight the social inequalities of that era. In "Feasts," Parajanov not only displays many of Pirosmani's famed paintings of Georgian feasts, he also creates amusing juxtapositions by filming pairs of paintings next to each other. A seemingly innocent painting of a sow with her piglets and another of a paschal lamb take on a new connotation when a painting of a cook sharpening his knife magically appears next to them. "A Bouquet for Marguerite" depicts the pretty French dancer whom Pirosmani loved. In "Requiem for Niko," images of winemaking and grape harvesting are accompanied, perhaps not terribly originally, by the Georgian hymn used earlier in *The Color of Pomegranates*, "Thou Art a Vineyard" ("Shen khar venakhi"). Pirosmani's status as a Christ figure is emphasized by introducing, once again, the aforementioned painting of a paschal lamb. In the last section, "A Step to Immortality," Parajanov moves fully into the timeless space of myth: Pirosmani and his Muse, the latter a transfigured vision of the actress Marguerite, stand before a fanciful, shambling folk iconostasis constructed out of Pirosmani paintings, window frames, and door frames (Fig. 7.5). Now dressed in white and holding up the painting of the lamb, Pirosmani departs through the open doorway with his Muse. The camera tracks through

Figure 7.5. Marguerite, Pirosmani's Muse (*Arabesques on the Theme of Pirosmani*). Courtesy of Yuri Mechitov.

the doorway, revealing a large field behind it. Saint George gallops on a horse around Pirosmani and his Muse, with the tall white apartment buildings of modern-day Tbilisi in the distant background.

For all its whimsy and deliberate primitivism, the most striking aspect of *Arabesques on the Theme of Pirosmani* is the way it foregrounds, in a systematic and sophisticated manner, the process of cinematic representation. In this respect it goes well beyond *The Legend of the Surami Fortress* and shares a great deal in common with another film about a painter from almost twenty years earlier, *Hakob Hovnatanyan*. The opening shot depicts a hand applying black and white paint to a dark-colored palette. This is followed by a painted representation of a flock of birds (probably gulls) from one of Pirosmani's paintings, juxtaposed with the recorded sound of real gulls on the soundtrack. (The brilliantly mixed soundtrack is arguably the high point of sound engineer Gari Kuntsev's collaborations with Parajanov during the 1980s.) In this sequence Parajanov edits together close shots of details from a painting as if constructing an ordinary film scene through montage. Elsewhere the film depicts paintings in their frames and even an original assemblage that Parajanov constructed for the film out of cut-up reproductions from Pirosmani's paintings, further extending his play on the concept of representation. This theme culminates in the final shot of a fish writhing on a white palette. Besides recalling the prologue to *The Color of Pomegranates*, it seems to be saying that whereas Pirosmani's medium was oil paint, Parajanov paints in the medium of cinema using physical objects. *Arabesques on the Theme of Pirosmani* may be difficult to see today, but is by no means a negligible entry in the director's canon.

Parajanov's Artworks

Parajanov continued to create drawings, collages, and assemblages regularly throughout the 1980s after his release from prison, and in January 1985 an exhibition of his works entitled "A Visit in a Director's Workshop" was held at the House of Cinema in Tbilisi. Subsequent exhibitions were organized in Armenia in 1988 and 1989. Though Parajanov's interest in collages and assemblages dated back long before his return to Tbilisi, he was undoubtedly spurred by other artists in Georgia employing these techniques, including Gogi Mikeladze, Georgi Alexi-Meskhishvili and Otar Chkhartishvili. (Alexi-Meskhishvili, a noted theatrical designer at the Rustaveli Theater in Tbilisi, later served as the lead production designer on *Ashik-Kerib*.)

In a very concrete sense, Parajanov's artworks are intimately connected with his filmmaking aesthetics. The stylistic inspiration that he finds in Renaissance painting, religious icons, and medieval Armenian and Persian miniatures is reflected in the frequent use of cut-out reproductions from these works as a form of visual quotation in his own artworks. Decorative elements such as seashells, patterned fabrics, and jewelry, which play such an important role in the visual texture of his films, often serve as encrustations adorning the subjects of his collage-portraits. He also likes to create visual puns, the most obvious example being the red plastic combs that make up the assemblage *The Gallic Rooster* (*Gall'skii petukh*, 1986).[28] Underlying all this is the principle of creative transformation: taking mundane, often discarded objects and creating something new with them, or taking something familiar and using it in an unexpected way.

The artworks also share broader thematic concerns with his films. Thus we find the world of Transcaucasia and the Near East in assemblages such as *King Erekle on the Throne* (*Tsar' Iraklii na trone*, 1984) and the installation entitled *Wall of the 26 Baku Commissars* (*Stena 26 Bakinskikh Komissarov*, 1984), or that of Hans Christian Andersen in *Andersen's Birthday* (*Den' rozhdeniia Andersena*, 1986). One even finds frequent homoerotic elements; among the most striking examples of this is the assemblage *Remorse* (*Raskaianie*, 1989) (Fig. 7.6). Using reproductions of actual Renaissance artworks, he creates a portrait of an older, bearded man with an earring (an actual piece of costume jewelry glued to his ear) about to kiss

Figure 7.6. *Remorse* (1989). Assemblage. Courtesy of the Sergei Parajanov Museum.

a beautiful youth. The youth has a rose glued to his cheek and is decorated with peacock feathers, shells, pearls, and pieces of brocaded fabric. The assemblage *Saint George in Blue (Sviatoi Georgii v golubom*, 1984) most likely alludes to Picasso's "blue period," but it is probably not accidental that *goluboi*, the adjective meaning "light blue," is also slang in Russian for "gay," and that this particular

Saint George is decorated with pearls and bits of lace. Lastly, the postmodern elements of parody, irony, and self-reflexivity that crop up in his films of the 1980s find their counterpart in Parajanov's handling of Soviet iconography in many of his artworks. For example, the collage entitled *Soviet Union* (*Sovetskii soiuz*, undated) combines representations of Stalin and Lenin with a picture of the Virgin Mary holding the infant Jesus.[29] Here his use of Soviet kitsch and sly commentary on Lenin and Stalin as religious figures clearly shares something in common with (and was possibly inspired by) Vitaly Komar and Alex Melamid's Sots Art movement of the late 1960s and early 1970s. Thanks to the efforts of Zaven Sargsyan and Karen Mikaelyan, the Armenian government later established a home-museum intended to house Parajanov's works and to serve as a new residence. Though Parajanov planned to live there during the last years of his life, the devastating 1988 earthquake in Armenia halted construction and the museum was not completed until 1991, after his death.

The Passion of Shushanik (1987) and Nationalist Backlash

One of the most bitter political conflicts of Parajanov's career arose from his decision to adapt the earliest surviving original work of Georgian literature, the fifth century hagiographic narrative *The Passion of Queen Saint Shushanik* (*Tsamebay tsmidisa shushanikisi dedoplisay*), attributed to Iakob Tsurtaveli.[30] The tale is narrated in the first person by Shushanik's confessor Iakob, a witness to the events. (His last name, Tsurtaveli, indicates that he is a resident of Tsurtavi, the township in which the story is set.) Shushanik was the daughter of Vardan Mamikonian, the military commander who courageously led the Armenians against the Persians at the battle of Avarayr in AD 451. (As mentioned earlier, this battle was the subject of one of the hymns used in *The Color of Pomegranates*.) Shushanik had married Varsken, the *Pitiakhsh* (Viceroy) of the Hereti region in Georgia. In approximately AD 466, Varsken abjured Christianity for Zoroastrianism, even taking up a second, Persian wife in order to strengthen his ties with Peroz, the Shah of Iran. Varsken further promised the conversion of his first wife, Shushanik, and his children. However, Shushanik refused to abandon her faith and condemned her husband, Varsken, for doing so. Feeling betrayed as a husband, Varsken was overcome with rage; during a confrontation over dinner he beat Shushanik savagely with a poker, nearly killing her. Later, he had her dragged into a dungeon where she was kept for six years, suffering from ill health and eventually dying from ulcerated sores. During that time her faith remained steadfast and she performed a number of miracles such as healing the sick and restoring sight to the blind. Other major figures in the legend are Aphots, the bishop serving the *Pitiakhsh*, Varsken's brother Jojik, and Jojik's wife. Although it is not recounted in Iakob Tsurtaveli's narrative, Varsken was later put to death by the Georgian king Vakhtang Gorgasali.

For a hagiographic narrative, *The Passion of Queen Saint Shushanik* is remarkably modern in tone, vividly conveying the emotional and physical violence of Varsken and Shushanik's relationship and the difficult conditions under which people lived during that time. One should note that there is some controversy about the origins of the work. Traditionally it is ascribed to Iakob Tsurtaveli and it is assumed to have been written shortly after the events took place. However, literary scholar Donald Rayfield argues that certain linguistic anomalies and allusions within the text suggest that it may be a "modernization, reconstruction, or mystification" from a hypothetical, now-lost original written a few centuries later. Another possibility is that the Georgian text may have been "filtered" through a parallel Armenian version.[31] (The hagiography also exists in multiple versions in the Armenian language.) Regardless of its provenance and its exact date of composition, it remains a masterpiece of Georgian literature.

The surviving manuscript for Parajanov's *The Passion of Shushanik* (*Muchenichestvo Shushanik*) is dated the summer of 1986. The film script consists of an elaborate handwritten document meant to suggest a medieval illuminated manuscript in its use of decorative motifs and illustrations, albeit executed with a ballpoint pen. Some of these crudely rendered but expressive illustrations are reproduced in *Ispoved'*, the Russian-language edition of his writings. A complete English translation of the script is available in the *Armenian Review* special issue on Parajanov.[32]

The dynamism of the prologue, besides evoking the vital energy of Christianity in its early days, suggests that Parajanov may have wanted to incorporate aerial shots in the beginning of the film:

> The rusty hills of Tsurtavi, their north slopes covered in gray ash.
> The hills were chasing after one another, blending into one, hill covered itself with hill, spawning and turning into stone.
> Naked stonemasons were pounding out the stone . . .
> The hammers resonated off the tuff of Bolnisi . . .
> The Bolnisi tuff precisely defined the contour of Bolnisi Sioni.[33]
> Gray-roseate hills were running . . .
> Roseate-gray hills were overtaking them . . .
> On the hills' horizon rows of pilgrims appeared . . .[34]

This passage strongly recalls the description of "Syria" (*Siriia*, presumably Assyria) from the opening section of *Ara the Fair*, written some fourteen years previous (see chapter 5 for a discussion of that project):

> Syria!
> Endless rust-colored hills . . .
> Brown hills that look like humps . . .
> Humps were hiding behind humps . . . they ran toward the horizon.
> They diminished . . . teased one another . . . repeated themselves . . .
> In the endlessness they melted into a rust-colored jumble, united with the rust-colored sky . . .[35]

Such similarities suggest that Parajanov had a precise notion of visual concepts that he wanted to reuse, in the same way that specific images from *Kyiv Frescoes* found their way into later projects. The rest of the prologue depicts Shushanik, her children, and her brother-in-law Jojik at a carnival celebrating the 100th anniversary of Christianity in Georgia. Shushanik urges Jojik to pray for his brother, who has renounced Christ.

The next section is set presumably in Ctesiphon at the court of Peroz, the Shah of the Persian Empire at that time. While Varsken's conversion to Zoroastrianism to gain favor with the Persian king is mentioned only briefly in Iakob Tsurtaveli's narrative, Parajanov naturally uses it as an opportunity to evoke the sumptuous world of the Sassanid Persian Empire:

> Persia . . . The marble palace of the King . . . Marble wells . . . Baths . . . Marble benches . . .
> From the jaws of a lion hot water was rushing . . .
> King Peroz was licking boiled rice from the palm of his hand . . .
> The Georgian king patiently rocked back and forth, his eyes closed . . .
> Persian attendants rubbed the body of the Georgian king with pungent gray taro-mud.
> The Persian king continued to eat boiled, steaming pilaf . . .
> Attendants were rubbing a thick layer of mud on the face and head of King Varsken . . .
> The King crosses his hands in front of his groin with a look of embarrassment . . .
> They washed Varsken and cast him into the pool, where they were throwing herbs and rose petals . . .[36]

This trope represents Varsken under the political influence of the Persian Empire. Once again Parajanov is referring back to an earlier script, in this case the scene in *The Color of Pomegranates* depicting a Tatar bath attendant rubbing gray "Turkish mud" over King Erekle II.

The rest of the script follows the outline of the original narrative in general terms, but with significant amplifications and additions, some of them quite startling. The hagiography does mention that Varsken and Shushanik bore children and that Varsken planned to have them converted to Zoroastrianism, but in Parajanov's script Varsken is depicted as turning the children against their mother, even encouraging them to hurl stones at her. Parajanov also dramatizes Shushanik's inner conflicts relating to her estranged family. Confined to a dungeon, she continues to perform miracles such as healing the sick. A young man with a skin disease is brought to her and she removes an infectious poultice of cabbage leaves from his face, applying a paste instead. When the boy is carried away and someone points out to her that it was her son — Parajanov implies that she was aware of this from the start — she mounts a horse, races up to the entourage, and replaces the cabbage leaf.

Most startling of all is the physical aspect of Varsken and Shushanik's relationship as portrayed in Parajanov's script. In Tsurtaveli's original narrative, when Queen Shushanik leaves Varsken to live in a cottage by the church, he complains: "How could my wife allow herself to do such a thing to me? Now go and tell her that she has degraded my person and sprinkled ashes upon my bed and forsaken my rightful place and gone elsewhere."[37] While the wounded pride and spurned affections of a husband come through clearly enough in Tsurtaveli's narrative, Parajanov takes the idea of marital desire much further, imagining a lurid primal scene of animalistic passions in which Shushanik expresses her contempt for Varsken when he signals his interest in making love with her again. She succumbs when he crawls at her feet, and the couple makes love on animal skins while "the royal children were watching them."[38]

In fact, forbidden or frustrated sexual desire is a recurring theme throughout the script. In the section immediately following this, Parajanov implies repressed incestuous feelings between Shushanik and Jojik. While picking mulberries together, she asks him to hug her and he replies, "Queen, I don't dare to touch you . . . I have dreams, and you appear to me in a radiant light." (Ellipses his.) Shushanik then describes a dream of her own: "It is raining . . . You, naked, are running in the rain . . . Lightning illuminates you. A downpour is washing you and you are struggling against it and step onto the shore in a cassock. You want to remove it . . . you remove it, but it, the cassock, again appears on your naked body."[39] Later in the script he portrays another Jojik, Shushanik's eldest son, as sexually attracted to Varsken's new wife:

The son of the Queen, already a prince, lean, with golden down above his passionate lips, fell against a dank wall . . . greedily watching . . .

Against the stone wall a pool was located. Green water washed over the pink body of Varsken's new wife. Black hair, like arrows, stuck to the wet, naked body . . . they floated like snakes in the water, again coming to rest on the pink body.

Luxuriant young breasts were floating in the water, as if accompanying the young wife . . .

The youth writhed against the stone wall . . . froze, and then again writhed . . .

The Queen was singing something . . . Something strange and distant . . .

The eyes of the youth clouded over . . . The youth fell with a crash against the stones . . . Above him stood the King . . . The father had caught the son in his lechery.[40]

Thus, Parajanov deliberately presents a world in which the torments of the flesh play as large a role as those of the spirit.

Parajanov's unorthodox interpretation of this hagiography almost certainly would have raised eyebrows even with the advent of glasnost, but no one involved with the project anticipated the vehement response it provoked in some Georgian intellectuals, who accused him of "profaning" a classic of Georgian literature. Beyond the very legitimate question of profanation, this response arose to no small degree from the fact that Parajanov, an ethnic Armenian, was adapting one of the key works of Georgian literature, and one that happened to have an Armenian heroine at that. In other words, one of the subtexts underlying the controversy was the question of cultural ownership. Giorgi Gvakharia recalls the near-riot that erupted at the 1987 Congress of the Union of Cinematographers in Georgia when the project was rejected by a sizable contingent of union members. Sofiko Chiaureli, stepping down from the rostrum, addressed those attending: "Why don't you want Parajanov to produce *The Passion of Shushanik?*" Such a din rose in the hall that Sofiko said afterwards, "For the first time in my life I was afraid of those people."[41] Chiaureli, who felt that Shushanik could have been one of her strongest roles to date, encouraged Parajanov to press forward with *The Passion of Shushanik* in spite of the criticism it had engendered. Nonetheless, due to political pressure the project was ultimately abandoned, much to Parajanov's disappointment.

The quarrel surrounding *The Passion of Shushanik* was by no means an isolated incident; rather, it was symptomatic of the increasingly nationalistic atmosphere in Georgia that coincided roughly with the advent of glasnost in the mid-1980s. This nationalism was partly a reemergence of long-standing desires for independent nationhood among many Georgians (a "return of the repressed," if you will), partly a reflection of preexisting tensions between various ethnic groups in the region, and partly a specific outcome of demographic changes and Soviet ideology and policies. Historian Ronald Suny argues that, alongside more commonly noted processes such as urbanization and industrialization, one of the fundamental drivers of social transformation within the Soviet Union was what he terms "renationalization." This entailed a range of factors that depended on the individual situation of each nationality, such as broad demographic changes. Specific Soviet policies and initiatives that contributed to renationalization included *korenizatsiia* (during the early Soviet period through the Stalin era, the preferential selection and promotion of the titular ethnic group in party cadres and state apparatuses within a given republic), the implementation of new alphabets, and even written languages for nationalities that still lacked one.[42]

For ethnic Georgians, one important aspect of renationalization was the consolidation of political power within their republic through mechanisms such as *korenizatsiia*; another was the ongoing outmigration of ethnic groups such as Armenians, Russians, and Jews. Whereas in 1939 61.4 percent of the population in the Georgian SSR was of Georgian ethnicity, by 1979 the percentage had increased to 68.8. The percentage of Armenians decreased from 11.7 to 9.0, and the percentage of Russians decreased from 8.7 to 7.4. As Suny points out, an overwhelming percentage of ethnic Georgians live within the Georgian republic, further contributing to a strong sense of cohesion. Finally, by 1975 the Georgian population of Tbilisi reached an absolute majority, thus cementing their hold on the historically diverse capital city.[43]

Moreover, the Soviet state actively supported Georgian-language university education and artistic production in fields such as literature, theater, opera, and folk dance, contributing to the cultural revival in Georgia that had begun in the late nineteenth century. The remarkable ascent of Georgian cinema in particular provides an example of how the Soviet state supported institutions that contributed to the growth of national identity and ultimately nationalism. During the postwar years Georgian feature film production grew from an average of 5.6 films per year during 1955–1959 to 11.9 films per year during 1980–1987, a doubling of output.[44] To put this growth into perspective, the total population of the republic grew from four million in 1959 to five million in 1979, or 25 percent. Using those dates as markers, the average number of films produced in the five year period surrounding 1959 (1957–1961) was 6.2; this figure increased to 10.6 in the five year period surrounding 1979 (1977–1981). Either way, one can see that the rate of growth in film production outstripped the rate of population growth. Georgia's film industry was also an important source of cultural pride. Thanks to directors such as Tengiz Abuladze, Rezo Chkheidze, Otar Iosseliani, Eldar and Giorgi Shengelaia, and Lana Gogoberidze, it developed a reputation in the Soviet Union as the strongest national cinema outside of Russia. Unusually for non-Russian republics, it possessed its own film school and thus was able to train a number of important younger directors domestically, among them Temur Babluani, Nana Djordjadze, Nodar Managadze, and Aleko Tsabadze.

However, the otherwise solid standing of Georgians as an ethnic group within their own republic did not erase the kinds of fears about long-term survival that "small nations" commonly experience. Because of the relative decline of the Georgian birthrate compared to some other groups in the republic — mainly Muslim, in keeping with the higher birthrates for Muslims in the USSR as a whole — the Georgian Communist Party began to emphasize "demographic concerns" during the 1980s and even started a program designating Georgian women who bore five or more children with the honorary title of "Mother Georgia."[45] Ethnic minorities within the republic also became increasingly concerned about their own status relative to the Georgians. In 1988–1989 the Abkhazians, long a minority group within the region of Abkhazeti and concerned about their status within the Georgian republic, stepped up their efforts to secede. The Ossetians constituted a majority in the South Ossetian Autonomous Oblast, and in 1990 they declared independence from Georgia and sought to align with the USSR in the face of rising Georgian nationalism.[46] The situation for ethnic Armenians in Georgia was hardly as dire, but Armenian-Georgian relations were fraught with tension nonetheless. In early 1986, a satirical novel by Levan Chelidze entitled *There, on a Distant Planet . . . Or Thirteen Throws from the Life of Artem Gasparov* (*Tam, na otdalennoi planete . . . ili trinadtsat' broskov iz zhizni Artema Gasparova*), which depicted an Armenian employee at a Georgian film studio, was published in the Russian-language version of *Literaturnaia Gruziia* (*Literary Georgia*). It resulted in letters of protest and public criticism both in a subsequent issue of *Literaturnaia Gruziia* and from the Central Committee of the Communist Party in Georgia, due to its negative portrayal of another ethnic group, which violated the "internationalist traditions of Soviet literature."[47]

Thus, it seems inevitable that Parajanov, because of his international stature, his Armenian ethnicity, and his provocative choice of subject matter, would become a focus of controversy. In the March 27, 1987, issue of the Georgian-language version of *Literary Georgia* (*Literaturuli sakartvelo*), the noted literary scholar Vakhtang Rodonaia published a lengthy diatribe against *The

Legend of the Surami Fortress. He accused the co-directors Sergei Parajanov and Dodo Abashidze of departing both from the legend and from Vazha Gigash-vili's screenplay. He writes:

> Ideologically and artistically, the screenplay shows a well-defined national spirit, but the result in the film is completely the opposite. The protagonists' surroundings, outfits, behavior, and speech bear resemblance with the strangers of another faith. (Al. Janshiev, the film's art director, tries to make the reality of the film even more foreign, Oriental looking. He does the same in the design of the brochure for the film.)
>
> When the story is told as a legend, it obviously has some nonspecific details in it. We are not demanding that the authors of the film recreate reality with ethnographic precision, BUT WHEN THEY INTENTIONALLY ALTER GEORGIAN REALITY, THE GEORGIAN CHARACTER, AND ARE METICULOUSLY TRANSFERRING ANOTHER PARTICULAR RE-ALITY INTO THE GEORGIAN, WHAT IS LEFT FOR US EXCEPT TO EXPRESS OUR INDIGNATION AND DISMAY?![48]

Rodonaia also criticizes Parajanov's treatment of Pirosmani in *Arabesques on the Theme of Pirosmani*, arguing that the director "tries to cut the artist from his roots, from his national soil."[49] In particular, he decries Parajanov's fascination with Oriental motifs in the section of the film entitled "Pages from History," noting that Pirosmani's painting, "Shamil and his Crew," which has obvious Islamic content, is followed by the aforementioned painting of King Erekle II in a Persian-style hat. Rodonaia continues: "Parajanov attracts our atten-tion to the surface, to clothing and makes the conclusion that is valuable for him: foreign dress and foreign, non-Georgian/Oriental faces prevail in Piros-mani's paintings. That is why he uses another painting, "Queen Tamar and the Poet" — and now he goes further into history to support his conclusion. Look at how Rustaveli dresses and even Tamar does not resemble a Georgian woman. That's how Parajanov brings "Pages from History" to life. He has the same revisionist approach in *Surami Fortress* and tries to put down our history in the tales of the joker/pipe-player."[50]

It is undeniably true that, in general, Parajanov is fascinated with the Orient and that his films of this period often foreground Persian and Turkish influences within the cultures of Transcaucasia. (Indeed, the Russian Empire and the West commonly regarded the region, including Georgia, as part of the Orient.) But it is an unavoidable fact that here Parajanov draws exclusively upon images from Pirosmani's paintings. Also, this particular section is only a small part of the film; as a whole the film incorporates a broadly representative selection of paintings, most of which would not be perceived in any way as "Oriental." Besides, if one is to extend Rodonaia's argument to its logical conclusion, one may as well criticize Pirosmani's painting of Queen Tamar and Rustaveli for not being Georgian enough. It is also difficult to see how Parajanov is "putting down" Georgian history and myth via Simon the Piper's stories to Zurab in *The Legend of the Surami Fortress*, since they are among the more unambiguously patriotic elements of the film.

Rodonaia further contrasts *The Legend of the Surami Fortress* unfavorably with *Shadows of Forgotten Ancestors*, which he characterizes a "masterpiece" that "brought great joy to the Ukrainian art world." In his view, *The Legend of the Surami Fortress* failed because Parajanov did not "find in Georgian reality the possibility of true creativity."[51] This point is worth considering, since *Shadows of Forgotten Ancestors* arguably achieves greater artistic unity through its intensive engagement with Hutsul culture. However, Parajanov's underlying aims in *The Legend of the Surami Fortress* are fundamentally different; in the latter film he envisions Transcaucasia as a kind of multiethnic bazaar and deliberately strives for an eclectic sensibility to reflect that idea.

Finally, Rodonaia warns his readers of Parajanov's plans to make a film on *The Passion of Shushanik*, concluding: "Parajanov proved that he does not know Georgian reality, Georgian culture and history. That is why he should refrain from realizing certain projects. Only those who have KNOWLEDGE, RESPONSIBILITY, AND LOVE can lead us to the sources of Georgian culture."[52]

While Rodonaia's essay created a minor scandal and shocked some members of the Georgian intelligentsia when it was published, it hardly appeared out of the blue. Rather, it was part of a larger project by certain Georgian nationalist intellectuals to promote a more wholesome and "pure" image of Georgian culture, weeded of "foreign" or "cosmopolitan" elements, especially Armenian and Persian influences. Targets included the figure of the *kinto* (traditional street vendor), described in chapter 1. In an article entitled "Old Tbilisi and . . . the *kinto*," published in the January 30 issue of *Literaturuli sakartvelo*, Archil Sulakauri complained about how the *kinto* had become a fetishized stereotype of Tbilisi culture.[53] He felt that this tendency was embodied most clearly in a soccer poster showing a *kinto* with a soccer ball balanced on his head. Sulakauri further characterized the *kinto* with a quote from Ioseb Grishashvili's book *Literary Bohemia of Old Tbilisi*: "[H]is activities include gambling, he uses filthy language, he commits Sodom-Gomorrah sins and petty theft."[54] The reference to "Sodom-Gomorrah" sins, like Rodonaia's characterization of the dancing in *The Legend of the Surami Fortress* as "saccharine and effeminate," is a clear example of how nationalist movements typically involve a reassertion of traditional gender boundaries and sexual mores. In that respect, it is hardly surprising that Parajanov, given his open homosexuality at this point in his life and his fondness for camp aesthetics, would be regarded with suspicion. More significantly, as Giorgi Gvakharia points out, the *kinto*—like the petty craftsman (the *qarachokheli*)—was "mainly of Armenian origin."[55] This may add a possible ethnic subtext to Sulakauri's argument. Thus, in Gvakharia's account, attacks on Parajanov and cultural icons such as the *kinto* were, on a deeper level, directed against the cosmopolitan heritage of Tbilisi. Gvakharia characterizes it as a city "of many customs and mores, the traditions of the Georgians, Armenians, Persians, Kurds, Jews, Russians, and others [. . .] coexisting but almost never fusing. Tbilisi, a city that had served as a bridge between Asia and Europe, became the main enemy of the nationalists, since their cherished goal of a 'return to origins' contradicted the very spirit of this city, which had always been marked by a thirst for openness and freedom, for the variegated colors and textures of the spectacular and the carnivalesque."[56]

In September 1987, Aleksandre Baramidze and Bondo Arveladze published an article in *Literaturuli sakartvelo* criticizing the Armenian scholar Paruir Sevak for his characterization of Sayat-Nova as "a peak in Georgian and Armenian art and literature" who significantly influenced writers in both traditions.[57] While recognizing Sayat-Nova's value as a "socially conscious" poet who "introduced the moods and opinions of craftsmen and the city's underprivileged citizens," Baramidze and Arveladze argued that "*ashugh* poetry stands outside the main axis of development of classical Georgian literature." In addition, they protested that far from liberating "Georgian and Armenian *ashugh* art from Arabic and Persian slavery," as Sevak supposedly had claimed, Sayat-Nova's work "continued the Oriental tradition."[58] They also criticized Sevak's scholarly methods, particularly his decoding of Sayat-Nova's poems to prove that they contained hidden references to Princess Ana, his conventionally ascribed beloved.

In the second part of the article, Baramidze and Arveladze further criticized the Russian-language book *Armenian Medieval Literature* by V. Nalbandian, V. Nersesian, and G. Bakhchinian for its handling of the biographical facts of Sayat-Nova's life. Almost as an aside, Baramidze and Arveladze closed the article with a quote from that book regarding Tsurtaveli's *The Passion of Queen Saint Shushanik*:

> One of the most outstanding monuments of Armenian hagiography of the early period is the narrative about the heroic life, courage, and steadfastness of Shushanik Vardeni, the daughter of the military leader Vardan

Mamikonian — *The Passion of Shushanik Vardeni* (5th century; there is also a Georgian version of this narrative).[59]

Baramidze and Arveladze countered: "In Georgian and not only Georgian scholarly circles it is widely acknowledged that Iakob [Tsurtaveli's] *The Passion of Shushanik* is a brilliant, original work of Georgian literature."[60] In fact, as Rayfield argues above, some controversy lingers about the origins of the Georgian version. However, like the debate surrounding the invention of the Georgian alphabet (which some sources claim was developed by the Armenian theologian Mesrop Mashtots, who also invented the Armenian alphabet[61]), this understandably remains a sensitive issue for many Georgians. At any rate, in case the reader has overlooked the subtext of ethnic rivalry underlying Baramidze and Arveladze's article, they concluded: "We believe that the variety of opinions about the issues discussed in this article do not stand in the way of the continuing tradition of Georgian-Armenian literary friendship. Polite academic arguments were and always are the best means to determine the truth."[62]

Parajanov's return to his home city of Tbilisi and his return to filmmaking in the 1980s illustrates how rapidly the political situation was changing during this period in the Soviet Union and in Georgia specifically. One the one hand, he clearly benefited from the increasing political liberalization under glasnost and perestroika. On the other hand, he found himself caught between two factions within the Georgian intelligentsia: secular, cosmopolitan individuals who largely shared his outlook, and increasingly vocal nationalists who viewed ethnicity as something primordial and sacred. Thus Parajanov's basic artistic identity — his attraction to Oriental motifs, his sexuality, and his playful and freely imaginative treatment of sacred legends — inevitably dragged him into the middle of this larger cultural fray.

8

Ashik-Kerib

The End of a Career

Parajanov's next project was supposed to be his long-delayed adaptation of
Lermontov's *The Demon*, using mountain locations. The Russian painter
Mikhail Vrubel's famed paintings of episodes from *The Demon* were to serve as a
main source of inspiration for its visual style. The film's cinematographer Albert
Yavurian recalls that by the time everything was ready for shooting to begin
in August 1987, Parajanov and he decided that the light was too harsh for the
visual effect that they wanted and that they needed to film either in the spring
or the fall.[1] Ultimately, Parajanov's longtime dream to adapt *The Demon* would
never be realized. The crew instead began work on *Ashik-Kerib* (co-director
David Abashidze, Georgia Film Studio 1988).[2]

The source material, Lermontov's 1837 story "Ashik-Kerib," subtitled a
"Turkish fairy tale" (*Turetskaia skazka*), is a transcription of a folktale heard during his 1837 trip to Tbilisi. Elizabeth Papazian characterizes Lermontov's story
as "a typical example of Russian 'Orientalism,' beginning with its simple, naïve
narrative style, which imitates the 'oral storytelling' of a native insider." Citing the Turkish scholar Ilhan Başgöz, Papazian also points out that the story
apparently originates from a historical figure named Âşık Garip.[3] In fact, a
surviving 1851 copy of a book purportedly authored by Âşık Garip is held at
the Bayerische Staatsbibliothek. Regardless, Âşık Garip became a figure of late
Ottoman popular culture, and oral versions resembling Lermontov's story have
been recorded even in recent times.[4]

In Lermontov's version, Ashik-Kerib, a poor *ashugh* from Tiflis, is in love with Magul-Megeri, the daughter of a wealthy Turk.[5] Determined to build his fortune so he can marry her, he sets out on a seven-year journey. His rival Kurshud-Bek steals his clothes and convinces everyone that he is dead, but Magul-Megeri holds out hope for his eventual return. The bulk of Parajanov's film loosely follows the outline of the Lermontov story, but there are some significant departures. In Parajanov's version, Ashik-Kerib's marriage proposal is rejected outright by Magul-Megeri's clownish father, who turns around and pats his behind in a vulgar gesture of contempt. Ashik-Kerib does not depart for seven years, but only for a thousand days. The brief mention of Ashik-Kerib's performances at various villages in Lermontov's story is expanded into full episodes: "The Wedding of the Blind" and "The Wedding of the Deaf and Dumb." Furthermore, Ashik-Kerib falls under the control of not one but *two* separate despots—the Nadir Pasha and Sultan Aziz—both of whom command him to sing their praises. When the *ashugh* declares that he is unable to sing, they threaten him but he manages to escape in both cases.

In view of Ashik-Kerib's travails and his encounter with "wild beasts and evil spirits," Papazian convincingly suggests a parallel with the Orpheus myth.[6] Parajanov's narrative emphasis on the two Oriental despots and the motif of "the poet and the tsar" has also caused a number of critics to argue for an autobiographical subtext as a tale of the vicissitudes and tribulations of the artist in the Soviet regime. Such an interpretation is supported by the last scene, entitled "Honors for the Bride's Father," in which Ashik-Kerib, with a trace of bitterness on his face, releases a white dove. This is followed by a shot of the dove landing on a movie camera. The closing title card states that the film is "dedicated to the memory of Andrei Tarkovsky." Thus Parajanov seems to suggest that the bride's father in the film represents the repressive apparatus of the Soviet state, which imprisoned Parajanov and ultimately forced Tarkovsky into exile. Another significant instance of personal commentary is Parajanov's last-minute interpolation of two entirely new episodes toward the end of the film: "The Desecrated Monastery" and "God is One," discussed below.

With regard to the film's visual style, Parajanov declares his main source of inspiration from the first images that appear onscreen: Persian arts such as miniature painting, calligraphy, inlaid woodwork, and metalwork. The Art Museum of Georgia has a fine collection of Persian art that Parajanov was especially fond of visiting, and he uses these pieces to create the many still-life compositions in the film. The museum's collection of Qajar-era paintings, which includes rare nudes, is especially noteworthy; a number of them are referenced throughout the film. These real objects, with all of their decorative richness, serve as a creative wellspring for his Orient of the imagination. His appropriation of Persian aesthetics even extends to putting joined eyebrows on the female actors, reflecting the standard of beauty in medieval Iran as represented in miniature paintings.

According to Karen Kalantar, Parajanov originally wanted to shoot *Ashik-Kerib* in Iran, but due to practical considerations the bulk of the film was shot in Azerbaijan instead.[7] The beautifully decorated nineteenth-century wooden mosque featured in the opening and closing sections of the film is actually located in the outdoor Tbilisi Ethnographic Museum, moved from its original location in Ajara.[8] In addition to electronic music and instrumental music written by the Azerbaijani composer Dzhavanshir Kuliev, the soundtrack incorporates singing by Alim Qasimov, one of Azerbaijan's leading performers of classical *Muğam* (multi-movement suites containing improvisations on traditional modal scales). Qasimov has also recorded Azerbaijani *aşıq* (*ashugh*) music. The score's playfully eclectic style embraces everything from traditional *ashugh* music to pop, even using a snippet from Schubert's *Ave Maria* at one point.

The dialogue of the film is likewise in Azerbaijani. However, it is deliberately not synchronized with the actors' lips. Instead, the actors perform mute tableaux, adding to the whimsical primitivism that permeates the film. The dubbing also gives the film a lighter, more playful feel than either *The Color of Pomegranates*, which also lacked dramatic dialogue in the normal sense but played with sound in a more vigorously experimental way, or *The Legend of the Surami Fortress*, in which the dubbing more or less matched the characters' lips. In the Georgian release version of *Ashik-Kerib*, the version initially distributed overseas, voice-over narration in Georgian was recorded on top of the Azerbaijani dialogue, although it blends much better with the rest of the soundtrack than the usual Russian monotone overdubs one finds on prints of non-Russian Soviet films. In some prints of the film a Russian overdub was even added *on top* of the Georgian overdubbing, making the Azerbaijani dialogue almost inaudible and altogether ruining the soundtrack's carefully designed texture.[9]

In his highly enthusiastic review of the film — calling it one of the finest films released worldwide in recent years — Miron Chernenko characterized *Ashik-Kerib* as the "ecstasy of a brilliant aestheticizer of all manner of second-hand goods, gathered from the most varied cultures and the most varied styles, and transformed into beauty."[10] In his view, one of the film's strongest influences is that of silent cinema, especially its acting style, use of makeup, and Méliès-inspired frontal compositions.[11] He further implied, quite perceptively, that the film's aesthetic principles have a strong connection with Parajanov's prison art and his more recent collages. Thus the director "[builds] his artistic microcosm out of makeshift materials — from masticated bread crumbs [*khleb-nyi miakish*] and scraps of cardboard, from tin cans and old shoes, from old cloths and rags, from pieces of broken bottles and mirrors crushed underfoot in searches."[12] While one can find aspects of the same handmade aesthetic in *The Legend of the Surami Fortress*, in this film Parajanov pushes it to the foreground.

The film's visual style is looser than *The Legend of the Surami Fortress*, and certainly much more so than *The Color of Pomegranates*. The compositions are not always as meticulously arranged, and the cinematographer Albert Yavurian makes extensive use of zooms and tracking shots. While the film's camera is still nowhere near as active as that in *Shadows of Forgotten Ancestors*, in a sense it represents a return to mobile camerawork. The most effective example of this is the scene depicting Ashik-Kerib's departure. It begins as an overhead shot of dancers dressed in black, who perform an elaborately choreographed dance while the hero leaves his home. The camera cranes down behind a pair of bushes with black pomegranates, and Ashik-Kerib and his sister step into the foreground between the bushes. This nicely executed shot is mirrored during Ashik-Kerib's return at the end of the film, only with the dancers clothed in white. In other places, the zoom lens seems overused when a simple, precisely composed tableau would have been more effective. The color is also not as vivid as that in *The Legend of the Surami Fortress*, or Parajanov's major 1960s films for that matter. Yavurian subsequently complained in an interview that because Parajanov's position at the Georgia Film Studio was not as "privileged" as the leading Georgian filmmakers, the crew had to work with inferior quality equipment and film stock. They also had to process the exposed film in Georgia rather than in Moscow or Saint Petersburg, where Yavurian was accustomed to having it sent when he worked at the Armenfilm Studio.[13] In an interview with Patrick Cazals, Parajanov likewise complained that the film was designated as a lower category of production and thus was not accorded the preparation time, budget, and quality of film stock that he had wanted.[14]

Another example of the overall looseness of Parajanov's approach is how he uses still-life compositions — what Chernenko terms "epigraphs" — to frame many scenes (Fig. 8.1). These shots are sometimes repeated, whereas in Parajanov's earlier films each "epigraph" had a unique and precise, if sometimes indirect, association with a particular scene. Such recurring shots are brief, though they are in danger of becoming repetitious by the end of the film. As a result of all this, the film as a whole appears more improvisatory, something of a lark.

Figure 8.1. Epigraphic still life (*Ashik-Kerib*).

The opening section of the film, entitled "Harvest Festival" (*mosavlis zeimi*), provides an example of the kind of playful pseudo-ethnography that abounds in Parajanov's work. In it, Ashik-Kerib chases his beloved around a courtyard and throws rice at her. Yavurian recalls that Parajanov originally wanted to have them toss water at each other, along the lines of the Armenian festival of Vardavar. (Vardavar is a summer holiday marking Christ's Transfiguration; it originated as a pagan harvest festival dedicated to the goddess Astghik, and the water-tossing is obviously a practice from the pre-Christian era.) However, because of the cold weather—the scene was shot in December—they decided to use rice instead.[15] To the viewer this does not necessarily look out of place since rice-throwing is associated with weddings or, more generally, fertility rites, as anthropologist Levon Abrahamian points out.[16] However, Parajanov adds a further, subversive twist to the "ritual": while Ashik-Kerib happily tosses rice at his beloved Magul-Megeri, Kurshud-Bek's spurned affections for the same woman are signified by his lack of someone to toss rice at, so he throws it bitterly to the side. Suddenly, a stream of rice falls upon Kurshud-Bek's head; the camera pans up to reveal another *man* pouring a bowl of rice on him.

While the latter joke might escape many viewers, it is by no means the only gay element in the film. The lead actor Yuri Mgoian, with whom Parajanov was in love at the time, is unmistakably put on display as an icon of masculine beauty. The most obvious instances of this are when his mother and sister bathe him in preparation for the betrothal, his undressing to cross the river, and the shot of him reclining semi-nude after he has performed at the wedding of the blind. Other images of male beauty in the film include Ashik-Kerib's guardian angels Aziz and Vale, represented as a pair of curly-haired ephebes.

Parajanov's Oriental Drag

One could argue further that the question of sexuality is intimately connected with Parajanov's aesthetics as a whole. His lifelong fascination with the Orient, which reaches a culminating point in the disarming dime-store fantasies of *Ashik-Kerib*, carries deeper implications than simply a love for the region's aesthetics. As Edward Said argues in his classic 1978 study *Orientalism*, Western artistic representations of the Orient are connected in complex and often subtle ways with questions of empire and cultural power. In Parajanov's case, the Orient is also closely tied to his conception of selfhood. Perhaps the most striking example of this is a late 1980s photo that Parajanov decorated, transforming himself into some kind of exotic Oriental prince (Fig. 8.2).

This gesture of making the self exotic, of performing as an Oriental, has often been tied to sexuality. As Said has pointed out, in the West historically the Orient was associated with sex: "not only fecundity but sexual promise (and threat), untiring sexuality, unlimited desire, deep generative energies."[17] For many writers and artists — Said cites Flaubert in particular — the Orient became a site for "self-discovery" and for pursing sex supposedly free of the restrictions of Western society. It performs a similar role in Parajanov's work, most obviously in the sexually charged atmosphere of his script for *The Slumbering Palace*. It also provides a vehicle for articulating same-sex desire or ambiguous sexuality.

This trope had partly to do with the widespread appearance of classical Arabic and Persian poetry in translation and its availability as a source of inspiration for Western artists. Thus, one began to see the appearance of works such as Goethe's *West-östlicher Diwan*. The explicit or implicit representation of the beloved as male was a standard literary convention among medieval Persian Sufi poets such as Hafiz and Rumi, although Franklin Lewis argues in his

Figure 8.2. Oriental drag: *Self-portrait in Istanbul* (1989). Photograph decorated with markers. Courtesy of the Sergei Parajanov Museum.

authoritative study of Rumi that this should be understood more as a literary and theological convention than as a manifestation of homoerotic desire per se.[18] In fact, translators of such poems have often switched the gender of the beloved to female to make them more palatable to Western readers. However, one does find overtly homoerotic verse in the Islamic tradition at least as far back as Abu Nuwas (AD 760–814). Furthermore, it is possible that Persian miniatures with homoerotic subject matter or reproductions of them may have circulated privately in the West. At the very least, Safavid-era miniatures with heterosexual but markedly androgynous couples would have begun to disseminate more widely thanks to increased trade with Iran. But the main point is that such poetry and art became available to Western readers both for consumption as a representation of same-sex desire and as a convention for articulating it.

In the same vein, the gay Russian poet Mikhail Kuzmin traveled to Egypt in 1895 and was sufficiently moved by his experiences to write the 1906 cycle *The Alexandrian Songs*, though these poems evoked classical Egypt as opposed to Islamic Egypt. More directly relevant for our purposes was the private club known as the *Hafiz-Schencke* (Hafiz-Tavern) that Vyacheslav Ivanov and his wife established and that Kuzmin frequented. Many of its members were either gay or at least sexually ambivalent. The gatherings entailed donning elaborate Oriental robes and meeting in a room decorated with Persian carpets, pillows, and patterned fabrics. In addition to poetry readings, some of the activities involved sexual experimentation or "deliberately confused gender boundaries," as Kuzmin biographers Malmstad and Bogomolov describe.[19] In the Western European context, the gay German photographer Wilhelm von Gloeden, who specialized in nude portraits of Sicilian youths, made a pair of self portraits in Arab garb in 1890. One may also view Thomas Phillips' 1814 portrait of Lord Byron in Albanian costume in the same light. Thus, in a rather self-conscious manner, the adoption of Oriental drag has functioned as a catalyst for releasing culturally imposed inhibitions and pursuing an ideal of freely expressed sexuality.

As one may have gleaned so far, to a striking extent Parajanov's three Transcaucasian feature films involve putting on costumes, cross-dressing, androgyny, and at times overt gay or bisexual elements. To recap, Sofiko Chiaureli plays both the young poet Sayat-Nova and his beloved, Princess Ana, in *The Color of Pomegranates*; these androgynous lovers who closely resemble each other were in fact inspired by Persian miniatures, as mentioned earlier. One also cannot help but be struck by the young Arutin's awakening to the sensual world when he peers down into the baths in Tbilisi and observes both a nude female torso and a handsome male figure (King Erekle II), the latter being bathed and massaged by a Kurdish bath attendant. In *The Legend of the Surami Fortress*, the character of Nodar Zalikashvili flees Georgia after killing a prince, crossing the border disguised as a female and later converting to Islam and changing his name to Osman-Agha. In *Ashik-Kerib*, the title character puts on a Chinese robe and a false beard before performing in front of the Nadir Pasha. Once he manages to escape, he peers down from the top of the wall at the Pasha and defiantly removes his false beard and moustache; the punch line to this sequence consists of the Pasha removing a false moustache as well. During the "Wedding of the Blind" sequence, the bridegroom wears a gauzy white veil topped with large

Figure 8.3. The groom at the Wedding of the Blind (*Ashik-Kerib*).

purple flowers, hardly traditional attire for grooms in any culture (Fig. 8.3). This is to say nothing of the more overt, aforementioned homoerotic elements in *Ashik-Kerib*.

There is, of course, a fundamental difference between Parajanov's conceptualization of the Orient and that of European writers such as Flaubert, Goethe, or perhaps even Kuzmin. Insofar as Parajanov was a native of Transcaucasia, the Orient was a basic component of his identity and part of his lived experience. Not only are Armenia, Georgia, and Azerbaijan adjacent to Iran and Turkey, they also fell under both empires' direct influence at various points in their history and served as avenues of crossing between the East and the West. Accordingly, the caravansary is a stock image of Old Tbilisi lore and crops up frequently in Parajanov's work. Moreover, Russian writers such as Lermontov understood and represented Transcaucasia in terms of the Orient. Thus, for Parajanov the Orient is not merely some place that he imagines "out there." It is, in a certain sense, a part of his homeland, and a part of himself is the exotic Other.

Ashik-Kerib and Karabagh

Ashik-Kerib did not arouse any particular political controversy in Georgia in the way that *The Legend of the Surami Fortress* and *The Passion of Shushanik* did. Instead, the completion and subsequent release of the film were complicated by rising tensions between the Armenians and the Azerbaijanis, which included clashes in the Karabagh region of the Azerbaijani SSR. In January 1988, thousands of Karabagh Armenians sent a petition to Moscow requesting a referendum on the issue of the enclave's status. Albert Yavurian recalled that although the film was "already shot and edited" by December 1987, Parajanov insisted on adding two interconnected episodes — "The Desecrated Monastery" and "God is One" — as a personal response to the unfolding conflict.[20] In the first episode, Ashik-Kerib takes refuge in an abandoned Christian church complex when marauders (probably Turkish) invade it and threaten him. In the second episode, Ashik-Kerib stands together with a group of children inside the church (Fig. 8.4). On February 29, 1988, barely a week after the episodes were filmed,

Figure 8.4. The episode "God is One" (*Ashik-Kerib*).

riots erupted in Sumqayit, Azerbaijan, resulting in over thirty dead—mostly Armenians at the hands of roaming mobs.[21] Parajanov, who shot much of *Ashik-Kerib* in Azerbaijan and was particularly fond of Baku, was wounded deeply by the events at Sumqayit.

Despite this, he continued to express his humanistic, transnational vision in public appearances and the press. In an interview with Parajanov out of Baku published in the September 29, 1988, issue *Sovetskaia kul'tura* (*Soviet Culture*), the author stressed the international character of Parajanov's work, pointing out that he made films in Ukraine, Georgia, Armenia, and Azerbaijan, and that Sayat-Nova, the subject of *The Color of Pomegranates*, "composed his songs in Azerbaijani, Armenian, and Georgian." Parajanov himself stated in the interview: "The cultures of peoples, especially of neighbors, are vessels for communicating with each other. Art, and first of all cinema, as the most popular art form, should further the mutual drawing together [*sblizheniiu*] of people. It has become practice to make films jointly with foreign partners, and this, of course, isn't bad. But is everything all right in our own home in this respect? For example, we, the filmmakers of Transcaucasia, the spokesmen of brotherly peoples [*narodov-brat'ev*], have never filmed a single picture together."[22] Some of the specific terms used here—namely, *sblizhenie* and *narody-brat'ia*—suggest the extent to which Parajanov's view of nationalities in the Soviet Union, and of Transcaucasia in particular, was shaped by official Soviet ideology. While undoubtedly sincere, noble, and even necessary in a certain sense, Parajanov's ideals were proving increasingly remote from the painful divisions taking hold in the region. His use of locations around Baku and his choice of an Azerbaijani soundtrack may have been in keeping with the internationalist spirit of Soviet ideology, but the unfortunate timing of the film's production made it problematic for Armenian audiences. As a result, it did not receive a general release in Armenia until the spring of 1996, well after Parajanov's death.[23]

The Treasures at Mount Ararat

Reflecting his increasing identification with Armenia toward the end of his life, Parajanov discussed with the Catholicos of All Armenians Vazgen I the possibility of making a documentary film about the treasures and cultural heritage of Etchmiadzin, to be entitled *The Treasures at Mount Ararat* (*Sokrovishcha u gory Ararat*). Some of the church's religious paraphernalia had already appeared in *The Color of Pomegranates*. Parajanov completed the script in the summer of 1987, just before beginning production on the ill-fated *The Demon*. The planned production team included Albert Yavurian as cinematographer, Karen Davydov as production designer, Tigran Mansurian as composer, and the noted art historian Nonna Stepanian as a consultant.

The script opens with the image of Ararat, then shifts focus to the volcanic rock that is the basic building material in Armenia:

> The camera slowly lowers its gaze toward the earth, fixing on the lifeless foundation of a pile of stones. For a long time it searches for something, passing from one pile to another and, finally, stops at some basalt with a lilac hue . . .
>
> The camera abruptly moves into the stones . . .
>
> In the frame is a piece of basalt that looks like a cathedral . . .
>
> Two pairs of hands hold the stone on opposite sides. The hands take the stone and raise it. The stone lies in rough palms for a long time, as if they were warming it with their heat . . .
>
> Against the background of the hands holding the stone the title appears:
>
> ARMENIA—A MOUNTAINOUS COUNTRY
>
> Inside a golden frame is a map of Armenia. Three borders gird a single country. Three Armenias on the map. The camera slowly moves into the map and for a long time peers into the territory of Soviet Armenia . . .
>
> With great solemnity the hands of the stonemasons-builders raise the piece of basalt with the lilac hue. Already it is not simply a stone, but a granite model of a cathedral, the creation of a skillful master. Against the background of mountains, hands hold the cathedral. The camera moves into the stone model, dissolving into it and abruptly moving away . . .
>
> In the shot: the bas-relief of the Haghpat Cathedral: "King Bagrat [*sic*] hands the model of the cathedral to Gurgen."[24]

The script then calls for a series of shots depicting famous monasteries and churches throughout Armenia before returning to Etchmiadzin. After various locations and activities at the Etchmiadzin complex, the bulk of the script focuses on Armenian religious art across the centuries; it includes a long series of *khachkars*, metalwork crosses encrusted with precious stones, other metalwork such as the right hands of various religious figures, bishops' croziers, works by the noted eighteenth-century icon-painter Hovnatan Hovnatanyan (an ancestor of Hakob Hovnatanyan), carpets, fabrics, and embroidered items (including gonfalons and vestments such as amices), medieval Armenian manuscript illuminations, and so on. The script closes with a scene depicting Vazgen I as the living representative of Armenia's religious heritage; the camera follows him as he leads the Easter celebration at Etchmiadzin.

Significantly, Parajanov inscribed the manuscript with the name "Sarkis

Paradzhan*ian*" in Russian, thus pointedly emphasizing his Armenian identity. (As mentioned earlier, his family's original Armenian name was in fact Paraja-niants, though Parajanov himself may have been unaware of that at the time.) Some of Parajanov's Armenian friends feel, not unreasonably, that his turn toward Armenia at the end of his life was partly in response to the blow he suf-fered from the rejection of *The Passion of Shushanik* in Georgia. At the same time, his awakened interest in his Armenian heritage dates at least as far back as the mid-1960s, before he began work on *The Color of Pomegranates*; it also crops up as an explicit theme in *Confession*. Furthermore, it is hardly uncommon for people to return to their roots during the final years of their life. Because of the inter-vening production of *Ashik-Kerib*, the planned production of *Confession* and Pa-rajanov's deteriorating health, he was unable to realize the Etchmiadzin project.

Final Years

In spring of 1988, Yuri Illienko recorded one of the many colorful prison stories that Parajanov liked to tell his friends. Illienko later reworked it into a script and filmed it as *Swan Lake: The Zone* (*Lebedinoe ozero: Zona*, Dovzhenko Film Studio 1990).[25] Shooting locations included one of the prison camps where Parajanov stayed during the 1970s. In the film, a prisoner escapes and seeks refuge inside a hammer-and-sickle shaped monument, where he is discovered by a young boy and his mother. The mother carries out a furtive affair with the fugitive. When he is caught and returned to prison, he attempts suicide but is resurrected thanks to a blood transfusion from a prison guard. Sharing a guard's blood brands him as anathema within the prison culture, and ultimately he commits suicide by slitting his wrists. The remarkable first half hour, much of which is set inside the cramped metal interior of the hammer-and-sickle monument, is entirely free of dialogue. More generally, the film's grim depiction of Soviet life both inside and outside of prison shares much in common with other works of the glasnost era, albeit with occasional surreal touches such as a flock of geese landing in the prison courtyard and the man drinking water from the impression of a hand in cement. The Canadian-US-Swedish-Ukrainian co-production was awarded the FIPRESCI prize and the Prix de la Jeunesse for Best Foreign Film at the 1991 Cannes Film Festival.

Leonid Osyka, another filmmaker of the Ukrainian poetic school who had remained friends with Parajanov over the years, directed the little-seen *Etudes on Vrubel* (*Etiudy o Vrubele*, Dovzhenko Film Studio 1989), based on a script that the two wrote collaboratively. The film focuses on Mikhail Vrubel's stay in Kyiv during the 1880s, when he painted new frescoes for the twelfth-century Church of Saint Cyril and unsuccessfully submitted sketches for interior decorations in the newly constructed Saint Volodymyr Cathedral. It also depicts the painter's incipient madness. While the lead actor Edisher Giorgobiani cuts a handsome figure as Vrubel and the film contains a number of compellingly imagined details, it ultimately fails to cohere and its visual style suffers from heavy overuse of the zoom lens, a common flaw of later Soviet productions.

During this period Parajanov also began to travel outside the Soviet Union for the first time. In February 1988, he attended the Rotterdam Film Festival to accept a special award as one of "Twenty Directors of the Future" and screen the short *Arabesques on the Theme of Pirosmani*.[26] In June, he accompanied the international festival premiere of *Ashik-Kerib* at the Munich Film Festival, which included a retrospective of his films and a filmmaking workshop led by him.[27] In September *Ashik-Kerib* screened out of competition at the Venice Film Festival, where it was warmly reviewed by Deborah Young for *Variety*: "The moving camera brings still and almost-still images to life, creating a magical, exotic world in which every gesture, look, and detail in makeup and costume vibrates with significance." Young further described the lead actor Yuri Mgoian as "an enigmatic figure with hypnotic charm," and summed up, "Lensed with more freewheeling fantasy than cash, the film has a basic richness and sumptuousness that few Western megaproductions can boast."[28] For Parajanov, one of the highlights of the Venice trip was the island of San Lazzaro degli Armeni, the site of an important Armenian monastery. That same month he also flew overseas to attend the New York Film Festival. In November, he realized his lifelong dream to visit Paris, in this case for a retrospective of his films at the Cinéma Saint Germain.[29]

In January 1989, he wrote a brief treatment for an adaptation of the medieval epic *The Song of Igor's Campaign* (*Slovo o polku Igoreve*). The following month, he traveled to Porto to screen *Ashik-Kerib* at the Fantasporto Film Festival, which is devoted to fantasy and sci-fi films. At the Istanbul Film Festival (April 1989) he received a special prize for *Ashik-Kerib* "for his contribution to contemporary art."[30] Perhaps inevitably, the ongoing conflict in Karabagh followed him to Turkey. According to Cora Tsereteli, who accompanied him at the festival, he delivered a moving acceptance speech in which he spoke out against the violence between the neighboring Azerbaijanis and Armenians, pointed out that his film was about a Turkish *ashugh*, mentioned the friends he had made while working in Baku, and finished his speech by declaring, "God is one." Afterwards, Tsereteli recalls, a group of young men followed them and thrust into her hand a note which read thus (in English): "You miserable director. We forgive you. Don't talk about Karabag. Live Azerbaycan! Young Turkish Poets."[31]

Taking full advantage of the more open atmosphere under glasnost and perestroika, Parajanov also conducted regular interviews with journalists, leaving behind a substantial, if occasionally fanciful, body of testimony. Starting in 1986, the French journalist and filmmaker Patrick Cazals periodically visited Parajanov in Tbilisi and conducted a series of interviews that found their way into two documentary films and a book.[32] At the aforementioned Munich Film Festival Ron Holloway filmed a lengthy interview, which he later developed into a feature-length documentary.[33] In a June 1989 interview with Judy Stone, Parajanov spoke passionately about the terrible legacy of the Soviet system and the need for filmmakers to expose it: "It's time to make films of apology before the people, apology for the cruelty that was perpetrated by the system: x-ray films that penetrate. The fact remains that the tragedy of distrust, the tragedy of persecution, the tragedy of humiliation endured by the people in the Soviet Union is the cruelest tragedy from primitive times to the Middle Ages and up to the twentieth century that humanity has endured. The Soviet Union — besides creating massive construction projects and demonstrations on the Red Square — has also created an astonishing regime that destroys individual personality, and I fell into it."[34]

Parajanov's long-cherished project *The Confession* was finally approved for production by the Armenfilm Studio, more than twenty years after he had first written the script. He began shooting in August of 1989, starting with Vera's funeral, which he filmed at his family residence in Tbilisi. However, after only three days of shooting it became apparent that Parajanov was too ill to continue. He was diagnosed with lung cancer and the production was shut down. The unedited footage only amounts to several minutes' worth, but it does suggest intriguing possibilities. The core of the episode is a complex master shot: it begins with four musicians at the bottom of the stairs in the courtyard then pans up slightly to reveal Parajanov as a boy with his mother descending the stairs, followed by pallbearers carrying Vera's coffin and members of the grieving family. The camera zooms out to reveal the courtyard filled with musicians, nuns, and others attending the funeral, then tracks laterally to reveal a group of boys tending a ram that is about to be sacrificed. It concludes by zooming in to a large pot that is waiting for the ram. While the scene still draws upon Parajanov's basic frontal tableau aesthetic, it displays a more complex arrangement of actors within space than is usual for his mature, post-*Shadows* films. Other completed shots include a lovingly composed tableau of the young Parajanov standing next to his mother and feeding the same ram (Fig. 8.5). Thus, the episode's underlying thrust probably would have been about Parajanov's first awareness of death, both in terms of his cousin Vera and the sacrificial ram.

Figure 8.5. A young Parajanov feeds a sacrificial ram (*Confession*). Courtesy of Yuri Mechitov.

The last year of Parajanov's life was marked by poor health—one of his lungs had to be removed and he was subsequently hospitalized in Moscow, Yerevan, and Paris. At the same time, he received belated official recognition for his work in the Soviet Union. In March of 1990 he was named a People's Artist of the USSR, and work continued on the home-museum in Yerevan, located on the edge of a plateau in the middle of the city, with a clear view of Mount Ararat. He passed away on the night of July 20–21, and on July 25 a massive funeral procession was held, starting in front of the Yerevan Opera. He was buried in the Armenian Pantheon, next to such significant Armenian cultural figures as Martiros Saryan and Aram Khachaturian. The Sergei Parajanov Museum opened to the public in July 1991.

While Parajanov has become institutionalized as an Armenian cultural hero, a number of Georgians and other residents of Tbilisi have expressed regret that he was not given a proper memorial or museum there and insist, not without reason, that his sensibility is inseparable from the uniquely multicultural city. His identity is "Tbilisian" (*Tbilisets*) rather than "Armenian" or "Georgian," they argue, and Parajanov himself said essentially the same thing on occasion.[35] Some have also complained about the wholesale removal of Parajanov's artworks to Armenia. However, one should keep in mind that toward the end of his life, partly due to the Armenian invitation and partly due to the political unrest in Georgia, Parajanov himself accepted the offer to move all his artworks and house them there. Others close to Parajanov have expressed the concern that if the artworks had not been moved immediately at the time of his death, they would have disappeared altogether or they would not have been properly preserved due to the troubled situation in Georgia during that time. Finally, in November 2004 a statue of Parajanov in a flying pose — inspired by a collage that he had made from a photo by Yuri Mechitov — was erected in his home city of Tbilisi.

Sergei Parajanov, whose life spanned from the beginning of Stalin's rule to the unwinding of the Soviet state, in many ways embodies the fascinating complexities and contradictions that existed within the Soviet Union. As a filmmaker coming from the imperial periphery, he achieved international renown by re-envisioning local cultures through a synthesis of indigenous, Russian, and Western European artistic traditions. Obsessed with authentic objects and places, he played freely with them and even relished provocation. Thanks to his dazzling, immediately identifiable visual style, his four major films have become among the most widely seen films made in Ukraine, Armenia, Georgia, and Azerbaijan, respectively. The underlying economic structure and ideology of the Soviet film industry, especially where they intersected with Soviet nationality policies, arguably made it possible for him to create the kind of films that he wanted, but they also worked against him because of his artistic daring, outspokenness, and at times difficult personality. Those same nationality policies, even as they created a framework in which he could operate, ultimately contributed to the growth of nationalism in the Soviet Union, which proved problematic for a cosmopolitan artist like him.

In the course of his life and artistic output, Parajanov also demonstrated considerable courage with regard to his unconventional sexuality. Those same cultures that sparked his creative genius were deeply conservative, and even to this day one can still encounter a great deal of denial about sexual matters. He may have paid a heavy personal price for living in the open, but he left us with a uniquely rich artistic legacy that sheds light on an under-explored, yet fundamental aspect of life in that region. The other area where he demonstrated courage was his willingness to speak out about political injustices and oppressive artistic policies within the Soviet state. Some of Parajanov's acquaintances have ascribed this mainly to his impulsiveness and his penchant for attention-seeking, but the fact remains that he was one of the few Soviet filmmakers to criticize the state so openly in these areas, and again he paid a price. If there is any compensation, it is a body of work that remains innovative and vital more than twenty years after his death.

Epilogue

Parajanov's Afterlife

Parajanov's experimental film language and challenging, at times subversive, subject matter place him squarely within the global art film tradition. The question of his influence within the countries of the former Soviet Union remains complicated. Younger Soviet filmmakers such as Roman Balaian (Ukraine), Artavazd Peleshian and Mikhail Vartanov (Armenia), and Rustam Khamdamov (Russia) were undoubtedly influenced by their friendship with Parajanov, though they have retained distinct stylistic identities. Another of Parajanov's close friends, the Odessa-based Kira Muratova, has acknowledged that he served as a source of inspiration for what she calls "ornamentalism" (*dekorativnost'*) in her visual style, starting with her film *Getting to Know the Wide World* (1978).[1] Still, the very uniqueness of Parajanov's style and the dominating force of his personality meant that he ultimately lacks a clear successor. This stands in contrast to Tarkovsky, since Alexander Sokurov's work at once arises from and extends the boundaries of what Tarkovsky accomplished.

One post-Soviet filmmaker, Aktan Abdykalykov from Kyrgyzstan, borrows rather directly from Parajanov at the beginning of *Beshkempir: The Adopted Son* (1998). The opening sequence, which pertains to the title character's adoption, depicts a ritual in which a group of old women lay out a cradle, various tools, and a richly colored blanket. In one shot the camera focuses on the women's hands as they pass the blanket underneath their legs, echoing Parajanov's fondness for showing hands as they perform ritualistic actions. Other borrowings include a shot in which the iron implements are laid out into a still-life composition and another shot focused solely on the beautiful decorative pattern on the baby blanket. The stylization of the sequence contributes to the feel of archaism, of unchanging traditions. Thus, it becomes a way of asserting, or perhaps even marketing, cultural difference within the post-Soviet, international arena of the film festival and art house distribution circuits.

In the West, Parajanov's work remains somewhat less well-known than that of Tarkovsky, who has established something of a cult following as befits an artist with messianic tendencies. Still, his aesthetics have influenced a number of younger directors. The Armenian diaspora filmmaker Don Askarian, who is based out of Germany, clearly draws upon Parajanov's tableau style in *Komitas* (1988), a poetic biography of the great turn-of-the-century composer and ethnomusicologist. Indeed, Askarian's style is such a deliberate and thorough blend of Tarkovsky and Parajanov that at least in *Komitas* he fails to develop a distinct identity of his own despite the worthy subject matter. In keeping with his own love for dynamic camerawork, the Serbian director Emir Kusturica makes an unmistakable allusion to *Shadows of Forgotten Ancestors* in his film *Underground* (1995), during the scene where the camera peers up from underneath the surface of the water at Blacky as he gazes down into a well. The camera spins vertiginously as he is drawn down into the water, recalling Ivan's death in Parajanov's film. Derek Jarman, who is fond of tableau-style shots, borrows some compositions from *The Color of Pomegranates* in his film of Benjamin Britten's *War Requiem* (1996).

Parajanov is especially popular in Iran due to his decorative Orientalist aesthetics and his avowed interest in Persian art. Saeed Ebrahimifar's *Pomegranate and Reed* (1989) alludes to *The Color of Pomegranates* during its wool-dyeing scene. Certainly, this allusion is more artistically effective and apropos to Ebrahimifar's subject matter — the life and imagination of a poet — than the heavy-handed reference to *2001: A Space Odyssey* that closes that film. As Levon Abrahamian argues, Mohsen Makhmalbaf's art house hit *Gabbeh* (1996) borrows from Parajanov to a degree that verges on plagiarism.[2] Not only does this influence include his lavish use of color, tableau compositions, and an emphasis on the decorative richness of folk handicrafts such as rugs, but it extends to specifically Parajanovian techniques such as having a rug unroll before the camera and the repeated shots, joined by jump cuts, of Gabbeh carrying a jug of water on her shoulder and turning to face the camera. It is worth noting that the film is set among the Bakhtiar tribe; thus Makhmalbaf's aesthetics exoticize a people who are probably almost as remote to urban Tehran audiences as they are to viewers in the West. Albeit less obviously, Makhmalbaf continues to cite Parajanov in *The Silence* (1998), which he filmed in Tajikistan.

Parajanov's aesthetics have also had a significant impact on the medium of the music video. Not bound by the constraints of narrative filmmaking, music video directors are free to play with color, décor, movement, repetition, and the interaction between music and image more than mainstream feature film directors. As sources of inspiration they often turn to avant-garde filmmakers such as Maya Deren, Stan Brakhage, and Kenneth Anger. (The latter was, perhaps, the first true music video director in films such as *Scorpio Rising* (1964) and *Kustom Kar Kommandos* (1965), with their campy appropriation of pop music on the soundtracks.) They also lean heavily on the European art cinema tradition as embodied by directors such as Fellini, Tarkovsky, and Parajanov.

In this vein, Mark Romanek's video for Madonna's "Bedtime Story" (1995) contains images lifted more or less directly from *The Color of Pomegranates*, including a bare male foot crushing grapes on top of a stone slab inscribed in Arabic and a shot of two bishop's croziers falling into outstretched hands. These borrowings reflect the overall dreamlike and mystical atmosphere of the video, which incorporates other exotic Oriental imagery such as whirling dervishes. Romanek also borrows liberally from Tarkovsky, particularly the films *Stalker* (1979) and *Nostalgia* (1983).

Other notable examples of Parajanov's influence are two videos by Tarsem (Tarsem Singh). R.E.M.'s "Losing My Religion" (1991), which won several prizes at the MTV Music Awards, is especially successful at integrating such stylistic borrowings into an aesthetically coherent whole. In one tableau, a muscular African American man poses as an angel, crouching on a chair with a pair of small gilded wings on his back. The image is framed by a gaudy profusion of gilded Christmas ornaments, ribbons, tinsel, and even baby-doll heads, alluding to Parajanov's unique style of assemblages. In another tableau, Michael Stipe is shown wearing a pair of large, heavily feathered wings. When he collapses the wings remain in place behind him, revealing an open book in front of the wings; this evokes the trick effects commonly found in Parajanov's films. Tarsem's video is striking not just because of the systematic way he has incorporated Parajanov's aesthetics, but also because of how it uses these stylistic gestures to construct Michael Stipe as a pensive, sexually ambiguous persona. In this respect, one of the video's more cryptic stylistic gestures — recurring shots of pale, heavily made-up figures in lavish Indian (or pseudo-Indian) costumes — makes sense if understood as an example of Oriental drag used to express sexual ambiguity.

Deep Forest's "Sweet Lullaby" (1994), another acclaimed music video by Tarsem, borrows even more directly from Parajanov in its specific imagery, including shots of men dressed in pseudo-Georgian outfits waving semaphore flags, and other shots with long strips of cloth stretched out across the ground, both evidently inspired by *The Legend of the Surami Fortress*. The touristy imagery of the video reflects the benignly exoticized treatment of ethnicity represented in the song itself, a field recording of Baegu music set to a soft contemporary dance beat. Parajanov's influence continues more subtly in Tarsem's feature film debut, the stylish supernatural thriller *The Cell* (2000). In addition to lavishly composed tableau shots, one of the deleted scenes included on the DVD portrays a desert landscape with strips of blue cloth stretched out between trees, directly alluding again to *The Legend of the Surami Fortress*. The problem with *The Cell* is that despite its frequently stunning visual style, it remains a clichéd and nonsensical thriller. Compared to *The Cell*, Tarsem's film *The Fall* (2006) displays both a more assured narrative and a more consistently inspired visual style that synthesizes a wide range of influences.

As early as the 1980s, critics such as Gilbert Adair and Miron Chernenko had argued that Parajanov's poetic cinema demands new modes of spectatorship because of how it expands the boundaries of narrative film form. Their observations have proven on the mark, considering his persistent influence in new media such as music videos, and the widespread consumption of his works internationally through home video and the Internet. Today's hypersaturated media environment only sharpens our thirst for fresh and original images, assuring Parajanov's films and artworks a prominent place in this new world. At least some of their appeal stems from the desire for authentic experience. This risks becoming an easy commodification of difference — especially, but not exclusively ethnic difference. But at its best, this desire can open up different cultures and aesthetic traditions, enriching one's encounter with the moving image as a medium and — to invoke the essay "Art as Device" by Viktor Shklovsky — renewing one's perceptions of the world.

Filmography

Whenever possible, the credits given below have been checked against a print of the film. Since Soviet era film credits often provide only the first initial and last name, the full name has been supplied when other sources provide it. Additional sources consulted include: Sergei Paradzhanov, *Pis'ma iz zony*, ed. Garegin Zakoian (Yerevan: Filmadaran, 2000); Raisa Prokopenko, ed., *Anotovanyi kataloh fil'miv: 1928–1998* (Kyiv: Natsional'na kinostudiia khudozhnykh fil'miv imeni Oleksandra Dovzhenka, 1998); Armianskoe assotsiatsia kinokritikov i kinozhurnalistov, *Armianskoe kino, 1924–1999: Annotirovannyi katalog* (Yerevan: Artagers, 2000); Sergei Zemlianukhin and Miroslava Segida, *Domashniaia sinemateka: Otechestvennoe kino, 1918–1996* (Moscow, Dubl'-D, 1996); L. B. Pil'kevych, ed., *Kinolitopys: Anotovanyi kataloh kinozhurnaliv, dokumental'nykh fil'miv, kino- i telesiuzhetiv, 1956–1965* (Kyiv: Derzhavnyi komitet arkhiviv Ukrainy, 2003).

Films as a Director

A Moldovan Fairy Tale (*Moldavskaia skazka*, 1952)
   Parajanov's diploma film for the VGIK (All-Union State Institute of Cinematography), based on the narrative poem *Andriesh* by Emilian Bukov. This film is presumed lost.

Andriesh (1955)
   Produced by the Kyiv Feature Film Studio. Color, 62 minutes.
   Direction: Sergei Parajanov, Yakov Bazelian. Screenplay: Emilian Bukov, Grigori Koltunov, Sergei Lialin. Russian text in verse form: V. Korostylev. Cinematography: Vadim Vereshchak, Suren Shakhbazian. Composers: Igor Shamo, Grigori Tyrtseu. Art Direction: V. Nikitin, Oleg Stepanenko. Costumes: E. Gamburd. Makeup: Nina Tikhonova. Sound: Nikolai Medvedev. Film Editor: V. Bondina. Consultant: V. Angel. Script Editor: L. Chumakova. Assistant Direction: V. Gerlak. Production Manager: N. Vaintrob.

Cast: Kostia Russu (Andriesh), Nodar Shashik-Ogly (Voinovan), Liudmila Sokolova (Liana), Kirill Shtirbu (Pakala), Yevgeni Ureke (Strymba-Lemna the Giant), Dominika Darienko (the Blind Woman), Robert Vizirenko-Kliavin (Black Storm), Trifon Gruzin (Barba-Kot).

The Top Guy (Pervyi paren'/ Pershyy khlopets', 1958)

Produced by the Dovzhenko Film Studio, Kyiv. Color, 85 minutes.

Direction: Sergei Parajanov. Screenplay: Pavel Lubensky, Viktor Bezorudko. Cinematography: Sergei Revenko. Art Direction: Alexander Lisenbart, Valeri Novakov. Costumes: O. Lorens. Makeup: E. Shainer. Composer: Yevgeni Zubtsov. Sound: Nina Avramenko. Song lyrics: N. Khomenko, P. Glazovoi. Film Editor: N. Gorbenko. Script Editor: Renata Korol. Assistant Direction: O. Lentsius. Production Manager: A Yarmolsky.

Cast: Grigori Karpov (Yushka), Liudmila Sosiura (Odarka), Yuri Satarov (Danila), Valeriya Kovalenko (Katria), Andrei Andrienko-Zemskov (Zhurba), Nikolai Shutko (Sidor), Tatiana Alexeeva (Frosia), Liudmila Orlova (Yabdosha), Mikhail Kramar (Panas), Yaroslav Sasko (Makar), Nikolai Yakovchenko (Grandpa Tereshko), Yuri Tsupko (the Goalie of "Zaria"), Varvara Chaika (Odarka's mother), Ivan Matveev (Grandpa Karpo), and the villagers of Peschanoe.

Natalia Uzhvy (1959)

Produced by the Dovzhenko Film Studio (Kyiv) and the Kyiv Television Studio. Black and white, 35 minutes.

Direction: Sergei Parajanov. Screenplay: Yukhim Martich. Cinematography: Valentina Tishkovets. Art Direction: Mikhail Gantman. Sound: Georgi Salov. Text read by: Anatoli Reshetnykov. Script Editor: S. Vyshynsky. Production Manager: P. Dedov.

Dumka (Derzhavna zasluzhena akademichna kapela URSR "Dumka," 1960)

Produced by Dovzhenko Film Studio (Kyiv) and Kyiv Television Studio. Black and white, 26 minutes.

Direction: Sergei Parajanov. Cinematography: Alexei Pankratiev. Sound: A. Demidenko. Art Direction: L. Baikova.

Golden Hands (Zolotye ruki/ Zoloti ruky, 1960)

Produced by the Dovzhenko Film Studio, Kyiv. Color, 35 minutes.

Direction: Alexander Nikolenko, Alexei Pankratiev, and Sergei Parajanov.

Screenplay: Ivan Kornienko. Cinematography: Alexei Pankratiev. Musical Design: G. Gumbler. Art Direction: Mikhail Rakovsky, Georgi Lukashov, B. Fedorenko. Makeup: M. Blazhevich. Sound: Georgi Salov. Script Editor: G. Zeldovich. Consultant: V. Nagai.

Cast: M. Kindzersky, G. Kononenko, Tolia Zaitsev, G. Blagodarov, E. Shakhovsky, and G. Markevitch.

Ukrainian Rhapsody (Ukrainskaia rapsodiia/ Ukrains'ka rapsodiia, 1961)
Produced by the Dovzhenko Film Studio, Kyiv. Color, 87 minutes.

Direction: Sergei Parajanov. Screenplay: Alexander Levada. Cinematography: Ivan Shekker. Art Direction: Mikhail Rakovsky. Costumes: N. Braun. Makeup: E. Shainer. Composer: Platon Maiboroda. Song lyrics: Nikolai Nagnibeda. Sound: Nina Avramenko, Sofia Sergienko. Film Editor: Maria Ponomarenko. Script Editor: N. Luchina. Assistant Direction: A. Bocharov. Production Managers: B. Glazman, P. Dedov.

Cast: Olga Reus-Petrenko (Oksana), E. Miroshnichenko (singing voice of Oksana), Eduard Koshman (Anton), Yuri Guliaev (Vadim), Natalia Uzhvy (Nadezhda Petrovna), Alexander Gai (Vainer), Valeri Vitter (Rudy), Stepan Shkurat (Oksana's Grandfather), Sergei Petrov (Jury President), Valentin Grudinin, Nikolai Slobodian, Olga Nozhkina, Dmitri Kapka, Yekaterina Litvinenko, Yuri Sarychev, I. Kulikov, Konstantin Stepankov, Svetlana Konovalova, V. Bely, Yevgeni Kovalenko, villagers of Buchak and soldiers of the Soviet Army.

The Flower on the Stone (Tsvetok na kamne/ Kvitka na kameni, 1960–1962)
Produced by the Dovzhenko Film Studio, Kyiv. Original title: *Tak eshche nikto ne liubil.* Black and white, 73 minutes.

Direction: Anatoli Slesarenko (uncredited) and Sergei Parajanov. Screenplay: Vadim Sobko. Cinematography: Sergei Revenko, Lev Shtifanov. Art Direction: Mikhail Rakovsky. Costumes: O. Yablonskaya. Makeup: V. Shikin. Composer: Igor Shamo. Song lyrics: D. Dutsenko, L. Smirnova. Sound: Arkadi Lupal. Film Editor: Maria Ponomarenko. Script Editor: Renata Korol. Assistant Directors: L. Dzenkevich, V. Parkhomenko. Production Manager: N. Vaintrob.

Cast: Boris Dmokhovsky (Varchenko), Grigori Karpov (Griva), Liudmila Cherepanova (Liuda), Inna Burduchenko-Kiriliuk (Christina), Georgi Yepifantsev (Zagornyi), Mikhail Nazvanov (Zabroda), Dmitri Franko (Chmykh), Vladimir Belokurov (Christina's father), Borislav Brondukov, Alexander Gai, Anatoli Soloviev.

Shadows of Forgotten Ancestors (*Teni zabytikh predkov/ Tini zabutykh predkiv*, 1964)
Produced by the Dovzhenko Film Studio, Kyiv. Color, 96 minutes.
Direction: Sergei Parajanov. Screenplay: Sergei Parajanov and Ivan Chendei, based on the novella by Mykhailo Kotsiubynsky. Cinematography: Yuri Illienko. Art Direction: Georgi Yakutovich, Mikhail Rakovsky. Composer: Miroslav Skoryk. Sound operator: Sofia Sergienko. Film Editor: Maria Ponomarenko. Assistant Direction: Vladimir Lugovsky. Production Manager: Nonna Yureva.

Cast: Ivan Mikolaichuk (Ivan), Igor Dziura (Ivan as a child); Larisa Kadochnikova (Marichka), Valentina Glinko (Marichka as a child), Tatiana Bestaeva (Palagna), Spartak Bagashvili (Yura the Sorcerer), Nikolai Grinko (Batag the Shepherd), Leonid Yengibarov (Miko), Nina Alisova (Ivan's mother), Alexander Gai (Petro Paliichuk, Ivan's father), Neonila Gnepovskaya (Marichka's mother), Alexander Raidanov (Onufri Huteniuk, Marichka's father).

Festival Screenings and Awards: Mar Del Plata Film Festival, Argentina (March 1965), Best Production and honorable mention "for color photography and special effects." San Sebastian Film Festival, Spain (June 1965). Venice Film Festival, Italy (August 1965). Rome Film Festival, Italy (October 1965), Italian Tourist Office Award. San Francisco Film Festival (October 1965). International Week of Films in Color, Barcelona, Spain (October 1965). Soviet Film Week, London, England (December 1965). Montreal Film Festival (July 1966). Locarno, Italy (July 1966). New York Film Festival (September 1966). Salonika (October 1966), Best Director. Festival of Festivals, London (December 1966).

Kyiv Frescoes (*Kievski freski/ Kyivs'ki freski*, 1966)
Produced by the Dovzhenko Film Studio, Kyiv. Color, 13 minutes.
Direction: Sergei Parajanov. Screenplay: Sergei Parajanov and Pavlo Zahrebelnyi. Cinematography: Alexander Antipenko. Art Direction: Alexander Kudria. Film Editor: Maria Ponomarenko.
Cast: Tengiz Archvadze (The Artist), Via Artmane (The Widow), Afanasi Kochetkov (The Longshoreman), Antonina Lefty (The Artist's ex-wife), Nikolai Grinko, Mikhail Gluzsky, Zoya Nedbai.
Restored in 2011 by the Oleksandr Dovzhenko National Centre, Kyiv.

Hakob Hovnatanyan (*Akop Ovnatanian*, 1967)
Produced by the Yerevan Newsreel-Documentary Film Studio. Color, 9 minutes.
Direction and Screenplay: Sergei Parajanov. Cinematography: K. Mesian. Composer: Stepan Shakarian. Sound: Yuri Sayadyan.

Children — to Komitas (Deti — Komitasu, 1968)

Direction: Sergei Parajanov. Operator: Oleg Bagdasarian. Composer: Tigran Mansurian. Film Editor: Maria Ponomarenko.

According to Garegin Zakoian, this film was about an exhibit of children's drawings dedicated to Komitas. "The film was given by Parajanov to the international organization UNICEF; its subsequent fate is unknown" (*Pis'ma iz zony,* 346).

The Color of Pomegranates (Tsvet Granata/ Nran guyne, 1969)

Produced by Armenfilm, Yerevan. Color, 77 minutes, Armenian release version. The Soviet release version edited by Sergei Yutkevich runs 71 minutes.

Direction and Screenplay: Sergei Parajanov. Cinematography: Suren Shakhbazian. Art Direction: Stepan Andranikian and Mikhail Arakelian. Costumes: Elena Akhvlediani, Iosif Karalov, Jasmine Sarabian. Makeup: Poghos Aschian, Vladimir Asatrian. Composer: Tigran Mansurian. Sound operator: Yuri Sayadyan. Film Editor: Maria Ponomarenko. Architectural Consultant: Victor Jorbenadze. Production Manager: Alexander Melik-Sarkisian.

Cast: Sofiko Chiaureli (the Poet as a youth, the Poet's Beloved, the Nun in White Lace, the Angel of the Resurrection, the Pantomime), Melkon Alekian (the Poet as a child), Vilen Galustian (the Poet as a monk), Georgi Gegechkori (the Poet in Old Age), Hovhannes (Onik) Minasian (the King), Spartak Bagashvili (the Poet's father), Medea Japaridze (the Poet's mother), Grigori Margarian (Sayat-Nova's teacher), G. Matsukatov, Medea Bibileishvili, L. Karamian, Guranda Gabunia, V. Mirianashvili.

The Legend of the Surami Fortress (Legenda Suramskoi kreposti/ Ambavi suramis tsikhisa, 1984)

Produced by the Georgia Film Studio, Tbilisi. Color, 89 minutes.

Directed by Sergei Parajanov and David (Dodo) Abashidze. Screenplay: Vazha Gigashvili, based on the novel by Daniel Chonkadze and other sources. Cinematography: Yuri Klimenko. Art Direction: Alexander Janshiev. Costumes: I. Mikatadze. Makeup: E. Kandelaki. Composer: Jansug Kakhidze. Sound: Gari Kuntsev. Film Editor: Maria Ponomarenko. Script Editor: Cora Tsereteli. Assistant Directors: Kh. Gogiladze, M. Simkhaev. Production Manager: Sergo Sikharulidze. Consultants: Victor Jorbenadze, S. Eristavi.

Cast: Sofiko Chiaureli (Vardo as an older woman), Leila Alibegashvili (Vardo as a young woman), David Abashidze (Osman-Agha and Simon the Piper), Zurab Kipshidze (Durmishkhan), Levan Uchaneishvili (Zurab as a grown man), Veriko Andzhaparidze (the old oracle), Givi Tukhadze (prince's courtier), Dudukhana Tserodze, Tamara Tsitsishvili.

Festival Screenings and Awards: Moscow Film Festival, out of competition (July 1985). Melbourne Soviet Film Festival (April 1986). Cannes Film Festival, Market (May 1986). Pesaro Film Festival, Italy (June 1986). Sitges Fantasy Film Festival (October 1986), Best Director. Berlin Festival, Berlin Forum sidebar (February 1987). Rotterdam Film Festival (February 1987), Most Innovative Film. Cinédecouverte Prize, Belgium (1987).

Arabesques on the Theme of Pirosmani (*Arabeski na temu Pirosmani*, 1986)

Produced by the Georgia Documentary Film Studio, Tbilisi. Color, 20 minutes.

Direction: Sergei Parajanov. Screenplay: Cora Tsereteli. Cinematography: Sergei Parajanov. Art Direction: Alexander Janshiev. Music: Jansug Kakhidze. Sound: Garri Kuntsev. Film Editor: Maria Ponomarenko.

Cast: Alexander Janshiev (Pirosmani), Leila Alibegashvili (Marguerite).

Festival Screenings and Awards: Rotterdam Film Festival (February 1988), special prize for "Twenty Directors of the Future."

Ashik-Kerib (*Ashik-Kerib / Ashik-Keribi*, 1988)

Produced by the Georgia Film Studio, Tbilisi. Color, 78 minutes.

Direction: Sergei Parajanov and David (Dodo) Abashidze. Screenplay: Gia Badridze, based on the story by Mikhail Lermontov. Cinematography: Albert Yavurian. Art Direction: Giorgi Alexi-Meskhishvili, Shota Gogolashvili, Niko Zandukeli. Music: Dzhavanshir Kuliev. Songs: Alim Qasimov. Sound: Gari Kuntsev.

Cast: Yuri Mgoian (Ashik-Kerib), Sofiko Chiaureli (Ashik-Kerib's mother), Ramaz Chkhikvadze (Ali-Agha), Konstantin Stepankov (Ashik-Kerib's teacher), Varvara Dvalishivili (Ashik-Kerib's sister), Veronika Metonidze (Magul-Megeri), David (Dodo) Abashidze, Tamaz Bashakidze, Nodar Dugladze.

Festival Screenings and Awards: Munich Film Festival (June 1988). Venice Film Festival, out of competition (September 1988). New York Film Festival (September 1988). European Film Awards (November 1988), "Felix" for Best Art Direction. Fantasporto Fantasy and Science Fiction Film Festival, Porto (February 1989). Istanbul Film Festival (April 1989), Special Jury Prize "for his contribution to contemporary art." 1990 Nika Awards (Russian Academy of Cinema Arts and Sciences): Best Film, Best Director, Best Cinematographer, Best Production Design.

Confession (Ispoved', 1989)

    Produced by Armenfilm, Yerevan. Color.

    Direction and Screenplay: Sergei Parajanov. Cinematography: Albert Yavurian.

    Cast: Sofiko Chiaureli (the Mother), Nino Tarkhan-Mouravi (Vera).

    Production was cancelled after only two days of shooting. Excerpts from the surviving footage may be found in Georgi Paradzhanov's documentary *I Died in Childhood . . . (Ia umer v detstve . . .* , Paradzhanov-Film, 2004).

Films Based on Scripts by Parajanov

Etudes on Vrubel (Etiudy o Vrubele/ Etiudy pro Vrubelia, 1989)

    Produced by the Dovzhenko Film Studio, Kyiv. Color, 80 minutes.

    Direction: Leonid Osyka. Screenplay: Leonid Osyka and Sergei Parajanov. Cinematography: Valeri Bashkatov. Art Direction: Nikolai Reznik, Alexander Danilenko, Valeri Novakov, Vitali Shavel. Music: Scriabin, Rachmaninoff, Rubinstein. Sound: Bogdan Mikhnevich. Film Editor: Maria Ponomarenko.

    Cast: Edisher Giorgobiani (Mikhail Vrubel'), Anatoli Romashin (the patron Ardian Prakhov), Olga Gobzeva (Emilia Prakhova), Alexei Safonov (the artist Vasnetsov), Svetlana Kniazeva (Anna Gappe), Boris Khmelnitsky (Semen Gaiduk), Daria Kmelnitskaya (Vera), Mikhail Dementev (Nikolai), Konstantin Stepankov, Nikolai Kriukov, Nadezhda Markina, Dmitri Mirgorodsky.

Swan Lake: The Zone (Lebedinoe ozero: Zona, 1989).

    Produced by Video Ukraine (Canada-USA), Kobzar International Corp. (Canada), Sweo-Sov Consult (Sweden), Dovzhenko Film Studio. Color, 96 minutes.

    Direction and Cinematography: Yuri Illienko. Screenplay: Sergei Parajanov and Yuri Illienko. Music: Virko Baley. Art Direction: Alexander Danilenko. Costumes: Nadia Sovtus. Sound Operator: Bohdan Mikhoevych. Film Editor: Eleonora Summovska.

    Cast: Viktor Soloviev (Man), Liudmyla Yefimenko (Woman), Maya Bulgakova (Old Woman), Filipp Illienko (Boy), Viktor Demertash (Prison Guard).

Films on Which Parajanov Worked as an Assistant

The Third Blow (Tretii Udar, 1948)

    Produced by the Kyiv Film Studio. Black and white, 113 minutes.

    Direction: Igor Savchenko. Screenplay: Arkadi Perventsev. Cinematography: Mikhail Kirillov.

Cast: Alexei Diky (Stalin), Nikolai Bogoliubov (Voroshilov), Yuri Shumsky (Vasilevsky), Sergei Martinson (Hitler).

Taras Shevchenko (1951)

Produced by the Kyiv Feature Film Studio. Color, 115 minutes.

Director and screenwriter: Igor Savchenko. Cinematography: Arkadi Koltsaty, Daniil Demutsky, Ivan Shekker.

Cast: Sergei Bondarchuk (Taras Shevchenko), Vladimir Chestnokov (Nikolai Chernyshevsky), Nikolai Timofeev (Nikolai Dobroliubov), Gnat Yura (Mikhail Shchepkin), Ivan Pereverzev (Sigismund Serakovsky), Natalia Uzhvy (Yaryna Shevchenko).

Maximka (1952)

Produced by the Kyiv Feature Film Studio. Color, 78 minutes.

Direction: Vladimir Braun. Screenplay: Grigori Koltunov, based on *Sea Tales* by Konstantin Staniukovich. Cinematography: Alexei Mishurin.

Cast: Tolia Babykin (Maximka), Boris Andreev (Luchkin), Nikolai Kriuchkov (Taras Matveevich), Stepan Kaiukov (Vasili Andreevich), Sergei Kurilov (Nikolai Fedorovich).

Notes

Introduction

1. Jean-Luc Godard, quoted in Gideon Bachmann, "In the Cinema, It Is Never Monday," *Sight and Sound* 52, no. 2 (Spring 1983): 120.

2. Sergei Parajanov quoted in Patrick Cazals, *Serguei Paradjanov* (Paris: Cahiers du cinéma, 1993), 130.

3. This book uses the British distribution title of *The Legend of the Surami Fortress*, which is a more accurate translation than the US distribution title, *The Legend of Suram Fortress*. Surami is an existing town in Georgia.

4. Sergei Paradjanov, *Seven Visions*, ed. Galia Ackerman, trans. Guy Bennett (Los Angeles: Green Integer, 1998); Garo Keheyan, ed., *Parajanov Himself* (Nicosia: Pharos, 2005); Sergei Paradzhanov and Zaven Sarkisian, *Kaleidoskop Paradzhanova: Risunok, kollazh, assambliazh* (Yerevan: Muzei Sergeia Paradzhanova, 2008), published simultaneously in English as *Parajanov Kaleidoscope: Drawings, Collages, Assemblages*; special issue on Sergei Parajanov, ed. James Steffen, *Armenian Review* 47/48, nos. 3–4/1–2 (2001/2002).

5. Sergei Paradzhanov, *Ispoved'*, ed. Kora Tsereteli (St. Petersburg: Azbuka, 2001); Kora Tsereteli, ed., *Kollazh na fone avtoportreta: Zhizn'—igra* (Nizhnii Novgorod: Dekom, 2008); Vasilii Vasil'evich Katanian, *Paradzhanov: Tsena vechnogo prazdnika* (Nizhnii Novgorod: Dekom, 2001); R. M. Korohods'kii and S. I. Shcherbatiuk, eds., *Serhii Paradzhanov: Zlet, trahediia, vichnist'* (Kyiv: Spalakh, 1994); Karen Kalantar, *Ocherki o Paradzhanove* (Yerevan: Gitutiun NAN RA, 1998); Levon Grigorian, *Tri tsveta odnoi strasti: Triptikh Sergeia Paradzhanova* (Moscow: Kinotsentr, 1991); Levon Grigorian, *Paradzhanov* (Moscow: Molodaia gvardiia, 2011). Only a very small amount of scholarship has been published about Parajanov in other languages such as Armenian and Georgian.

6. The best-known instance of Parajanov's usage of the term "cardiogram" is found in his comments at an October 1981 Artistic Council meeting on Yuri Liubimov's suppressed production of the play *Vladimir Vysotsky*, during which he called the Taganka Theatre a "cardiogram of Moscow." Parajanov also used the precise phrase "cardiogram of the time" in the interview shot by journalist Ron Holloway at the 1988 Munich Film Festival and subsequently used in his documentary *Parajanov: A Requiem* (1994).

7. Ron Holloway, "Sayat Nova," *Variety*, June 21, 1978.

8. Frank Williams, "A Martyrdom Concealed," *Times Literary Supplement*, August 27, 1982, 922.

9. Ibid.

10. Jeanne Vronskaya, "The Paradzhanov Affair," *The Times* (London), June 20, 1974.

11. Leonid Alekseychuk, "A Warrior in the Field," *Sight and Sound* 60, no. 1 (Winter 1990/1991): 22.

12. Ibid., 24.

13. Ibid.

14. George Faraday, *Revolt of the Filmmakers: The Struggle for Artistic Autonomy and the Fall the of the Soviet Film Industry* (University Park: Pennsylvania State University Press, 2000), 52.

15. The following account is synthesized from: Valery S. Golovskoy with John Rimberg, *Behind the Soviet Screen: The Motion-Picture Industry in the USSR, 1972–1982* (Ann Arbor, MI: Ardis, 1986), 8–45; B. N. Konoplev, *Osnovy fil'moproizvodstva* (Moscow: Iskusstvo, 1969), 3–24 and 38–87; and my own observations based on Goskino documents at the Russian State Archive of Literature and Art (RGALI).

16. Golovskoy and Rimberg, *Behind the Soviet Screen*, 17.

17. Ibid., 13.

18. The term *kinofikatsiia* ("cinefication") referred to the expansion and improvement of film exhibition facilities.

19. Konoplev, *Osnovy fil'moproizvodstva*, 90.

20. Golovskoy and Rimberg, *Behind the Soviet Screen*, 24.

21. Konoplev, *Osnovy fil'moproizvodstva*, 20.

22. Ronald Grigor Suny, *The Revenge of the Past: Nationalism, Revolution, and the Collapse of the Soviet Union* (Stanford: Stanford University Press, 1993), 87.

23. Ibid., 102.

24. Yuri Slezkine, "The USSR as a Communal Apartment, or How a Socialist State Promoted Ethnic Particularism." *Slavic Review* 53, no. 2 (1994): 415

25. Ibid.

26. Terry Martin, *The Affirmative Action Empire: Nations and Nationalism in the Soviet Union, 1923–1939* (Ithaca: Cornell University Press, 2001).

27. Ibid., 13.

28. Rossiiskii Gosudarstvennyi Arkhiv Noveishei Istorii (hereafter RGANI), f. 5, op. 61, d. 77.

29. Martin, *Affirmative Action Empire*, 452–53.

30. Peter Kenez, "Films of the Second World War," in *The Red Screen: Politics, Society, Art in Soviet Cinema*, ed. Anna Lawton (New York: Routledge, 1992), 164–66.

31. Alexander Karaganov, "The Soviet Multinational Cinema," in *The Soviet Multinational State: Readings and Documents*, ed. Martha B. Olcott, Lubomyr Hajda, and Anthony

Olcott (Armonk, NY: M. E. Sharpe: 1990), 293. Originally published as "Skhodstva i razlichiia" in *Pravda*, October 10, 1982.

32. Karaganov, "The Soviet Multinational Cinema," 293.

33. Ibid., 294.

34. Ibid.

35. Ibid., 295.

36. Ibid., 296.

37. Ibid., 296–97.

38. See, for instance, Larysa Briukhovets'ka, ed., *Poetychne kino: Zaboronena shkola* (Kyiv: ArtEk/Kino-Teatr, 2001).

39. Anna Lawton, *Kinoglasnost: Soviet Cinema in Our Time* (Cambridge: Cambridge University Press, 1992), 33.

40. Jeanne Vronskaya, *Young Soviet Film Makers* (London: Allen and Unwin, 1972), 32.

41. Viktor Shklovsky, "Poetry and Prose in Cinematography," in *Russian Formalism*, ed. Stephen Bann and John E. Bowlt (New York: Barnes and Noble, 1973), 130.

42. Ibid., 129.

43. Ibid., 130.

44. Viktor Shklovsky, "Art as Device," in *Theory of Prose*, trans. Benjamin Sher (Normal, IL: Dalkey Archive, 1990), 6; emphasis in original.

45. Katerina Clark, *The Soviet Novel: History as Ritual*, 3rd ed. (Bloomington: Indiana University Press, 2000), 163.

46. For a good overview of Aitmatov's career within the context of the literary culture and politics of the Soviet Union, see Joseph P. Mozur, *Parables from the Past: The Prose Fiction of Chingiz Aitmatov* (Pittsburgh: University of Pittsburgh Press, 1994).

47. Katherine Verdery, *National Ideology under Socialism: Identity and Cultural Politics in Ceausescu's Romania* (Berkeley: University of California Press, 1991), 80. See 74–80 for her initial articulation of these ideas. Verdery has subsequently developed her theory more fully in *What Was Socialism, and What Comes Next?* (Princeton: Princeton University Press, 1996).

Chapter 1. An Artist's Origins

1. Karl Baedeker, *Russia with Teheran, Port Arthur, and Peking: Handbook for Travelers* (Leipzig: Karl Baedeker, 1914), 467–68.

2. Ronald Grigor Suny, *The Making of the Georgian Nation*, 2nd ed. (Bloomington: Indiana University Press, 1994), 116.

3. Giorgi Gvakharia, "Sergei Parajanov's Ecumenical Vision," trans. Harsha Ram, *Armenian Review* 47/48, nos. 3–4/1–2 (2001/2002): 95–96.

4. This birth certificate is on display at the Parajanov Museum in Yerevan and is reproduced in Sergei Paradzhanov and Zaven Sarkisian, *Kaleidoskop Paradzhanova: Risunok, kollazh, assambliazh* (Yerevan: Muzei Sergeia Paradzhanova, 2008), 8.

5. Karen Kalantar, *Ocherki o Paradzhanove* (Yerevan: Gitutiun NAN RA, 1998), 8.

6. Kora Tsereteli, "Khronika zhizni i tvorchestva Sergeia Paradzhanova," in *Kollazh na fone avtoportreta: Zhizn'—igra*, ed. Kora Tsereteli, 2nd ed. (Nizhnii Novgorod: Dekom, 2008), 17.

7. See especially Parajanov's interview in Patrick Cazals, *Serguei Paradjanov* (Paris: Cahiers du cinéma, 1993), 32–33.

8. Anne Williamson, "Prisoner: The Essential Parajanov," *Film Comment* 25, no. 3 (May/June 1989): 63.

9. "Khronika zhizni i tvorchestva Sergeia Paradzhanova (Sargisa Paradzhaniantsa)" in Paradzhanov and Sarkisian, *Kaleidoskop Paradzhanova*, 9.

10. Richard Taylor, "Ideology as Mass Entertainment: Boris Shumyatsky and Soviet Cinema in the 1930s," in *Inside the Film Factory: New Approaches to Russian and Soviet Cinema*, ed. Richard Taylor and Ian Christie (New York: Routledge, 1991), 193–216. *A Cinema of the Millions (Kinematografiia millionov)* was the actual title of Shumyatsky's 1936 book.

11. Aleksandr Troshin, "'A driani podobno Garmon' bol'she ne stavite?': Zapisi besed B. Z. Shumiatskogo s I. V. Stalinom posle kinoprosmotrov. 1934 g.," *Kinovedcheskie zapiski*, no. 61 (2002): 296.

12. The Kyiv Film Studio was renamed the Kyiv Dovzhenko Feature Film Studio after Dovzhenko's death in 1956.

13. Rostislav Iurenev, Introduction to *Igor Savchenko: Sbornik statei i vospominanii*, ed. Nina Ivanivna Luchyna and T. T. Derevianko (Kyiv: Mystetsvo, 1980), 3–16.

14. Aleksandr Alov and Vladimir Naumov, quoted in *Igor Savchenko*, 18.

15. Feliks Mironer, Marlen Khutsiev, and Latif Faiziev, quoted in *Igor Savchenko*, 29, 32.

16. Aleksandr Korchinskii, "Vsia pravda o sudimostiakh Sergeia Paradzhanova," *Segodnia* (Kyiv), January 29, 2008. Continuation in January 30, 2008, issue. Parajanov biographer Levon Grigorian cites an altogether different reason for Parajanov's first arrest, based on the account of Parajanov's fellow student at the VGIK, Grigori Melik-Avakian, who claimed that it was due to Parajanov decorating the facility of GOKS with drawings of saints and listening to foreign radio. See Levon Grigorian, *Paradzhanov* (Moscow: Molodaia gvardiia, 2011), 53. However, the preponderance of evidence points to charges stemming from alleged homosexual relations with Mikava.

17. Cazals, *Serguei Paradjanov*, 48.

18. According to Henry Gabay, the film was controversial due to the inherent sensitivity of the issue of Russian-Ukrainian relations, which necessarily figured prominently in the subject matter. Genrikh Gabai, "Moi drug Sergei Paradzhanov," *Vremia i My*, no. 110 (1990): 264.

19. Paradzhanov and Sarkisian, *Kaleidoskop Paradzhanova*, 10; Natal'ia Fokina, "Lev Kulidzhanov: Postizhenie professii" (interview with Kulidzhanov), *Kinovedcheskie zapiski*, no. 64 (2003): 151; Vasilii Vasil'evich Katanian, *Prikosnovenie k idolam* (Moscow: Zakharov/ Vagrius, 1997), 211–12; Tonino Guerra, "Les fantômes du destin, ou le monde de

Paradjanov," *Positif*, nos. 389–90 (July/August 1993): 30. Nigyar's family name is sometimes listed as Kerimova; this book relies on information supplied by the Parajanov Museum.

20. Rostislav Iurenev, "Sredstvami kinematograficheskoi zhivopisi," *Sovetskii ekran*, no. 10 (May 1986): 15.

21. Sergei Paradzhanov, "Vechnoe dvizhenie," *Iskusstvo kino*, no. 1 (1966): 60. My translation. A slightly abridged English translation is available as "Perpetual Motion" in Sergei Parajanov, "Shadows of Our Forgotten Ancestors," trans. Steven P. Hill, *Film Comment* 5, no. 1 (Fall 1968): 38–48.

22. Gabai, "Moi drug Sergei Paradzhanov," 267.

23. Sergei Paradzhanov, ". . . chtoby ne molchat', berus' za pero," *Iskusstvo kino*, no. 12 (1990): 33.

24. Ibid., 33–34.

25. Josephine Woll, *Real Images: Soviet Cinema and the Thaw* (London: I.B. Tauris, 2000), 3–13.

26. Ibid., 7.

27. Ibid., 36. As Woll points out, while the Komsomol received that film with ambivalence, on the whole it was popular with the public.

28. In Russian, the *bytovoi* genre in various art forms depicts the details and problems of everyday life. Classic Soviet *bytovoi* films include Fridrikh Ermler's *The Parisian Cobbler* (*Parizhskii sapozhnik*, Lensovkino 1927) and Abram Room's *Bed and Sofa* (*Tret'ia meshchanskaia*, Sovkino 1927).

29. Sergei Zemlianukhin and Miroslava Segida, *Domashniaia sinemateka: Otechestvennoe kino, 1918–1996* (Moscow: Dubl'-D, 1996), 62.

30. Emilian Bukov, *Andriesh: Moldavskaia skazka*, trans. Vladimir Derzhavin (Moscow: Detgiz, 1946).

31. Miron Chernenko, "Sergei Paradzhanov," *Soviet Union* 17, nos. 1–2 (1990): 4.

32. L. Viktorov, "Kazka na ekrani," *Vechirnyi Kyiv*, June 25, 1955.

33. Information about the film's theatrical run is taken from the newspaper *Vechirnyi Kyiv*.

34. Mikhail Beliavskii, "O serosti i posredstvennosti," *Iskusstvo kino*, no. 8 (1955): 44.

35. Chernenko, "Sergei Paradzhanov," 7.

36. Kalantar, *Ocherki o Paradzhanove*, 32.

37. V. Sosiura and Ia. Zorin, "Pervyi paren'," *Sovetskii ekran*, no. 23 (1958): 9.

38. Aleksandr Kiknadze, "Tykva pretknoveniia," review of *Pervyi paren'*, *Sovetskii sport*, September 3, 1959.

39. A. Levada, "O nekotorykh problemakh ukrainskoi kinodramaturgii," *Iskusstvo kino*, no. 6 (1959): 104–5.

40. Information about the film's theatrical run is taken from the newspaper *Vechirnyi Kyiv*.

41. Most of this data comes from Sergei Kudriavtsev, "Poseshchaemost' otechestvennykh i zarubezhnykh fil'mov v Sovetskom kinoprokate," http://kinanet.livejournal

.com/689229.html. The admission figures for *The Color of Pomegranates* and *The Legend of the Surami Fortress* come from Zemlianukhin and Segida, *Domashniaia sinemateka.*

42. Some sources list the dates for all three films as 1957. I am using the dates supplied in *Kinolitopys: Anotovanyi kataloh kinozhurnaliv, dokumental'nykh filmiv, kino- i telesiuzhetiv, 1956–1965* (Kyiv: Derzhavnyi Komitet Arkhiviv Ukrainy, 2003).

43. Paradzhanov, "Vechnoe dvizhenie," 61.

44. Sergei Paradzhanov, "Pectoral'," in *Ispoved'*, ed. Kora Tsereteli (St. Petersburg: Azbuka, 2001), 379–83.

45. Leonid Osyka, "Genii: Obyknovenyi," in Tsereteli, *Kollazh na fone avtoportreta*, 100.

46. Woll, *Real Images*, 123.

47. Oleksandr Levada, "Ukrains'ka Rapsodiia" in *Tvory v chotyr'okh tomakh* (Kyiv: Dnipro, 1980), 3:279.

48. Ibid., 266–67.

49. Ibid., 262.

50. Information about the film's theatrical run is taken from the newspaper *Vechirnyi Kyiv.*

51. Tat'iana Senchenko, "Vospitivat' vkus!," *Iskusstvo kino*, no. 1 (January 1962): 172–73.

52. For an account of the incident, see "Dorogoi nash chelovek," *Izvestiia*, September 8, 1960.

53. Volodymyr Luhovs'kyi in *Tini zabutykh predkiv: Rozkadrovky*, by Serhii Paradzhanov and Volodymyr Luhovs'kyi (Kyiv: Vydavnychyi dim Akademiia, 1998), 29.

54. *Encyclopedia of Ukraine*, ed. Volodymyr Kubiiovych and Danylo Husar Struk (Toronto: University of Toronto Press, 1984), s.v. "Sobko, Vadym."

55. Chernenko, "Sergei Paradzhanov," 7–8.

56. Ibid., 12.

57. Kalantar, *Ocherki o Paradzhanove*, 38.

58. Iu. Martynenko, "Vernyi put'—truden!," *Nauka i religiia*, no. 7 (1963): 91–93.

59. N. Lordkipanidze, "Derzhite marku, Dovzhenkovtsy!," *Izvestiia*, November 26, 1962.

60. Alexander Muratov, interview with the author, Kyiv, December 2000.

Chapter 2. *Shadows of Forgotten Ancestors*

1. Renata Korol, "Tak pochynavsia vydatni film," in *Poetychne kino: Zaboronena shkola*, ed. Larisa Briukhovets'ka (Kyiv: ArtEk/Kino-Teatr, 2001), 319–21.

2. Chendei (b. 1922) also occupied a number of important official positions, including the secretary of the Transcarpathia oblast section of the Writer's Union. During the crackdown of the early Seventies he fell under official disfavor "for idealizing the Transcarpathian past." See *Encyclopedia of Ukraine*, ed. Volodymyr Kubiiovych

and Danylo Husar Struk (Toronto: University of Toronto Press, 1984), s.v. "Chendei, Ivan."

3. Korol, "Tak pochynavsia vydatni film," 319.

4. For a good survey of Kotsiubynsky's life and work see Bohdan Rubchak, "The Music of Satan and the Bedeviled World: An Essay on Mykhailo Kotsiubynsky," in *Shadows of Forgotten Ancestors*, by Mykhailo Kotsiubynsky, trans. Marco Carynnyk with notes and an essay by Bohdan Rubchak (Littleton, CO: Ukrainian Academic Press, 1981), 79–121.

5. Ibid., 81.

6. Ibid., 90–91.

7. The characterization "democratic" is also found in Soviet-era criticism on Kotsiubynsky, namely S. Shakhovskii, "Zhizn' i tvorchestvo M. M. Kotsiubinskogo," in *Sobranie sochinenii v trekh tomakh*, by Mikhail Kotsiubinskii (Moscow: Goslitizdat, 1951), 1:8.

8. Rossiiskii Gosudarstvennyi Arkhiv Literatury i Iskusstva (hereafter RGALI), f. 2944, op. 4, d. 280, l. 1

9. Rubchak, "Music of Satan," 104–5.

10. RGALI f. 2944, op. 4, d. 280, l. 1.

11. Ivan Chendei, *Teni zabytykh predkov* po odnoimennoi povesti M. M. Kotsiubinskogo. Rezhisserskaia redaktsiia S. Paradzhanova (1963), Sergei Parajanov Museum.

12. RGALI, f. 2944, op. 4, d. 280, ll. 7–8.

13. RGALI, f. 2944, op. 4, d. 281, l. 5.

14. *Encyclopedia of Ukraine*, s.v. "Yakutovich, Heorhii."

15. *Encyclopedia of Ukraine*, s.v. "Skoryk, Myroslav."

16. Volodymyr Luhovs'kyi in *Tini zabutykh predkiv: Rozkadrovky*, by Serhii Paradzhanov and Volodymyr Luhovs'kyi (Kyiv: Vydavnychyi dim Akademiia, 1998), 69.

17. Ibid., 31.

18. Yuri Illienko quoted in Bohdan Nebesio, "*Shadows of Forgotten Ancestors*: Storytelling in the Novel and the Film," *Literature/Film Quarterly* 22, no. 1 (1994): 47.

19. R. M. Korohods'kii and Svetlana Shcherbatiuk, eds., *Serhii Paradzhanov: Zlet, trahediia, vichnist'* (Kyiv: Spalakh, 1994), 70–71.

20. Illienko made these comments during a March 1988 visit to the University of Nevada at Las Vegas, attended by the author.

21. Transcript of the September 4, 1964, meeting of the Artistic Council of the Dovzhenko Film Studio, Sergei Parajanov Museum.

22. RGALI, f. 2944, op. 4, d. 280, ll. 24–26.

23. David A. Cook, "*Shadows of Forgotten Ancestors*: Film as Religious Art," *Post Script* 3, no. 3 (1984): 22.

24. Nebesio, "*Shadows of Forgotten Ancestors*," 45.

25. Sergei Paradzhanov, "Vechnoe dvizhenie," *Iskusstvo kino*, no. 1 (1966): 64.

26. Ibid., 65

27. Ibid., 62–63. Dovbush actually wears a red *serdak* (short cloak) in the film, not

a red shirt. Such cloaks are common accessories in traditional male Hutsul costumes, though the film's symbolism is indeed obvious as Parajanov points out.

28. Ibid., 65. The *lubok* was a form of folk woodcut print found in Russia and Ukraine.

29. "Prizes at Argentine Festival," *Variety*, April 7, 1965. The Italian production *Gli Indifferenti* (1964) received Best Film.

30. Andrew Sarris, "Breaks Jaw: Best Actress," *Variety*, April 7, 1965.

31. Gene Moscowitz, review of *Teni Zabytykh Predkov*, *Variety*, September 8, 1965.

32. Mikola Bazhan, "Karpatskaia pesnia," *Literaturnaia gazeta*, December 5, 1964.

33. Vladimir Turbin, "Mir, otkrytyi zanovo: Zametki o filme 'Teni zabytykh pred- kov," *Komsomol'skaia pravda*, December 27, 1964.

34. Vladimir Turbin, "Zhivoi ogon'," *Molodaia gvardiia*, no. 2 (1965): 282–83.

35. Georgi Gachev, *Natsional'nye obrazy mira: Obshchie voprosy; Russkii, bolgarskii, kirgiz- skii, gruzinskii, armianskii* (Moscow: Sovetskii pisatel', 1988).

36. Kenneth Farmer, *Ukrainian Nationalism in the Post-Stalin Era: Myth, Symbols, and Ideology in Soviet Nationalities Policy* (The Hague: Martinus Nijhoff, 1980), 97.

37. Ivan Drach, "Otkrytie," *Ekran 1965* (Moscow: Iskusstvo, 1966), 29.

38. Ivan Dziuba, "Den' poiska," *Iskusstvo kino*, no. 5 (1965): 79.

39. As mentioned earlier, the documents in the Goskino file in Moscow in fact do not suggest any particular difficulty around the issue of retaining the original language soundtrack.

40. Undated report by F. Braichenko to S. P. Ivanov, Sergei Parajanov Museum.

41. Leonid Plyushch, *History's Carnival: A Dissident's Autobiography*, trans. Marco Carynnyk (New York: Harcourt Brace Jovanovich, 1979), 81.

42. "Interv'iu V. Chornovola gazeti 'Moloda gvardiia,'" in *Petro Shelest: The True Judgment of History Still Awaits Us; Memoirs, Diaries, Documents, Materials*, by Petro Iu. Shelest and Iuri Shapoval (Kyiv, Geneza, 2003), 702.

43. N. Mikhailov, "Zapiska Komiteta po pechati pri SM SSSR v TsK KPSS o nekotorykh voprosakh literatury i iskusstva," in *Apparat TsK KPSS i kul'tura, 1965–1972: Dokumenty*, ed. N. G. Tomilina (Moscow: ROSSPEN, 2009), 164.

44. Information about the film's theatrical run is taken from the newspaper *Vechirnyi Kyiv*.

45. "Ot komiteta po Leninskim i gosudarstvennym premiiam SSSR v oblasti liter- atury, iskusstva i arkhitektury pri Sovete Ministrov SSSR," *Izvestiia*, June 8, 1967.

46. Advertisement for *Les Chevaux de feu*, *Le Monde*, March 26, 1966.

47. Information about the film's Paris theatrical run is taken from the newspaper *Le Monde*.

48. Serge Paradjanov, "*Les Chevaux de feu* c'est l'histoire d'un coup de foudre," *Les Lettres Françaises*, March 24, 1966.

49. Samuel Lachize, review of *Les Chevaux de feu*, *L'Humanité*, March 26, 1966.

50. Jean De Baroncelli, "Les Chevaux de feu," *Le Monde*, March 30, 1966.

51. Sylvain Godet, "Le dernier cinéaste heureux," *Cahiers du cinema*, no. 178 (May 1966): 74.

52. For a good brief account of this period, see chapter 14, "Religion, Nationality and Dissent" in Geoffrey Hosking, *The First Socialist Society: A History of the Soviet Union from Within* (Cambridge, MA: Harvard University Press, 1990), esp. 402–26.

53. Michael Browne, ed., *Ferment in the Ukraine: Documents by V. Chornovil, I. Kandyba, L. Lukyanenko, V. Moroz, and others* (New York: Praeger, 1971), 3; Vyacheslav Chornovil, *The Chornovil Papers* (New York: McGraw-Hill, 1968), 52–53. Article 62, Criminal Code of the Ukrainian SSR, quoted in Chornovil, 6.

54. Chornovil, *Chornovil Papers*, 37.

55. Browne, *Ferment in the Ukraine*, 191.

56. Sources consulted in this section include: Bohdan Nahaylo, *The Ukrainian Resurgence* (Toronto: University of Toronto Press, 1999); Orest Subtelny, *Ukraine: A History*, 4th ed. (Toronto: University of Toronto Press, 2009); Bohdan Krawchenko, *Social Change and National Consciousness in Twentieth-Century Ukraine* (London: Macmillan, 1985); Zev Katz, ed., *Handbook of Major Soviet Nationalities* (New York: The Free Press, 1975); and Ronald Grigor Suny, *The Revenge of the Past: Nationalism, Revolution, and the Collapse of the Soviet Union* (Stanford: Stanford University Press, 1993).

57. Shelest's defense of Drach: Vladimir Gusev, "Dialogi so Shcherbytskim V.," *ZN,UA*, January 4, 1998. http://zn.ua/SOCIETY/dialogi_so_scherbitskim_v-9812.html. Shelest's discussion of Dziuba's essay: Iurii Shapoval, "Interv'iu V. Shelesta," in Shelest and Shapoval, *Petro Shelest*, 748–49.

58. Nahaylo, *Ukrainian Resurgence*, 26–28.

59. Ibid., 32.

60. Browne, *Ferment in the Ukraine*, 5. For a copy of the letter in the original Ukrainian, see *Ukrains'ka inteligentsiia pid sudom KGB: Materiialy z protsesiv V. Chornovola, M. Masiutka, M. Ozernoho ta in.* (Munich: Suchasnist', 1970), 187–88.

61. Browne, *Ferment in the Ukraine*, 192. On pages 192–96, along with the list of signatories Browne provides information about their individual fates. Documents about the trials were compiled by Chornovil and later published in *The Chornovil Papers*.

62. Luhovs'kyi in Paradzhanov and Luhovs'kyi, *Tini zabutykh predkiv*, 97.

63. Valentyn Moroz, "Chronicle of Resistance," in *Report from the Beria Reserve: The Protest Writings of Valentyn Moroz*, ed. and trans. John Kolasky (Chicago: Cataract Press, 1974), 59.

64. Ibid., 75–77.

65. Ibid., 76. The spelling has been changed from "Paradzhanov" to "Parajanov."

66. Ibid., 75.

67. Ibid.

68. Alexei Korotyukov, "Parajanov: The True Story Behind His Arrest," interview by Slavko Nowytski, *CTVD: Cinema-TV-Digest* 9, no. 4 (September 1975): 1–2.

69. Sergei Paradzhanov, "Voskhozhdenie k masterstvu," *Sovetskii ekran*, no. 24 (1971): 1.

70. "Stenograma zasidannia Khudozhnoi rady kinostudii im. O. P. Dovzhenka, 29 sichnia 1966 roku," in Briukhovets'ka, *Poetychne kino*, 59. For further information on the film's censorship history, see also Evgenii Margolit, "Rodnik dlia zhazhdushchikh," in *"Polka": Dokumenty, svidetel'stva, kommentarii. Vypusk 3*, ed. Valerii Fomin (Moscow: Materik, 2006), 67–86.

71. "Stenograma zasidannia Khudozhnoi rady kinostudii im. O. P. Dovzhenka," 58.

72. Ibid., 63.

73. Ibid., 65.

74. Larysa Briukhovets'ka, "Areshtovani fil'my Ukrainy: Tsenzura v ukrains'komy kino," in *Poetychne kino*, 247.

75. For a good overview of both Vasyl Stefanyk as a writer and Osyka's film, see Vitaly Chernetsky, "Visual Language and Identity Performance in Leonid Osyka's *A Stone Cross*: The Roots and the Uprooting," *Studies in Russian and Soviet Cinema* 2, no. 3 (2008): 269–80.

76. Briukhovets'ka, *Poetychne kino*, 145.

77. Joshua First, "Ukrainian National Cinema and the Concept of the 'Poetic,'" *KinoKultura*, Special Issue 9: Ukrainian Cinema (December 2009). http://www.kino kultura.com/specials/9/first.shtml.

78. Rossiiskii Gosudarstvennyi Arkhiv Noveishei Istorii (hereafter RGANI), f. 5, op. 60, d. 66, ll. 9–13.

Chapter 3. *Kyiv Frescoes*

1. Known during the Soviet period as the Kyiv Museum of Western and Oriental Art, the museum has a relatively small but impressive collection of Western European, as well as Egyptian, Greek, Roman, Chinese, Japanese, and Persian art. Founded in 1919, it is based on the private residence and collection of Bohdan and Varvara Khanenko. Velázquez's portrait of the Infanta Margarita is one of the best-known pieces in the museum. It is also notable for its fine collection of Italian ceramics.

2. Sergei Paradzhanov, *Ispoved'*, ed. Kora Tsereteli (St. Petersburg: Azbuka, 2001), 51.

3. "Stenograma zasidannia khudozhnoi rady (Obhovorennia rezhisers'koho stenariia S. I. Paradzhanova). Kyivs'ka kinostudiia khudozhnikh fil'miv im. O. P. Dovzhenka," "Kievskie freski" file, Sergei Parajanov Museum.

4. In Soviet film production, the initial script submitted for approval was written in prose with dialogue and was called a "literary scenario" (*literaturnyi stsenarii*). The director would develop a detailed shooting script (*rezhisserskii stsenarii*, or "director's scenario") after the film was approved to launch into production.

5. Sergei Paradzhanov, "Kievskie freski," *Iskusstvo kino*, no. 12 (December 1990): 42.

6. Ibid., 43.

7. *Parsuna* refers to a style of portraiture of the late sixteenth and seventeenth century, especially in Russia and Ukraine, that served as an intermediate stage between icon

painting and Western-style painting. It combines a more naturalistic rendering of detail with the flattened perspective of icons.

8. Paradzhanov, "Kievskie freski," 43. The sudden tense shifts are present in the original Russian here and subsequently.

9. *Kirza* is a thick oilcloth used in Russia and the Soviet Union for the making of army boots; this term is usually etymologically linked to "Kersey cloth," a heavy woolen fabric used to make uniforms, originally made in Kersey, England. Thanks to Vitaly Chernetsky for his help identifying this reference.

10. Paradzhanov, "Kievskie freski," 43–44.

11. Ibid., 44–46.

12. Here and following, Paradzhanov, "Kievskie freski," 51–52.

13. Ibid., 54. The definition in parentheses is Parajanov's.

14. Ibid.

15. Ibid. Kobzars were itinerant Ukrainian bards. The first book by Taras Shevchenko, Ukraine's national poet, published in 1840, was titled *Kobzar*. Since then, editions of Shevchenko's collected poems usually bear this title. When capitalized, in modern Ukrainian usage the word can refer to Shevchenko himself. Here Parajanov appears to refer to the Shevchenko monument located in the park between the Khanenko Museum and the main building of Kyiv University, a neoclassical structure unusually painted a deep red color. Thanks to Vitaly Chernetsky for his help identifying this reference.

16. "Kievskie freski" file, Sergeĭ Parajanov Museum.

17. Ibid.

18. Aleksandr Antipenko, "Ego deviz byl—otdavat'," *Iskusstvo kino,* no. 12 (1990): 64.

19. Shooting script dated May 30, 1965, "Kievski freski" file, Sergei Parajanov Museum.

20. Ibid.

21. "List golovnoho upravlinnia khudozhnoi kinematografii Golovi Derzhavnoho komitetu Radi Ministriv URSR po kinematografii. Ivanovu S. P. vid 29 chervnia 1965 r. No. 19/962," "Kievskie freski" file, Sergei Parajanov Museum.

22. Ibid.

23. Here and subsequently, undated shooting script draft, "Kievskie freski" file, Sergei Parajanov Museum. Cora Tsereteli has incorporated passages from it in the version of the script published in *Ispoved'*.

24. Svetlana Shcherbatiuk, interview with the author, Kyiv, December 2000.

25. Paradzhanov, "Ispoved'," in *Ispoved'*, 125.

26. Paradzahnov, "Kievskie freski," 50.

27. R. M. Korohods'kyi and Svitlana Shcherbatiuk, eds., *Serhii Paradzhanov: Zlet, trahediia, vichnist'* (Kyiv: Spalakh, 1994), 143–44.

28. Yuri Yegorov, quoted in Sergei Paradzhanov, ". . . chtoby ne molchat', berus' za pero," *Iskusstvo kino,* no. 12 (1990): 35–36.

29. Printed program located in the Parajanov files of the Dovzhenko Film Studio Museum, Kyiv, December 2000.

30. For an overview of Zahrebelny's career, see *Istoriia ukrains'koi literatury u dvokh tomakh*, ed. I. O. Dzeverin (Kyiv: Nauk. dumka, 1987), 2:614–26.

31. Here and following: "Protokol obsuzhdeniia literaturnogo stsenariia 'Kievskie freski' (avtory P. Zagrebel'nyi i S. Paradzhanov) na zasedanii stsenarno-redaktsionnoi kollegii 5 fevralia 1966 g.," "Kievskie freski" file, Sergei Parajanov Museum.

32. Ibid.

33. Ibid.

Chapter 4. *The Color of Pomegranates*

1. From "Dun en gelkhen imatsun is" ("You were ever wise"), translated in Charles Dowsett, *Sayat-Nova: An 18th-Century Troubadour; A Biographical and Literary Study* (Lovanii: In aedibus Peeters, 1997), 93.

2. "Soviet [*sic*] glorifies a poet of 1700s; cites Armenian in drive for cultural assimilation," *New York Times*, November 3, 1963.

3. "Sayat-Nova: Tsar' pesnopenii," in *Ekran 1969* (Moscow: Iskusstvo, 1969), 184.

4. Levon Grigorian, "Sayat-Nova," *Literaturnaia gazeta*, October 30, 1968.

5. The French critic and filmmaker Érik Bullot has made some fruitful comparisons between Parajanov's style and American experimental cinema; see Érik Bullot, *Sayat nova de Serguei Paradjanov: La face et le profil* (Crisnée, Belgium: Éditions Yellow Now, 2007), 58–60.

6. Karen Kalantar, *Ocherki o Paradzhanove* (Yerevan: Gitutiun NAN RA, 1998), 98.

7. See, for example, Laert Vagarshian, "Familiia moia Paradzhanov," *Iskusstvo kino*, no. 8 (August 1995): 132.

8. Rossiiskii Gosudarstvennyi Arkhiv Literatury i Isskustva (hereafter RGALI), f. 2944, op. 1, d. 324, ll. 38–40.

9. Vahagn Mkrtchian served as head of Armenfilm Studio from September 8, 1964, to July 1, 1967; Laert Vagarshian from July 1, 1967, to February 12, 1969; and Razmik Madoian from April 1969 to April 1974 and from April 20, 1982, to November 3, 1983. Information courtesy of Susanna Harutyunyan and Mikayel Stamboltsyan.

10. Sayat-Nova's biographical information was gleaned mainly from Dowsett, *Sayat-Nova*. Dowsett scatters these details throughout his text; I have attempted to present them in a clear chronological order.

11. Ibid., 70.

12. Ibid., 7.

13. Ibid., 71.

14. See especially Háfiz, *The Collected Lyrics of Háfiz of Shíráz*, trans. Peter Avery (Cambridge: Archetype, 2007). For an overview of the ghazal genre of poetry, see chapter 3 in J. T. P. de Bruijn, *Persian Sufi Poetry: An Introduction to the Mystical Use of Classical Persian Poems* (Richmond, Surrey: Curzon, 1997).

15. Dowsett, *Sayat-Nova*, 268, 377. For English translations of Sayat-Nova's poems in addition to Dowsett, see Aram Tolegian, trans. and ed., *Armenian Poetry, Old and New: A Bilingual Anthology* (Detroit: Wayne State University Press, 1979), 96–99; and Diana Der Hovanessian and Marzbed Margossian, trans. and ed., *Anthology of Armenian Poetry* (New York: Columbia University Press, 1978), 106–12.

16. One of Hovnatan's poems ("Song of Love") is available in English translation in Tolegian, *Armenian Poetry, Old and New*, 88–89.

17. Mania Kazarian, *Khudozhniki Ovnataniany* (Moscow: Iskusstvo, 1968), 10.

18. Dowsett, *Sayat-Nova*, 423.

19. Ibid., 16–21.

20. Ibid., 78–82.

21. Ibid., 21–22.

22. Ibid., 32.

23. Alexander Mikaberidze, "Battle of Krtsanisi," in *Historical Dictionary of Georgia* (Lanham, MD: Scarecrow Press, 2007).

24. Dowsett, *Sayat-Nova*, 26. Parajanov in fact shot footage depicting the raid upon the Haghpat Monastery, though he ultimately decided against using it in the finished film.

25. Viktor Jorbenadze, interview with the author, Tbilisi, July 1998; Mikhail Arakelian, *Sergei Iosifovich Paradzhanov: Kak sozdavalsia khudozhestvennyi fil'm "Tsvet granata" i drugoe* (Yerevan: Avtorskoe izdanie, 2006), 8.

26. Arakelian, *Sergei Iosifovich Paradzhanov*, 12.

27. Aleksandr Pushkin, *Bakhchisarayi shatrvane* (Yerevan: Haypethrat, 1964). The illustrations were originally published in Aleksandr Pushkin, *Bakhchisaraiskii fontan: Poema* (Moscow: Grosman i Knebel', 1899).

28. Kalantar, *Ocherki o Paradzhanove*, 98.

29. Some Soviet editions of Sayat-Nova's poetry published during that era: Sayat'-Nova and Morus Hasrat'yan, *Hayeren, vrats'eren, adrbejaneren khagheri zhoghovatsu* (Yerevan: Haypethrat, 1959), republished 1963; Saiat-Nova and S. Z. Gaisarian, *Stikhotvoreniia* (Leningrad: Sovetskii pisatel', 1961); Saiat-Nova and Valerii Iakovlevich Briusov, *Saiat-Nova v perevodakh V. Ia. Briusova* (Yerevan: Izd-vo AN Armianskoi SSR, 1963); Saiat'nova, *Saiat'nova: K'art'uli lek'sebi*, ed. Aleksandre Baramidze (Tbilisi, 1963). Biographies and essays: Suren Gaisarian, *Saiat-Nova: Zametki o zhizni i tvorchestve velikogo armianskogo poeta* (Moscow: Znanie, 1963); Mirali Seiidov, *Pevets narodov Zakavkaz'ia* (Baku: Izd-vo Akademii nauk Azerbaidzhanskoi SSR, 1963). Novel: Zarzand Darian, *Sayat'-Nova* (Yerevan: Haypethrat, 1960), translated into Russian as *Saiat-Nova: Roman* (Moscow: Sovetskii pisatel', 1973).

30. Saiat-Nova, *Lirika: Perevody s armianskogo, gruzinskogo, azerbaidzhanskogo*, intro. Ioseb Grishashvili (Moscow: Gosudarstvennoe izd-vo khudozhestvennoi literatury, 1963).

31. For a concise characterization of how this element of Soviet cultural policy fit within the framework of nationalities policies as a whole, see Yuri Slezkine, "The USSR as a Communal Apartment, or How a Socialist State Promoted Ethnic Particularism,"

Slavic Review 53, no. 2 (1994), 414–52. For an excellent study of the origins of these policies, see Terry Martin, *The Affirmative Action Empire: Nations and Nationalism in the Soviet Union, 1923–1939* (Ithaca: Cornell University Press, 2001).

32. Grishashvili, introduction to Saiat-Nova, *Lirika*, 3.

33. Ibid., 5.

34. Ibid., 15.

35. Ibid., 11.

36. Ibid., 15.

37. Sergei Paradzhanov, "Saiat-Nova," in *Ispoved'*, ed. Kora Tsereteli (St. Petersburg: Azbuka, 2001), 83.

38. For a more detailed account see James Steffen's essay "From *Sayat-Nova* to *The Color of Pomegranates*: Notes on the Production and Censorship of Parajanov's Film," in *Armenian Review* 47/48, nos. 3–4/1–2 (2001/2002): 105–47.

39. RGALI, f. 2944, op. 4, d. 1408, ll. 2–4.

40. Ibid., l. 9.

41. Ibid., l. 10.

42. RGALI, f. 2944, op. 4, d. 1409, ll. 91–93.

43. Arakelian, *Sergei Iosifovich Paradzhanov*, 19.

44. RGALI, f. 2944, op. 4, d. 1409, ll. 4–5.

45. Kalantar, *Ocherki o Paradzhanove*, 98.

46. Vagarshian, "Familiia moia Paradzhanov," 131.

47. RGALI, f. 2944, op. 4, d. 1408, ll. 53–56.

48. *Hakob Hovnatanyan* is available as a bonus feature on the DVD of the "director's cut" of *The Color of Pomegranates* released on DVD by Kino in the United States. The title on the most commonly circulated print is in Russian: *Akop Ovnatanian*.

49. Valerii Fomin, "Tsvet granata," in *"Polka": Dokumenty, svidetel'stva, kommentarii. Vypusk 3*, ed. Valerii Fomin (Moscow: Materik, 2006), 142.

50. Vagarshian, "Familiia moia Paradzhanov," 133.

51. Levon Abrahamian, "Toward a Poetics of Parajanov's Cinema," trans. Harsha Ram, *Armenian Review* 47/48, nos. 3–4/1–2 (2001/2002): 69.

52. Shostka is a city in Ukraine known for chemical products, including film stock. NIKFI is the Scientific Research Film-Photo Institute. Parajanov is perhaps suggesting that due to the poor quality of the film stock available, the shoot has become, in effect, a laboratory for testing stock.

53. RGALI, f. 2944, op. 4, d. 1408, ll. 57–58.

54. Ibid., ll. 73.

55. Vagarshian, "Familiia moia Paradzhanov," 133.

56. Stepan Andranikian, undated video interview, Sergei Parajanov Museum.

57. Arakelian, *Sergei Iosifovich Paradzhanov*, 9.

58. Andranikian, undated video interview.

59. RGALI, f. 2944, op. 4, d. 1408, ll. 81–82.

60. Ibid., ll. 113–14.

61. Paradzhanov, "Saiat-Nova," 99.

62. Here and following I have made slight modifications to the chapter title translations on the commonly available DVD version to more closely reflect the flavor and rhythm of the original Armenian texts written by Hrant Matevosyan. Many thanks to Vigen Galstyan for his translations and his insightful comments about Matevosyan's text.

63. Here and following: RGALI, f. 2944, op. 4, d. 1409, ll. 56–57.

64. Ibid.

65. Mikayel Stamboltsyan, interview with the author, Yerevan, July 1998.

66. Fomin suggests that Yutkevich reedited the film at his own initiative. See Fomin, "Tsvet granata," 154–56.

67. This is the version available on DVD in the United States through Kino Lorber.

68. Here the film is probably using Morus Hasratyan's previously published Armenian translation. Parajanov wrote the original script in Russian and quotes the same line in Russian, as he does with all of Sayat-Nova's poems: "Ia tot, ch'ia zhizn' i ch'ia dusha — stradaniia." This most likely comes from K. Lipskerov's translation of the poem entitled "Ia lish' sluga ashugov iskushennykh" (I am only the servant of experienced *ashughs*) in Saiat-Nova, *Lirika*, 255. Parajanov was certainly familiar with this edition and most likely kept it at hand when he wrote the script.

69. Patrick McGovern has identified wine residue in clay vessels at the Neolithic site of Shalveris-Gora (in present day Georgia), dating as far back as 6000 BC. McGovern, *Ancient Wine: The Search for the Origins of Viniculture* (Princeton: Princeton University Press, 2003).

70. *The Color of Pomegranates* was in fact Mansurian's first feature film project, though he had worked on several documentary shorts before this. Parajanov originally wanted to use the noted Geneva-born Russian composer Andrei Volkonsky. (See Arakelian, *Sergei Iosifovich Paradzhanov*, 38; various interview subjects also mentioned this.) An accomplished harpsichordist, Volkonsky founded the early music ensemble Madrigal. He was also known for his interest in twelve-tone and serial compositional techniques, which frequently put him into conflict with the Soviet authorities until he emigrated in 1973. No doubt his score would also have also been exceptional, though perhaps in a different style.

71. "La musique de Sayat Nova," interview with Tigran Mansurian by Naïri Galstanian in *À la recherche de Serguei Paradjanov: Publié à l'occasion du 18e festival ("Théâtres au cinéma"), 9 au 25 mars 2007, à Bobigny*, ed. Dominique Bax (Bobigny: Magic cinéma, 2007), 106–9.

72. The fortress-monastery at Akhtala, located in the Lori province like Sanahin and Haghpat, dates to the eleventh to thirteenth centuries and is known for its beautiful painted murals, which survive only in part. The dome containing the image of the Virgin Mary holding the infant Jesus is badly damaged and her face is missing, which served as the inspiration for Parajanov's fantasy.

73. The location here is the St. Hovhannes Monastery in the village of Ardvi (Lori

province, ca. seventh to seventeenth century). Though the monastic complex is not very large and has a plain-looking exterior, the nearby cemetery has a beautiful collection of *khachkars* and a picturesque view of the mountains that Parajanov uses to full advantage. In the Yutkevich version this chapter is mistakenly described as "the Poet buries his Love." It is likely that Yutkevich conflated the "Nun in White Lace" with the woman being buried, who is also dressed in white, though they are actually played by different actresses: Sofiko Chiaureli plays the Nun, whereas this appears to be Medea Japaridze. The latter makes more sense considering Parajanov's conception of that chapter of the film as a whole. Yutkevich's interpretation also fails to address why the funeral is taking place in a new locale far away from the convent, and why the deceased woman is surrounded by ordinary folk rather than people of the cloth.

74. "Saiat-Nova: Tsar pesnopenii," 187.

75. This section was in fact shot at the Alaverdi cathedral in the Kakheti region of Georgia, as is the subsequent episode and the earlier episode in which Sayat-Nova's family visits Surb Gevorg and sacrifices a rooster. Most likely this was done because the Surb Gevorg cathedral is closely surrounded by other buildings and would have been too difficult to film in the way that Parajanov wanted.

76. "Saiat-Nova: Tsar pesnopenii," 187.

77. Paradzhanov, "Saiat-Nova," 116.

78. Komitas Vardapet (1869–1935) was a priest and musicologist who transcribed literally thousands of Armenian folk songs and composed a number of original works. His role in preserving the Armenian musical heritage cannot be overestimated. A witness to the early days of the 1915 Armenian genocide in Turkey, he suffered psychological trauma as a result and spent the last twenty years of his life in a French psychiatric clinic. The most recent biography in English is Rita Soulahian Kuyumjian, *Archeology of Madness: Komitas, Portrait of an Armenian Icon* (Reading, England: Taderon Press, 2001).

79. Thanks to Irena Popiashvili for translating this passage.

80. In fact Parajanov's father Iosif had passed away in 1962, though his mother Siran did not pass away until 1975, while he was in prison.

81. This is sometimes identified as the pectoral cross of Queen Tamar, though it appears to be a different piece; Tamar's cross is of a simpler design.

82. Levon Abrahamian, interview with the author, Yerevan, July 1998.

83. Sabir Rizaev, "Saiat-Nova," *Literaturnaia Armeniia*, no. 12 (1970): 74.

84. "Muzhestvennyi" can also be translated as "courageous," but given the context I am translating it as "manly."

85. Rizaev, "Saiat-Nova," 75.

86. Ibid., 80.

87. Mikhail Bleiman, "Arkhaisty ili novatory?" *Iskusstvo kino*, no. 7 (1970): 55–76. The title of Bleiman's essay refers to Yuri Tynianov's classic 1926 essay "The Archaists and Pushkin."

88. Ibid., 70.

89. Ibid., 71.

90. Ibid., 73–74.

91. Here and following: ibid., 76.

Chapter 5. Silent Years

1. Sergei Paradzhanov, "Ispoved'," in *Ispoved'*, ed. Kora Tsereteli (St. Petersburg: Azbuka, 2001), 121. My translations here and following.

2. Ibid., 127.

3. Tsereteli: "A mountain resort in Georgia where tuberculosis is treated." See note 1 to "Ispoved'," 131.

4. According to Tsereteli, this refers to a folk belief that dog meat cures tuberculosis; see note 2, 131.

5. That is, she did not share a desk with other students because of her tuberculosis.

6. Paradzhanov, "Ispoved'," 130–31.

7. Ibid., 136.

8. Ibid., 145.

9. Given the time frame mentioned here, Parajanov may have been location scouting for *The Color of Pomegranates*.

10. Paradzhanov, "Ispoved'," 150.

11. Ibid., 159.

12. Ibid., 160.

13. Ibid., 160, note 1.

14. Nairi Zarian, *Ara Prekrasnyi*, trans. Mariia Petrovykh (Moscow: Sovetskii pisatel', 1947).

15. Paradzhanov, "Ara Prekrasnyi," in *Ispoved'*, 223–24.

16. Ibid., 225.

17. Kora Tsereteli, preface to Paradzhanov, "Ara Prekrasnyi," 220.

18. This information is summarized from the website of the Bakhchisaray Historical and Cultural State Preserve in Crimea, http://hansaray.iatp.org.ua.

19. Paradzhanov, "Dremliushchii dvorets," in *Ispoved'*, 165–66.

20. Ibid., 168.

21. *Shahsey-Vahsey* (*Shakhsei-Vakhsei* in Russian) is a colloquial term derived from the Persian chant "*Shah Hussein, vah Hussein.*" One place where the term is used is the predominantly Shia Azerbaijan, which may well be how it came into the Russian vernacular; it refers to the tenth day of Muharram, a day of fasting known as Ashura. For the Shiites, who also refer to this holy day as the *Ta'ziyeh*, it marks the death of Imam Hussein, son of Ali. In particular, it refers to the procession accompanying the passion play reenacting Hussein's martyrdom at the hands of the Umayyads. As a sign of devotion, males often flagellate themselves with whips or chains and cut themselves to draw blood, evoking Hussein's sufferings. This ritual is officially forbidden in many communities, though it is still widely practiced.

22. Paradzhanov, "Dremliushchii dvorets," 176–77.

23. Ibid., 179–80.

24. Kora Tsereteli, preface to Paradzhanov, "Dremliushchii dvorets," 164.

25. Viktor Shklovsky, quoted in Tsereteli, preface to "Dremliushchii dvorets," 163.

26. Ibid., 163–64.

27. To my knowledge, there was no cinematic treatment of the plight of the Crimean Tatars in Soviet cinema until 1988 with Alexander Sokurov's *Days of the Eclipse*, in which one character relates to the Russian protagonist the story of his family's deportation to Central Asia.

28. Sergei Parajanov, letter to Sviatoslav Ivanov dated July 14, 1970, Sergei Parajanov Museum.

29. "Sergei Parajanov's Speech in Minsk before the Creative and Scientific Youth of Byelorussia on 1 December 1971," trans. Nora Seligman Favorov and P. Elana Pick, *Armenian Review*, 47/48, nos. 3–4/1–2 (2001/2002): 18. The original document is located at RGANI (Rossiiskii Gosudarstvennyi Arkhiv Noveishei Istorii) under f. 5, op. 64, d. 135, ll. 1–24. While the original transcript of the speech does not set off the title in quotes since the person transcribing was no doubt unaware of the project's existence, its title *The Earth . . . Again the Earth!* is confirmed by Sviatoslav Ivanov's written notes.

30. Mykhailo Kotsiubynsky, "Intermezzo," in *Fata Morgana and Other Stories*, trans. Abraham Mistetsky (Kyiv: Dnipro, 1980), 328. The ellipses are Kotsiubynsky's.

31. Ibid., 337.

32. Parajanov is listed as sole author in the versions published in *Seven Visions* (ed. Galia Ackerman, trans. Guy Bennett [Los Angeles: Green Integer, 1998]) and *Ispoved'*. Both these versions differ significantly in places from each other and from the shooting script. It is difficult to tell at what stage they were written, though presumably they were completed before the shooting script. The version in *Ispoved'* ends with the section entitled "Hymn to the Sun." The version in *Seven Visions* closes, like the shooting script, with a section depicting the dissemination of the song "Eternal Revolutionary" both as a recording and as sheet music, and the Tsarist authorities' failed attempt to suppress it.

33. Paradzhanov, "Intermezzo," in *Ispoved'*, 196–97.

34. See notes to "Intermezzo" in Mykhailo Kotsiubyns'kyi, *Tvory v shesti tomakh* (Kyiv: Vydavnytstvo Akademii Nauk Ukrainskoi RSR, 1961), 2:403.

35. See N. L. Kalenychenko, *Mykhailo Kotsiubyns'kyi: Zhyttia i tvorchist'* (Kyiv: Vydavnytstvo Akademii Nauk Ukrainskoi RSR, 1956), 154–59; Z. Kotsiubynskaia-Efimenko, *M. M. Kotsiubinskii: Masterstvo pisatel'ia* (Moscow: Sovetskii pisatel', 1959), 214–22.

36. Paradzhanov, "Intermezzo," 204–5.

37. Rossiiskii Gosudarstvennyi Arkhiv Literatury i Iskusstvo (hereafter RGALI), f. 2944, op. 4, d. 2145a, ll. 3–4.

38. Ibid., ll. 5–7.

39. Tamara Shevchenko, "Ia sdelala stavku na ukhodiashchikh . . ." in *Kollazh na fone avtoportreta: Zhizn'—igra*, 2nd ed., ed. Kora Tsereteli (Nizhnii Novgorod: Dekom, 2008), 153–54.

40. RGALI, f. 2944, op. 4, d. 2145a, l. 17.

41. "Sergei Parajanov's Speech in Minsk," 14–15.

42. Memo by Andropov, quoted in "Sergei Parajanov's Speech in Minsk," 13.

43. Alla Bobkova, "Armianin Tiflisskogo razliva," *Vechernyi Minsk*, February 10, 1993.

44. December 28, 1971, memorandum from Pavlo Fedchenko to Petro Shelest. Document courtesy of Cora Tsereteli.

45. Undated letter from Sviatoslav Ivanov to Petro Shelest. Document courtesy of Cora Tsereteli.

46. Mikhail Lermontov, "Demon," in *Polnoe sobranie sochinenii v desiati tomakh* (Moscow: Voskresen'e, 2000), 4:219–65.

47. Paradzhanov, "Demon," in *Ispoved'*, 272.

48. Ibid., 266

49. Tsereteli, preface to Paradzhanov, "Demon," 254.

50. Viktor Shklovsky, quoted in Tsereteli, preface to Paradzhanov, "Demon," 253.

51. Tsereteli, preface to Paradzhanov, "Demon," 254.

52. Tamara Shevchenko, introduction to Sergei Paradzhanov, "Iz nasledii" ("Vystuplenie v Minske" and "Zolotoi obrez"), *Kinovedcheskie zapiski*, no. 23 (1994): 76.

53. Ibid., 77.

54. Sergei Paradzhanov, "Zolotoi obrez," *Kinovedcheskie zapiski*, no. 23 (1994): 99–100.

55. Konstantin Tsiolkovsky (1857–1935), a scientist specializing in aerodynamics, astronautics, and rocket design.

56. Here and following: "Inga: Rezhisserskii stsenarii," Sergei Parajanov Museum.

57. RGALI, f. 2944, op. 4, d. 2294, l. 23.

58. RGALI, f. 2944, op. 4, d. 2294, l. 24.

59. The background information about production of *A Miracle in Odense* comes from Kora Tsereteli, preface to Paradzhanov, "Chuda v Odense," in *Ispoved'*, 276–77; and Tamara Ogorodnikova, "Rok," in Tsereteli, *Kollazh na fone avtoportreta*, 254–57.

Chapter 6. Internal Exile

1. Here and following: Marta Dziuba, "KDB pro Paradzhanova. Dokumenty iz rozsekrechenoho arkhivu KDB URSR," *Kino-Teatr*, no. 1 (2011): http://www.ktm.ukma.kiev.ua/show_content.php?id=1067.

2. Ibid. Thanks to Yuri Shapoval for helping to identify Leonid Cherchenko.

3. Ibid. Presumably Cherchenko meant the aforementioned October 1965 letter of petition that Parajanov signed along with six other leading cultural figures, although this leaves out the April 1968 petition to Brezhnev, Kosygin, and Podgorny. See chapter 2.

4. Ol'ha Petrova, interview with the author, Kyiv, December 2000.

5. Iuri Shapoval, "Interv'iu V. Shelesta," in *Petro Shelest: The True Judgment of History Still Awaits Us; Memoirs, Diaries, Documents, Materials* (Kyiv: Geneza, 2003), 748–49.

6. Nikolai Rapai, "V chem-to on byl naiven," in *Kollazh na fone avtoportreta: Zhizn'-igra*, 2nd ed., ed. Kora Tsereteli (Nizhnii Novgorod: Dekom),156.

7. Orest Subtelny, *Ukraine: A History*, 4th ed. (Toronto: Univ. of Toronto Press, 2009), 512–13.

8. For a good account of the 1972–1973 crackdown, see *Ukraine After Shelest*, ed. Bohdan Krawchenko (Edmonton: Canadian Institute of Ukrainian Studies, 1983), especially Roman Solchanyk, "Politics and the National Question in the Post-Shelest Period," 1–29; and Bohdan Nahaylo, "Ukrainiain Dissent and Opposition after Shelest," 30–55.

9. Subtelny, *Ukraine: A History*, 521

10. Shelest and Shapoval, *Petro Shelest*, 13.

11. Gagik [Garegin] Karapetian, "Kto 'zakazal' Paradzhanov: Versiia Aleksandra Iakovleva," interview with Aleksandr Iakovlev, *Iskusstvo kino*, no. 1 (January 2006), 141.

12. Alexei Korotyukov, "Parajanov: The True Story Behind His Arrest," interview by Slavko Nowytski, *CTVD: Cinema-TV-Digest* 9, no. 4 (September 1975): 4.

13. Aleksandr Korchinskii, "Vsia pravda o sudimostiakh Sergeia Paradzhanova," *Segodnia* (Kyiv), January 29, 2008. Continued in January 30, 2008, issue.

14. Korchinskii, "Vsia pravda o sudimostiakh," January 29, 2008.

15. Ol'ha Petrova, interview with author, Kyiv, December 2000.

16. Korchinskii, "Vsia pravda o sudimostiakh," 29 January, 2008.

17. Court verdict (*prigovor*) dated April 25, 1975, Sergei Parajanov Museum.

18. Korchinskii, "Vsia pravda o sudimostiakh," 29 January, 2008.

19. Korotyukov, "Parajanov," 4.

20. Svetlana Shcherbatiuk, quoted in Vasilii Katanian, *Prikosnovenie k idolam* (Moscow: Zakharov/Vagrius, 1997), 234.

21. Ibid., 234–35.

22. Evgenii Makashov, "Narod ne znaet takogo rezhissera," interview by Alla Bossart in Tsereteli, *Kollazh na fone avtoportreta*, 212.

23. Court verdict, Sergei Parajanov Museum.

24. Korotyukov, "Parajanov," 3–5.

25. Court verdict, Sergei Parajanov Museum.

26. P. Dolins'kyi, "Imenem zakona," *Vechirnyi Kyiv*, March 1, 1974.

27. Marta Dziuba, "KDB pro Paradzhanova. Dokumenty iz rozsekrechenoho arkhivu KDB URSR," *Kino-Teatr* 2 (2011): http://www.ktm.ukma.kiev.ua/show_content.php?id=1123.

28. V. V. Shcherbytskii, "O zadachakh partiinykh organizatsii respubliki po dal'neishemu uluchsheniiu ideologicheskoi raboty v svete reshenii XXIV s"ezda KPSS. Doklad na Plenume TsK Kompartii Ukrainy 16 maia 1974 goda," in *Izbrannye rechi i stat'i* (Moscow: Politizdat, 1978), 164.

29. Newspaper publication of the speech: V. V. Shcherbyts'kyi, "Pro zavdannia partiynykh orhanizatsiy respubliky po dal'shomu polipshenniu ideolohichnoi roboty v svitli rishen' XXVI z'izdu KPRS," *Vechirniy Kyiv*, May 17, 1974.

30. Karapetian, "Kto 'zakazal' Paradzhanov," 140.

31. Tsereteli, "Khronika zhizni i tvorchestva," in *Kollazh na fone avtoportreta*, 19.

32. See especially Sergei Paradzhanov and Garegin Zakoian, *Pisma iz zony* (Yerevan: Fil'madaran, 2000); and Sergei Paradzhanov, *Pis'ma v zonu* (Yerevan: Muzei Sergeia Paradzhanova, 2005).

33. Judy Stone, "Sergei Paradjanov," in *Eye on the World: Conversations with International Filmmakers* (Beverly Hills: Silman-James Press, 1997), 557.

34. Sergei Paradzhanov and Zaven Sarkisian, *Kaleidoskop Paradzhanova: Risunok, kollazh, assambliazh* (Yerevan: Muzei Sergeia Paradzhanova, 2008), 77.

35. Patrick Cazals, *Serguei Paradjanov* (Paris: Cahiers du cinéma, 1993), 52.

36. "Journée du comité contre la répression," *Le Quotidien de Paris*, November 30, 1976.

37. "U.S. Prof. Got No Info From Soviets on Parajanov," *Variety*, October 1, 1975; Herbert Marshall, "The Case of Sergo Parajanov," *Sight and Sound* 44, no. 1 (Winter 1974–1975): 8–11.

38. Antonín J. Liehm, ed., *Serghiej Paradjanov: Testimonianze e documenti su l'opera e la vita* (Venice: La Biennale di Venezia/Marsilio, 1977).

39. "Paradjanov Libéré," *L'Humanité*, January 3, 1978.

40. Zaven Sarkisian, "Khronika zhizni i tvorchestva," in *Kaleidoskop Paradzhanova*, 13.

41. Paradjanov, Serge. "Serge Paradjanov, cinéaste indésirable," interview by H. Anassian, *Le Monde*, January 27, 1980.

42. Rossiiskii Gosudarstvennyi Arkhiv Noveishei Istorii (hereafter RGANI), f. 5, op. 77, d. 196, ll. 88–93.

43. RGANI, f. 5, op. 84, d. 1014, l. 1; reprinted in Iurii Liubimov, *Rasskazy starogo trepacha* (Moscow: Novosti, 2001), 417.

44. Liubimov, *Rasskazy starogo trepacha*, 418–19.

45. Ibid., 429–31.

46. Nikolai Gubenko is a noted Odessa-born actor and director. At that time he was a member of the Taganka Theatre troupe.

47. Svetlana Sidorina, ed., "Ozhidanie dlilos', a provody byli nedolgi . . ." *Sovremennaia dramaturgiia*, no. 4 (1991): 187–88.

48. Kora Tsereteli, "Khronika zhizni i tvorchestva," in *Ispoved'*, by Sergei Paradzhanov (St. Petersburg: Azbuka), 25.

49. Iurii Mechitov, *Sergei Paradzhanov: Khronika dialoga* (Tbilisi: GAMS-print, 2009), 111.

50. The details in this account come from Mechitov, *Sergei Paradzhanov*, 107, 111, and 125. Mechitov reconstructed the events with the help of Eteri Gugushvili and Georgi Parajanov. (Georgi has changed his last name from Khachaturov to Parajanov in order to continue the family name.)

51. Ibid., 111.

52. Ibid., 131.

53. Tonino and Laura Guerra, "Ia dyshal vozdukhom ego skazok . . . ," interview by Garegin Karapetian in Tsereteli, *Kollazh na fone avtoportreta*, 47.

Chapter 7. *The Legend of the Surami Fortress*

1. Iurii Mechitov, *Sergei Paradzhanov: Khronika dialoga* (Tbilisi: GAMS-print, 2009), 142.

2. *Repentance*, also undertaken with the support of Eduard Shevardnadze, was originally produced for Georgian television, which had a certain degree of autonomy from Gosteleradio, the central television agency in Moscow. The script for Abuladze's film was written in 1981–1982 and the film was finished in December 1984, shortly after *The Legend of the Surami Fortress*. Due to concerns over its subject matter, it was only shown in Moscow professional circles (such as Dom Kino and the Writer's Union) in early 1986 and was released generally in 1987. See Josephine Woll and Denise J. Youngblood, *Repentance* (London: I. B. Tauris, 2001), 90–91.

3. The edition consulted is Daniel' Chonkadze, *Suramskaia krepost'*, trans. Elisbara Ananiashvili (Tbilisi: Zaria Vostoka, 1939).

4. Donald Rayfield, *The Literature of Georgia: A History* (Surrey, UK: Curzon, 2000), 153.

5. The emancipation of serfs in Georgia was a protracted process that happened in different parts of the country through the 1860s. See chapter 5 of Ronald Grigor Suny, *The Making of the Georgian Nation*, 2nd ed. (Bloomington: Indiana University Press, 1994).

6. Perestiani's work as a whole deserves to be better known. Trained in Russia, he and his colleagues brought crucial technical expertise to Georgia; at the same time, he and directors such as Hamo Bek-Nazarov and stars such as Nato Vachnadze provided a reliable source of income for the fledgling Soviet industry as a whole due to the popularity of their melodramas. Perestiani would shortly achieve fame with *The Red Imps*, one of the first true popular successes in Soviet cinema. See Denise J. Youngblood, *Movies for the Masses: Popular Cinema and Soviet Society in the 1920s* (Cambridge: Cambridge University Press, 1992), esp. 76–78, table 5 on p. 40 and table 7 on p. 92.

7. Niko Lortkipanidze, "Nepreklonnye," in *Izbrannoe*, trans. Elena Gogoberidze (Tbilisi: Zaria Vostoka, 1948), 382–459. Lortkipanidze's name is generally transliterated as "Lordkipanidze" in Russian.

8. Giorgi Gvakharia, "Sergei Parajanov's Ecumenical Vision," trans. Harsha Ram, *Armenian Review* 47/48, nos. 3–4/1–2 (2001/2002): 95–96.

9. Rossiiskii Gosudarstvennyi Arkhiv Literatury i Iskusstva (hereafter RGALI), f. 2944, op. 4, d. 7324, l. 2.

10. Ibid., l. 12.

11. RGALI, f. 2944, op. 4, d. 7113, l. 2.

12. Ibid., l. 3.

13. Ibid., l. 30.

14. Ibid., ll. 46–47.

15. Rostislav Iurenev, "Sredstvami kinematograficheskoi zhivopisi," *Sovetskii ekran*, no. 10 (May 1986): 16.

16. Miron Chernenko, "Svoevremennost' vechnosti," *Iskusstvo kino*, no. 5 (1987): 57.

17. Ibid., 61–62.

18. Ibid.

19. Ibid.

20. Gilbert Adair, "Poet's Blood," review of *The Color of Pomegranates, Sight and Sound* 53, no. 1 (Winter 1983/1984): 66.

21. Iurii Lotman, *Semiotics of Cinema*, trans. Mark E. Suino (Ann Arbor: Dept. of Slavic Languages and Literature, University of Michigan, 1976).

22. Iurii Lotman, "Novizna legendy," *Iskusstvo kino*, no. 5 (1987): 63.

23. Ibid., 64.

24. Ibid., 65.

25. Ibid., 67.

26. Ibid.

27. For biographical information on Pirosmani, see Niko P'irosmanašvili, E. Kuznetsov, and K. Bagratišvili, *Niko Pirosmani, 1862–1918* (Leningrad: Aurora Art Publishers, 1983), 5–24; and Niko P'irosmanašvili, *Pirosmani* (Tbilisi: GAT, 2010), 10–11. For Pirosmani as a holy innocent or Christ figure, see Peter Nasmyth, *Georgia: In the Mountains of Poetry*, 2nd rev. ed. (New York: St. Martin's Press, 2001), 99–100; and Giorgi Shengelaia's film *Pirosmani* (Georgia Film Studio 1969).

28. This and other artworks by Parajanov are reproduced in the album Sergei Paradzhanov and Zaven Sarkisian, *Kaleidoskop Paradzhanova: Risunok, kollazh, assambliazh* (Yerevan: Muzei Sergeia Paradzhanova, 2008).

29. Plate 31 in Sergei Paradzhanov, *Ispoved'*, ed. Kora Tsereteli (St. Petersburg: Azbuka, 2001).

30. An English translation is available as Iakob Tsurtaveli, "A Martyred Princess: The Passion of St. Shushanik," in *Lives and Legends of the Georgian Saints*, ed. and trans. David Marshall Lang (London: Allen and Unwin, 1956), 45–56.

31. Rayfield, *Literature of Georgia*, 43–44. The primary Armenian version has been translated into English as *The Passion of Saint Shushanik*, trans. with an introduction by Father Krikor Maksoudian, ed. Christopher H. Zakian (New York: St. Vartan Press, 1999).

32. Sergei Parajanov, "The Passion of Shushanik," ed. with notes and commentary by Cora Tsereteli, trans. Nora Seligman Favorov and E. Elana Pick, *Armenian Review* 47/48, nos. 3–4/1–2 (2001/2002): 35–65. The original Russian script is available as Sergei Paradzhanov, "Muchenichestvo Shushanik," in *Ispoved'*, 303–40.

33. Bolnisi Sioni: a fifth-century basilica in Georgia.

34. Parajanov, "Passion of Shushanik," 38.

35. Paradzhanov, "Ara Prekrasnyi," in *Ispoved'*, 221.

36. Parajanov, "Passion of Shushanik," 40.

37. Tsurtaveli, "A Martyred Princess," 47–48.

38. Parajanov, " Passion of Shushanik," 48.

39. Ibid., 48–49.

40. Ibid., 52.

41. Giorgi Gvakharia, "Paradzhanov: Khoziain 'Kavkazskogo doma'," interview

with Naira Mansucharova, *Vremia* (Yerevan), October 16, 1996. Clipping located at the Sergei Parajanov Museum.

42. Suny, *Making of the Georgian Nation*, 298.

43. Ibid., 298–99.

44. Nineteen-fifty-five was chosen as a starting date because it marks the real renaissance of the Georgian film industry with the appearance of a new generation of directors such as Tengiz Abuladze and Rezo Chkheidze and relaxation of controls during the Thaw. Nineteen-eighty-seven was the last date for which I was able to find a reliable list of all the feature films produced in Georgia, but it also coincides with the period described in this chapter. Data calculated from "Les longs métrages géorgiens, 1912–1987," in *Le Cinema Géorgien*, ed. Jean Radvanyi (Paris: Centre Georges Pompidou, 1988), 175–83.

45. Stephen F. Jones, "Glasnost', Perestroika and the Georgian Soviet Socialist Republic," *Armenian Review* 43, nos. 2–3 (Summer/Autumn 1990): 130.

46. See Jones, "Glasnost', Perestroika," 131–35; and Suny, *Making of the Georgian Nation*, 320–33.

47. Elizabeth Fuller, "A Georgian-Armenian Literary Polemic," *Radio Liberty Research*, no. 375 (September 1986): 1–4. The novel was published as Levon Chelidze, *Tam, na otdalennoi planete . . . ili trinadtsat' broskov iz zhizni Artema Gasparova*, in *Literaturnaia Gruziia*, no. 2 (1986): 44–95 and no. 3 (1986): 66–121.

48. Vakhtang Rodonaia, "Shvilo zurab sadamdi," *Literaturuli sakartvelo*, March 27, 1987, 11. Translated by Irena Popiashvili. Emphasis in original.

49. Ibid., 11.

50. Ibid., 13.

51. Ibid.

52. Ibid., 13. Emphasis in original.

53. Archil Sulakauri, "Dzveli tbilisi da . . . kinto," *Literaturuli sakartvelo*, January 30, 1987, 11. Translation by Irena Popiashvili.

54. Ibid.

55. Gvakharia, "Sergei Parajanov's Ecumenical Vision," 96.

56. Ibid.

57. Aleksandre Baramidze and Bondo Arveladze, "Cheshmaritebis dasadgenad," *Literaturuli sakartvelo*, September 25, 1987, 3. Translation by Irena Popiashvili.

58. As mentioned in chapter 4, Sayat-Nova's work is indeed influenced by the Arabic and Persian poetic traditions. I will not address here the question of the extent to which he contributed to a uniquely Armenian or Georgian tradition.

59. V. Nalbandian, V. Nersesian, and G. Bakhchinian, quoted in Baramidze and Arveladze, "Cheshmaritebis dasadgenad," 3.

60. Baramidze and Arveladze, "Cheshmaritebis dasadgenad," 3.

61. Rayfield, *Literature of Georgia*, 19.

62. Baramidze and Arveladze, "Cheshmaritebis dasadgenad," 3.

Chapter 8. *Ashik-Kerib*

1. One of Armenia's leading cinematographers, Albert Yavurian (1935–2007) was perhaps best known for his work for the director Frunze Dovlatian on films such as *Hello It's Me!* and *A Lone Nut-Tree* (*Odinokaia oreshina*, Armenfilm 1986). Parajanov admired Dovlatian's work and wrote an appreciation of the latter film, reprinted as Sergei Paradzhanov, "Odinokaia oreshina," in *Armiane v mirovom kino*, ed. Garegin Zakoian (Yerevan: Armianskaia Natsional'naia fil'moteka, 1995), 61–63.

2. Al'bert Iavurian, "Zapozdavshaia prem'era: Kak sozdovalsia 'Ashik-Kerib' i kak ego vernuli erevanskomy zriteliu," interview with Albert Yavurian by Susanna Harutiunyan, *RA* [*Respublika Armeniia*], April 30, 1996.

3. Elizabeth A. Papazian, "Ethnography, Fairytale and 'Perpetual Motion' in Sergei Paradjanov's *Ashik-Kerib*," *Literature / Film Quarterly* 34, no. 4 (2006): 306.

4. For example, see the version retold by Ishak Kemâli (d. 1971) and published in F. Türkmen, *Âşık Garip hikâyesi üzerinde bir araştırma* (Ankara, 1974), 242–56, and translated into Italian in Giampiero Bellingeri, "Non solo *Aşik-Kerib*: Quale altro aşuğ?," in Gianroberto Scarcia, ed. *Aşik-Kerib* (Venice: Università degli studi di Venezia, Diparmento di studi Eurasiatici, 1991), 91–105.

5. Mikhail Lermontov, "Ashik-Kerib," in *Polnoe sobranie sochinenii v desiati tomakh* (Moscow: Voskresen'e, 2000), 6:203–11.

6. Papazian, "Ethnography," 304.

7. Karen Kalantar, *Ocherki o Paradzhanove* (Yerevan: Gitutiun NAN RA, 1998), 155.

8. Giovanni Curatola, "Una moschea di legno per un aşuğ," in Scarcia, *Aşik-Kerib*, 112.

9. The DVD of *Ashik-Kerib* recently released by the Russian Cinema Council includes the original Azerbaijani language version *without* Georgian overdubbing, which is presumably preferred. However, the mono soundtrack has been remixed to 5.1 stereo and the new track contains ambient effects not present in the original.

10. Miron Chernenko, "Puteshestvie na krai poetiki," *Iskusstvo kino*, no. 5 (1989): 71.

11. Ibid., 72–73.

12. Ibid., 71. *Khlebnyi miakish*: in the former Soviet Union prisoners commonly used the soft interior of bread loaves to create sculptures since it was one of the few materials available to them.

13. Iavurian, "Zapozdavshaia prem'era."

14. Patrick Cazals, "Le maître du Caucase grisonnant," *Cahiers du cinéma*, no. 410 (July–August 1988): 10.

15. Ibid.

16. Levon Abrahamian, "Toward a Poetics of Parajanov's Cinema," *Armenian Review* 47/48, nos. 3–4/1–2 (2001/2002): 74.

17. Edward W. Said, *Orientalism* (New York: Vintage Books, 1979), 188.

18. Franklin Lewis, *Rumi: Past and Present, East and West, The Life, Teaching and Poetry of Jalâl al-Din Rumi* (Oxford: Oneworld, 2000), 321–24.

19. John E. Malmstad and Nikolay Bogomolov, *Mikhail Kuzmin: A Life in Art* (Cambridge, MA: Harvard University Press, 1999), 104–5.

20. Yavurian, quoted in Kalantar, *Ocherki o Paradzhanove*, 154. Although Yavurian claims that Parajanov filmed the episodes specifically in response to the massacre at Sumqayit, Yuri Mechitov's photo log book indicates that he filmed the episodes at Ninotsminda on February 20, 1988, before the actual massacre took place. See Iurii Mechitov, *Sergei Paradzhanov: Khronika dialoga* (Tbilisi: GAMS-print, 2009), 379.

21. For a brief overview of these events see chapter 12 of Ronald Grigor Suny, *Looking toward Ararat: Armenia in Modern History* (Bloomington: Indiana University Press, 1993).

22. "Ekrannyi mir Paradzhanova," *Sovetskaia kul'tura*, September 29, 1988.

23. Iavurian, "Zapozdavshaia prem'era."

24. "Sokrovishcha u gory Ararat," Sergei Parajanov Museum, pp. 7–9. "Bagrat" is a misidentification. Scholarly sources commonly interpret the image as Smbat and Gurgen both holding up the church as an offering to God. See Jean-Michel Thierry, *Armenian Art*, trans. Célestine Dars (New York: Harry N. Abrams, 1989), 140.

25. Sergei Paradzhanov, "Lebedinoe ozero: Zona," in *Ispoved'*, ed. Kora Tsereteli (St. Petersburg: Azbuka, 2001), 364.

26. Lenny Borger, "A Warm Reception Greets Paradjanov at Rotterdam Fest," *Variety*, February 10, 1988.

27. Jack Kindred, "Munich's 6th Annual Film Fest Matched City's Unclouded Skies," *Variety*, July 6, 1988.

28. Deborah Young, "Ashik-Kerib," *Variety*, September 14, 1988.

29. Joël Magny, "Quelques fleurs poussées sur la terre d'Ukraine," *Cahiers du cinéma*, no. 414 (December 1988): 45–48.

30. B. Samantha Stenzel, "Sociopolitical Films Big Winners at Eighth Istanbul Film Festival," *Variety*, May 3–9 1989.

31. Kora Tsereteli, "Khochu umeret' kak Griboedov!," in *Kollazh na fone avtoportreta: Zhizn'-Igra*, 2nd. ed. (Nizhnii Novgorod: Dekom, 2008), 259–60. A photograph of the note is reproduced on p. 260.

32. *Serguei Paradjanov, un portrait*, directed by Patrick Cazals (France, Les Films du Horla, 1988); *Serguei Paradjanov, le rebelle*, directed by Patrick Cazals (France, Les Films du Horla, 2003); Patrick Cazals, *Serguei Paradjanov* (Paris: Cahiers du cinéma, 1993).

33. *Paradjanov: A Requiem*, directed by Ron Holloway (Germany/US, O-Films, 1994). The film is available on DVD in the United States from Kino Lorber.

34. Judy Stone, "Sergei Paradjanov," in *Eye on the World: Conversations with International Filmmakers* (Beverly Hills: Silman-James Press, 1997), 558–59.

35. See, for example, the comments by individuals such as Manana Chkonia, Sofiko Chiaureli, Giorgi Gvakharia, Rezo Chkheidze, Eldar Shengelaia et al., in the January 9, 1997, issue of *Saiatnova*, the newspaper of the Parajanov Foundation in Tbilisi.

Epilogue

1. Jane Taubman, *Kira Muratova* (London: I. B. Tauris, 2005), 5.

2. Levon Abrahamian, "Toward a Poetics of Parajanov's Cinema," trans. Harsha Ram, *Armenian Review* 47/48, nos. 3–4/1–2 (2001/2002): 81.

Selected Bibliography

This bibliography lists the core books and articles cited throughout the text. It does not include newspaper articles cited in the notes or books that are mentioned only in passing. Names are spelled (or transliterated) according to the original language of publication to ensure that works are easily findable.

Abrahamian, Levon. "Toward a Poetics of Parajanov's Cinema." Translated by Harsha Ram. *Armenian Review* 47/48, nos. 3–4/1–2 (2001/2002): 67–91.

Adair, Gilbert. "Poet's Blood." Review of *The Color of Pomegranates. Sight and Sound* 53, no. 1 (Winter 1983/1984): 66.

Alekseychuk, Leonid. "A Warrior in the Field." *Sight and Sound* 60, no. 1 (Winter 1990/1991): 22–26.

Anderson, Benedict R. *Imagined Communities: Reflections on the Origin and Spread of Nationalism.* Revised and extended edition. New York: Verso, 1991.

Antipenko, Aleksandr. "Ego deviz byl — otdavat'." *Iskusstvo kino,* no. 12 (1990): 64–67.

Arakelian, Mikhail. *Sergei Iosifovich Paradzhanov: Kak sozdavalsia khudozhestvennyi fil'm "Tsvet granata" i drugoe.* Yerevan: Avtorskoe izdanie, 2006.

Armianskoe assotsiatsia kinokritikov i kinozhurnalistov. *Armianskoe kino, 1924–1999: Annotirovannyi katalog.* Yerevan: Artagers, 2000.

Baedeker, Karl. *Russia with Teheran, Port Arthur, and Peking: Handbook for Travelers.* Leipzig: Karl Baedeker, 1914.

Baramidze, Aleksandre, and Bondo Arveladze. "Cheshmaritebis dasadgenad." *Literaturuli sakartvelo.* September 25, 1987, 3.

Bax, Dominique, ed. *À la recherche de Serguei Paradjanov: Publié à l'occasion du 18e festival ("Théâtres au cinéma"), 9 au 25 mars 2007, à Bobigny.* Bobigny: Magic cinéma, 2007.

Beliavskii, Mikhail. "O serosti i posredstvennosti." *Iskusstvo kino,* no. 8 (1955): 35–45.

Bleiman, Mikhail. "Archaisty ili novatory?" *Iskusstvo kino,* no. 7 (1970): 55–76.

Briukhovets'ka, Larysa, ed. *Poetychne kino: Zaboronena shkola.* Kyiv: ArtEk/Kino-Teatr, 2001.

Browne, Michael, ed. *Ferment in the Ukraine: Documents by V. Chornovil, I. Kandyba, L. Lukyanenko, V. Moroz, and others.* Foreword by Max Hayward. New York: Praeger, 1971.

Bukov, Emilian. *Andriesh: Moldavskaia skazka*. Translated by Vladimir Derzhavin. Moscow: Detgiz, 1946.

Bullot, Érik. *Sayat Nova de Serguei Paradjanov: La face et le profil*. Crisnée, Belgium: Éditions Yellow Now, 2007.

Cazals, Patrick. "Le Maître du Caucase grisonnant." *Cahiers du cinéma*, no. 410 (July–August 1988): 9–11.

——. *Serguei Paradjanov*. Paris: Cahiers du cinéma, 1993.

Chernenko, Miron. "Puteshestvie na krai poetiki." Review of *Ashik-Kerib*. *Iskusstvo kino*, no. 5 (1989): 70–74.

——. "Sergei Paradzhanov." *Soviet Union* 17, nos. 1–2 (1990): 1–53.

——. "Svoevremennost' vechnosti." *Iskusstvo kino*, no. 5 (1987): 55–62.

Chernetsky, Vitaly. "Visual Language and Identity Performance in Leonid Osyka's *A Stone Cross*: The Roots and the Uprooting." *Studies in Russian and Soviet Cinema* 2, no. 3 (2008): 269–80.

Chonkadze, Daniel'. *Suramskaia krepost'*. Translated from Georgian by Elisbara Ananiashvili. Tbilisi: Zaria Vostoka, 1939.

Chornovil, Vyacheslav. *The Chornovil Papers*. New York: McGraw-Hill, 1968.

Clark, Katerina. *The Soviet Novel: History as Ritual*. 3rd ed. Bloomington: Indiana University Press, 2000.

Cohen, Louis Harris. *The Cultural-Political Traditions and Developments of the Soviet Cinema, 1917–1972*. New York: Arno Press, 1974.

Cook, David A. "Shadows of Forgotten Ancestors: Film as Religious Art." *Post Script* 3, no. 3 (1984): 16–23.

Der Hovanessian, Diana, and Marzbed Margossian, trans. and ed. *Anthology of Armenian Poetry*. New York: Columbia University Press, 1978.

Dowsett, Charles. *Sayat-Nova: An 18th-Century Troubadour; A Biographical and Literary Study*. Lovanii: In aedibus Peeters, 1997.

Drach, Ivan. "Otkrytie." In *Ekran 1965*, 29–32. Moscow: Iskusstvo, 1966.

Dzeverin, I. O., ed. *Istoriia ukrains'koi literatury u dvokh tomakh*. Kyiv: Nauk. dumka, 1987.

Dziuba, Ivan. "Den' poiska." *Iskusstvo kino*, no. 5 (1965): 73–82.

——. *Internationalism or Russification?: A Study in the Soviet Nationalities Problem*. New York: Monad Press, 1974.

Dziuba, Marta. "KDB pro Paradzhanova. Dokumenty iz rozsekrechenoho arkhivu KDB URSR." Parts 1 and 2. *Kino-Teatr* 1 (2011): http://www.ktm.ukma.kiev.ua/show_content.php?id=1067; 2 (2011): http://www.ktm.ukma.kiev.ua/show_content.php?id=1123.

Encyclopedia of Ukraine. Edited by Volodymyr Kubiiovych and Danylo Husar Struk. Toronto: University of Toronto Press, 1984.

Faraday, George. *Revolt of the Filmmakers: The Struggle for Artistic Autonomy and the Fall of the Soviet Film Industry*. University Park: Pennsylvania State University Press, 2000.

Farmer, Kenneth C. *Ukrainian Nationalism in the Post-Stalin Era: Myth, Symbols, and Ideology in Soviet Nationalities Policy*. The Hague: Martinus Nijhoff, 1980.

First, Joshua. "Ukrainian National Cinema and the Concept of the 'Poetic.'" *Kino-Kultura*, Special Issue 9: Ukrainian Cinema (December 2009): http://www.kinokultura.com/specials/9/first.shtml.

Fokina, Natal'ia. "Lev Kulidzhanov: Postizhenie professii." *Kinovedcheskie zapiski*, no. 64 (2003): 125–65.

Fomin, Valerii. *Kino i vlast: Sovetskoe kino, 1965–1985 gody*. Moscow: Materik, 1996.

———, ed. *"Polka": Dokumenty, svidetel'stva, kommentarii. Vypusk 3*. Moscow: Materik, 2006.

Fuller, Elizabeth. "A Georgian-Armenian Literary Polemic." *Radio Liberty Research*, no. 375 (September 1986): 1–4.

Gabai, Genrikh. "Moi drug Sergei Paradzhanov." *Vremia i My*, no. 110 (1990): 255–74.

Gellner, Ernest. *Nations and Nationalism*. Ithaca: Cornell University Press, 1983.

Godet, Sylvain. "Le dernier cinéaste heureux." *Cahiers du cinéma*, no. 178 (May 1966): 74–75.

Golovskoy, Valery S., with John Rimberg. *Behind the Soviet Screen: The Motion-Picture Industry in the USSR, 1972–1982*. Ann Arbor, MI: Ardis, 1986.

Grigorian, Levon. *Paradzhanov*. Moscow: Molodaia gvardiia, 2011.

———. *Tri tsveta odnoi strasti: Triptikh Sergeia Paradzhanova*. Moscow: Kinotsentr, 1991.

Guerra, Tonino. "Les fantômes du destin, ou le monde de Paradjanov." *Positif*, no. 389–90 (July/August 1993): 30–31.

Gvakharia, Giorgi. "Sergei Parajanov's Ecumenical Vision." Translated by Harsha Ram. *Armenian Review* 47/48, nos. 3–4/1–2 (2001/2002): 93–104.

Hobsbawm, E. J. *Nations and Nationalism since 1780: Programme, Myth, Reality*. Cambridge: Cambridge University Press, 1990.

Hobsbawm, Eric, and Terence Ranger, eds. *The Invention of Tradition*. Cambridge: Cambridge University Press, 1983.

Hosking, Geoffrey. *The First Socialist Society: A History of the Soviet Union from Within*. Cambridge, MA: Harvard University Press, 1990.

Iurenev, Rostislav. "Sredstvami kinematograficheskoi zhivopisi." *Sovetskii ekran*, no. 10 (May 1986): 14–16.

Jones, Stephen F. "Glasnost', Perestroika and the Georgian Soviet Socialist Republic." *Armenian Review* 43, nos. 2–3 (Summer/Autumn 1990): 127–52.

Kalantar, Karen. *Ocherki o Paradzhanove*. Yerevan: Gitutiun NAN RA, 1998.

Kalenychenko, N. L. *Mykhailo Kotsiubyns'kyi: Zhyttia i tvorchist'*. Kyiv: Vydavnytstvo Akademii Nauk Ukrains'koi RSR, 1956.

Karaganov, Alexander. "The Soviet Multinational Cinema." In *The Soviet Multinational State: Readings and Documents*, edited by Martha B. Olcott, Lubomyr Hajda, and Anthony Olcott, 293–97. Armonk, NY: M. E. Sharpe, 1990. Originally published as "Skhodstva i razlichiia." *Pravda*, October 10, 1982.

Karapetian, Gagik [Garegin]. "Kto 'zakazal' Paradzhanova: Versiia Aleksandra Iakovleva." *Iskusstvo kino*, no. 1 (2006): 139–44.

Katanian, Vasilii Vasil'evich. *Paradzhanov: Tsena vechnogo prazdnika* (Nizhnii Novgorod: Dekom, 2001).

————. *Prikosnovenie k idolam.* Moscow: Zakharov/Vagrius, 1997.

Katz, Zev, ed. *Handbook of Major Soviet Nationalities.* New York: The Free Press, 1975.

Kazarian, Mania. *Khudozhniki Ovnataniany.* Moscow: Iskusstvo, 1968.

Keheyan, Garo, ed. *Parajanov Himself.* Nicosia: Pharos, 2005.

Kinolitopys: Anotovanyi kataloh kinozhurnaliv, dokumental'nykh filmiv, kino- i telesiuzhetiv, 1956–1965. Kyiv: Derzhavnyi Komitet Arkhiviv Ukrainy, 2003.

Konoplev, B. N. *Osnovy fil'moproizvodstva.* Moscow: Iskusstvo, 1969.

Korohods'kyi, R. M., and Svitlana Shcherbatiuk, eds. *Serhii Paradzhanov: Zlet, trahediia, vichnist'.* Kyiv: Spalakh, 1994.

Korotyukov, Alexei. "Parajanov: The True Story Behind His Arrest." Interview by Slavko Nowytski. *CTVD: Cinema-TV-Digest* 9, no. 4 (September 1975): 1–7.

Kotsiubynskaia-Efimenko, Zoia. *M. M. Kotsiubinskii: Masterstvo pisatelia.* Moscow: Sovetskii pisatel', 1959.

Kotsiubynsky, Mykhailo. *Fata Morgana and Other Stories.* Translated by Abraham Mistetsky. Kyiv: Dnipro, 1980.

————. *Shadows of Forgotten Ancestors.* Translated by Marco Carynnyk with notes and an essay by Bohdan Rubchak. Littleton, CO: Ukrainian Academic Press, 1981.

————. *Tvory v shesti tomakh.* Kyiv: Vydavnytstvo Akademii Nauk Ukrainskoi RSR, 1961.

Krawchenko, Bohdan. *Social Change and National Consciousness in Twentieth-Century Ukraine.* London: Macmillan, 1985.

————, ed. *Ukraine After Shelest.* Edmonton: Canadian Institute of Ukrainian Studies, 1983.

Lawton, Anna. *Kinoglasnost: Soviet Cinema in Our Time.* Cambridge: Cambridge University Press, 1992.

————, ed. *The Red Screen: Politics, Society, Art in Soviet Cinema.* New York: Routledge, 1992.

Lermontov, Mikhail. *Polnoe sobranie sochinenii v desiati tomakh.* Moscow: Voskresen'e, 1999–2002.

Levada, A. "O nekotorykh problemakh ukrainskoi kinodramaturgii." *Iskusstvo kino,* no. 6 (1959): 97–107.

Levada, Oleksandr. *Tvory v chotyr'okh tomakh.* Kyiv: Dnipro, 1979–1980.

Lewis, Franklin. *Rumi: Past and Present, East and West; The Life, Teaching and Poetry of Jalâl al-Din Rumi.* Oxford: Oneworld, 2000.

Liehm, Antonín J., ed. *Serghiej Paradjanov: Testimonianze e documenti su l'opera e la vita.* Venice: La Biennale di Venezia/Marsilio, 1977.

Liubimov, Iurii. *Rasskazy starogo trepacha.* Moscow: Novosti, 2001.

Lortkipanidze, Niko. *Izbrannoe.* Translated by Elena Gogoberidze. Tbilisi: Zaria Vostoka, 1948.

Lotman, Iurii. "Novizna legendy." *Iskusstvo kino,* no. 5 (1987): 63–67.

————. *Semiotics of Cinema.* Translated by Mark E. Suino. Ann Arbor: Dept. of Slavic Languages and Literature, University of Michigan, 1976.

Luchyna, Nina Ivanivna, and T. T. Derevianko, ed. *Igor Savchenko: Sbornik statei i vospominanii.* Kyiv: Mystetsvo, 1980.

Madoian, Razmik. "Pochemu 'Tsvet granata?'" *Literaturnaia Armeniia*, no. 3 (1991): 92–99.

Magny, Joël. "Quelques fleurs poussées sur la terre d'Ukraine." *Cahiers du cinéma*, no. 414 (December 1988): 45–48.

Malmstad, John E., and Nikolay Bogomolov. *Mikhail Kuzmin: A Life in Art.* Cambridge, MA: Harvard University Press, 1999.

Marshall, Herbert. "The Case of Sergo Parajanov." *Sight and Sound* 44, no. 1 (Winter 1974–1975): 8–11.

Martin, Terry. *The Affirmative Action Empire: Nations and Nationalism in the Soviet Union, 1923–1939.* Ithaca: Cornell University Press, 2001.

Mechitov, Iurii. *Sergei Paradzhanov: Khronika dialoga.* Tbilisi: GAMS-print, 2009.

Mikhailov, N. "Zapiska Komiteta po pechati pri SM SSSR v TsK KPSS o nekotorykh voprosakh literatury i iskusstva." In *Apparat TsK KPSS i kul'tura, 1965–1972: Dokumenty*, edited by N. G. Tomilina, 150–76. Moscow: ROSSPEN, 2009.

Moroz, Valentyn. *Report from the Beria Reserve: The Protest Writings of Valentyn Moroz.* Translated and edited by John Kolasky. Chicago: Cataract Press, 1974.

Nahaylo, Bohdan. *The Ukrainian Resurgence.* Toronto: University of Toronto Press, 1999.

Nasmyth, Peter. *Georgia: In the Mountains of Poetry.* 2nd revised edition. New York: St. Martin's Press, 2001.

Nebesio, Bohdan. "*Shadows of Forgotten Ancestors*: Storytelling in the Novel and the Film." *Literature / Film Quarterly* 22, no. 1 (1994): 42–49.

"Nezakonchennaia ispoved': Vospominaniia o Sergee Paradzhanove." Reminiscences by Ivan Dziuba, Ivan Drach, Pavlo Zagrebel'nyi, Leonid Cherevatenko, Iurii Il'enko, Mikhail Belikov and Georgii Iakutovich. Translated from Ukrainian by Georgii Tamosian. *Literaturnaia Armeniia*, no. 2 (1998): 89–128.

Papazian, Elizabeth A. "Ethnography, Fairytale and 'Perpetual Motion' in Sergei Paradjanov's *Ashik-Kerib*." *Literature / Film Quarterly* 34, no. 4 (2006): 303–12.

Paradjanov, Serge. "Serge Paradjanov, cinéaste indésirable." Interview by H. Anassian. *Le Monde*, January 27, 1980.

Paradjanov, Sergei. *Seven Visions.* Edited by Galia Ackerman. Translated by Guy Bennett. Los Angeles: Green Integer, 1998.

Paradzhanov, Sergei. ". . . chtoby ne molchat', berus' za pero." *Iskusstvo kino*, no. 12 (1990): 32–41.

———. *Ispoved'.* Edited by Kora Tsereteli. St. Petersburg: Azbuka, 2001.

———. "Iz nasledii" ("Vystuplenie v Minske" and "Zolotoi obrez"). Introduction by Tamara Shevchenko. *Kinovedcheskie zapiski*, no. 23 (1994): 76–100.

———. "Kievskie freski." Edited by E. Levin. *Iskusstvo kino*, no. 12 (1990): 41–54.

———. "Odinokaia oreshina." In *Armiane v mirovom kino*, edited by Garegin Zakoian, 61–63. Yerevan: Armianskaia Natsional'naia fil'moteka, 1995.

———. *Pis'ma v zonu.* Yerevan: Muzei Sergeia Paradzhanova, 2005.

———. "Slovo o polku Igoreve: Zaiavka na fil'm." In *Armiane v mirovom kino*, edited by Garegin Zakoian, 37–40. Yerevan: Armianskaia Natsional'naia fil'moteka, 1995.

————. "Vechnoe dvizhenie." *Iskusstvo kino*, no. 1 (1966): 60–66.

————. "Voskhozhdenie k masterstvu." *Sovetskii ekran*, no. 24 (1971): 1.

Paradzhanov, Sergei, and Garegin Zakoian. *Pis'ma iz zony*. Yerevan: Fil'madaran, 2000.

Paradzhanov, Sergei, and Zaven Sarkisian. *Kaleidoskop Paradzhanova: Risunok, kollazh, assambliazh*. Yerevan: Muzei Sergeia Paradzhanova, 2008. Published simultaneously in English as *Parajanov Kaleidoscope: Drawings, Collages, Assemblages*.

Paradzhanov, Serhii, and Volodymyr Luhovs'kyi. *Tini zabutykh predkiv: Rozkadrovky*. Kyiv: Vydavnychyi dim Akademiia, 1998.

Parajanov, Sergei. "The Passion of Shushanik." Edited with notes and commentary by Cora Tsereteli. Translated by Nora Seligman Favorov and E. Elana Pick. *Armenian Review* 47/48, nos. 3–4/1–2 (2001/2002): 35–65.

————. "Sergei Parajanov's Speech in Minsk before the Creative and Scientific Youth of Byelorussia on 1 December 1971." Translated by Nora Seligman Favorov and P. Elana Pick with notes and an introduction by James Steffen. *Armenian Review* 47/48, nos. 3–4/1–2 (2001/2002): 11–33.

————. "Shadows of Our Forgotten Ancestors." Translated by Steven P. Hill. *Film Comment* 5, no. 1 (Fall 1968): 38–48.

The Passion of Saint Shushanik. Translated with an introduction by Father Krikor Maksoudian. Edited by Christopher H. Zakian. New York: St. Vartan Press, 1999.

P'irosmanašvili, Niko. Pirosmani. Tbilisi: GAT, 2010.

P'irosmanašvili, Niko, E. Kuznetsov and K. Bagratišvili. *Niko Pirosmani, 1862–1918*. Leningrad: Aurora Art Publishers, 1983.

Plyushch, Leonid. *History's Carnival: A Dissident's Autobiography*. Translated by Marco Carynnyk. New York: Harcourt Brace Jovanovich, 1979.

Prokopenko, Raïsa. *Anotovanyi kataloh fil'miv: 1928–1998*. Kyiv: National'na kinostudiia khudozhnikh fil'miv imeni Oleksandra Dovzhenka, 1998.

Radvanyi, Jean, ed. *Le Cinéma arménien*. Paris: Centre Georges Pompidou, 1993.

————, ed. *Le Cinéma géorgien*. Paris: Centre Georges Pompidou, 1988.

Rayfield, Donald. *The Literature of Georgia: A History*. Surrey, UK: Curzon, 2000.

Rizaev, Sabir. "Saiat-Nova." Review of *The Color of Pomegranates*. *Literaturnaia Armeniia*, no. 12 (1970): 74–80.

Rodonaia, Vakhtang. "Shvilo zurab sadamdi." *Literaturuli sakartvelo*, March 27, 1987, 11–13.

Saiat-Nova. *Lirika: Perevody s armianskogo, gruzinskogo, azerbaidzhanskogo*. Introduction by Ioseb Grishashvili. Moscow: Gosudarstvennoe izdatel'stvo khudozhestvennoi literatury, 1963.

Said, Edward W. *Orientalism*. New York: Vintage Books, 1979.

"Sayat-Nova: Tsar' pesnopenii." In *Ekran 1969*, 184–87. Moscow: Iskusstvo, 1969.

Scarcia, Gianroberto, ed. *Ašik-Kerib*. Venice: Università degli studi di Venezia, Diparmento di studi Eurasiatici, 1991.

Senchenko, Tat'iana. "Vospitivat' vkus!" *Iskusstvo kino*, no. 1 (1962): 172–73.

Shakhovskii, S. "Zhizn' i tvorchestvo M. M. Kotsiubinskii." In *Sobranie sochinenii v trekh tomakh*, by Mikhail Kotsiubinskii, 1:7–32. Moscow: Goslitizdat, 1951.

Shcherbytskii, V. V. *Izbrannye rechi i stat'i*. Moscow: Politizdat, 1978.

Shelest, Petro Iu., and Iuri Shapoval. *Petro Shelest: The True Judgment of History Still Awaits Us; Memoirs, Diaries, Documents, Materials*. Kyiv: Geneza, 2003.

Shklovsky, Viktor. "Poetry and Prose in Cinematography." Translated by T. L. Aman. In *Russian Formalism*, edited by Stephen Bann and John E. Bowlt, 128–30. New York: Barnes and Noble, 1973.

———. *Theory of Prose*. Translated by Benjamin Sher. Normal, IL: Dalkey Archive, 1990.

Sidorina, Svetlana, ed. "Ozhidanie dlilos', a provody byli nedolgi." *Sovremennaia dramaturgiia*, no. 3 (1991): 155–74; no. 4 (1991): 179–201.

Slezkine, Yuri. "The USSR as a Communal Apartment, or How a Socialist State Promoted Ethnic Particularism." *Slavic Review* 53, no. 2 (1994): 414–52.

Smith, Anthony D. *The Ethnic Origins of Nations*. Oxford: Basil Blackwell, 1986.

———. *Nationalism: Theory, Ideology, History*. Cambridge: Polity, 2001.

Steffen, James. "From *Sayat-Nova* to *The Color of Pomegranates*: Notes on the Production and Censorship of Parajanov's Film." *Armenian Review* 47/48, nos. 3–4/1–2 (2001/2002): 105–47.

———. "*Kyiv Frescoes*: Sergei Paradjanov's Unrealized Film Project." *KinoKultura*, Special Issue 9: Ukrainian Cinema (December 2009): http://www.kinokultura.com/specials/9/steffen.shtml.

———. "Parajanov's Playful Poetics: On the 'Director's Cut' of *The Color of Pomegranates*." *Journal of Film and Video* 47, no. 4 (Winter 1995/1996): 17–33.

Stone, Judy. "Sergei Paradjanov." In *Eye on the World: Conversations with International Filmmakers*, 555–59. Beverly Hills: Silman-James Press, 1997.

Subtelny, Orest. *Ukraine: A History*. 4th ed. Toronto: University of Toronto Press, 2009.

Sulakauri, Archil. "Dzveli tbilisi da . . . kinto." *Literaturuli sakartvelo*, January 30, 1987, 11.

Suny, Ronald Grigor. *Looking toward Ararat: Armenia in Modern History*. Bloomington: Indiana University Press, 1993.

———. *The Making of the Georgian Nation*. 2nd ed. Bloomington: Indiana University Press, 1994.

———. *The Revenge of the Past: Nationalism, Revolution, and the Collapse of the Soviet Union*. Foreword by Norman M. Naimark. Stanford: Stanford University Press, 1993.

Taubman, Jane. *Kira Muratova*. London: I. B. Tauris, 2005.

Taylor, Richard. "Ideology as Mass Entertainment: Boris Shumyatsky and Soviet Cinema in the 1930s." In *Inside the Film Factory: New Approaches to Russian and Soviet Cinema*, edited by Richard Taylor and Ian Christie, 193–216. New York: Routledge, 1991.

Thierry, Jean-Michel. *Armenian Art*. Translated by Célestine Dars. New York: Harry N. Abrams, 1989.

Tolegian, Aram, trans. and ed. *Armenian Poetry, Old and New: A Bilingual Anthology*. Detroit: Wayne State University Press, 1979.

Troshin, Aleksandr. "'A driani podobno *Garmon'* bol'she ne stavite?': Zapisi besed B. Z. Shumiatskogo s I. V. Stalinom posle kinoprosmotrov. 1934 g." *Kinovedcheskie zapiski*, no. 61 (2002): 281–346.

Tsereteli, Kora, ed. *Kollazh na fone avtoportreta: Zhizn'–igra.* 2nd ed. Nizhnii Novgorod: Dekom, 2008.

Tsurtaveli, Iakob. "A Martyred Princess: The Passion of St. Shushanik." In *Lives and Legends of the Georgian Saints*, edited and translated by David Marshall Lang, 45–56. London: Allen and Unwin, 1956.

Turbin, Vladimir. "Zhivoi ogon'." *Molodaia gvardiia*, no. 2 (1965): 280–91.

Ukrains'ka inteligentsiia pid sudom KGB: Materiialy z protsesiv V. Chornovola, M. Masiutka, M. Ozernoho ta in. Munich: Suchasnist', 1970.

Vagarshian, Laert. "Familiia moia Paradzhanov." *Iskusstvo kino*, no. 8 (1995): 130–38.

Verdery, Katherine. *National Ideology under Socialism: Identity and Cultural Politics in Ceausescu's Romania.* Berkeley: University of California Press, 1991.

———. *What Was Socialism, and What Comes Next?* Princeton: Princeton University Press, 1996.

Vronskaya, Jeanne. *Young Soviet Film Makers.* London: Allen and Unwin, 1972.

Williamson, Anne. "Prisoner: The Essential Parajanov." *Film Comment* 25, no. 3 (May/June 1989): 57–60, 62–63.

Woll, Josephine. *Real Images: Soviet Cinema and the Thaw.* London: I. B. Tauris, 2000.

Woll, Josephine, and Denise J. Youngblood. *Repentance.* London: I. B. Tauris, 2001.

Youngblood, Denise J. *Movies for the Masses: Popular Cinema and Soviet Society in the 1920s.* Cambridge: Cambridge University Press, 1992.

Zabrodin, Vladimir. *Igor' Andreevich Savchenko, 1906–1950: Materialy k retrospektive fil'mov; Oktiabr' 1996.* Moscow: Muzei kino, 1996.

Zarian, Nairi. *Ara Prekrasnyi.* Translated by Mariia Petrovykh. Moscow: Sovetskii pisatel', 1947.

Zemlianukhin, Sergei, and Miroslava Segida. *Domashniaia sinemateka: Otechestvennoe kino, 1918–1996.* Moscow: Dubl'-D, 1996.

Index

8½ (film), 89, 99, 101, 108, 157

Abashidze, David "Dodo," 202, 227, 231, 257, 258
Abdykalykov, Aktan, 249
Abrahamian, Levon, 129, 152, 235, 250
Abuladze, Tengiz, 18, 20, 122, 202, 226, 282n2
Accordion, The (film), 27–28, 38
Adair, Gilbert, 213, 252
adaptation. See literary adaptations
aesthetics: connection to ideology in Soviet Union, 9, 16, 17, 20–21, 22; of Parajanov, 7–8, 23, 30, 34, 37, 53, 88, 103, 107, 115–16, 128, 194, 218–20, 233–34
Aitmatov, Chingiz, 21, 183
Alekseychuk, Leonid, 8–9
Alexi-Meskhishvili, Georgi, 218
Alov, Alexander, 29, 33, 47, 55, 112. See Naumov, Vladimir
Andersen, Hans Christian. See Miracle in Odense, A (script)
Anderson, Benedict, 13
Andranikian, Stepan, 126, 130–31, 257
Andrei Rublev (film), 82, 87, 108, 112, 132
Andriesh (Bukov poem), 30, 34–35
Andriesh (film), 33, 34–37, 46, 253–54; as a fairy-tale film, 34, 35–37; reception of, 37; visual style of, 36. See also Moldovan Fairy Tale, A (film)
Andropov, Yuri, 78, 176–77, 198
Anger, Kenneth, 116, 251
Antipenko, Alexander, 98, 256
Arabesques on the Theme of Pirosmani (film), 44,
127, 166, 173, 215–18, 258; soundtrack of, 216, 217; visual style of, 216–18
Aragon, Louis, 197
Arakelian, Mikhail, 120, 130–31, 257
Ara the Fair (script), 162–64, 197
archaism, 4, 116, 139, 155–56, 213, 214
Armenfilm Studio, 21, 112, 116–17, 123, 126, 128, 129–30, 132, 184–85, 234, 245, 272n9
Armenia: culture and history, 8, 24, 25, 120–21, 137, 148–49, 154, 161, 162–63, 220–21, 230, 235, 239, 246; film industry in, 14, 15, 117. See also under identity; Karabagh conflict; nationalism
Armenian Apostolic Church, 22, 117, 119, 129, 148–49, 150, 241–42
Armenians in Tbilisi and Georgia, 4, 13, 15, 25, 26, 27, 29, 126, 127, 128, 225, 226, 229
Artistic Councils: description of, 11–12; at Armenfilm Studio, 126; at Dovzhenko Film Studio, 61, 84, 89; at Taganka Theatre, 198, 199, 261n6
Ashik-Kerib (film), 5, 231–36, 258; autobiographical elements in, 232; awards and festivals, 238–39, 240–41, 244, 258; cinematography and camerawork in, 234; distribution of, 14, 241; effect of Karabagh conflict on, 14, 240–41; historical figure of Âşık Garip, 213; origins of project, 231; Persian art in, 232–33; production of, 233, 234, 235, 240; reception of, 233–34, 240, 244; shooting locations, 233; soundtrack of, 233, 285n9; visual style of, 232–33, 234

WISCONSIN FILM STUDIES

Patrick McGilligan, Series Editor